# NTC's
# Dictionary
# of
# WORD
# ORIGINS

# NTC's
## Dictionary
## of
# WORD
# ORIGINS

Adrian Room

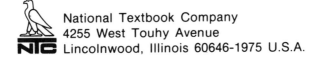

National Textbook Company
4255 West Touhy Avenue
Lincolnwood, Illinois 60646-1975 U.S.A.

This edition first published in 1991 by National Textbook Company,
a division of NTC Publishing Group, 4255 West Touhy Avenue,
Lincolnwood (Chicago), Illinois 60646-1975 U.S.A.
© Adrian Room 1986. Originally published by Routledge & Kegan Paul plc.
Library of Congress Catalog Card Number 89-64133
Manufactured in the United States of America
0 1 2 3 4 5 6 7 8 9 BC 9 8 7 6 5 4 3 2 1

# CONTENTS

Almost all of us are etymologists at heart.

Raymond Mortimer, *Sunday Times*, 25 December 1960

# INTRODUCTION

We almost all of us have what might be called an inbuilt 'wordwonder' facility as part of our mental and psychological make-up. We see unfamiliar words and wonder what they mean, wonder how to pronounce words, how to spell them, wonder how they relate to one another, how they originated. The whole thing is a part conscious process, part unconscious. Words generate other words in our minds.

The process usually happens something like this. We read a line in a story or newspaper report which runs as follows (let us assume): 'The two men raced up the spiral staircase and came out on the roof of the church'. We think 'spiral staircase' 'church spire', and wonder if the two words are related. (They are not, in fact.) Or we get an attractive picture postcard from a friend on holiday in the Lake District 'Arrived Windermere yesterday,' we read, 'wonderful scenery'. We see that name 'Windermere' and think of wind and winding waters and even windows opening on to a mere or lake. We may even recall Lady Windermere and her fan, and begin a series of secondary associations. All these thoughts are involuntary, of course, and quite pleasant. But when it comes to the real, etymological meaning of the name, they are all false, since the lake is actually named after a Viking leader called Vinandr! One final example: We meet a friend in the street. 'I see Jack's bought a new greyhound', says the friend. Instantly we conjure up a mental picture of that dog, with its thin, grey coat and slinky-looking tail. So would anyone, of course. But there is something wrong here, for greyhounds are not grey, despite their name. What has happened? The name has altered over the years and the centuries, and the first part of the word, which was formerly Old English *grīg*, meaning 'bitch', has become assimilated to another, different word, 'grey', which in this particular context is logical enough: if you can have a grey owl, a grey squirrel and a grey wolf, why not a grey hound?

This involuntary or sometimes even wilful attempt to link two similar words, or turn a meaningless one into a meaningful one, is technically known as 'popular etymology', or 'folk etymology'. It can occur purely in a single individual's mind, as with the false 'spiral/spire' association mentioned, or the words that sprang to mind on seeing 'Windermere', or it can have already been made in the general consciousness, as with the 'greyhound'. The word has thus become fixed in the language as something of a paradox: it is the right word to define or describe the object or action, in this case a particular breed of racing dog, but the wrong word to supply its origin. The dog is *not* so called because of its grey coat, but because originally such dogs were bred as bitches.

There are in fact hundreds of words and names in English that are either already established etymological delusions, like the greyhound, or potential ones, like the

I

spiral staircase and the name of the lake. The object of this dictionary is to give the *true* origins for a small selection of them (in fact just under 1200). The book concentrates much more on the words than the names, however, since the latter are legion, and anyway a more specialized field. Even so, a very few well known ones are included, such as the two City of London streets of Cripplegate and Crutched Friars. Neither has any connection with cripples.

Many 'false origin' words belong to a particular category of specialized or semi-specialized words. That is, it is not so much the ordinary everyday words of speech and writing that have become, or could become, distorted, but those that are associated with a particular 'subject area'. Even so, they are well enough known to most people, who may therefore be quite unaware that things are not really what they seem, and that a word's origin lurks in a coat of quite a different hue. Discovering such true origins is not only interesting, of course, and even entertaining, but also can be important, since it gives us a new insight into the meaning of the word, its *real* meaning, and the object or action that it describes. (Many such words are nouns, in fact.) Here, now, are some of the general areas in which such words occur and, in each of the categories, the representative selection of five words includes those that are actually entered in the dictionary, so that their true origins can be found there:

1. PLANTS AND FLOWERS: **artichoke, candytuft, cowslip, hollyhock, pennyroyal**
2. FOOD: **Bombay duck, cutlet, gingerbread, pettitoes, sparerib**
3. RELIGION: **aisle, anchorite, Gentile, homily, sect**
4. ANIMALS: **filly, husky, mongoose, polecat, reindeer**
5. BIRDS: **barnacle goose, fieldfare, hen harrier, lapwing, turtledove**
6. SPORTS AND GAMES: **cannon, checkmate, chessman, court card, gymkhana**
7. HISTORY: **argosy, casemate, footpad, gallowglass, Picts**
8. SHIPS AND THE SEA: **conning tower, hold, lanyard, outrigger, taffrail**
9. FABRICS AND TEXTILES: **cordwain, drugget, kerseymere, mohair, tweed**
10. COMMERCIAL PRODUCTS: **ambergris, boxcalf, catgut, isinglass, train oil**
11. MEDICINE: **boil, dropsy, hangnail, midwife, pustule**
12. WEAPONS AND AMMUNITION: **blunderbuss, cutlass, dumdum, knobkerrie, Maxim gun**

These categories are recorded in order of frequency, at least in the present dictionary, and it thus appears that most etymological red herrings are in the natural world, and relate to the creatures great and small that inhabit it. A combined selection of all words in the dictionary for plants, animals, birds, reptiles, fishes, insects and the like would easily outnumber any other. This says much for man's primitive method of naming the fauna and flora around him, using a basically descriptive or even imitative word which subsequently became distorted. (Many of the bird names in the book turn out to be based on an imitative origin, with the source lying in an onomatopoeic word that suggested the bird's call or cry. This is generally true of bird names, including those that have not become corrupted with the passage of time, so that such common names as those of the cock, crane, crow, cuckoo, curlew, dove, finch, grouse, gull, heron, owl and pigeon are all ultimately imitative, as many of them are in languages other than English.)

An important feature in the development of false etymologies is the desire to make a meaningless word meaningful in one's own language. This particularly applies to foreign words adopted by English, not only from modern foreign languages but from ancient Latin and Greek, often through Old French. Up to a point, in fact, it can be said that *all* modern false etymologies have been derived through the medium of a foreign language, since with the passing of time even Old English itself became something of an alien tongue, and many formerly meaningful words were no longer understood. (That, after all, is what happened with 'greyhound', when the Old English word that meant 'bitch' was no longer regarded as meaningful.) Of course, any language that adopts a foreign word usually adapts it to its own patterns of pronunciation, spelling and grammar. It is just that the insular English appear to have been particularly good at abandoning any original native form of nuance in a word, and remarkably adept at corrupting it and redesigning it to fit their native speech as rapidly as possible. Even today many English are scornful or at least suspicious of foreign words and 'lingos', and the mocking or aping of a foreign language is generally regarded as a perfectly acceptable way to raise a laugh. Those funny foreigners! (This attitude is also reflected in the manner in which many quite well educated English pronounce a non-English word or name, if finally brought to it. One typical example was the way in which a high-ranking public figure, when asked his views in the course of a radio interview on the newly emigrated Russian writer Solzhenitsyn, consistently and apparently quite obliviously referred to the author as 'Soldier Neatskin', thereby suggesting not a native talent of Russia but a fairy-tale figure from Grimm or Andersen, a sort of grotesque blend of Constant Tin Soldier and Rumpelstiltskin.)

Several of the words listed by way of example in the twelve categories above are ones that have been borrowed quite recently by English from some modern foreign language, among them 'husky', 'gymkhana' and 'knobkerrie'. Most current false etymology words, however, have long been established in the language, and entered it from one of the ancient tongues mentioned – to which may also be added Hebrew and Arabic. Hence the frequency with which such terms as 'Old English', 'Old French,' 'Medieval Latin' and so on occur in the various entries. These are all explained, with the necessary dates, where appropriate, in the 'Language List' that follows this Introduction.

One of the factors that naturally assists and encourages the formation of a popular etymology is an actual similarity of sense or sound to an existing English word. Sometimes one has one without the other, sometimes one finds both. The famous 'greyhound', for example, came about by a development of sense (even though this was not the correct one, and the wrong coat colour for this particular dog). In many cases, however, there is an agreeable if fortuitous matching of both sense and sound, and these are among the most interesting false etymologies that can be found. For example, 'jubilee' arose from a Hebrew word meaning 'ram's horn' which happened to resemble both Latin *jubilare*, 'to rejoice' and English 'jubilant'. Since the original sense was also used for a special festival (announced by blasts on ram's horn trumpets), the final product was an ideal match of sense, sound and background. To call such an origin 'false' seems almost a misnomer, since everything falls into place so well! But of course it *is* false as the resemblance of the Hebrew word to the Latin one was simply fortuitous. Again, and to take a more modern borrowing, it seems quite appropriate that 'plimsoll' should be used as a word for a shoe that has a distinctive sole (with even the 'plim' sounding right, as if representing a blend of 'pliant' and 'trim', or imitative of the soft 'plumping' sound the shoe makes). But it actually derives from the name of Samuel Plimsoll who advocated the Plimsoll line for marking a ship's loading capacity! In cases like this, too, one even finds an alteration of spelling, so that the word for the shoe is often spelt 'plimsole'. Perhaps this may even ultimately supersede the present spelling – assuming that the shoe itself remains in use as footwear, which seems a little doubtful. (Doubtless the true successor will be another word altogether, such as the current 'trainer'.)

In a few instances English forms develop that are quite obviously completely unrelated to the origin word, and that are also even inappropriate for the object or action. Thus 'lutestring' is hardly the best word to describe a glossy silk fabric, yet this is what the English musically made out of the original Italian *lustrino*. Some of the best mealtime misnomers are of this type, too, so the Jerusalem artichoke does not come from Jerusalem (the word is a typical happy-go-lucky English corruption of Italian *girasole*, 'sunflower'), and Palestine soup did not originate in Palestine. (So successful was the name 'Jerusalem artichoke', that punsters used it as the basis for 'Palestine soup', thereby compounding the etymological confusion. Not that the perpetrators seem to have cared!)

On occasions, a more or less generic or standard word can develop from a personal name or place name, whose own presence becomes subsequently obscured. One ('plimsoll') has already been mentioned, and in the categorized examples listed earlier there are others: personal names lurk behind 'boxcalf' and (perhaps more obviously) 'Maxim gun', and place names behind 'argosy', 'kerseymere' (not Kersey, however!) and 'dumdum'. As is to be expected, many names of manufactured objects derive from that of a person (others are 'leotard', 'shrapnel', 'silhouette' and 'Bakelite'), but otherwise the disguised name may have originally been that of the object's discoverer or developer, such as 'nicotine', 'trudgen', 'guppy' and 'bel'. Two semi-slang adjectives that are based on a personal name are 'ritzy' and 'titchy', the latter on a nickname which later became a stage name.

Included in the dictionary, inevitably, are a sizeable proportion of what might be called 'hoary stories'. These are words whose true origin is usually quite well documented, but which nevertheless have acquired a well known folk etymology. Among them are the familiar toddlers' tales about 'butterfly' coming from 'flutter by', about 'news' actually standing for '*N*orth, *S*outh, *E*ast, *W*est' as the four parts of the world from which news comes, and about the sirloin being so called since a certain king (maybe Henry VIII, maybe not) 'knighted' a joint of beef as 'Sir Loin'. Most people have heard of these and similar 'derivations'. What is slightly worrying

4

is that there was a time not so long ago when people actually believed such fancies, and really did think that the tram was named after one Outram and that 'barmy' referred to the patients at Barming Lunatic Asylum (as it was then called). Indeed, there seems to have been no end to the ingenuity and imagination of a number of amateur etymologists, many of whom took themselves and their scholarship most seriously. No holds were barred in the game of origins, and no language immune from involvement in a desperate derivation. Latin and French were a particular favourite, especially the former, since it gave a spurious air of authority and authenticity: if this word comes from the Latin, its origins are both ancient and honourable.

The reader will come across instances of such pseudo-scholarship in the book. Many more examples could have been included, but there was simply no room. In any case, the retelling of such romances is hardly the primary aim of the book. However, here on the doorstep are one or two examples (not included in the dictionary) of the sort of thing that was hatched up, some by scholars quite genuinely eminent in their field (name of perpetrator in brackets): 'ostler' comes from 'oat-stealer' (Jonathan Swift); 'apothecary' from 'a pot he carries' (ditto); 'star' because it does not 'stir' (Thomas Adams, seventeenth-century religious writer); 'marriage' from 'merry age' (Henry Smith, known as 'Silver-tongued Smith', sixteenth-century puritan divine); 'elf' because it is 'alive' (Spenser, *The Faerie Queene*); 'German' as he is a 'Guerre-man' or 'man that wars' (Thomas Carlyle, *History of the French Revolution*); 'world' because it 'whirled' round (Sir John Davies, sixteenth- and seventeenth-century philosophical poet); 'heaven' from 'haven' (Giles Fletcher, sixteenth- and seventeenth-century poet). Such curiosities resemble the transformation of the name of their ship from 'Bellerophon' to 'Bully Ruffian' by the sailors on board her, and the assurance apparently made by the hostess of a north-country inn to Wordsworth that the river Greta was so called from the bridge over it, which, as he could see for himself, formed a 'great A'.

It will be noted that many of the false etymologies above, and also a number quoted in the dictionary entries, were devised by clergymen and 'divines' of one form or another. There must be a message in this somewhere, but this is not the time or place to find it. Suffice it to say that there was one nineteenth-century cleric who did much to sort the whole thing out and, while quoting many false etymologies, took great care to give the true ones, as far as he was able within the limits of his own resources and references.

This was the Reverend Abram Smythe Palmer, and the monumental work in which he produced the results of his researches was his dictionary *Folk-Etymology*, published in 1882 (see Bibliography for its full title). Here in a thick volume of nearly 700 pages he gives the true origins (with limitations as mentioned) of hundreds of words, backed up with a wealth of quotations, translations, references and examples, making a unique assembly of material on the subject. If the reader would wish for more than is contained in the present book, he could do no better than seek out Palmer (possibly with some difficulty, as the work is now rare). True, there are errors – Palmer denies any link between 'ointment' and 'anoint', for example, whereas these words are actually related to each other – and many of the words he includes are dialect forms or obscure terms, but taken for what it is, it is a remarkable

5

work, and a survey of the phenomenon as a whole that has not since been matched.

Palmer was a graduate of Trinity College, Dublin, and his first foray into folk etymology resulted in the publication in 1876 of his *Leaves from a Word-Hunter's Note-Book* (again, see Bibliography, as for other works by him). This rather uneven work, in which he devotes over twenty pages to deriving 'tree' from 'true' (!), was self-confessedly something of an experiment, but at least it was a start. Subsequent work at a deeper and more sustained level resulted not only in the publication of his great dictionary (by now he was a curate in Staines), but in the appearance of his more 'approachable' work of 1904, *The Folk and Their Word-Lore*. Palmer was also interested in place-names and edited and updated Isaac Taylor's famous *Words and Places,* which appeared a few years later (see Bibliography). Shamefully, the *Dictionary of National Biography* has no place for this great innovative scholar.

As already implied, the approach of this present dictionary is rather different to that of Palmer. He based his entries on nothing but well attested printed (or at least written) material, quoting liberally from numerous sources. Here I have included not only known popular etymologies, for whatever reason, but also likely ones of the 'spiral/spire' type as mentioned at the beginning of this Introduction. I have tried to let such false trails appear as naturally as possible, without deliberately hunting for them or trying to create them. Some entries arose as a result of discussions with friends. Others are concerned with etymologies that I have myself wondered about, and even mistakenly believed in the past. I am sure it is likely that many concepts or 'images' that we have of particular words stem from our first encounter with them in childhood, when we are most impressionable. Such impressions stick well into adult life. Moreover, it is not just the self-generating impressions that remain, but the explanations behind the words that we may have been given by well meaning (or simply pun-making) teachers or relatives. We may long remember the teacher who quipped 'Didn't you know that's why it's called an opera – because it was an uproar?'. Of course, we as children have delighted in similar (and probably better) puns, and we no doubt recall these, too!

Apart from the various 'subject' categories, as mentioned earlier, many popular etymologies occur in colloquial and slang words, which is a category of a different kind. Many of these feature in the book (examples are 'batty', 'cheesed off', 'fogey', 'geezer', 'plonk' and 'tacky''), as well as words that occur in particular sayings or idioms, such as the last word of 'kick the bucket' or the first of 'coign of vantage'. Here it is not usually the etymology that is misunderstood, but the meaning. What sort of image does 'kick the bucket' have for you? What do you visualize for the phrase 'from pillar to post'? The true origin here will be the origin of the phrase itself, as far as it can be established.

It goes without saying that in some cases it is still not possible to state what the precise origin of a word actually is. In such cases the entry will obviously state the fact. But at least it will also state what the origin is *not*. So while not able to give a true origin, at least it will not give a false one. The various degrees of 'clouds of unknowing' for the different etymologies are stated as honestly as possible, I hope, so that where there is doubt, the entry will say so. But naturally the most satisfactory entries are the ones that kick out popular origin A and replace it with proper origin B.

Each headword is followed by a brief and often rather casual definition in brackets, simply so that the reader knows which word is being dealt with. It is advisable not to overlook the definition, since the word in question may be in one of its less common meanings: see for example 'arch', 'baggage', 'bustle', 'cashier', 'charm', 'spade' and 'wrinkle'.

As with Palmer, too, but on nothing like the same scale, a few 'backup' quotations are given. These are often designed to show the actual origin of a false etymology, or the evolution of a true one. The wording of the quotations (the source is usually given) is as in the original, which may thus appear rather 'Olde Englishe' at times but at least is authentic. Exceptions to this rule are for quotations from those familiar old English classics, the Bible and Shakespeare. For biblical quotations, the texts are those of the Authorized Version of 1611, which many people still regard as the 'real' English version of the Bible. For Shakespeare, the quotations have been taken from the *Oxford Standard Authors* edition edited by W. J. Craig, first published in 1905 and since reprinted several times in different formats.

The attention of the reader is specially drawn to the Bibliography (page 189) and to the note that precedes it. The matter is dealt with in a little more detail there, but suffice it to say here that some works are included in the Bibliography not because they give the true origin of a word (although many of them do), but because they were used for furnishing false etymologies. The Bibliography is thus recommendatory only in the sense that it will provide a general background to the true and false origins of words, and to the subject as a whole.

Finally, although in places some of the material may seem more like Alice's Wonderland than the entries in a conventional dictionary, I hope that overall the present book may provide the reader with much that is informative and enjoyable, and that it may prompt him or her to make further researches into the true origins of many of the hundreds of words that flock into our daily lives.

Petersfield, Hampshire                                           Adrian Room

# LANGUAGE LIST

The list below gives brief information regarding some of the language terms used in the Dictionary, together with the approximate dates when early forms of a language were spoken. Any language described as 'modern' in the entries will mean the form of the language as it exists today, and as it developed after the dates given here for the 'Middle' form of it.

*Anglo-French:* the form of French used in medieval England.

*Anglo-Norman:* the form of *Anglo-French* used by Normans living in England after the Conquest.

*Germanic:* the original *Indoeuropean* language from which developed modern German, English, Dutch, the Scandinavian languages and a few others such as Flemish.

*Greek:* the language spoken by the ancient Greeks until about 200 A.D.

*Indoeuropean:* the original parent language that developed in about 4000 B.C. into the separate languages now spoken in most of Europe and as far east as north India.

*Late Greek:* the form of *Greek* spoken from about 200 to 600 A.D.

*Late Latin:* the form of *Latin* spoken from about 200 to 600 A.D.

*Latin:* the language spoken by the ancient Romans until about 200 A.D.

*Medieval Latin:* the form of *Latin* used for liturgical and literary purposes from about 600 to 1500.

*Middle Dutch:* the form of Dutch spoken from about 1100 to 1500.

*Middle English:* the form of English spoken from about 1150 to 1500.

*Middle French:* the form of French spoken from about 1300 to 1600.

*Middle Greek:* the form of *Greek* spoken from about 600 to 1500.

*Middle High German:* the form of German spoken in southern Germany (where the land is higher than in the north) from about 1100 to 1500; this was the language that became modern standard German.

*Middle Low German:* the form of German spoken elsewhere than in southern Germany from about 1100 to 1500; see also *Middle High German*.

*New Greek* (also known as *Modern Greek*): the form of *Greek* spoken since about 1500.

*New Latin:* the form of *Latin* used from about 1500 for scientific and learned texts.

*Old English:* the form of English spoken in medieval times until about 1150.

*Old French:* the form of French spoken in medieval times until about 1300.

*Old High German:* the form of German spoken in southern Germany until about 1100; see also *Middle High German*.

*Old Norse:* the common language of Scandinavia and Iceland spoken until about 1350.

*Old North French:* the dialects of *Old French* spoken mainly in Normandy and Picardy.

9

*Romance:* the original *Indoeuropean* language that developed in about 300 A.D. from *Latin* into French, Italian, Spanish, Portuguese and Romanian; see also *Vulgar Latin.*

*Sanskrit:* the ancient sacred language of India and Hinduism, dating from about 1200 B.C.

*Vulgar Latin:* the informal (spoken) language of ancient Rome that was the main source of the *Romance* languages.

# DICTIONARY

**abominable** (hateful)
For many years from medieval times it was believed that the word derived from Latin *ab homine*, 'from a man', in the sense 'inhuman', 'unnatural', and Shakespeare punned on the word with this supposed origin in *Love's Labour's Lost* where Holofernes, talking of Don Adriano's strange pronunciation, says: 'This is abhominable, which he would call abominable'. (See Act V, Scene i for some whimsical language play.) In fact the word comes from Latin *abominari*, 'to regard as an evil omen', from *ab-*, 'from' and *omen*, 'evil omen'.

**aborigine** (native inhabitant)
Like **abominable** (above), this word is still sometimes regarded as having a Latin derivation, in this case from *ab origine*, since such a native was in the country 'from the beginning'. The actual origin was probably the proper name, *aborigines*, of a pre-Roman tribe in Latium and Italy. In Italian, French and other Latin-based languages, the word appears with *-gen-* (Italian *aborigeni*, French *aborigènes*), as if deriving from Latin *gens*, 'people'.

**abracadabra** (magic word)
This word has cast its spell over many linguists, and a popular nineteenth-century theory was evolved that derived it from the Aramaic initials of *ab* ('Father'), *ben* ('Son'), and *ruach hakōdesh* ('Holy Spirit'), with the final section based on Hebrew *davar*, 'word'. The reference was thus seen as being to the Trinity. In fact the word, first found in a second-century Latin poem, comes from Greek, where the fifth letter, rendered by the Roman *c*, was actually the Greek sigma (equivalent to *s*), and the whole formula relates to some name such as *Abrasax*. This was the name of a god worshipped by an early Christian gnostic sect (the so called Basilidians), who thus evolved *abracadabra* as their cabalistic or 'charm' word. The god's name contains the number 365, which is the number of heavens that emanated from him. It is, however, quite possible that the last part of the weird word does indeed derive from the Hebrew for 'word', as stated.

**absinthe** (kind of liqueur)
The word is sometimes thought of as linking up, in French or English, with 'absent', perhaps because of its powerful alcoholic effect or its associations with despairing love ('absinthe makes the heart grow fonder', as it were). In fact the origin goes back to Greek *apsinthion*, '**wormwood**', since the drink has, or at least used to have, a high content of this particular herb (which see for its own supposed and true origin).

**abstemious** (modest in eating and drinking)
It certainly looks as if the word is related to 'abstain', since this is what an abstemious person does, while others indulge. In fact the origin lies in Latin *abstemius*, where *ab-* is the usual 'from', 'away' prefix, and the main word is *temetum*, 'intoxicating drink'.

**accomplice** (associate)
An accomplice is not so called as he is an 'accomplished' criminal, but because he is 'a complice', or simply an associate. This is now an obsolete word, but was still in use in the time of Shakespeare, where in *Richard II* Bolingbroke says that Bristol Castle is held by 'Bushy, Bagot, and their complices'

11

(the 'caterpillars of the commonwealth'). The old word survives, however, in modern 'complicity'.

**accordion** (musical instrument)
The vulgarly named 'squeezebox' is not so called as it can produce 'chords', at least not directly, but because its music has harmony, or 'accord', that is, it is 'to the heart' (Latin *ad*, 'to' and *cor, cordis*, 'heart'). The instrument is sometimes spelt *accordeon*, and this comes from the French, which was itself influenced by the Greek *ōideion*, a theatre for musical contests. (Hence, incidentally, the well-known cinema name Odeon).

**acorn** (fruit of the oak)
The word has long been popularly associated, understandably enough, with 'corn' and 'oak', and was spelt as *akecorn* and *okecorn* only a few centuries ago. Its real origin lies in Old English *æcern*, related to Latin *ager*, 'field' (as in 'agriculture') and modern English 'acre'. The link is in the source of the acorn, which is the natural fruit of a tree that grows in fields.

**acrobat** (gymnastic performer)
The agile entertainer is not so called as he 'acts with bats', or even performs 'aerobatics', but because he was originally a Greek *akrobatēs*, or 'point walker', that is, 'one who walks on tiptoe'. Aerobatics is *aerial acrobatics*, although no word 'aerobat' has evolved for the person who performs them.

**acrostic** (type of poem or puzzle)
An acrostic is not so called since its letters go 'across', and in fact they actually go down, since it is a type of linguistic entertainment where the first letters (and sometimes the last) of each line spell out a word, name or sentence. The term derives from Greek, where the *acro* is 'end', 'point' (as for **acrobat**, above) and the *stic* denotes a 'line of verse' (Greek *stichos*, 'row'). Acrostics are an agreeable way for lovers or doters to send seasonal greetings, like this:

Just a line to say you're mine,
And to send this valentine;
Now you know I'm close to you,
Ever faithful, ever true.

**adjust** (arrange more precisely)
For some time the word has been associated with 'just' (to adjust something is to make it 'just right'), but the true origin is in Late Latin *adjuxtare*, 'to bring near'. This came into English via Old French *adjuster* (modern *ajuster*), which was itself influenced by Latin *justus*, 'right'.

**admiral** (senior naval officer)
The rank looks as if it is an 'admirable' one, one to be looked up to (especially if it is a 'Lord High Admiral'). But although the *d* did indeed come from 'admirable', the historic origin of the name lies in Arabic *amīr-al-baḥr*, 'commander of the sea' (the first part of this gives the title of 'emir'). One sixteenth-century 'linguist', applying the word to Columbus, said it derived from Latin *admirans mare*, 'admiring the sea'! However, the butterfly known as the red admiral has a name where the derivation may well be from 'admirable'.

**adultery** ('violation of the marriage-bed')
[*Chambers*, see Bibliography.]
The deed is performed by adults, but is not so called for this reason. The origin goes back, through Old French, to Latin *adulterare*, 'to corrupt', 'to debase', itself possibly deriving from *alter*, 'another', so that the implication is 'corruption of another' (although in modern terms, since the engagement is voluntary, the distinction of who is corrupting who is more blurred). 'Adult', on the other hand, comes from Latin *adultus*, the past participle of *adolescere*, 'to grow up' (as in 'adolescent'), so that an adult is someone who has grown up.

**aghast** (astounded)
There is no direct link with 'ghastly' or 'ghost', even though someone who is aghast may well be horror-struck as if they had seen a ghost. The *h* was added, however, under the influence of 'ghastly', which means that the early spelling of the word was *agast*. This comes from the Old English verb *gæstan*, 'to frighten'. In *Henry VI*, Part I, Shakespeare makes a messenger, speaking of the overthrow of Talbot, say that 'All the whole army stood agaz'd on him', as if the origin was in *gaze*.

**agnostic** (one who holds that nothing is known beyond material phenomena)
The term was devised in 1869 by the Darwinian biologist T. H. Huxley, when a member of the Metaphysical Society. He coined the word from Greek, with *a-* meaning 'not' and *gnōstos* meaning 'known', 'knowable'. However, he was not referring to the 'unknown god' mentioned in the Bible (in Acts 17:23), where the original Greek for the inscription 'TO THE UNKNOWN GOD' was *Agnōsto Theo*, but to his own views as contrasting with those of contemporary 'gnostics'. (Those who wish to go into this further should see his own account in 'Agnosticism' and 'Agnosticism and Christianity' in his *Collected Essays*, published in 1900.) The modern English word is often popularly understood to mean 'one who does not know if there is a God or not', which is not its original sense, as defined by Huxley (for more about whom, see **trade wind**).

**agog** (expectant)
The word looks as if it ought to link up with 'goggling', like a greedy child eagerly awaiting the appearance of a birthday tea, but it probably came into English from the French phrase *en gogues*, 'in merriment', itself of uncertain origin.

**air** (manner, melody)
The two basic senses of 'air' given here, as in 'an independent air' and the 'Londonderry Air', are sometimes subconsciously linked with the other, basic 'air' ('fresh air of morning'), but the origins are really quite distinct. 'Air' in the 'manner' sense comes from Old French *aire*, 'place', 'quality' (seen more obviously in English 'debonair', from the French *de bon air*). 'Air' in the musical sense comes, through French, from Italian *aria*, although this in turn may have been influenced by French *aire*. The basic 'air' can be traced back, through Latin, to Greek *aēr*, itself from the verb *aēmi*, 'I blow'. For another 'airy' link see **eyrie**.

**aisle** (passage between rows of seats in a church)
Today the word is popularly used of the central passage between the seats that leads to the altar 'up the aisle', and it also has its non-church sense in the gangway between seats in a theatre (where the actors aim to delight their audience or 'lay them in the isles'). In both these usages, and in the spelling of the word, there is an association with 'isle', as if the passageway was a stretch of water passing between 'islands' of seats. In a church, too, this particular association is reinforced by the link with 'nave', itself a word related to ships. Originally, however, the term 'aisle' applied not to the central passage but to one or other of the two on each side, flanking the nave or chancel. Each of these was seen as a 'wing', Latin *ala*, and that is the ultimate derivation. The spelling, however, was influenced by both 'isle' and the French word for 'wing', *aile*. For a related misspelling, see **island**.

**aitch-bone** (bone of the rump)
When spelt in this, the most usual way, it looks as if the origin may lie in the letter 'H', to refer to the shape of the bone, on a parallel with a 'T-bone', which actually is shaped like a 'T'. But the word has 'done an adder', that is, just as 'an adder' was once 'a nadder', so 'an aitch-bone' was 'a naitch-bone', as it were, with the original first letter *n* thought to be that of *an*. In Middle English it was spelt *nache-bone*, and this derives, through Old French *nache*, from Latin *natis*, 'rump', 'buttock'. But clearly the true origin has long been obscured, since other variant spellings for the word have been 'edge-bone', 'haunch-bone' (which makes a little more sense, but is still wrong), 'ash-bone', 'each-bone' (as there are two) and even 'ice-bone'. These all reflect a desperate bid to make sense out of a meaningless word.

**alabaster** (kind of opaque or translucent gypsum)
There is sometimes an association with 'plaster', which even obscures the precise concept of what alabaster actually is. Its ultimate origin, however, is in Greek *alabastros*, itself of non-Greek origin, although possibly linked with the ancient town of Alabastron in Egypt.

**albatross** (large sea-bird)
The name of this bird, feared of old by mariners as an ill omen, is traditionally

derived from Latin *albus*, feminine *alba*, 'white', from its colour. It probably originated, however, as a corruption of Portuguese *alcatraz*, which actually means 'pelican' (and which incidentally gave the name of the former prison island in San Francisco Bay, California, which pelicans frequented). See also **alcove** (below).

**alcove** (recess)
An alcove can quite easily be seen to be a little 'cove' in a room, but the two words are not related. As with a small but significant group of words beginning 'al-', the origin is in Arabic. In this case it is *al-qubbah*, 'the vault', 'the arch'. (There are even those who like to derive **albatross**, above, from Arabic *al-qadus*, 'the pitcher', alluding to its – or the pelican's – large pouch, in which it was said to carry water.)

**alderman** (civic dignitary)
The title goes back to historic times, but it does not originate in a person who led 'all the men', as has been sometimes explained. Instead, it means more or less what it says, so that an alderman is an 'elder man' or chief.

**alimentary canal** (food tract from mouth to anus)
This basic and essential anatomical feature is sometimes written and pronounced 'elementary canal', as if it performed the simple act of processing food (which in a sense it does). But its true origin is in Latin *alimentum*, 'food', from *alere*, 'to feed'. See also **alimony** (below).

**alimony** (allowance for support, especially to a wife by a husband after a divorce)
The word looks as if it ought to be connected with 'money' or even 'alms'. In fact it is not linked with either, but comes from Latin *alimonia*, 'sustenance', itself from the same verb *alere*, 'to feed', that eventually produced the **alimentary canal** (above). Similarly, 'matrimony', 'patrimony' and **parsimony** have no connection with 'money': the final four letters simply represent the Latin ending *-monia* or *-monium*.

**allegiance** (loyalty, obligation by a servant to his lord and master)

The origin here is not in 'allege' or in some such word as 'legal', but in the relation in which a man stood to his 'liege' lord. A liege lord was one entitled to feudal service, and 'liege' ultimately relates to English 'let', since the lord was one whom the law 'let' have his servant. There is thus also no link with 'ligament', even though a man who gives allegiance is in a sense 'tied' to his master. It is probable that the initial 'al-' of the word was added by association, again, falsely, with 'alliance'.

**alligator** (crocodile-type reptile)
The fearsome creature's name looks so Latin that attempts have been made to interpret it as 'binder', from *alligare*, 'to bind', since an alligator's jaws 'bind' their prey. A nice idea, but the true origin is even better. The word is a corruption of Spanish *el lagarto*, 'the lizard'. Doubtless early scientific explorers, even if they knew the true origin of the name, wanted an English name that was more imposing and learned, like the Greek-derived 'rhinoceros' and 'hippopotamus'. They therefore devised, or at any rate tacitly accepted, the name 'alligator'. However, in modern times all these former wondrous animals have become well known worldwide, and the once grand names of the four mentioned here are now shortened and trivialized as ''gator', 'croc', 'rhino' and 'hippo'. See also **avocado** (below).

**almanac** (calendar-type register)
This is a difficult word, but it does not derive from 'all the months', as has been sometimes innocently explained. Nor does it even derive, apparently, from the more learned Arabic *al-manākh*, since this is a nonexistent word. Its true origin is still not precisely known, although there was a Late Greek word *almenichiaka*, said to mean something like 'calendars', and this may be at least one strand of the origin.

**altruism** (devotion to the welfare of others above oneself)
This lofty-principled word does not derive from Latin *altus*, 'high', however appropriate this might be. It is actually a concocted word in origin, devised by the French philosopher Auguste Comte in the

nineteenth century, and based by him on the Italian *altrui*, 'someone else', as the opposite to 'egoism'. The word was introduced into English by lawyers translating and commenting on Comte's works.

**amaranth** (flower of the 'love-lies-bleeding' genus)
The '-anth' of the name does not mean 'flower' (Greek *anthos*) as it does in most other flower names, such as 'polyanthus' and 'chrysanthemum', but is part of the Greek *amarantos*, 'unfading'. The word was originally used in poetry for a mythical flower that never fades.

**Amazons** (mythical race of female warriors)
The name of the race is usually traditionally derived from a Greek word meaning 'breastless' (*a-*, 'not', and *mazos*, 'breast'), and this explanation was devised by the ancient Greeks themselves, who duly accounted for it by saying that the women deliberately burnt off or cut off one breast of their all-female offspring so that the girls could shoot their arrows better in battle. But the true origin is almost certainly nothing like this, and may be from some non-Greek language altogether. (It could be, however, that the origin may lie in the Greek *a-*, 'not' and 'maza' meaning cereal food, referring to the fact that the Amazons were a tribe of meat-eaters.) The river Amazon is so called after some female or female-looking (i.e. long-haired) warriors encountered there by early Spanish explorers.

**ambergris** (waxy substance secreted by the sperm whale)
The still rather mysterious and exotic substance, also formerly spelt 'ambergrease', has nothing to do with 'grease', but derives from Old French *ambre gris*, 'grey amber'. Not that it *was* amber, of course, but it was confused with it as both substances were found by the seashore, the amber (yellow in colour) as a fossil resin, and the ambergris (grey) as something that had been washed ashore. See also **sperm whale** and compare **verdigris**.

**ambush** (surprise attack from a place of concealment)

The word is not directly related to 'bush'. Indirectly and historically it is, however, since it can be traced back ultimately to Late Latin *boscus*, 'wood', which is linguistically linked to English 'bush' as well as French *bois*.

**amuck, amok** (frenzied)
Someone who 'runs amuck', thirsting for blood, vengeance or whatever, does not do so because he is in 'a muck sweat' or because he causes 'a muck'. The word is Malay in origin (*amoq*), meaning 'furious attack'.

**anchorite** (hermit, religious recluse)
Anchorites are (or were) not so called as they are the 'anchors of the church', but because they have retired or 'withdrawn back' from the world. The derivation of the name is thus Greek, from *ana-*, 'back', and *chōrein*, 'to withdraw'.

**andiron** (metal support for logs in a hearth, 'firedog')
There is no original connection with 'iron' in the word, even though attempts have been made to derive it from 'anti-iron', since andirons are in pairs and stand opposite ('anti-') each other. The word came into English from Old French *andier*, whose own origin is uncertain: one possibility is a derivation in a Gaulish conjectured word *andero*, meaning 'young bull', since the devices are usually decorated with animal heads. (But see also **firedog** itself, below.) The modern French word for an andiron is *landier*, itself originally *l'andier* but with the definite article fused to the noun. For a similar phenomenon in English (but involving the indefinite article) see **nickname**.

**anthem** (special kind of church hymn)
Anthems were originally sung antiphonally, that is, with the singing passing from one side of the choir to the other. For this reason, some have tried to explain the name as being an 'anti-hymn', with 'anti-' in the accepted sense of 'opposite'. This is only half correct, however, since the word actually originates in 'antiphon' itself, or rather in the Late Latin word for it, *antiphona*. The term thus means 'sounding opposite', or

'responding to the sound'. The Old English word for 'anthem' was *antemne*. This came to be pronounced 'an*temny*' and the spelling with *h* was probably brought about by association with 'hymn'.

**anticipate** (expect)
Many words beginning with 'anti-' have an original sense 'opposite', as in 'antiphony' (see **anthem** above), 'anticlimax', 'antidote', and so on. But in 'anticipate' the original sense is not 'opposite taking', as if one were taking (Latin *capere*, 'to take') from another person, but in 'ante-' meaning 'before'. A person who anticipates, therefore, is one who 'takes before'. There are one or two other words where 'ante-' is disguised as 'anti-', one tasty example being 'antipasto', which is the hors d'oeuvre eaten 'before food' in an Italian meal. See also **antique** (below).

**antique** (old, valuable object)
The word does not directly derive from 'ancient', or even from this adjective in its earlier spelling of 'antient'. 'Antique' is a sixteenth-century word deriving from Latin *antiquuus*, 'ancient', while 'ancient' itself is an earlier word coming into English, via Old French *ancien*, from a deduced Vulgar Latin word *anteanus*. But the ultimate root of both words is certainly Latin *ante*, 'before'.

**April** (fourth month of the year)
The popular explanation of the name is a derivation from Latin *aperire*, 'to open', since April is the month when the buds open. However, a more likely origin is in an old Etruscan word related to the name of Aphrodite, the goddess of love and beauty, as after all, 'In the Spring a young man's fancy lightly turns to thoughts of love', and noticeably so in Mediterranean countries. On the other hand, the name could perhaps go back to some Indoeuropean root meaning 'later', 'second', since originally April was the second month of the year. The link with Aphrodite seems more probable, however.

**arbour** (tree-shaded bower)
The word seems so obviously to derive from Latin *arbor*, 'tree', and its present spelling and even sense have been certainly influenced by this. The true origin, however, lies in Old French *erbier*, itself from *erbe*, 'herb' (from Latin *herba*), so that an arbour was originally a grassy plot or flower garden, not a shady bower as it is today. See also **bower** itself.

**arch** (cunning, knowing)
There is no connection with 'arch' in the common sense 'lofty curved structure', as if an 'arch' person was superior in some way (or supercilious, with arched eyebrows). The derivation is from the other 'arch' meaning 'chief', as in 'arch-rogue', 'arch-thief', 'archbishop'. An 'arch-rogue' was originally a pre-eminent one, and therefore a cunning one, who knew the tricks of his trade.

**argosy** (large fleet of ships, or large abundantly laden ship)
The word is a historic one, as is the concept. Only nine lines into Shakespeare's *The Merchant of Venice*, for example, there is a mention of 'argosies with portly sail'. For many years the word was believed to derive from the classical name *Argos*, and in particular that of the *Argo*, the ship in which Jason sailed with the Argonauts in search of the Golden Fleece. But the actual origin is in the former (Italian) name of the city of Ragusa, from which such merchant ships originally came. The name of this port, now Dubrovnik, Yugoslavia, was formerly spelt in various ways, including *Aragouse* in one sixteenth-century text.

**arithmetic** (branch of mathematics)
A popular derivation of the word, from about the thirteenth century to the fifteenth, was from Latin *ars metrica*, 'measuring art'. But the term's real origin is in Greek, not Latin, since it comes from *arithmein*, 'to count', itself from *arithmos*, 'number'.

**Armageddon** (final destructive conflict)
In modern, militaristic times, the name has come to be associated with 'army' and 'armament'. The actual source of the biblical word is in Hebrew *har megiddōn*, 'mountain district of Megiddo', with Megiddo itself in the plain of Esdraelon and famous as the scene of several great battles, from biblical times, well BC, to Allenby in

1917. Megiddo is mentioned more than once in the Old Testament, for example Joshua 12:21 ('the king of Megiddo'), Judges 1:27 ('the inhabitants of Megiddo'), 2 Kings 9:27 ('he fled to Megiddo'), and the final battle of Armageddon is foretold in Revelation 16:16.

**arrant** (notorious, utter)
The word is not a variant of 'arrogant', as if 'arrant disobedience' was the act of someone who regarded himself as superior to others. It is, however, a variant of 'errant', that is 'wandering', so that the original 'arrant thief' was a wandering vagabond, just as a 'knight errant', his opposite number, was a roving knight.

**arrowroot** (plant yielding starch)
Perhaps the plant is so called as its roots are arrow-like? In fact its tubers *were* originally used to absorb poison from wounds caused by poisoned arrows, but the real source of the name of this West Indian plant is a native one, *aru-aru*, meaning 'meal of meals' (the starch is easily digestible), and this was assimilated to the present spelling by association with the medicinal properties of the plant's juice. For a similar development, although in the opposite direction, see **asparagus**.

**artichoke** (plant with edible flower head)
The plant is not so called as it makes you 'choke', but derives its name ultimately from Arabic *al-kharshūf*, 'the artichoke', via Old Spanish and Italian. Yet the 'choke' association developed quite early in English and former spellings such as *hortichock* and *hartichoke* suggest that the plant was seen as one that either 'choked the garden' or 'choked the heart' (or itself had a 'heart that choked'). Even the French had problems over how to understand the name. The French for 'artichoke' is *artichaut*, suggesting a false association with words such as *chou* ('cabbage'), *chaud* ('hot') and *haut* ('high'). See also **Jerusalem artichoke, Jordan almond**, and **Palestine soup** for some Middle East cousins.

**asparagus** (plant whose succulent young shoots are eaten as a delicacy)
As is well known, this tasty plant was long popularly known as 'sparrow grass', as if eaten or otherwise favoured by sparrows. However, this form of the name was so widespread that it almost looks as if *asparagus* was evolved as a 'learned' name for what was, after all, rather a delicacy, not just a 'grass for sparrows', which is really rather common. Moreover, although the name is said to go back to Latin or Greek, no one has yet explained its original sense in either of these languages, or its ultimate source. Even if the name is regarded as a version of 'spear grass', or the other way round, the same argument applies. However, this theory is not conclusive and until further facts come to light perhaps we must accept that 'sparrow grass' is, after all, a corruption of 'asparagus', and not vice versa.

**asphalt** (pitch or composition used in road-surfacing and roofing)
Since asphalt is often used in combination with other materials, such as gravel, it may be felt that its name is a similar compound, of words such as 'ash' or 'salt' (or even 'felt', from its uses in roofing). But the term goes back to Greek *asphaltos*, itself probably deriving from *a-*, 'not' and *sphallein*, 'to cause to fall', referring to the binding or cementing property of asphalt.

**atone** (make amends)
The apparent connection with 'tone' is false here, despite the fact that someone or something having the same 'tone' as another means that there is accord, and that all is well. The word actually derives from the noun 'atonement', which originated as a sixteenth-century invention to express the state of being 'at one' (i.e. 'at-one-ment'), in the sense of a religious reconciliation. So by coincidence, the idea of harmony and 'rightness' suggested by 'tone' were in the original, even though this was different.

**auburn** (reddish-brown, especially of hair)
The origin does not lie in 'brown' or 'burn' (as in 'sunburnt'), although the shade expressed by the word certainly became associated with 'brown'. The word originally meant 'blond', and derives from Middle French *alborne*, itself ultimately from Latin *albus*, 'white'. As the association with

17

the word 'brown' grew in English, so the actual meaning of 'auburn' changed colour.

**aureole** (border of light round the head or body)
An aureole is a type of halo, seen in portraits of holy persons, and suggesting an 'aura' of sanctity. The two words are not related, however, and 'aureole' derives from Medieval Latin *corona aureola*, 'golden crown', while 'aura' goes back to the identical Latin and Greek words that means 'breeze'.

**avalanche** (downpour of rocks or other objects)
An origin in some such word as 'launch' or 'lava' or even 'valley' may suggest itself. The word came into English from French, however, from a dialect word such as *lavanche* that is itself of obscure origin. There was an association, however, with French *avaler*, 'to swallow', which is itself related to *val*, 'valley'.

**avast** (nautical command to stop)
The word does not relate to 'vast', even in the 'vasty deep', nor does it derive from Italian *basta*, 'stop!', 'enough!'. As with many maritime terms, the origin is from Dutch, where the phrase was *hou' vast*, 'hold fast'. The first part of this became 'a-' on a line with similar nautical words such as 'abeam', 'astern' and 'abreast'.

**avocado** (pear-shaped fruit)
The word is obviously foreign, and is sometimes thought to mean 'lawyer', as if the fruit was favoured by lawyers or advocates, just as the slightly exotic drink called advocaat was. But although 'lawyer' is *avocat* in French (as is the name of this fruit), no

language actually produced an 'avocado' in this sense, so there must be a different origin. This is Spanish *aguacate*, which in turn derives from a Central American or Mexican native word meaning, somewhat surprisingly, 'testicle'. (The reference is to the shape of the fruit. The word 'orchid' has the same origin, although from Greek.) A once common alternative name for the avocado was the 'alligator pear', which is simply a fanciful corruption of 'avocado' itself. See also **alligator**, for its own corrupt background.

**avoirdupois** (system of weights)
Yes, the origin is indeed French, but the meaning is not 'have some weight', as sometimes believed by some. The Old French phrase for the system was *aveir de peis*, meaning 'goods of weight', although admittedly the first word here does derive from Latin *habere*, 'to have'. With luck, Britain will one day finally abandon avoirdupois and go fully metric, so that we will no longer need to ponder on the origin and spelling and pronunciation of such outlandish terms.

**aweigh** (of an anchor: no longer hooked in the bottom)
Strange things happen with nautical words, and this one looks like a variant spelling of 'away', since once the anchor is raised it is 'away' from the bottom and the ship can sail 'away' (or get 'under way'). But what has happned in this manoeuvre is that the anchor has been 'weighed', that is, taken up like a weight. So the spelling of the word reflects its true origin. However, the phrase 'chocks away' used of an aircraft ready to take off really does contain 'away'.

**Babel, Tower of** (biblical tower where the confusion of languages took place)
'Therefore is the name of it called Babel; because the Lord did there confound the language of all the earth' (Genesis 11:9). But there should be no confusion between 'Babel' and 'babble', although it is known that 'Babel' and 'Babylon' (one and the same place biblically) derive from a common root word, this perhaps being Assyrian *bāb-ilu*, 'gate of God' or *bāb-ili*, 'gate of the gods'. 'Babble', on the other hand, is a word of imitative origin, as it is in many other languages (French *babiller*, German *plappern*, for example). However, the translators of the Bible, as can be seen, related the name to *balal*, 'to confuse', perhaps as a deliberate pun, perhaps out of ignorance.

**bacon** (meat from the back and sides of a pig)
Incredibly, some sources say the word derives from a form of 'bake'. In fact, the origin is Germanic, and related to 'back' (i.e. of a pig). Bacon is not baked, anyway, but fried, grilled, roasted, and the like.

**badger** (animal that lives in sets and that has black and white stripes on its face)
Some modern dictionaries derive the animal's name from 'badge', referring to the white mark ('badge') on its forehead. The difficulty here is that 'badge' (unlike 'blaze') has nowhere been recorded in this sense. However, a dialect sense of 'badger' was 'middleman', 'huckster', and the animal could have been so called as it was thought to hoard corn (which in fact it doesn't). A similar connection can perhaps be seen between the French name of the animal, *blaireau*, and the French for 'corn', *blé*, although it must be said that the origin here could be an Old French word *bler*, meaning 'spotted with white'. So the true etymology here remains unresolved.

**baggage** (saucy girl)
Can this semi-slang word derive from 'baggage' in the sense of 'luggage', 'goods accompanying a traveller'? The answer is yes, with the link being the sense 'camp followers', 'women travelling with wagons' (in modern terms, 'groupies'). There is thus no need to derive the word from French *bagasse* or Italian *bagascia*, 'whore', although these words may have influenced the sense. Shakespeare was one of the first to use the word in its 'worthless woman' meaning, and at the very beginning of *The Taming of the Shrew* (the 'Induction'), Christopher Sly, when called a rogue by the Hostess, retorts, 'Y'are a baggage: the Slys are no rogues'.

**Bakelite** (type of resin used for making certain plastic goods)
'Bakelite' is a trade name, but does not derive from 'bake' or 'light', despite the association with kitchen ware, electric insulators, and the like. The name actually represents the surname of its Belgian-born inventor, L. H. Baekeland, who originally produced the substance when a chemical engineer working in America. The name first appeared in German (as *Bakelit*) in 1900.

**bald** (having little or no hair on the head)
Here's a nice fanciful origin: the word comes from 'balled', since a bald head is 'reduced to the smoothness of a ball' (so stated in Edwards, see Bibliography). In fact derivation is in Middle English *ballede*, meaning literally 'having a white spot'. In this connection, compare **piebald** and **skewbald**.

**ball** (dance)
The name derives from 'ball' (round object for sport), say some hopeful wordsmiths, since in early dances a ball was thrown among the dancers. The true origin, going

19

back through French and Latin, is in Greek *ballizein*, 'to dance'.

**ballyhoo** (uproar, rowdy publicity)
There are people who like to blame much that is wordy or noisy on the Irish, so that these good people are apparently responsible not only for 'blarney' but also for 'hooligan', respectively from the place name and surname. Similarly, there are those who like to see the origin of 'ballyhoo' in the place name 'Ballyhooly', as if the residents of this Cork village were the originators of this particular kind of racket. In point of fact they are not to blame, since the actual derivation is probably the word *ballahou*, said to be a native Central American name for a type of wood from which clumsy sailing boats were made. This in turn gave rise to the expression 'ballyhoo of blazes', used contemptuously by sailors for a ship they disliked. The phrase was still actively used in the present century.

**bandanna** (type of handkerchief or neckerchief)
The word, also spelt 'bandana', does not derive from 'band' or 'bandage', but from a Hindi word *bādhnū*, meaning what today is called 'tie-dyeing', that is, dyeing a cloth but tying sections of it together so that they will not absorb the dye. Hence the spotty or patchy appearance of a genuine large silk bandanna.

**bang** (hairstyle)
The once popular style had the hair cut straight across the forehead, and this could have quite a striking effect, i. e. give a shock or aesthetic 'bang' to the sensitive beholder, who was used to long locks. But the origin is not quite in this sort of 'bang', but in the resemblance of this hairstyle to the 'bang-tail', or short tail of a horse, which was so called as it had been 'cut bang off'. Other hairstyles also derive from animals, such as the 'pigtail', 'ponytail', 'cowlick' and even the 'duck's arse' (or 'D.A.') favoured by teddy boys in the 1950s.

**bangle** (kind of bracelet)
The bangle is not so called as it dangles or jangles, but because it originated as an Indian coloured glass bracelet, called in Hindi *bangrī*.

**banksia** (kind of shrub)
Some flower and shrub names are misleadingly suggestive (compare, for example, the **gardenia**). This particular one is not so called as it grows on or by banks, but because it was introduced by the eighteenth-century botanist and explorer Sir Joseph Banks, who sailed round the world with Captain Cook.

**banns** (official proclamation of a forthcoming marriage)
The word is not a special variant of 'bands', as if implying a future **wedlock** (see this word also), but derives quite normally from the Old English verb *bannan*, 'to proclaim'. It is, however, related to 'ban', since such a proclamation enables an objection to be made to the marriage, which can therefore, in theory, be banned. (Hence the inclusion, in the Prayer Book formula, of the sentence: 'If any of you know cause, or just impediment, why these two persons should not be joined together in holy Matrimony, ye are to declare it'.)

**barbecue** (outdoor meal cooked over an open fire)
A rather ingenious origin of this word has been proposed in French *barbe*, 'beard' and *queue*, 'tail', since the animal from which the meat is cut is cooked whole, i. e. from 'beard' to 'tail'. But the word actually comes from Spanish America, where *barbacoa* was the term for a special cooking frame made out of sticks.

**barberry** (spiny shrub with yellow flowers and orange berries)
The barberry bush does indeed have berries, but the origin of its name lies in Old French *berberis*, which is also the scientific name of its genus. The source of this generic name is not known. (It is sometimes said to be from the Arabic *barbārīs*, although this is likely to be simply a transcription from the Latin made by Arabian botanists.)

**barbican** (type of fortification)
Why is a barbican so called? Because it

'barred' the enemy? Because it served as a 'barricade'? Because it was a 'bastion'? Because it was 'barbed' with defences? These origins suggest themselves, but the true derivation is uncertain. All that is known is that the word came into English from Old French *barbacane*, itself from Medieval Latin *barbacana*. And the derivation of that is unknown.

**bargain** (agreed transaction, especially one at a satisfactorily low price)
The origin is not in a 'gain' made at or over a 'bar', but in Old French *bargaignier*, 'to trade', which may itself be related to English 'borrow'.

**barley sugar** (kind of hard, clear sweet)
Some etymologists have sought to derive the name from French *brûlé*, 'burnt', as if the substance was originally *sucre brûlé*, 'burnt sugar'. But why such ingenuity? The name means what it says, since barley sugar, even if not now, at least once was made with a barley extract.

**barmy** (crazy)
This slang word, also spelt 'balmy', has had a number of ingenious fabrications to account for it. One tells how the origin lies in the name of St Bartholomew, since he was the patron saint of the feeble-minded. Another derives the name from Barming Asylum near Maidstone, in Kent, where this was the former county lunatic asylum (or mental hospital, as we would say today). The truth of the matter probably lies in the simple adjective derived from 'barm', that is, 'full of barm'. Barm is a term for yeast, and so is here used to produce a sense 'frothy', 'excitable'.

**barnacle goose** (kind of north European goose with black and white body and grey wings)
What is the connection between this bird and the shellfish that is identically named? The answer lies in the curious old belief that the bird was born or 'hatched' out of the shellfish as they held fast to trees and other objects over the water. But this may well not be the whole story, and it is just possible that the two similar words originate from different sources independently. The mystery of the geese and the barnacles has not yet been finally solved. (To complicate matters, there is a special kind of barnacle called a 'goose barnacle'.)

**baron of beef** (double sirloin joined at the backbone)
Is the joint so called as it is 'rich' like a baron? Or perhaps it is a corruption of 'barrel of beef'? The answer seems to be that the name is a punning reference to the **sirloin** (which see, for its own popular history). 'Baron of Beef' is sometimes found as an evocative inn name.

**barracking** (loud vocal criticism)
The semi-colloquial word suggests that it is somehow connected with 'barracks', and especially 'barrackroom language'. But the true origin appears to be a dialect word, perhaps Australian *borak*, a native word occurring in the phrase 'to poke borak'. However, according to the *English Dialect Dictionary*, the derivation may be in a Northern Ireland word meaning 'to boast'. Either way, the source does not seem to be 'barrack'.

**basalt** (kind of dark rock)
Perhaps because basalt rocks are often found by the sea (as at the famous Giant's Causeway in Northern Ireland), it is sometimes supposed that the word derives from 'salt', with an additional association in 'rock salt'. But the name actually goes back, through Latin, to Greek *basanitēs lithos*, 'touchstone', with this in turn ultimately deriving from some Egyptian word.

**bassoon** (woodwind musical instrument)
Some popular reference sources still derive the name from 'bass horn', perhaps confusing the instrument with the 'basset horn'. But as with many musical instruments, the origin lies in an Italian word, here *bassone*, meaning 'deep' with the so called augmentative (or 'big') ending *-one* (as in 'minestrone', which is literally a 'big serving' of soup). By contrast, the basset horn actually derives its name from the opposite, the diminutive or 'small' form of Italian *basso*, which is *bassetto* (not to be confused with a *cornetto*, which is a post-

man's horn or, in another context, a delicious icecream).

**bastard** (illegitimate offspring)
The designation is often thought to derive from 'base'. Certainly Shakespeare seemed to think so, when in *King Lear* Edmund, the bastard son of the Earl of Gloucester, declaims:

'Why bastard? wherefore base?
. . . Why brand they us
With base? with baseness? bastardy?
base, base?'

The true origin of the word is probably much more interesting, and very likely the source is the French phrase *fils de bast*, 'son of the packsaddle', that is, a son born of a union elsewhere than in the marriage bed.

**bated** (of breath: held in suspense or fear)
The word is not an alternative spelling of 'baited', as if the breath had been 'caught' (although if you catch your breath you do hold it). It is simply a short form of 'abated'. The verb 'abate', meaning 'diminish' (originally 'beat down', from Old French *abatre*), was formerly often shortened to 'bate', and occurs in this form several times in Shakespeare, for example.

**bath chair** (kind of invalid chair)
The chair was not one in which originally a patient went to a bath. It was, however, first in use in the town of Bath, which is famous for its baths, and that is the source of the name. Doubtless this false etymology arose since the phrase today is usually spelt with a small letter, and since many other terms, such as 'bath cube', 'bath salts' and so on, are indeed connected with a bath. Bath the spa and resort has produced a number of 'healthy' terms, including also the tasty Bath bun and Bath Oliver, and the attractive Bath stone.

**batman** (officer's personal servant)
This functionary is not so called as he carries a bat, or looks after the officer's baton, or even because he 'bats for', his senior, or defends his interests. Nor does the name originate in his authority to act 'off his own bat'. The word's derivation lies in Old French *bat* or *bast*, from Medieval Latin

*bastum*, 'packsaddle' (see in this respect **bastard**, above). He thus originally looked after the officer's luggage or baggage when it was transported by horse.

**batty** (crazy)
Another slang word for 'mad', like **barmy** (above). In her 'little etymology of eponymous words', Rosie Boycott (see Bibliography) derives 'batty' from an eccentric barrister in Jamaica called Fitzherbert Batty. But it seems much more likely, if less colourful, that the word simply has its origin in the phrase 'bats in the belfry'. In passing, it is interesting that many slang words for 'crazy' end in '-tty', among them not only 'batty', but also 'dotty', 'potty', 'scatty' and 'nutty'. See also **belfry**, in its own right.

**bawbee** (former Scottish coin)
It has been suggested that the former silver coin known as a bawbee was so called since it was a small or 'babby' coin, or because it had the head of the baby king on it. The truth is much more likely to be a historical derivation, from the name of Alexander Orok, laird of Sillebawby, who was master of the mint from 1538. The bawbee was worth sixpence, and was anyway first struck some time after the 'babby' one-year-old king James V came to the throne in 1513.

**bazaar** (colourful market)
A bazaar is not so called because of its bizarre variety, but because the word came into English from a Persian word meaning 'market'. The origin of 'bizarre' itself is still uncertain. It seems to have come into English from some Italian word.

**beaker** (drinking vessel)
The beaker is not related to 'beak', even though drinkers 'dip their beak' into it. The word's ultimate derivation, through Germanic languages, is Greek *bikos*, 'drinking bowl'.

**bear garden** (scene of disorder or chaos)
It would be nice to think that the term was a corruption of 'beer garden', as some imagine it is, referring to the scenes and sounds of noisy, drunken revelry. In fact the words refer to a place, such as a garden or enclosure, where bear-baiting took place.

Hence the association of uproar and confusion.

**beatific** (showing great happiness or calm)
A 'beatific' smile may be a beautiful one, but the two words are not related. 'Beatific' means literally 'made blessed', from Late Latin *beatificus*, while 'beautiful' comes from Latin *bellus*, 'handsome', via French *beau*. For something else also occasionally regarded as beautiful, see **beaujolais** (below).

**beaujolais** (popular red or white wine)
Beaujolais is an attractive wine, but its name does not derive from a combination of French *beau*, 'beautiful' and *joli*, 'pretty'. Like most wines, the name refers to its region of origin, which here is Beaujolais in southern Burgundy.

**bedlam** (disorderly scene)
For some reason, the word is often thought to derive from 'bed', perhaps by association with an apple-pie bed or with a mental picture of a pillow fight (which could well be bedlam). The actual origin, rather surprisingly, is in 'Bethlehem', or more precisely in the former London lunatic asylum called the Hospital of St Mary of Bethlehem, whose name is now preserved in the Bethlehem Royal Hospital at Beckenham, in Kent.

**beefeater** (yeoman warder at Tower of London)
Because the apparent meaning, 'eating of beef', seems too obvious, a more 'learned' alternative origin was provided for the word, which derived it from French *buffetier*, denoting an official who served at a *buffet*, or 'side-table' (doubtless one groaning with beef). But the apparent origin is the true one, and arose as a nickname for a plump, well-fed servant, especially a 'beefy' one.

**behemoth** (huge monstrous creature)
The behemoth is not so called because it resembles a gigantic moth, even though a large moth can also be a frightening monster. The origin of the word is in Hebrew *běhēmōth*, which is the plural of *běhēmāh*, 'beast'. (The plural here is a so called 'plural of dignity' to indicate a great and awesome beast.) The behemoth first came to the attention of English readers and listeners in the Bible, where it occurs in Job 40:15 ('Behold now behemoth . . . he eateth grass as an ox.'). It is thought that the beast was probably a hippopotamus, and it is interesting that in Russian the word for 'hippopotamus' today is *begemot*.

**bel** (unit of comparison in measurement of, e.g., noise, making ten decibels)
The name of the unit does not derive from 'bell', but from 'Bell', that is, from the appropriately named Scottish-born engineer, Alexander Graham Bell, who invented the telephone. For another word that does not derive from 'bell', see **belfry** (below).

**belfry** (part of a tower or steeple in which bells are hung)
The word has long been associated with 'bell', understandably enough. It originated, however, in Old French *berfrei*, which itself derived from two Germanic words meaning respectively 'fort', 'protector', and 'peace'. The tower that later came to house bells was thus originally a 'peace-protector', or defensive tower. In the thirteenth century the word was used in English to denote a movable siege tower.

**bergamask** (kind of rustic dance)
This is one of those agreeable but rarish words whose meaning often remain elusive, the sort of word where we think, 'Yes, I've heard of that – now *what* is it?' In such cases we seize one any familiar association in the word, and here it is usually 'mask', with special reference to masked dances. But the true origin is in the region of the original dance, which is Bergamo in Italy. Natives of Bergamo are known as 'Bergamasks' (or 'Bergomasks'), so the dance itself is a 'Bergamask' one. The false association with 'mask' is further encouraged by the musical piece called a 'bergamask' (or 'berga-masque' or 'bergamasca'), and in particular by Fauré's suite entitled *Masques et bergamasques*. For Bergamo's own role in false etymologies, see **bergamot** (below).

**bergamot** (kind of pear)
The name 'bergamot' applies not just to a

variety of pear but to a kind of tree yielding an aromatic oil, a kind of mint, and a type of tapestry. It is just possible that one or two of these, perhaps the last, may derive from the name of Bergamo, the city in northern Italy, but the pear's name goes back, through Italian, to some word of Turkic origin, possibly associated with Turkish *bey-armadu*, 'prince's pear'. For further involvement of Bergamo, see **bergamask** (above).

**bevy** (group or gathering of some kind)
A 'bevy' is usually a gathering of pleasant or colourful creatures of some kind, such as quails, roedeer or 'beauties', and perhaps for this reason it is often thought to derive from 'bevvy' in the sense of 'drinking party'. But this is almost certainly not the true derivation. Originally, from the fifteenth century, it was applied almost always to women (a 'bevy of ladies'), and a sixteenth-century writer, commenting on the word's use in Spenser's *Shepherd's Calendar* ('this bevie of ladies bright'), says, 'the terme is taken of larkes'. But although there *may* be a link with drinking, even with the modern Liverpool dialect 'bevvy', the source still remains uncertain.

**bidding prayer** (special prayer in church service)
The term is usually understood as 'prayer bidding the people to pray'. It originated, however, as the phrase 'bidding of the prayer' or 'bidding of the prayers', where 'bidding' was used in its now obsolete sense of 'praying'. So the historicc sense is 'praying of the prayers'.

**bigamy** (the illegal marriage of an already married person to someone else)
The semi-legal term does not originate in the 'big' crime, or in the fact that the person has gone in for marriage in a 'big' way, but has a more scholarly derivation in Latin *bi-*, 'two' and Greek *gamos*, 'marriage'. Perhaps knowledge of 'monogamy' (marriage to one person) and 'polygamy' (marriage to many), with their Greek prefixes, subconsciously suggest that 'marriage to two' should be 'digamy', since the Greek numeric sequence usually goes 'mono-', 'di-', 'tri-' while the Latin equivalent goes 'uni-', 'bi-',

'tri-'. Or possibly the pronunciation of 'bi-' in the word (unlike its usual sound in such words as 'bicycle' and 'binary') disguises its true sense.

**bigot** (opinionated and intolerant person)
One rather nice tale behind the word derives it from a French pronunciation of the English exclamation 'by God!', with a story how Rollo, Duke of Normandy, is said to have declared *Nese bi god* ('No, by God') when pressed to kiss the foot of Charles the Simple, his father-in-law. But the word is really of obscure origin. It may perhaps somehow relate to the name of the Visigoths, who set up a kingdom in present Spain and southern France in the fifth century. But if the French did not call the Normans the 'by Gods', they did at least call the English the 'God damns' ('goddams').

**bikini** (women's two-piece swimming costume)
It is generally recognized that the name derives from Bikini atoll in the North Pacific, where an American atom bomb was tested in 1946, but the reason for the transfer of name in this unlikely manner is often misunderstood. It is not because the bomb blew the atoll into two small halves, but because the effect of first seeing women in the brief garment was, for Frenchmen (where the name originated), as 'explosive' as the atom bomb that was still in the news when the garments were first worn. At the same time, it must be admitted that there could be a more subtle link between the scantiness of the costume and the minuteness of atoms (an 'atomy' is an old word for a minute particle or creature). However, despite the emergence of the 1960s 'monokini' (lower half only), it is generally realized that the 'bi-' of 'bikini' does not mean 'two', however apparently appropriate!

**billycock hat** (kind of round-crowned hat)
The hat is (or was) not so called as it was worn by 'bully cocks', that is, 'swells' who fancied themselves, but because it was created for William Coke, a nineteenth-century English gentleman, whose wearing of it started a new fashion. It was really a sort of **bowler** (which see below).

**billyoh** (in the phrase 'like billyoh': 'very much')
Rosie Boycott (see the Bibliography) derives the word, which she spells 'billio', from the name of a zealous seventeenth-century Puritan minister called Joseph Billio. But the word was not first recorded until the nineteenth century, and this origin therefore seems unlikely. There may, of course, have been some topical or local William or 'Billie' whose enthusiasm or fanaticism led to the expression. Similar phrases are usually based on more infernal sources, such as 'like the devil', 'like blazes' and 'like hell'.

**bistro** (kind of small restaurant)
The usual story behind this French word is that when Russian troops invaded Paris after the fall of Napoleon in 1815, they raced into restaurants and cafés to eat and drink with shouts of *bystro! bystro!* ('quick! quick!'). (A command they might well have made in their own restaurants, where service was notoriously slow.) But the much more likely origin of the word is in the French *bistouille*, or cheap wine, that was sold in such places.

**bitter end** (the absolute end)
The phrase ('to the bitter end') usually implies danger and difficulty. Hence, it is commonly supposed, the bitterness. But there may well be truth in the derivation from the nautical 'bitter end', the term for the final part of the rope or cable that was left round the bitts (special posts on the deck) when the rest was overboard. When the rope was paid out 'to the bitter end', that was it, there was no more to go.

**black magic** (magic for evil purposes)
The derivation would seem to be obvious and lie in the evil 'powers of darkness'. The true origin is probably more prosaic. The phrase is a translation of Medieval Latin *nigromantia* (where *nigro-* means 'black'), But this was a corruption of *necromantia,* 'necromancy', that is 'corpse conjuring' (more precisely, 'corpse divination'), and 'black' was not originally in the picture. However, both darkness and corpses are sinister, so that the end result is similar. As a counter to the evil 'black magic', there also developed 'white magic', which is good and kindly.

**blackmail** (use of threats or intimidation to obtain money or other favours)
The popular image is of a shady or corrupt knight in armour, but 'mail' here, now obsolete in the sense, means 'monetary payment', especially in rent or taxes. 'Black' payment of this kind would have been one that was extorted unfairly.

**blanket** (bed covering)
The cosy covering is not so called as it is 'blank', or undecorated, but because originally it was white (French *blanc*). The word came into English from French. Rosie Boycott (see the Bibliography) says that blankets are so called as they were originally woven by one Thomas Blanket of Bristol!

**blasphemy** (violation of a holy name)
If you blaspheme, you may say 'blast', but the two words are not linked, and a blasphemer is not someone who 'blasts God', as has been sometimes suggested. The origin is in Greek *blasphēmos*, 'evil-speaking', from *blapsis*, 'evil', 'harming' and *phēmē*, 'speech'.

**blazer** (colourful jacket, especially as worn by members of a sports team)
In an attempt to explain the name of the garment, a story has arisen that such jackets were first worn by members of the crew of the ship HMS 'Blazer'. In fact, however, the name simply refers to the bright or 'blazing' colours of the blazer, as worn by university boating crews and other sportsmen.

**blindfold** (bandage over the eyes)
Although a blindfold is usually devised from a folded piece of cloth, such as a handkerchief, the origin has nothing to do with 'fold'. The word comes from Old English *blindfellian*, 'to strike blind', and down to the sixteenth century a blindfold was called a *blindfelle*. The 'fell' here is the same as the modern 'fell a tree'. Because of the way blindfolds were prepared, however, the word became associated with 'fold'.

**bliss** (state of great happiness or ecstasy)
The derivation of the word is not from 'blessed' but from an Old English word related to 'blithe'. ('Bless,' unexpectedly, is related to 'blood'.)

**bloody** (as swearword: 'bad', 'very')
Many swearwords are distorted versions of older expressions, such as 'struth' from 'God's truth', and 'bloody', for this reason, is often stated to be a contraction of 'by Our Lady'. It probably means what it says, however, since blood is a fearsome yet vital thing. It is likely, however, that the curse was influenced by the swearword 'sblood', meaning 'by God's blood'.

**bloomers** (women's baggy knickers)
Were they so called as they 'bloomed' or were voluminous? Were they a 'blooming' disgrace in their day? The answer is no to both, since they were introduced (about 1850) by the American social reformer Mrs Amelia Bloomer, who recommended them (but did not invent them) as a 'rational dress' for women. As originally conceived, they consisted of a pair of 'Turkish' trousers gathered round the ankle worn with a short jacket and a skirt coming down below the knee. A modified form of bloomers was subsequently worn by women cyclists.

**blowsy** (of a woman: untidy, slovenly in appearance)
The epithet, also spelt 'blowzy', suggests a derivation in 'blouse', perhaps with a touch of 'blowy' or 'blown'. But there is no connection with these words, and 'blowsy' comes from an obsolete term *blowze* used to describe a beggar girl or sluttish woman (defined by Dr Johnson as 'a ruddy, fat-faced wench').

**bludgeon** (kind of heavy club)
The word conjures up a possible origin in a blend of 'blunt' and 'truncheon', but its actual derivation is unknown. It could have come into English from some French word. For another misascribed weapon, see **blunderbuss** (below).

**blunderbuss** (type of old musket)
Since the blunderbuss scattered shot all over the place, it often proved inaccurate (which is probably why it was mostly fired at short range), and for this reason it could be thought that the name comes from 'blunder'). It certainly came to be associated with this word, but in actual fact orig-

inated in the Dutch *donderbus*, literally 'thunder gun'. Either way, it's a good name.

**blurb** (promotional description on the cover of a book)
The semi-jargon term does not derive, except subconsciously, from 'blurt', as if the publisher or author had 'blurted' a lot of 'blah' about the book. It is in fact a coined word, devised in the early twentieth century by the American author Gelett Burgess to promote his book *Are You a Bromide?*. The jacket of the book had a picture of a sweet but sickly-looking girl called 'Miss Belinda Blurb', and Burgess later referred to her as shown to be 'blurbing a blurb to end all blurbs, I fondly hoped'. But doubtless subconsciously Burgess had invented the name and word under the influence of other 'blabbing' words such as 'blurt', 'bluff' and even 'blarney'.

**bodice** (type of corset or undergarment)
The bodice is not so called since it is (or was) worn next to the body, but because it was originally called a 'pair of bodies', with 'body' in the sense used to describe the part of the dress above the waist. The garment was originally worn by men, too, so that Dr Johnson, in his *Life of Pope*, tells us that 'he was invested in bodice made of stiff canvass'.

**bogus** (false, sham)
This word does not derive from 'bogey', even though both words suggest something unpleasant or at any rate mischievous. The actual source of 'bogus' is uncertain, but the term originated in the United States to apply to false coins, and it could, perhaps, be related to 'bogie' in the sense of 'wheeled assembly', referring to the device (the so called 'bogus press') that was used to produce such coins.

**Bohemian** (unconventionally or extravagantly artistic)
Bohemian artists were not so called because they came from Bohemia in central Europe, but because such an artist was like a gypsy, the French for which is *bohémien*. The word was introduced into English in this sense by Thackeray in *Vanity Fair*, where he says of Becky Sharp, 'she was of a wild, roving

nature, inherited from father and mother, who were both Bohemians, in taste and circumstances'.

**boil** (painful swelling)
A boil is not so called because it is hot and tender, as if it had arisen by being 'boiled', but because it was originally a 'bile', this word being related to Latin *bulla*, 'bubble'. A boil has thus been 'blown up', not boiled up.

**bombast** (pompous talk)
Bombast may have a 'battering' effect on the hearer or captive audience, but this is not because it 'bombs' or has a powerful 'blasting' effect. Nor, as sometimes stated, is the word derived from the middle name of the great Phillippus Aureolus Theophrastus Bombastus von Hohenheim, better known as Paracelsus, the sixteenth-century Swiss physician and alchemist. Bombast was originally a word meaning 'cotton wool used for padding', and derives, through French, from Latin *bombyx*, 'silk'. (Hence the name of the fabric known as bombazine.) So bombast is all padding, not all bombing and blasting.

**Bombay duck** (type of fish, eaten dried with curry)
This is one of those weird foods, like the **Jerusalem artichoke**, whose name betrays its true nature or provenance. In this case, the Bombay duck was indeed exported originally from Bombay, but it is a fish, not a duck. It came to be so called since it was regarded as a substitute for roast duck, and since with a heavy accompaniment of curry and other spicy Indian dishes, its taste can be suitably disguised. It is thus in the same category as Scotch woodcock, which is not woodcock (an exotic meat) but anchovies and egg on toast. However, although exported from Bombay, and thus associated with this city, Bombay duck really got its name as a corruption of its native name of *bombila*, and this came to give the dish its alternative name of 'bummalo'.

**bonfire** (outdoor fire)
A bonfire is not so called because it was, in French, a *bon feu*, or 'good fire', but because it was originally a 'bone fire', that is, a funeral pyre. There are some odd coincidences in associated words, however, so that the French phrase *faire un bon feu* means 'to burn bodies', and 'pyre' (funeral fire) and 'fire' are related words. However, for most people a bonfire is a festive one, which is why it is known in French as a *feu de joie*. Doubtless this 'good' association also encouraged the false derivation from *bon*.

**boomerang** (type of Australian throwing stick that returns to the thrower)
The boomerang is not so called because it 'booms' back to the thrower, or because it is used for catching 'boomers' (kangaroos). The word is a native one, recorded in Port Jackson as *wo-mur-rang* and elsewhere as *bumarin*.

**boon** (benefit, blessing)
A boon is not so called because it is something 'good' (French *bon*, Latin *bonus*), but because it originally meant 'prayer', 'petition', from some rather obscure Germanic source. In the phrase 'boon companion', however, the source actually is French *bon*.

**boot** (compartment for luggage in a car)
A boot is not so called for its shape, despite the fact that other parts of a car have 'dress' designations, such as 'bonnet' and 'hood'. The origin of the word is almost certainly French *boîte*, 'box', although it could also perhaps be *botte*, 'cask'. Either way, it is not 'boot'. For more about boots, see **boot and saddle** (below).

**boot and saddle** (historic order for cavalry to mount)
The command seems to say 'Put your boots on and get in the saddle', or something similar, but the phrase originates in French *boute-selle*, literally 'put saddle'. This was the trumpet call to mount, having first, of course, made sure to *bouter* (put) the *selle* (saddle) on the horse. In the United States, the command was more usually given in the form 'boots and saddles'.

**bore** (tidal wave)
This kind of wave, such as the famous 'Severn Bore', is not so called because it

'bores' its way up the river, but because the word comes from Old Norse *bāra*, 'billow'.

**borstal** (corrective training centre for young offenders)
A borstal is now usually called a 'detention centre', but when more widely used did not derive as a kind of corruption of 'board school', as sometimes imagined. The establishment took its name from the place where the first such centre was set up in 1902, Borstal in Kent (now part of Rochester). By an odd coincidence, the actual place name Borstal means 'security place', from Old English *borg* and *steall*.

**bound** (travelling to)
If you are 'bound' for the coast, say, this is not because you are 'bound' or destined to go there, or because you are 'bound' or certain to make the journey. There are at least four distinct words 'bound' in English, and this one is not related to the others. It ultimately derives from an Old Norse word *būinn*, meaning 'prepared'. So when you are 'homeward bound' you are all set to return to your native land or house.

**bow** (front, curved part of a ship)
A ship's bow is curved, but its name is not related to 'bow' in the sense 'arc'. Both words are ultimately of Germanic origin, but a ship's bow is related to 'bough' while the other 'bow' (rhyming with 'slow') is related to 'bow and arrow'.

**bower** (leafy shelter)
A bower has come to be associated with trees, just as an **arbour** has (which see), and Tennyson in his *In Memoriam* wrote of 'branchy bowers'. The poetic word does not derive from 'bough', however, but from Old English *būr*, 'dwelling', which was its original sense. The old meaning survives as the second half of the word 'neighbour', since he lives in a 'nearby dwelling'.

**bowler** (type of round-crowned hat)
It would be agreeable to think that the bowler hat is so called because it is shaped like a bowl, or because it 'bowls' along when the wind sends it flying. In point of fact it is named after its designer, the London hatter John Bowler. The bowler hat appeared in the mid-nineteenth century, just about the same time as the **billycock** (which see), which resembled it.

**boxcalf** (kind of patterned calfskin leather)
The name of the leather suggests its use for 'boxing' or packing, or perhaps points to the pattern of fine creases on it, resembling little boxes. But the word, or at any rate the first part of it, comes from the name of its originator, the London bootmaker Joseph Box. The leather was promoted, and the name actually devised, by an American, Edward L. White, of Boston, and rather naughtily (or purely commercially) he advertised the product by means of a picture of a calf in a box. Boxcalf first appeared on the market at the end of the nineteenth century.

**brand-new** (newly made)
A brand-new object or product is not so called as it is a 'new brand', but because it is, as it were, 'fresh from the furnace', like newly forged iron. However, both senses of 'brand' ('mark made with hot iron' and 'class of goods') are from one and the same word.

**breeze block** (kind of light brick for building)
The brick or block has a name that suggests it is porous, or that the breeze can blow through it. The word derives from French *braise*, however, meaning 'live coals' (as in English 'brazier'), referring to its manner of manufacture from the ashes of coal, coke, and the like. In America, less ambiguously, breeze blocks are usually known as 'cinderblocks' or 'clinker blocks'.

**briar pipe** (kind of tobacco pipe)
Possibly the fragrance of some tobaccos suggests a connection with the briar that is the wild rose. The pipe is so called, however, since it is made from the woody root of the other shrub called 'briar' (or 'brier'), which is the tree heath or *Erica arborea*, growing in southern Europe.

**bridal** (relating to a bride or wedding)
The word looks like a standard adjective formed, as several are, by adding '-al' to the noun, as in 'sectional', 'tonal' and the like.

But the origin of 'bridal', somewhat unexpectedly, is in an Old English word corresponding to 'bride-ale', that is, a noun denoting a wedding feast. There were other types of 'ales' or feasts in 'merry old England' as well, including a 'leet-ale' (manorial court feast), 'church-ale', 'clerk-ale' and 'bid-ale' (in a particular person's honour, to which there was a general 'bidding' or invitation). The 'ale' of all these is beer, of course. For more relating to brides, see **bridegroom** (below).

**bridegroom** (man who is about to marry, or who has just married)
The word originated from Old English *brȳdguma*, literally 'bride man'. Later, under the influence of 'groom', the form (and popular understanding) of the word changed. There are thus two sorts of grooms in modern English, of different origin: the one who is properly a 'bridegroom', and the one who looks after horses (and who was originally simply a servant or 'man'). The Old English word quoted here is related to the modern German word for 'bridegroom' (normally used on the day only) which is *Bräutigam*. For a related word (and person), see **bridal** (above).

**broach** (pierce [a cask], initiate [a subject])
Since a form of 'breaking' is involved in both the actions expressed by 'broach', it might be supposed that the word is related to 'breach' or even to 'break' itself. In fact the words are unrelated, and 'broach', which *is* related to 'brooch', originally meant 'pointed rod', 'roasting spit', coming into English from Old French *broche*, in turn from Latin *broccus*. 'Breach' and 'break', however, are related words deriving from a Germanic source. See also **broker** (below).

**Broadmoor** (mental hospital in Berkshire)
Because of open expanses such as Dartmoor (famous for its prison), Broadmoor is often wrongly identified or incorrectly located. The name certainly means 'broad moor', but only in a local sense, and today the hospital is not on a rolling heath but surrounded by pine woods near the modern town of Crowthorne. Probably the 'confinement' image of Dartmoor prison and Broad-

moor mental hospital also blurs the correct identification of the latter place.

**broker** (commercial or other agent)
There is no connection with 'break' here, not even with people who are 'broke' and need financial aid. A broker originated as a 'broacher', that is, as a tapster or buyer and seller of casks. The word is thus related to **broach** (which see, above).

**brown study** (reverie)
According to some sources, the phrase originated as 'brow study', as if one were sitting with furrowed brow. But there is no evidence that this is the derivation, and the sense seems to be 'brown' meaning 'dark', 'gloomy'. The expression dates from the sixteenth century, so cannot be related to 'browned off', which is a much more modern phrase (although it also uses 'brown' in a dreary or depressing sense). 'Melancholy' has a similar 'dark' origin, since it derives from the Greek for 'black bile'.

**buccaneer** (pirate)
A mutineer is someone who mutinies, and a cannoneer is someone who fires a cannon, but a buccaneer is not someone who 'bucks' in any sense of the word, or who fancies himself as a sort of 'buck' of the high seas. The word comes from French *boucanier* itself derived from an old native word of West Indian origin meaning 'frame for smoking meat'. Original buccaneers were thus French and English hunters who trapped and killed animals in the West Indies (in particular San Domingo, now the Dominican Republic, and Tortuga) and dried the flesh of their prey on such frames. The name then transferred to Spanish pirates, whose habits were somewhat similar. There are curious parallels here between 'buccaneer' and 'barbecue', both in the sound and sense of the original words (see **barbecue**) and in the Spanish American connection.

**buck** (in phrase 'pass the buck': shift responsibility onto someone else)
It is often widely felt, especially by the English, perhaps, that the buck involved here is a dollar, which for some reason is being passed on to someone else as being

too 'hot' or as having some illegal connection with gambling. The 'buck' is not a dollar, although there is indeed a link with gambling, or rather with poker, since the word originated as a term for the marker in the jackpot that reminded the winner of his obligation to set up a new jackpot when he dealt. The word 'buck' has many senses (even the *Concise Oxford Dictionary* has nine), and its origin here is uncertain.

**bucket** (in phrase 'kick the bucket': die)
The phrase is sometimes explained, rather grimly, as referring to the upturned bucket that a suicide stood on, when roped to a beam, before he kicked it away. More probably, the word is not the familiar kind of bucket but a dialect word for the beam itself (perhaps related to French *trébuchet*, 'trap', 'balance') from which, equally grimly, a pig would be suspended for slaughter. In its throes the animal would thus 'kick the bucket'.

**buckram** (material used for lining and bookbinding)
The material is nothing to do with buckskin, but ultimately derives, through French, from the name of the city of Bukhara or Bokhara, now in the Soviet Union, and long famous for its textiles.

**buckwheat** (kind of cereal)
Buckwheat does not serve as a grain food for bucks, but has a name that derives from Middle Dutch *boecweite*, 'beech wheat', from the resemblance of the grains to beechnuts.

**budgerigar** (kind of small Australian parrot kept as a cagebird)
The homely 'budgie' is not so called because it likes to 'budge' from its perch or cage (or because it refuses to), but because it has a native Australian name. This is a compound of *budgeri*, 'good' and *gar*, 'cockatoo', which simple description seems to sum it up quite well. In America the name was sometimes corrupted (and elevated) to 'beauregarde', as if in allusion to the bird's handsomeness.

**bugle** (kind of plant having small blue or white flowers)
Perhaps on an analogy with other names such as 'trumpet flower' and 'harebell', it is

sometimes thought that this small flower resembles a bugle. The true derivation, however, can be found in Late Latin *bugula*, itself a word of uncertain origin. The bugle, incidentally, is not related to the bugloss, whose own name is more meaningful since it derives from the Greek for 'ox tongue'.

**bulldog** (breed of fierce-looking, thick-bodied dog)
The head of a bulldog can certainly look something like that of a bull, pugnacious and stocky, but the dog is very likely so named as it was used in bull-baiting, and not for its appearance.

**bully beef** (canned corned beef)
The name may suggest 'beef for bullies', that is, suitable for tough and aggressive people, but it actually originates from French *boeuf bouilli*, 'boiled beef'. The second of these two words was anglicized in what was thought to be a meaningful way by the people who ate the beef. There is also, therefore, no connection with 'bull', even though beef comes from bulls. Compare **corned beef**.

**bulwark** (stout defence, especially one on a ship)
The word 'bull' (or 'bul-') begins many words with 'stout' meanings, such as the bulrush, which is a thick kind of rush, and the bullfinch, which has a stocky body and thick neck. In the case of 'bulwark', however, the origin is not in 'bull work', suitable though it might seem, but, via Dutch, in Middle High German *bolwerk*, literally 'plank work'. Compare English 'bole' as a related word.

**bum-bailiff** (former official authorized to collect debts and arrest debtors)
Here is the genteel explanation: a bum-bailiff was really a 'bound' bailiff, that is one whose bounden duty it was to execute his task, under threat of penalty if he did not. In reality, the name means what it says: he was a bailiff who followed hard on the heels of the debtors, or who harassed them from the rear until they paid up.

**bumper** (glass filled to the brim)
A bumper is traditionally a glass from which

a toast is drunk, and this has prompted some ingenious word-processors to declare that the origin of the name lies in the French *au bon père*, 'to the good father', i. e. a toast to the pope. But the true derivation is almost certainly much more prosaic, and the reference is either to an old verb 'bump' meaning 'bulge', describing the brimming drink, or simply to 'bumping' in the sense 'thumping', 'very large'. The 'French' explanation is thus an attempt to give a more refined origin to a rather basic word. For a similarly concocted etymology, see **bum-bailiff** (above).

**bumpkin** (yokel, lout, rustic person)
The word would seem so obviously to link up with other 'loutish' words such as 'bump', 'bum' and 'bumble'. The most likely derivation, however, is in Dutch *boomken*, 'little tree', with the term first used as a derogatory nickname for a Dutchman, seen as a small and thick-set person. The wretched Dutch have a hard time of it in English terms, as witness all the 'Dutch' phrases: the Dutch uncle who criticizes and reproves, the Dutch treat that is no treat at all, the false Dutch courage gained by alcohol, the Dutch auction where the prices get lower, not higher. Builders even call a piece of wood or metal used to repair or patch up poor workmanship a 'dutchman'. See also **yokel**, for another rustic source.

**bungalow** (small, single-storied house)
In English terms, a bungalow has a name that suggests a 'low' house into which the residents can 'bung' their belongings. But the word is of Indian or Bengali origin, as is the house itself, and the native term for it is *bangla*, 'Bengali' ('house' understood). This word today forms the first half of the name of Bangladesh, meaning 'Bengali nation'.

**burden** (main theme of a book or speech)
The 'burden' of a speech is not so called as it is the main 'weight' or 'burden' of it, but because it runs through it like a constantly recurring chorus or 'burden' in the musical sense, this in turn deriving from Old French *bourdon*, the word for a bass horn that droned on and on. (In English, 'bourdon' is still used as a musical term for a bagpipe drone or organ stop.)

**bust** (sculpture of upper half of the body)
A bust looks as if it so called because it has been 'bust' off from the rest of the body below the shoulders. The precise origin of the word, which came into English from Italian *busto* (via French *buste*), is not clear, but it is certainly not this. The other sense of the word, 'chest of a human being', 'bosom', is the same in origin, although the 'sculpture' sense came first, not the other way round.

**bustle** (frame formerly used for padding out a skirt behind)
The word is not connected with the other 'bustle' meaning 'hurry along busily', although no doubt women wearing bustles did bustle about. The term probably derives from German *Büschel*, 'bunch', 'pad', although this particular origin is not absolutely certain. Originally, a bustle seems to have been part of the dress itself, as seen in these lines from Thomas Monro's *Olla Podrida* written in 1788:

> Such locks the nymphs now wear (in silks who rustle,)
> In rich luxuriance reaching to the bustle.

**butterfly** (flying insect with large, often brightly coloured wings)
No doubt many young children are still being told by granny (or 'nan') that the butterfly is so called because it 'flutters by'. As indeed it does, of course. But the name means what it says, and the insect really is a 'butter' fly. In what sense, however, is still not finally resolved. The name could refer to the pale or even dark yellow colour of the wings of many butterflies, including the brimstone and all the 'whites', or it could derive from the old belief that butterflies stole butter and milk, or it could even refer to the colour of their excrement. Some good research is needed into the most likely of these.

**buttery** (room for storing food or wine)
Although some university colleges and other establishments have butteries that today serve bread and butter and sandwiches, the

original source of the word is in Anglo-French *boterie,* with this in turn coming from Latin *butta,* 'cask'. The word is thus directly connected with butts of wine. For a similar misleading room name, see **pantry**.

**buttonhole** (detain a person in conversation)
If you wish to emphasise the point you are making in conversation, or seek to make someone listen to what you have to say, you can of course grab him or her by the buttonhole. The word is, however, really an alteration of 'button-hold', this deriving in turn from 'button-holder', that is, a person who seizes one of your buttons to gain further attention. The whole strategy is only of nineteenth-century origin. The New York magazine *Home Journal* reported in 1880 that 'Charles Lamb, being button-held one day by Coleridge', cut the button off.

**buxom** (full-bosomed)
The word suggests a variant spelling of 'bustsome'. Originally, however, it meant 'pliant', 'yielding', from the stem of the Old English verb *būgan,* 'to bow', 'to bend'. The sense then developed gradually like this: 1) 'obedient', 2) 'flexible', 3) 'good-natured', 4) 'plump and amiable and jolly', 5) 'full-bosomed'. So there was never a 'bust' behind the word, at least etymologically.

**bye-bye** (as a children's word: sleep)
If you talk of 'going to bye-byes' it sounds as if you are saying 'bye-bye' as you (or whoever it is) go to bed or to sleep. But the second 'bye-bye' here is simply a familiar or 'baby' form of 'goodbye', while the 'sleep' one is simply a lulling sound. But at the end of the day, especially at the end of a party when the guests leave, the two senses just about coincide, if that is the way you wish to announce your departure.

**bylaw** (law made by a local authority)
The term, also spelt 'bye-law', looks as if it means 'subsidiary law', 'extra law', as in words such as 'by-product' and 'by-election'. But in 'bylaw' the origin is in the Old Norse word for 'town', still seen in the '-by' that ends many place names (such as Whitby and Grimsby). So such a regulation is of Scandinavian origin, applying locally in a community.

**cabal** (group of plotters)

The pleasant fiction arose that the word derives from the initials of the group of five ministers who governed for six years in the reign of Charles II, namely Clifford, Ashley, Buckingham, Arlington and Lauderdale. But this was simply a coincidence (seized on, of course, by political opponents), and the word is actually a form of the ancient Jewish mystical tradition known as a 'cabbala' (or 'kabbala', or some other spelling), which itself ultimately comes from Hebrew. However, proponents of the seventeenth-century ministerial 'Cabal' were delighted when a near-repetition of the acronym arose in 1910. In that year, ministers assembling for a representative conference were Asquith, Balfour, Birrell, Lord Cawdor, Chamberlain, Lord Crewe, Lloyd George, and Lord Lansdowne. Only one of the names begins with 'A', but there are enough 'Bs', 'Cs' and 'Ls' to produce something like a 'cabal' (or rather, a 'cab'l').

**caddy** (container for tea)

An association with the golf 'caddy' or 'caddie' springs to mind, since the tea caddy holds tea and the golf caddy holds clubs. But the words are of quite different origin: the former comes ultimately from a Malay word indicating a particular weight (equal to nearly 1½ lbs and first called a 'catty' in English); the latter, via the Scots, ultimately goes back to French *cadet*, 'young person'.

**Caesarean** (type of birth in which a baby is delivered by means of an incision)

The name is popularly said to allude to the fact that Julius Caesar was himself delivered by such a means ('Caesarean section'), and that he was so named because of this (i.e. from Latin *caedere*, 'to cut', or *caesus,* 'having been cut'). But there is no firm ground for this belief, and Caesar's name probably derives in fact from Latin *caesaries,* 'head of

hair'. This could have originated as a kind of nickname for a person with thick hair. Of course, Caesar was not the first of the name anyway. So the term is both historically suspect and etymologically unattested.

**cafeteria** (self-service restaurant)

A cafeteria is not so called because it is a type of café. The word came into English (first in the United States) from American Spanish, itself from Spanish *cafeteria,* deriving from *cafetero*, 'coffee-seller', ultimately from French *café*, 'coffee', which also led to the English 'café'. So the word had a longer journey to travel than directly from an already existing English word.

**calico** (type of cotton fabric)

Calico originated in India. It is not named after Calcutta, however, but the town formerly called Calicut (now Kozhikode). This is in south-west India, whereas Calcutta is way over in the east of the country.

**camel** (in Bible: animal that went 'through the eye of a needle')

Because of the bizarre image, several scholars have made repeated attempts to say that 'camel' in the famous quotation should really be 'cable', even claiming that in the original Greek, the word for 'camel' (*kamēlos,* based on Hebrew *gamal*) should really be *kamīlos,* 'ship's cable'. The full quotation, referring to the difficulty with which a rich man can enter the kingdom of God, occurs in three of the Gospels (e.g. Matthew 19:24), and in an English text of 1534 the word actually was 'cable', not 'camel', as follows: 'For as harde a thynge it is to plucke through the small nedels eie a greatte caboull rope, as to brynge a rich man in at heuens wycket'. This was probably the source of the error, and those who felt that 'camel' really *should* be 'cable' have

33

quoted it triumphantly ever since. It is now usually held, however, that the word really was 'camel' after all, and that the two Greek words were unrelated. However, debunkers of the 'cable' theory who refer to a postern gate called a 'Needle's Eye' (through which a camel might have passed with difficulty), are on rather shaky ground since this name was not known in biblical times. This means that the simile is simply an amusing and colourful one after all: a camel is something big, and the eye of a needle is something small. Together, they are quite incompatible.

**Canary Islands** (group of Spanish islands off north-west Africa)
The islands are not so called since canaries fly freely there, but because of the large wild dogs (Latin *canes*) encountered here by the Romans when they landed. Pliny the Elder, writing in the second century A.D., called the island of Gran Canaria (or Grand Canary) *Canaria insula*. The birds, however, do get their name from the islands, since they are native to them.

**candidate** (person applying for a qualification, job, etc)
A candidate is not so called because he must be candid in answering questions and the like but because, historically, Romans seeking high office in state wore white togas, and so were called *candidati*, from Latin *candidus*, 'white'. This same word, of course, led also to 'candid', since a candid person is 'pure and white', as it were.

**candytuft** (plant with clusters of white, red or purple flowers)
The flower is not so called since it is multi-coloured, like candy, but because it originated from 'Candy', as Crete (or Candia) used to be called in English. The tufts are genuine, however, and are the plant's clusters (what horticulturists call its 'corymbs').

**canister** (metal container)
The word was almost certainly influenced by 'can', but does not derive from it. Its ultimate origin is Latin *canistrum*, 'reed basket', which in turn is related to modern 'cane'. The familiar tin 'can' is a word that has a Germanic origin.

**cannibal** (eater of human flesh)
For many years attempts were made to relate this word to Latin *canis*, 'dog', since cannibals were greedy and ate flesh voraciously, as a dog does. But the word actually relates to 'Caribbean', and came into English from Spanish *Caníbal*. This was the word used by Columbus to refer to the native Caribs of Cuba and Haiti, who subsequently acquired a reputation (possibly unfairly) for being cannibals. The native name is said to mean 'brave people'.

**cannon** (shot in billiards where the cue ball makes contact with two others)
The cannon is a powerful stroke, and can easily be seen as a kind of 'cannon' fire. But although influenced by this word, the term is actually a corruption of 'carom', which is still the American word for this stroke. This itself comes from an earlier word *carambole* (shortened to 'carom' as it was understood as 'carom ball'), which developed out of *carambola*, the Spanish name for a kind of fruit.

**canter** (easy gait of a horse)
The term is not related to 'cant' in any sense (e.g. 'inclination from the vertical'), as is sometimes assumed, but is an abbreviated form of the original 'Canterbury trot' or 'Canterbury gallop', the special pace (halfway between a trot and a gallop) at which pilgrims used to ride to Canterbury. The word was first widely used in English only as late as the eighteenth century, however. (In 1706 the *London Gazette* referred to a horse that 'Trots, Paces, and Canters very fine'.)

**cantilever** (kind of bracket or framework)
There is no firm evidence that the word is related to 'lever', although the first part may well come from 'cant' (in the sense 'tilt'). Perhaps the origin is in some Germanic language such as Dutch or German. So even if the apparent etymology here is not quite 'false', it has not yet conclusively been proved to be 'true'.

**canting arms** (coat of arms making punning reference to surname of bearer)
The reference is not to the shape or design of the arms, as if they were tilting or

'canting', but to 'cant' in the other sense of 'specialised vocabulary' (as of thieves, for example). Instances of canting arms can be in trumpets to indicate the name Trumpington, shells to point to Shelley, and a tree in a well to denote Wellwood. Anne Boleyn's coat of arms had a black bull's head. (Her name was also spelt 'Bullen'.)

**car** (automobile)
Because 'cab' is a shortened form of 'cabriolet', just as 'van' is of 'caravan', 'bus' or 'omnibus', and 'plane' of 'aeroplane', so it is sometimes assumed that 'car' is an abbreviation of 'carriage'. In fact the two words are unrelated, and 'car' is quite an old word (ultimately of Latin origin), dating from the fourteenth century. It is, however, related to 'chariot', which was the regular term for a type of light four-wheeled carriage in the eighteenth century, as well as a 'car' or vehicle in ancient warfare. See also **jaunty**. A 'carriage' is simply a vehicle that 'carries'.

**carboy** (large glass or plastic container)
The word has all the wrong associations, suggesting chemical words like 'carbolic' or 'carbon' and the 'tallboy' (and even 'caddy') that is also a container. As often happens in such cases, the origin is an exotic one, in this case from a Persian word for large flagon (*qarāba*).

**carcass** (dead body of an animal)
A false association has developed here with 'case', especially since there was a former verb 'to case' in English meaning 'to skin' (hence the misquoted cookery tip 'First catch your hare', which was originally 'Take your hare when it is cased'). Some classical dabblers, too, liked to derive the word from Latin *caro casa*, 'fallen flesh'. The word is actually of uncertain origin, coming into English from French. An alternative spelling, less commonly used, is 'carcase'.

**care** (worry, concern)
Church preachers of old have been known, in their sermons, to derive this word from Greek *kēr* or even French *coeur*, both meaning 'heart', since 'care lies near the heart'. The word is actually, as might be imagined, an Old English one, of Germanic origin.

**caricature** (exaggerated drawing of a person)
The word is not a variation on 'character', but comes from Italian *caricatura*, 'distortion', in turn from the verb *caricare,* 'to load' (so that the drawing is a 'loaded' one, out of the true). The word 'character' is of Greek origin (*charaktēr*), meaning 'that which is cut in or marked' such as the stamp on coins. This eventually came to mean a distinctive mark of any sort, or character, when referring to people.

**carnation** (plant with white, pink or red flowers)
The flower was originally called a 'coronation' in English, especially by sixteenth-century herbalists, and it was subsequently supposed that this was the true origin of the name (as if from its use in adorning the head in crownings, or referring to the flower's own little 'crownlets'). But the true origin is in the other, now less common use of 'carnation', meaning 'flesh-pink colour'. This obviously refers to the shade of the flower that is, after all, known also as a 'clove pink'. (In this connection, see both **clove** and **pink**.)

**carnival** (festive occasion, public show or display)
Carnivals were particularly associated with Shrovetide, when people 'let rip' before the austerities of Lent. For this reason, the word was supposed to derive from Latin *carnis vale* (or perhaps *carnem vale*), meaning 'farewell to meat'. Even Byron alludes to this origin in his mock-heroic poem *Beppo*, where he writes,

This feast is named the Carnival,
    which being
Interpreted implies 'farewell to flesh'.

Later, it was also felt that another kind of 'fleshly' appetite was involved in the word, as a writer in the *Standard* of 22 February 1882, reported: 'The Carnival was really and truly what its name implies, farewell to all carnal enjoyments'. The source of the word does involve meat, but not 'farewell', since it lies in Italian *carnevale*, itself from an earlier *carnelevare*, i. e. 'removing of meat'. This originally referred to the Lenten fast, when meat was 'removed'. Later, it came to be used, as mentioned, for the great and greedy days before the fast.

**carouse** (drink freely)
The word looks as if it is linked to 'rouse' or 'carousel' (after all, a drinking spree can be a 'merry-go-round'). Rather unexpectedly, however, the origin is in the German expression, *trinken gar aus*, 'drink right out'. When a drinker's glass or mug is *gas aus* it is quite finished. He refills it, therefore, until it is *gar aus* again. In other word, he starts to carouse, and repeats the process ad nauseam.

**casemate** (chamber or compartment in which guns are mounted)
Some old castles or forts have impressive casemates for visitors to admire, and the old word suggest a connection with the equally old (or poetic) 'casement', since the walls have openings like windows through which the guns can fire. The two words are not connected, however, and a casemate (also not related to 'case') is so called since it derives ultimately from Greek *chasmata*, 'apertures', (singular *chasma*), itself related to 'chasm'. The word came into English through Italian and French, and its Italian form of *casamatta* may well have been influenced by Italian *casa*, 'house'.

**cashier** (dismiss from the armed forces with dishonour)
What can the connection with the more familiar 'cashier' be? Perhaps a man who is cashiered is so called as his pay is stopped? After all, he is in effect being given a real 'payoff'. But the words are not connected at all, and 'cashier' in this sense comes from a Middle Dutch verb *kasseren*, meaning 'to disband'. This itself came from Old French (and also modern) *casser*, 'to break'. The word was first used in English in the late sixteenth century, probably as a result of the Netherlands campaign of 1585 against Spain. Thomas North's famous translation of the 'Lives' of Plutarch, published in 1595, has the sentence, 'He could not abide very fat men, but cashiered a whole band of them

for that cause onely'. (Things are somewhat less partisan today.)

**caste** (class of Hindu society, or any social class or system)
The word is not derived from, or related to, any meaning of 'cast', whether as a troupe of actors, or a special 'cast' of people (in a special mould, as it were), or even with some suggestion of 'outcast'. The origin is actually in Portuguese *casta*, 'race', and so is related to 'chaste', since a race contains people who fully and 'purely' belong to it. The term was originally used by the Portuguese of men of difference classes in India. See also **outcaste**, however.

**catchpenny** (designed to have instant commercial appeal by means of crude advertising)
According to some sources (e.g. Radford, see Bibliography), the term is a corruption of 'Catnach Penny', this alleged to derive from the name of a London hawker of songs and sayings called James Catnach. But this is almost certainly an ingenious (and ingenuous) fabrication, and the word really means what it says, 'catch penny'. Catchpenny goods were designed to 'catch the pennies' without any regard for quality.

**catchpole** (in medieval times, a sheriff's officer who arrested debtors)
Did the catchpole (or catchpoll) aim to 'catch polls', i. e. count (and arrest) the heads? Or perhaps he carried a pole to trap the offenders? The answer is neither of these. The term comes from Medieval Latin *cacepollus*, which was a word for a tax gatherer that literally meant 'chicken chaser' (or 'catcher of pullets', to take the phrase nearer the English). This unexpected name was a reference to the tax gatherer's custom of seizing a debtor's poultry if he could not find the money to pay. The historic word still survives today as a surname. Compare **polecat**.

**caterpillar** (larva of butterflies and moths)
There have been some strange stories to account for this admittedly strange-seeming word. One of the most far-fetched, yet touchingly attractive, is that the creature is so called because it 'caters' for itself by

'pillaging' (with the second half of the word alleged to derive from French *piller*, to 'rob'). But the true origin of the name is more straightforward: it derives from Old French *chatepelose*, 'hairy cat' (or from some French dialect word meaning this). This refers to the caterpillar's appearance, especially that of some of the larger, hairier ones. Something similar seems to have happened in French, where *chenille*, the word for 'caterpillar', derives from Latin *canicula*, 'little dog'. In English, too, it is worth recalling that tiger moth caterpillars are often nicknamed 'woolly bears'.

**catgut** (cord made from the dried intestines of an animal and used for stringed instruments)
Catgut is indeed made from 'gut', but certainly not that of a cat. The usual animal source is the sheep, although the gut of horses and donkeys has also been used. The origin of 'cat' is something of a mystery. Perhaps there was some kind of punning origin for the name, or an allusion to a 'kit', which was the name of a small kind of fiddle. It is tempting to think that there may even have been a sort of reference to caterwauling, from the sounds produced on violin strings by amateur or amatory players.

**causeway** (raised road or path over marshland or the like)
A causeway is not so called because it is a 'course way', or way where the road follows a particular course. Earlier spellings of the word show it as *cauceway* or *cauciwey*, and this derives from Medieval Latin *via calciata*, 'paved way', 'way paved with limestone' (Latin *calx*).

**cave in** (collapse)
The mental picture is of the collapsing roof of a cave. This is not the origin, however, and the phrase was probably 'calve in' initially. This was an East Anglian dialect term, and may even have been introduced to East Anglia by Dutch workmen engaged to drain the fens, since modern Dutch *afkalven* and Flemish *inkalven* have the same meaning. Undoubtedly, the term was influenced by English 'cave', however.

**cayenne pepper** (kind of very hot, red pepper)
Anyone can be forgiven for thinking that cayenne pepper comes from Cayenne, the capital of French Guiana, and some reference sources (e.g. *The Penguin Encyclopedia of Places*) do derive the word from this town. But the ultimate source is a Tupi (South American Indian) word *kyinha*, which was the native name of the pepper. The place-name Cayenne certainly influenced the meaning and spelling, however.

**centipede** ('insect with lots of legs')
Many people will confidently tell you that this creature (not actually an insect) is so called as it has a hundred legs. Some centipedes do, but most do not, however, and the true number can vary from fifteen pairs of legs to 190. So why 'cent-'? The sense here is not exactly 'hundred' but simply 'large number' (as when a cross parent says 'I've told you a hundred times'). A former name for the centipede in English was 'forty-legs', with the same use of 'forty'. (By coincidence, or in corroboration, the standard Russian word for 'centipede', with exactly the same sense as this, is *sorokonozhka*.) See also **millipede**.

**cesspool** (cistern, pool or sump for sewage)
This word is a real dark horse, suggesting a first half related to 'cesspit' and a latter half from 'pool'. If the word is traced back it will gradually change to quite a different origin, however. Earlier it was *cesperalle* and before that *suspiral*. This meant 'vent', 'water-pipe', and in turn came from Old French *souspirail* (related to modern English 'suspire'). The later forms of the word were wrongly associated with 'pool', and 'cesspit' was in turn based on it, as if 'cess' was sewage. (In the phrase 'Bad cess to you!', said to be popular among Irish imprecators, 'cess' is probably short for 'success'.)

**chagrin** (annoyance, mortification)
In an attempt to explain this word, obviously of French origin, some etymologists have done their best to derive it from *chagrin* in the sense 'shagreen', that is, from the kind of rough sharkskin that is used as an abrasive. Thus the feeling of annoyance

called 'chagrin' is one that 'rasps' or 'frets'. But the true origin lies in the other French *chagrin*, used as an adjective to mean 'sad', 'distressed', 'fretful', and as a noun in virtually the same sense as the English (although basically in a meaning that is more 'grief', 'affliction'). So both English words 'chagrin' and 'shagreen' come from the French, but the source of the French 'grief' *chagrin* is unknown. (The other one, the sharkskin, comes from a Turkish word.) '**Shagreen**' also has its own folk etymology, which see separately.

**chaplet** (wreath of flowers on the head; string of beads on a rosary)
The religious sense of 'chaplet' has led to a false association with 'chapter' or 'chapel', although the word actually came into English from Old French *chapelet*. This meant 'garland of roses' and was a diminutive of *chapel*, which was not the word for 'chapel' but the old word for 'hat' (now *chapeau*).

**charcoal** (kind of black fuel made by heating wood or other matter)
There simply must be a derivation from 'char', surely. But there isn't. Moreover, 'coal' originally meant 'charcoal', so does not have its popular meaning here. What the 'char' means is obscure. Perhaps it relates to 'chore' and 'charwoman', so that the substance has been 'worked' or converted in some way. The final origin is uncertain, although it is clear that the modern verb 'to char' meaning 'burn partially' must come from 'charcoal'. See also **charnel house**.

**charlatan** (impostor, 'quack')
One story formerly put forward assiduously by the good Dr Brewer to account for this word, was that a French quack dentist named Latan used to tour Paris in a fine car or carriage, which he used as a sort of mobile dispensary, and that when people saw it (and him) they would exclaim *Voilà le char de Latan!* The original Dr Brewer, who was the author of the *Dictionary of Phrase and Fable* (see Bibliography), claimed he had even seen him, wearing either a feathered hat or a brass helmet. But this is really just a piece of mischief, and if there *was* a M.

Latan he presumably adopted this false name just for fun as part of his evidently eccentric way of conducting his business. The word 'charlatan' actually comes from Italian *ciarlatano*, from the verb *ciarlare*, 'to chatter'. Obviously, charlatans would need the 'gift of the gab' more than anything, to compensate for the skill they actually lacked.

**charm** (collective term for birds, especially finches)
Some collective nouns are weird and wonderful ('exaltation of larks' and so on). This one looks as if it comes from the ordinary 'charm' meaning 'attractive or magic feature or object'. It probably comes from the old noun 'chirm', however, which meant 'chirping of birds'. If you have heard finches *en masse*, you will appreciate this. But the word was almost certainly influenced by 'charm' in the well-known sense, or even by Latin *carmen*, 'song'. Milton used it in the 'chirping' sense in *Paradise Lost:*

> Sweet is the breath of morn, her rising sweet,
> With charm of earliest birds.

The 'group' sense of the word, and its revived popularity, was promoted by Viscount Grey of Falloden's book *The Charm of Birds*, published in 1927. See also **school**.

**charnel house** (special kind of building or vault where bones were deposited)
By a false association with 'char', this now outdated word is often misunderstood to mean 'place where bones are burnt', as if it was a sort of primitive (and grisly) crematorium. But this is neither the meaning nor the origin of the word, which comes ultimately, through Old French, from Latin *carnalis*, 'fleshly' (as in modern related 'carnal'). In its earliest use in English, the word meant simply 'burial place', 'cemetery'.

**Charterhouse** (1 Carthusian monastery; 2 English public school)
The question here is, what is a 'charterhouse'? Is it a sort of charthouse, or a kind of chapterhouse? The answer, of course, is neither. The word is a corruption of Anglo-French *chartrouse*, itself from the French

village of *Chartrosse* (now called St-Pierre-de-Chartreuse), near Grenoble, where the Carthusian monastic order was founded in the late eleventh century by St Bruno. (Compare the liqueur called 'chartreuse', which was made at the monastery.) The public school Charterhouse was founded in London in 1611 on the site of a Carthusian monastery in London. In 1872, however, it moved to Godalming, in Surrey. Many of the original monastery buildings survive in London, despite severe damage by bombing in the Second World War.

**charwoman** (woman who does domestic work, 'daily')
Despite semi-facetious allegations otherwise, a charwoman is not so called as she is always drinking cups of 'char', but because she does (or did) chores in the home.

**checkmate** (winning position in chess, when an opponent's king cannot move)
The term looks as if it derives from 'check', or as if a player has at last 'checked his mate'. But the term actually comes, via French, from Arabic *shāh māt*, 'the king is dead'. One or both of these words gave the actual name of chess in many languages including English 'chess', French *échecs*, and Russian *shakhmaty*. Compare **stalemate**.

**cheerio** (farewell greeting)
One hardly serious account explains the word as deriving from the days of travel by sedan chair, when a departing guest would call 'Chair-o!' just as a Londoner might call 'Taxi!'. But the word is much more recent than that, and is obviously based on 'cheer' or 'cheery'. In fact, the expression seems to be of late nineteenth or early twentieth century origin. One of the earliest written records of the greeting is in a copy of *Punch* dated 12 January 1910, where one loafer says to another, 'Cheero, Charlie'.

**cheesed off** (fed up)
This slang phrase does not come from 'cheese' in the regular sense, or even from 'hard cheese' meaning 'bad luck'. It originates in nineteenth-century thieves' slang, where 'cheese' meant 'stop', 'leave off'. ('Cheese it!' meant, or even still means, 'Get

away quick!' or 'Stop what you're doing!') The source of this particular 'cheese' is not clear, although Eric Partridge (see Bibliography) thinks it may be a form of 'cease'.

**cheroot** (cigar with both ends cut off)
The name perhaps suggest a connection with 'root', but hardly surprisingly the word turns out to be a native one. It comes from Tamil *curuṭṭu*, meaning 'curl', 'roll', implying a roll of tobacco. Cheroots themselves originate from southern India, which is where Tamil is spoken.

**chessman** (chesspiece)
'Man' in the sense of 'piece' has been in use in chess since the fifteenth century, but before this the word for 'chessmen' (plural) was chessemeyne. This means 'chess company', with the second part of the word related to modern 'menage' or (less directly) 'mansion', and this is therefore the origin of the apparent 'man'. The earlier sense may still be preserved, or at any rate implied, in the familiar nursery rhyme reference to 'all the king's horses and all the king's men'. The association with 'man', too, is understandable when so many chesspieces are human figures (pawn, knight, bishop, king, queen, etc).

**chestnut** (edible or inedible kind of nut, best known as the 'conker')
Some names of nuts have a first half suggesting wrong associations ('**walnut**', which see, is another). Here there is no connection with 'chest' (as if the shiny brown surface of a horse chestnut resembled an old oak chest, perhaps, or alluding to some former 'nature remedy' for chest ailments), but simply a derivation in Old French *chastaine* (modern *châtaigne*), itself ultimately from Greek. If a good related word is required in English, there is one in 'castanet' (via the Spanish, naturally). See also **conker** itself.

**chickenpox** (contagious disease common among children)
What can the link with chickens be? Perhaps they have it, too, or spread it? There is no actual link with these birds at all. The name seems to have come about since chickenpox was regarded as being less

severe than smallpox, i. e. it was 'chick-enfeed', so to speak. However, there may be some connection with the word '**chickpea**' (see next entry), with reference to the spots that appear. 'Pox', after all, implies pustules (that is, 'pocks'), and these might be fancifully compared to the pealike seeds of the chickpea. See also **smallpox** itself.

**chickpea** (kind of bushy plant with edible pealike seeds)
The chickpea has nothing to do with chicks. Its name ultimately derives, through French, from Latin *cicer*, which was the Roman name for the plant. (This same word gave the name of the famous Roman writer Cicero, at any rate according to Plutarch, since he had a prominent wart, 'a flat excrescence on the tip of his nose', like the seed of a chickpea.) The English spelling of the name was *ciche pease* down to about the eighteenth century, when an apparent error or misprint produced the present form.

**chiffchaff** (kind of bird that is properly a warbler)
There is no relation between this bird and the chaffinch, nor is it so called as it eats chaff (as the chaffinch does). Its name is simply imitative of its two sharp repeated notes. Other birds are similarly named for their song or call, such as the peewit and the cuckoo.

**chignon** (fashion in which long hair is arranged at the back of the head)
The obviously French word looks as if it derives from some proper name, such as that of a designer or French town. It even conjures up other fashion words such as 'chic' and 'chiffon'. The true origin is more anatomical, since the word comes from Old French *chaignon*, 'link', itself from *chaine*, 'chain', referring to the 'chain' of muscle or sinew in the nape of the neck, or possibly the top of the spinal column. However, this word was probably in turn influenced by Old French *tignon*, 'coil of hair'. The French place-name that probably falsely springs to mind here is Chinon.

**Childe Harold** (hero pilgrim of one of Byron's best-known works)
The first word here (and also in that of a

similar hero, Childe Roland) does not mean 'child' in the modern sense, as is sometimes thought, but is a sort of title to refer to a young man of noble birth. In the thirteenth and fourteenth centuries, 'child' (or 'childe') was the term used for a young man who was about to be made a knight. In fact Byron deliberately used the 'archaic' spelling 'childe' to indicate the old sense of the word.

**Chink** (derogatory nickname for a Chinaman)
Are (or were) Chinks so called because the Chinese are 'chink-eyed'? This phrase may have influenced the word, but the actual origin is almost certainly 'China', rather fancifully altered. (It may be relevant that the actual Chinese word for 'China' is *chung-hua*, sometimes spelt *chung-kua*.) The term came into use in English only in the twentieth century, apparently on the rise to prominence of the Chinese laundry.

**chipmunk** (kind of burrowing rodent with black-striped fur)
Those not familiar with the small animal, or acquainted with it only through cartoons or synthesized 'chipmunk' voices, may perhaps be forgiven for supposing that it is some kind of monkey or somehow connected with 'chips' of wood, say. As often happens, the English spelling is an attempt to produce some sort of meaning for a native name, in this case an Algonquian one. The creature is certainly not a monkey but a kind of squirrel. Compare the similar-sounding **woodchuck**.

**chipolata** (kind of small sausage)
The name suggests the accompaniment or association of 'chips', a sort of slightly upmarket 'bangers and mash', perhaps. But of course there are no chips behind the name, and the chipolata, very properly, is a word of Italian origin, where *cipollata* strictly speaking means not a sausage but a dish flavoured with onions (Italian *cipolla*).

**chirpy** (happy, 'merry and bright')
The mental picture here is of chirping or chirruping birds, and this indeed is the basis of the semi-slang word. But the phrase 'to feel chirpy' is also probably influenced by

'cherry' or 'cheer up'. This, however, is not the actual origin of the expression.

**chit** (note or voucher)
The word looks as if it is a sort of blend of 'check' and 'ticket', or something similar. Its original common form in English was 'chitty', and this came, via Anglo-Indian connections in the eighteenth century, from Hindi *chitthī*, 'note'. The word is not the same as the 'chit of a girl', incidentally, which is of quite separate origin. (It was initially a word for the young of an animal.)

**chock-full** (absolutely full, full right up)
The word is not related to 'chock' but to 'choke', and an earlier form of it in English was in fact 'choke-full', implying something that 'filled to choking'. However, the word 'chock' came to be used first in English at about the same time, in the seventeenth century, and there must have been an association, if not a precise derivation. Meanwhile, to cloud the issue somewhat, 'chock-a-block' developed as a virtual equivalent to 'chock-full' (but perhaps suggesting a 'tighter' fullness). This was originally a nautical term, based on 'chock', in its proper sense used of tackle pulled as tight as possible so that the two blocks (of the 'block and tackle') were brought close together above and below the pulley. Finally, 'chock-a-block' in turn produced the slangy 'chocker', used of a person who is fed up or 'choked off'.

**chop and change** (continually alter, vacillate)
The familiar expression suggests that a vacillating person keeps giving a 'chop' or halt to thoughts or action in one direction while then 'changing' to another. But the original meaning was 'barter and exchange', so was somewhat different. The Old English verb that meant 'to barter', 'to trade' gave not only modern 'cheap' but also such place-names and street-names as Chipping Ongar and Cheapside. Of course, the basic actions of bartering and exchanging are closely linked anyway.

**chopsticks** (thin sticks for eating, used by the Chinese and Japanese)
The sticks are not so called because you chop your food with them (this would be quite a feat), but because their name is based on the Chinese *k'wâi*, 'quick', 'nimble'. The word came into English via Pidgin English, as did the related 'chop-chop' meaning 'hurry-up', 'get a move on'. (Hence also the 'chopsticks' executed on the piano as a quick tune played with the forefinger of each hand.) For another wrongly apprehended 'chop' see the next entry.

**chop suey** (Chinese-type dish of meat, chicken, etc served with beanshoots and rice)
To English speakers the name suggests 'chopped suet', or at least meat or vegetables that have been chopped. As with '**chopsticks**', however (see above), the origin is quite different, since the phrase comes from Chinese Cantonese dialect *tsap sui*, which rather attractively means 'mixed bits', 'odds and ends'.

**chukka** (period of continuous play in polo)
In no way is the 'chukka' (or 'chukker') connected with any sense of 'chuck'. Instead, and as might be expected in view of the sport's Indian origin, the word comes from Hindi *cakkar*, itself deriving from Sanskrit *cakra*, 'circle', referring to the 'round' of play. Chukka boots, of course, are named after the chukka, since they are properly worn for playing polo.

**chute** (sloping passage or channel down which water, coal etc may be poured)
If you pour coal down a chute it certainly looks (and more precisely, sounds) as if you 'shoot' it down. Yet the two words are not properly connected, despite the fact that you do 'shoot the rapids' which are themselves a kind of 'chute'. ('Shoot' here has the sense 'pass quickly through', and it is probably because the rapids slope downwards that the 'chute' association developed. You can after all 'shoot' through many places that do not resemble a chute.) The basic derivation of 'chute' is Latin *cadere*, 'to fall', hence related words such as 'parachute' (itself colloquially called a 'chute'). In this last connection, see **parasol**.

41

**clam** (kind of mollusc adhering fast to rocks)
The clam is not so called because it is 'clammy' (cold, damp, sticky, slimy, etc), although it actually may be. It was earlier known as a 'clamshell', which simply means a 'shell that clamps', either in the sense that it keeps its two bivalves tightly shut or because it clings firmly to the rock.

**clan** (group of people related by blood, especially in Scotland)
'Contrary to popular belief', wrote a feature-writer in *The Times* of 2 January 1984, 'the word itself has nothing to do with "clandestine" '. He then went on to give the actual origin, for the benefit of any readers who held this belief – in Latin *planta*, 'sprout' (in the sense 'shoot' of a plant), with the initial 'p' of this becoming Gaelic 'c'.

**claret** (type of red wine)
Since many names of wines derive from their regions or places of origin (such as Bordeaux, Champagne, Graves, and the like), it may occasionally be thought that claret itself is so named. Looking at a fairly detailed map of France one can indeed find a little village near Montpellier in the south called Claret, and another, smaller one east of it, in the *département* of Alpes-de-Haute-Provence. But this is not the origin of the name, and claret is so called since in Old French it was known as *vin claret*, that is, 'clear wine'. Claret was originally a yellowish or light red wine, and was so named to distinguish it from the two basic groups of 'red wine' (*vin rouge*) and 'white wine' (*vin blanc*). Today, in English, 'claret' is the word mostly used to apply to a wine from the Bordeaux region.

**climax** (peak, supreme moment)
Despite the apparently apt association, the word is not related to 'climb', but comes (as the final 'x' doubtless suggests) from the Greek (through Latin), where *klimax* means 'ladder'. As originally used, it was a learned and specialized word applying to an ascending series of expressions in rhetoric ('If A, then B; if B, then C; if C, then D', etc). The *Oxford English Dictionary* says that the modern sense of 'climax' is 'due to

popular ignorance and misuse of the learned word'.

**clinker-built** (of a boat: having a hull made with overlapping planks)
'Clinkers' do not feature in the construction of a clinker-built boat, and the true origin of the term can be seen in the alternative form 'clincher-built'. In such a construction, each plank overlaps and 'clinches' (or 'clenches') the one below. The opposite is a boat that is 'carvel-built', i. e. has its planks laid flush. (The word comes from *caravel*, a former type of sailing ship built in this way.)

**clove** (dried flower used as a fragrant spice)
There is no relation between this clove and the clove that is the division of a bulb such as garlic, shallot, etc., even though both have their culinary uses. The 'spice' clove comes from French *clou*, 'nail' (in full *clou de girofle*, 'nail of clove', referring to the shape of the bud), whereas the 'bulb' clove is of Old English origin and relates to 'cleave'. The 'clove pink' is so called since it is scented like the first clove here, while the knot called a 'clove hitch' belongs to the second sort. For more about cloves, see **gillyflower**.

**club** (association of people with a common interest)
A rather ingenious theory maintains that a club is so called since it originally consisted of the band of people who were called together by a club-bearer (to support him in battle). This seems rather fanciful, although there may be a connection with 'club' in the other sense if a club (of people) is regarded as a gathering of members as a kind of club-like mass. There could also be a link with 'clump' (as in 'clump of trees').

**clumber spaniel** (type of thickset spaniel)
Many breeds of dog are named after their actions or appearance (e.g. boxer, **cocker spaniel, lurcher, whippet, bulldog**: see these as indicated), and the clumber spaniel might well be so called because it 'clumps' along, or because it is clumsy (or even because it is 'lumbered', or burdened with its duties as a working dog). But other breeds of dog also have names deriving from their places of origin, and this is the source

of the clumber spaniel, which was first bred in the late eighteenth century at Clumber Park, the Duke of Newcastle's estate in Nottinghamshire.

**coach** (teach or train students or sportsmen individually)

Perhaps a coach is so called since he has to 'coax' his students, who may be uncertain or unpromising? After all, a coach does train sports teams, including boat crews (who have a confusingly named **'cox'**, whom see separately). In fact the origin is the familiar 'vehicle' coach, and the coach who teaches or instructs perhaps came to be so called as he was seen to 'carry' his students along. (The road vehicle derives its name from Hungarian *Kocsi szeker*, literally 'wagon of Kocs', since this village in Hungary was where coaches were first made.)

**Cockaigne** (imaginary land of luxury)

Originally the name of a 'never-never land', where all was luxury and idleness, Cockaigne came to be associated, in the nineteenth century, with London and with 'Cockneydom'. It is therefore sometimes popularly thought that there is a connection between the two names. This is not the case, and the 'London' link was simply a humorous one. The actual origin of the name Cockaigne (also sometimes spelt as Cockayne) is rather obscure. It seems to be based, via French, on some Germanic word meaning 'cook' or 'cake'. An early fourteenth-century quotation describes Cockaigne as a land where:

Fluren cakes beth the scingles alle,
Of cherche, cloister, boure, and halle.

('Scingles', i. e. modern shingles, are roof tiles.) This means that the houses were actually covered in cakes. Perhaps to some cockneys, London is a city where life is as sweet as that. See also '**cockney**' itself.

**cockatrice** (legendary monster, part snake and part cock)

Although the monster was part cock, its name does not derive from this. Instead, it comes, through Old French *cocatris*, from Medieval Latin *cocatrix*, itself from Late Latin *calcatrix* meaning 'tracker' and translating Greek *ichneumōn*, 'ichneumon'. (This

creature, a kind of mongoose also known as Pharaoh's rat, has a name that also means 'tracker', from its alleged ability to track down or locate the eggs of crocodiles.) The word has had a complex history, and has also had a muddled association with 'crocodile', while in the Bible 'cockatrice' somehow came to be used for 'basilisk' (a serpent that could kill by simply breathing or looking at you). The heraldic sense of the word was, however, doubtless influenced by 'cock', and this false association even gave rise to a story that the creature hatched out of a cock's egg. (For more about cock's eggs, see **cockney**.)

**cocker spaniel** (kind of spaniel with silky hair)

How does the dog get its name? Perhaps it cocks it ears up when game is scented? Or its tail, to indicate the presence of game? Or is it simply 'cocky'? It is an established working dog, used when hunting game. The derivation of the name is almost certainly from the actual quarry which it is trained to flush up, and this is woodcock. The term 'cocking' was formerly used in English to mean 'hunting woodcock' and this word was used as recently as the nineteenth century by Charles Kingsley in his novel *Two Years Ago*, where he writes that there 'ought to be noble cocking in these woods'. Compare the name of the **clumber spaniel**, above.

**cockney** (native Londoner)

The cockney is not so called because he is cocky (although typically he is), or because London is sometimes known as **Cockaigne** (which see, above). The name in fact derives from its original sense of 'cock's egg' (the former word for 'egg' was *ey* or *ay*). This was used for a small or misshapen egg (unlike the proper hen's egg), and later came to be a term used, almost as a contemptuous nickname, for a town dweller, who would have been out of place in the country, and who allegedly lived a pampered life, unlike the 'real' life of the countryman. But most cockneys are proud of their name now, just as they are of their distinctive rhyming slang.

**cockroach** (kind of beetle)

There are a number of creatures with names

beginning 'cock' (the cockatoo, cockatrice and cockchafer among them), but in most cases there is no connection with 'cock', and even 'cockatoo' comes from a native word. With 'cockroach' the origin is similar, and the word derives from Spanish *cucaracha*. This is also apparently some native word, but its exact source is still uncertain.

**cocktail** (mixed drink with a spirit base, usually drunk as an aperitif)
The name obviously suggest 'cock's tail', and the ultimate origin, although still disputed, may really be this. It is known, however, that an earlier meaning of 'cocktail' was 'horse with a docked tail', i. e. one that was cocked up, and this may be the true derivation. Whatever kind of tail it was, it seems to have been one that served as a good name for a drink that 'perked you up', or made you feel 'bright-eyed and bushy-tailed', as it were. In fairness, however, it should be said that many other origins have been proposed, including a source in some non-English word.

**coconut** (fruit of the coconut palm)
The coconut, also spelt 'cocoanut', is some-times said to derive its name from 'cocoa', doubtless because of some association between coconut milk and cocoa as a drink, or simply the similarity of the words. But the root of the coconut is Portuguese *coco*, 'grimace', referring to the 'face' seen on the nut with its three holes. 'Cocoa', on the other hand, comes via Spanish from a native Central American word for cocoa beans (properly 'cacao' beans), *cacauatl*.

**codger** (slang word for an elderly or eccentric man, an 'old codger')
Age can bring wisdom, and so perhaps a codger is so called since he is cogent, or because he cogitates, or even because, of his kind, he is one of the 'cognoscenti'. With due respect to the 'Old Codgers' of the *Mirror*, who answer readers' queries in their 'Live Letters' page, the origin of 'codger' seems to be 'cadger'. Unless, of course, the *Mirror*'s Old Pair know different?

**coign** (position, especially in 'coign of vantage' as a favourable viewpoint)
The word often seems to be associated with

'coin', perhaps with the idea of tossing a coin and winning an advantage, or with some sporting allusion. This particular phrase became memorable when it was used by Shakespeare in *Macbeth*, and Banquo describes Macbeth's castle in Inverness as a building favoured by the 'temple-haunting martlet' (i.e. swift):

>                    no jutty, frieze,
> Buttress, nor coign of vantage, but this bird
> Hath made his pendent bed and procreant cradle.

Following this, Walter Scott popularized the phrase still further by using it in *Heart of Midlothian*. The derivation *is* from 'coin', but here as a different spelling of 'quoin', meaning 'corner'. So all three spellings ('coign', 'quoin' and 'coin') all mean the same thing.

**coil** (disturbance, confusion)
Because of Shakespeare's 'shuffle off this mortal coil' (in Hamlet's famous 'To be or not to be' speech), a mental picture emerges of some kind of encircling loop like a binding coil of rope. When you 'shuffle off the mortal coil' you die, of course, and this even more suggests an escape from some kind of mortal chains. But 'coil', although having a special sense in this phrase, simply means 'commotion' when used on its own, and was still used as a dialect word with this meaning until quite recently. Its origin is unknown.

**coleslaw** (salad made of shredded cabbage and other vegetables with mayonnaise)
The tasty side dish is frequently understood as 'cold slaw', and even spelt as such on chalked-up pub menus. In a way, this makes sense, since it *is* cold and since 'slaw' exists as a word for a salad like this. But 'slaw' is actually a short form of 'coleslaw' and the 'cole' is the cabbage. The word as a whole comes from Dutch *koolsla,* and there are also related words 'cole' and 'kale' in English to denote various kinds of cabbage.

**coltsfoot** (plant with daisy-like yellow flowers and heart-shaped leaves)
Some plant-name explainers, seeing no obvious resemblance anywhere to a 'colt's foot', have preferred to derive the word from

'cold's food', since the leaves were regarded as good for treating colds or chills. But the leaves, although heart-shaped, are actually the source of the name, and the English is a translation of Medieval Latin *pes pulli*, 'foot of colt'. At any rate, that was how they appeared to the early scholars who devised the name. (One popular French name for the plant is virtually the same, *pas d'âne*.)

**comely** (handsome, good-looking)
This rather poetic word seems so clearly to be derived from 'come' or 'becoming', if only because a comely person is attractive or 'come-hitherish'. Rather disappointingly, this is not the case, and the word derives from Old English *cymlic*, meaning 'beautiful', and itself related to modern German dialect *kömmlich*, 'convenient', 'comfortable'. Having said this, etymologists in the past have had other explanations to account for the word, and Professor Skeat (see Bibliography) actually does prefer to derive it from 'come'. Compare **winsome**.

**comfit** (kind of sugar-coated sweet, typically a 'liquorice comfit')
The sweet is not, alas, so called because it gives you comfort, even though it can. The word comes from Old French *comfit* which in turn derives from Latin *confectum*. And there the true origin of the name can be seen. The sweet, after all, is confectionery (which is literally something 'put together').

**compound** (enclosure)
The true origin of this word comes as quite a surprise, especially as 'compound' means 'combination of things' (i.e. people, buildings, and the like). It does not even derive from 'pound', which is also the word for an enclosure of some kind. The actual source is Malay *kampong*, 'village', and this seems to have been adopted by Englishmen working in factories in the Malay Archipelago in the seventeenth century. Of course, the word was soon influenced by the already existing English 'compound'.

**comptroller** (alternative title for 'controller')
It is the spelling here that has a false origin, since 'comptroller' was believed to contain the French *compte* that means 'count', 'account' (as in *tenir les comptes*, 'keep the accounts'), with English 'count' in turn associated with words beginning 'cont-' (e.g. 'countermine' and 'contradict'). The term is still in use in the titles of various financial executives, and *Whitaker's Almanack* for 1985, for example, includes 'Comptroller of the Household' (for the royal household) and 'Comptroller and Auditor General of the Exchequer and Audit Department'. (On the other hand, as the same book notes, there is a 'Controller of the Navy' and, on the Board of Inland Revenue, a 'Controller of Development Land Tax Office'. Her Majesty's Stationery Office, too, is headed by a 'Controller and Chief Executive'.)

**Confessor** (title of King Edward)
Edward the Confessor was king of England in the mid-eleventh century, and also gained fame as the founder of Westminster Abbey. But was not a 'confessor' in the sense that a priest is, who hears people's confessions, but a man who confessed his Christian faith by his deeds and words, despite many dangers and threats to his life. Compare the equally misleading title of his father, Ethelred the **Unready**.

**conger eel** (kind of large eel)
Because of its size, attempts have been made to derive 'conger' from some Germanic word meaning 'king' (Icelandic *kongr* would do very nicely, especially in view of the fishing associations). But the word actually comes, through French, from Latin *conger* and Greek *gongros*, the word for the 'sea eel'.

**conker** (horse chestnut, especially as annually sported with by boys)
Through the actual method of play of the great game of conkers, a derivation of 'conquerors' has been proposed for the word, since the object of the sport is after all to win and vanquish your opponent. But the name actually comes from a dialect word 'conker' meaning 'snail-shell' (compare related 'conch'), since the game was originally played with snail shells which were pressed together, apex to apex, until one broke. The switch to horse chestnuts was doubtless made (apparently as recently as the late nineteenth century) when either

the players tired of such a tame entertainment or when they could no longer be bothered to look for the shells. Certainly, the new conkers was a much more exciting game, even with an element of danger. See also **chestnut**.

**conning tower** ('bridge' of a submarine when it is on or just below the surface)
The term looks as if it indicates a tower to 'con' or examine things from. But the 'con' here is a special nautical word, deriving ultimately from Old French *conduire* and Latin *conducere*, 'to lead', and itself meaning 'direct the steering' (i.e. 'conduct' it).

**consensus** (general agreement)
The word is sometimes misspelt 'concensus', reinforcing the concept that the derivation lies in 'census', that is, as if a 'census' had been taken of people's views or opinions, and they all agreed. But the word actually means 'feeling together' and is related to 'consent', so there is no question of a 'census'.

**consommé** (clear soup of meat or chicken stock)
The 'starter' is not so called because it is 'consumed' before the main meal, but because the last nourishment or 'goodness' of the meat is 'consumed' or used up in making it. The word is French, of course.

**coolie** (cheaply hired native servant in India)
The coolie is not so called as he keeps his employer cool (by fanning him), but because his native Hindi name means 'hireling'. The word has undertones of the British Raj.

**cor anglais** (type of woodwind instrument of the oboe family)
The name is French for 'English horn', as which the instrument is also known, but it does not seem to be English in origin, any more than the oboe was (French *haut bois*, 'high wood'). Nor is it a sort of English 'French horn' (which is anyway a brass instrument). The hoary old story that the name is a corruption of *cor anglé*, 'angled horn', may therefore be correct. The instrument does have a bent metal crook at its top end, and was formerly also bent in the middle.

**corduroy** (heavy cotton fabric with vertical ribbing)
The origin of the name is usually explained as deriving from either French *corde du roy* or Old French *colour de roy*, meaning respectively 'king's cord' and 'king's colour'. (The latter was said to refer to the original purple or tawny shade of corduroy.) But there are no good grounds for either derivation, and the true origin may lie in the name of the original designer, who was called Corderoy. Even this has still not been substantiated, however, and the word still remains of uncertain origin. This means, of course, that at least one of these etymologies is false, and possibly they all are. For another fabric name, see the next entry.

**cordwain** (kind of fine leather made from horsehide)
The word is now, perhaps, an outdated one, with the modern equivalent being 'cordovan'. This actually explains the real source, since the leather was originally made in Cordoba, Spain. There is thus no connection with 'cord' or 'wain'.

**corned beef** (kind of specially salted and preserved beef)
Corned beef is canned beef, and the word is often said to derive from this, as if a corruption. (Most people rule out a link with 'corn'.) But the actual origin really is 'corn', in the sense 'preserve in brine'. The semantic link is 'make granular by preserving', 'make look like corn'. For a related food, see **bully beef** and **jerked beef**.

**corporal** (army rank below a sergeant)
From the spelling of the word, it looks as if the corporal was, or is, the man in charge of a body or corps of men. The actual origin can be seen, however, in French *caporal* and Italian *caporale*, which gave the English word and which themselves derive from Latin *caput*, 'head'. As historically conceived, therefore, a corporal was a soldier at the head of his men. There must certainly have been an influence of French *corps*, 'body', however.

**costermonger** (person who sells fruit from a barrow)
A costermonger looks as if he was so called because he 'accosted' his potential customers. But originally he sold costards, a kind of large ribbed apple. Both they and he are now virtually things of the past.

**counterpane** (bedspread)
The word suggests a quilt with 'panes' or panels that somehow run counter to one another. But the origin had neither 'counter' nor 'pane', as can be seen in the word's ultimate source, which is Medieval Latin *culcita puncta*, literally 'stitched pillow', i. e. a sort of early duvet. This developed into Old French *contepointe*, meaning 'quilt', and was adopted into English as *counterpoint* before acquiring its present spelling. No doubt the modern form was influenced by the now obsolete use of 'pane' to mean 'coverlet'. Even 'counterpane' is now rarely used, since the object itself has mostly been replaced by a bedspread or a duvet (or both). For a related bedroom history, see **coverlet** (below).

**country dance** (kind of folk dance)
Some wordmongers like to point out, knowledgeably, that the English country dance is so called since it developed from the French *contredanse*. In fact, however, it was the other way round. The English country dance came first, then was (flatteringly enough) adopted by the French some time in the seventeenth century, when it came to be called *contredanse*. The name seemed suitable enough, since the dancers were *contre* ('opposite') one another. Finally, the kind of dance that evolved in France was borrowed back in English under the name of 'contradance'. Thus did folk etymology make a positive contribution to folk dancing.

**court card** (playing card that is a king, queen or jack)
The three court cards must surely be so called since they portray the members of the royal court. Yet in point of fact the origin of the term is 'coat card', since the figures portrayed are 'coated' or dressed up. In most other languages the court cards are called something like 'figure cards', as in French *figure*, Italian *figura*, German *Figur* and Russian *figurnaya karta*.

**coverlet** (bedspread)
Like many words ending in '-let' ('notelet', 'booklet' and so on), it would appear that 'coverlet' means 'little cover'. But the word's French origin shows it to be what is actually is, a 'bed cover' (Anglo-French *covrelit*, modern French *couvre-lit*).

**coward** (person who avoids danger or difficulty)
Is a coward so called because he cowers, or because he is cowed? Was he even originally a 'cow-herd' (or 'cow-heart'), so named contemptuously by some enemy in battle? The answer is almost certainly none of these, and the true origin very likely lies in Old French *coue* (modern *queue*), 'tail', since a coward was seen to be like a dog that runs away with its tail between its legs. Certainly, cowards are apt to 'turn tail' when some danger appears. Or, if the comparison with a dog slinking away is not the precise derivation, there may well have been an influence from another animal, Old French *coart*, 'hare'. Hares are often cowardly, timid creatures, after all, and a former English equivalent for 'timid' was 'hare-hearted'. There is certainly no link between 'coward' and the verbs 'cower' and 'cow'. For more about the '-ard' ending, see **witch**.

**cowslip** (kind of primrose found in fields and on banks)
Flower names quite frequently arise from some resemblance to animal features (see **coltsfoot**, above). But a cowslip is not so called since the flower of the plant or its leaves look like a cow's lip. Divide the word differently and the true origin will appear: 'cow slip', i. e. 'cow's slippery stuff'. The reference is to cow dung (especially as 'cowpats'), since the plant grows well in naturally manured surroundings. The plant called the oxlip has a name of similar origin.

**cox** (helmsman of a boat)
The theory is sometimes put forward that a cox is so called since he 'coaxes' the boat or the crew. The allusion is apt, but 'cox' is actually short for 'coxswain', which itself is

47

short for 'cockboat swain'. A 'cockboat' was a word for a small boat, and 'swain' here has a sense similar to that of 'boatswain'. So the proud aunt who tells friends how her nephew used to 'coax the boat' of his college eight has unfortunately got her rudder lines crossed.

**crabbed** (surly and 'crusty')
Although a 'crabbed' old man is mean and 'sour', the adjective that describes him probably comes from crabs rather than crab-apples. Crabs, after all, have a wayward gait. However, the general sense of the word may well have been influenced by the small, sour-tasting crab-apple. The crustacean origin also seems more likely when applied to the other sense of 'crabbed', since used of handwriting it means 'cramped', 'crooked'. There may even be a hint of an association in the two mental equations 'crabbed' = 'crusty' and 'crab' = 'crustacean'.

**craven** (cowardly)
This historically associated word ('thou craven knight!' and the like) does not derive from the fact that the bearer 'craves' for mercy, and the true source almost certainly lies in Old French *crevant*, 'bursting', 'dying', with the ending of this assimilated to other English adjectives ending in '-en'.

**crayfish** (kind of crustacean)
The crayfish (or crawfish, as it is usually known in America) is not so called because it is a fish, but because the word comes from Old French *crevice* or *crevis* (modern (*écrevisse*), its name in that language. The latter part of this was anglicized as 'fish' (which it is not anyway).

**cremona** (type of organ stop)
Not a widely used word, but one still found labelling one or more of the stops on church organs, where it indicates a clarinet-sounding eight-foot reed. The Italian town of Cremona is famous for its musical associations, notably for the fine violins made there from the sixteenth century. But this is not the origin of the organ stop, which is a deviant spelling of 'cromorna' or 'cromorne', this word in turn deriving from 'krummhorn' or 'crumhorn', from German

*Krummhorn*, literally 'curved horn' (like the well-known 'cow with the crumpled horn'). The krummhorn or crumhorn was a medieval woodwind instrument of bass pitch with a curved end, and the 'cremona' organ stop was regarded as producing a tone something like it.

**Cripplegate** (street in City of London)
Cripplegate was originally a gate in the north wall of the City. It is not so called because cripples and beggars sat there asking for alms, however, but because there was an Old English *crepel* or 'covered way' there. The name was corrupted to 'Cripplegate' after reports that cripples had been cured there when the body of St Edmund the Martyr had been carried through it. For a similarly corrupt London street name apparently involving cripples, see **Crutched Friars**.

**crisscross** (crossing in different directions)
The word looks as if it is one of the common English reduplications, such as 'dilly-dally', 'ding-dong', 'fiddle-faddle' and the like. But there are good grounds for deriving it from the figure of a cross known formerly as a *chris-crosse*, i. e. a *Christscrosse*. This in particular was used of the cross printed at the beginning of a 'christ-cross row', an alphabet on a 'hornbook' or primer. Such primers were in use from the sixteenth down to the nineteenth century.

**crosier** (bishop's crook)
The word, also spelt 'crozier', would seem to derive from 'cross', especially since it often has one on the top. But it also has a crook, hence the origin, which is in Old French *crosse*, 'hooked stick'. The same word also lies behind the game of lacrosse, which is played with a special stick actually called a 'crosse'.

**crucial** (very important, decisive)
The origin of the word is of course ultimately in Latin *crux*, *crucis*, 'cross'. But the reference is not to something painful or tortuous, as if 'crucifying' on a cross, but to 'cross' in the sense 'crossroads'. When you reach a crossroads, literal or metaphorical, you have to take a very important decision: which way to go? The actual origin of this

lies in the phrase *instatia crucis,* 'crucial instance', occurring in Francis Bacon's *Novum Organum* of 1620. Somewhat later, the scientists Boyle and Newton used the phrase *experimentum crucis,* 'crucial experiment', in the same sense. The adjective then came to acquire its present, more general meaning. But see also **crux**.

**crude** (vulgar, unrefined)
Many pairs of words beginning respectively 'cr-' and 'r-' are near doublets, with the 'cr-' word often a more 'severe' equivalent, for example 'rumple' and 'crumple', 'wrinkle' and 'crinkle', 'ram' and 'cram'. There is no etymological link, however, between 'rude' and 'crude', although there is, oddly enough, between 'raw' and 'crude', since the latter word derives from Latin *crudus* in this sense. The origin of 'rude', on the other hand, is Latin *rudis,* 'unwrought', 'coarse'.

**crumpet** (kind of soft cake eaten toasted)
There is no proven link with 'crumb' for this word, and the derivation is almost certainly not 'crumb-bread', as has been sometimes stated. The precise origin is still uncertain, but there may well be an association with 'crumple', somehow referring to a cake that has turned-up edges. Crumpets have changed their shape and consistency over the years, and in the seventeenth century they were more a form of thin griddle cake. (For something about these, see **gridiron**.)

**Crutched Friars** (street in City of London)
The street so named does not refer to friars on crutches, but to 'crouched' friars, i. e. ones who wore a cross on their habit. The title denoted a so called mendicant or begging order of friars, properly named Friars of the Holy Cross, that was suppressed in 1656. The friars had their house here, near what is now the Barbican Centre. Only a mile away is **Cripplegate**, another street-name mistakenly associatd with cripples.

**crux** (decisive stage or point)
The word is of course Latin for 'cross', and the implication seems to be a kind of 'cross-roads' or turning point, where an important decision has to be made. But the term orig-

inated as a reference to a real 'cross', with its association of torment and trouble. The usage (and the preservation of the Latin word) sprang from the scholastic phrase *crux interpretum* or *crux philosophorum,* respectively 'torment of interpreters' or 'torment of philosophers'. From this, Swift and Sheridan extracted the 'crux' to mean 'riddle', 'conundrum', a linguistic entertainment (and mental torment) in which they both delighted. Thus Sheridan would write to Swift:

'Dear dean, since in cruxes and puns you and I deal,
Pray, Why is a woman a sieve and a riddle?'

And Swift would reply something like:

'As for your new rebus, or riddle, or crux,
I will either explain, or repay it in trucks.'

This was in 1718, when the original crux was born. But see also **crucial**.

**culvert** (drain or covered channel)
This word looks as if it should come from some French origin, such as *couvert,* 'covered', or *couler,* 'to flow'. But there is no evidence for such a source, and in fact the word is comparatively recent, appearing towards the end of the eighteenth century in connection with the construction of canals, when it was a sort of aqueduct. It is possible that the word derives from some proper name, such as that of the engineer or bridge builder who invented it. (Perhaps he was named Culver). If this is so, the word has a history similar to that of 'macadam' and (properly a trade name) 'tarmac', which both also came from the surname of the same engineer, their Scottish inventor, John McAdam.

**cur** (dog)
A once popular explanation used to say that a cur was so called since it had been 'curtailed', i. e. had its tail docked. This is not as fanciful as it seems, when the original of '**curtail**' itself is considered (see below). But the snappy cur is probably so called since it was a 'cur-dog', with the first part of this representing a Germanic word imit-

ating a growl (Old Norse *kurr*, for example, meant 'grumbling'). A cur, therefore, was probably a 'grrr-dog'.

**curmudgeon** (surly or mean person)
The actual origin of this impressive word is unknown, but it is here because it was the victim of one of the most wayward false etymologies on record. The tale began when the great Dr Johnson, in his *Dictionary of the English Language*, defined the word as 'An avaricious, churlish fellow; a miser; a niggard', adding an etymology (credited 'Fr. an unknown correspondent') that derived it as a corrupt pronunciation of *coeur méchant* (i.e. 'wicked heart'). So far so good. Then another lexicographer John Ash, entering the same word in his own dictionary published in 1775, used Johnson as a source for the etymology, which according to him was 'from the French *coeur* unknown and *méchant* a correspondent'! The incident is an amusing but also awful warning to lax lexicographers.

**curry favour** (ingratiate oneself)
However unlikely it may seem, the original phrase was nothing to do with 'favour'. The expression was properly 'curry favell', this itself meaning 'curry (i.e. groom) the chestnut horse', and coming partly through French (*torcher fauvel*) from some fourteenth-century story. Thus 'Favell' was the name of the horse, perhaps in turn influenced by an old word *favel* that meant 'flattery' (related to Italian *favola*, 'fable'). For some reason – perhaps because chestnut horses were regarded as unreliable – the phrase came to acquire an implication of duplicity or 'deviousness'. Later, the meaningless 'favell' was altered to a meaningful similar word, 'favour', although 'curry' remained unchanged.

**curtail** (cut short)
The word is not directly related to 'tail', but derives from an old word *curtal* which, however, does mean 'horse with a docked tail'. This word itself comes from French *courtault*, and the last part of this, when adopted into English, was naturally

(although falsely) assimilated to 'tail' because of its sense. See also **cur** for more about docked tails.

**cushy** (easy, comfortable)
This slang word could so easily derive from 'cushion', since a 'cushy' job, for example, is a nice, soft, easygoing one, as if one were comfortably 'cushioned'. But, however attractive, the real origin of the word is, via Anglo-Indian, from Hindi *khush*, 'pleasant'. The term is a quite modern one, apparently originating in the First World War (when some soldiers were lucky enough to find themselves in 'cushy billets').

**cutlass** (kind of curved sword)
The cutlass is not so called because of its cutting blade, but because the word comes from French *coutelas*, related to modern *couteau*, 'knife', and therefore to 'cutlery', which see. ('Cutlass' also relates to 'coulter' as a word for the blade or sharp disc attached to a plough so that it can cut the soil).

**cutlery** (implements used for eating and cutting)
'Cutlery' includes knives, of course, but as with **cutlass** (see previous entry), there is no association with 'cut'. The original sense of 'cutlery' was 'trade or art of the cutler', later becoming the actual knives, scissors, and so on with which he carried on his trade. 'Cutler' itself derives from Old French *coutelier*, and this word has the same relation to English words that 'cutlass' has.

**cutlet** (piece of 'best end of neck')
As a meat dish, 'cutlet' is a word that suggests it is a 'little cut', with the diminutive '-let' ending seen in other words such as 'booklet' and 'piglet' (see also the similarly misleading **coverlet**, above). Cutlets, too, are small enough. However, a cutlet is not a 'little cut', but a 'little rib', since it comes from French *côtelette* (where, however, the final *-lette* is the same sort of diminutive as the English '-let'). Today some so called 'cutlets' do not even contain meat.

**dairy** (factory or shop supplying milk and milk products)
For some years an etymology was proposed for this word that derived it from 'day' (or the Old English equivalent), since the dairy was the place where a woman did a day's work on a homestead, milking cows, preparing cheese, and so on. The true origin, however, is not in 'day' but actually in 'woman', or more precisely in the Old English word (*dæge*) that meant 'servant girl', itself based on words that literally meant 'dough lady', i. e. one whose job it was to knead the dough for the bread. This particular derivation doubtless explains the fact that the modern word 'dairy' contains no obvious reference to 'milk', as words do in other languages (French *laiterie*, German *Milchraum*, Italian *latteria*, Russian *molochnaya*, and so on). Young children sometimes misspell 'dairy' as 'diary' (or the other way round), and of course 'diary' actually *is* related to 'day'.

**dandelion** (common plant or weed with bright yellow flower and edible leaves)
Suspecting that the 'lion' may be a false clue, as such word elements often are, some people may suppose that the flower is so called because it is 'dandy' (although there must be many much 'dandier'). But the 'lion' is real enough, and the name is Old French *dent de lion,* 'lion's tooth'. This refers to the appearance of the leaves. The German name for the plant, *Löwenzahn,* means exactly the same. However, the modern French name for it, as schoolchildren learn with some delight, is *pissenlit,* referring to the diuretic property of the leaves when eaten, not their appearance. The corresponding English 'pissabed' may still survive as a dialect name.

**darbies** (handcuffs)
This is a slang or even a cant word, so its etymology must be treated with due caution. Its origin is unlikely to be 'Darby and Joan', however, with punning reference to a 'pair of inseparables', for this happily married virtuous couple first appeared only in the seventeenth century (in a ballad dated 1735), and 'darbies' were in use some time before this. They may get their name from the expression 'Father Darby's bonds' or 'Father Darby's bands', which was a term of literary origin that came to be used for a binding agreement between a debtor and a usurer.

**D-day** (the day when the Allied forces invaded Europe in the Second World War)
The code name is often popularly thought to stand for 'Deliverance day'. In fact 'D' is here arbitrarily used to mean simply 'day', and the military term was in use long before the special 'D-day' of 6 June 1944. It denoted the start of any military operation, as did the similar 'H-hour' (where 'H' in the same way just stands for 'hour'). Both terms were in use in the First World War, and some Field Orders dated 7 September 1918 read: 'The First Army will attack at H-hour on D-day with the object of . . .', etc. 'D-day' later came to be popularly and even semi-officially used to mean 'Decimal day' (or 'Decimalization day'), referring to the day (15 February 1971) when Britain adopted decimal currency.

**dearth** (scarcity)
Since the word has an association with famine, it is sometimes thought to have derived as a former spelling of 'death'. In fact it originates as a noun from 'dear' (like 'broad' and 'breadth', 'deep' and 'depth'). When food or some other commodity is dear, it is often scarce – and conversely, when it is dear, it is because it is scarce.

**decadence** (state of decay or degeneration)
The word was formerly pronounced 'de*cay*dence', with the stress on the second syllable, and this almost certainly came about by false association with 'decay'. The actual origin is in Medieval Latin *decadentia*, literally 'a falling away'. However 'decay' itself also derives from a closely related verb, Late Latin *decadere*, which similarly means 'to fall away'.

**decoy** (lure)
From the word's sporting associations, the explanation arose that it was really 'duckcoy'. The most likely source, however, is in Dutch *de kooi*, which is simply 'the decoy', or literally 'the cage' (ultimately from the Latin word for 'cage', *cavea*). This was blended in the sixteenth century, however, with another word *decoy* that was the name of a gambling card game (now obsolete). The 'duck' link, on the other hand, did actually produce an alternative spelling 'duckoy' in the seventeenth and eighteenth centuries.

**demeanour** (behaviour)
The word is not associated with 'demean' in the sense 'lower onself in dignity', as if this was a desirable thing to do in one's behaviour. The origin is actually in the Old French verb *demener*, 'lead', 'exercise'. On the other hand, it is quite possible that the present sense and even spelling of the word was influenced by its synonym, 'behaviour', or by some earlier form of this, such as the now obsolete 'haviour' or 'havour'.

**demerara** (kind of brown crystallized sugar)
Demerara is a rather 'special' sort of sugar, and for this reason its name has occasionally been interpreted as 'demi-rare', rather like (and even because of) a 'demitasse', which is literally a 'half cup' and actually a small cup of coffee. But demerara sugar comes from the West Indies and other countries nearby, and its name is that of the river Demerara, in Guyana. For another misunderstood 'demi', see **demijohn**, below.

**demijohn** (kind of large bottle, traditionally encased in wickerwork)
The name of the bottle looks as if it can hold half a 'john', whatever that is. Almost certainly, however, it is a corruption of French *dame-jeanne*, literally 'Lady Jane', which seems to fit the French pattern of using women's names for various receptacles. (Among others are the Normandy dialect *christine* for a large stone jar and northern France *jacqueline* for a stone jug.) Perhaps in the case of the *dame-jeanne* the name was prompted by the resemblance of the wicker-covered bottle to a lady in period costume.

**Derby** (famous horserace)
Those who are not regular punters or at all interested in the sport may suppose (and on occasions even do suppose) that the Derby is run at Derby. It is actually run annually at Epsom, of course. So why is it called the Derby? The answer lies in the title of the founder of the race in 1780, the twelfth Earl of Derby. (He also instituted The Oaks, the 'Ladies' Race' for three-year-old fillies run two days after the Derby, and named after his hunting lodge near Epsom.)

**dervish** (member of Muslim order of ascetics, typically a 'whirling dervish')
The word is not related to 'devil' or 'devilish', but derives from Turkish *derviş*, itself coming from a Persian word meaning 'poor person', 'begging monk'.

**despot** (tyrant, absolute ruler)
There is a strong association here with the word 'pot', as in other prominent but undesirable persons such as a 'tinpot king', a 'big pot', or even a 'fleshpot'. But the actual source is in Greek *despotēs*, 'master', 'lord', and the word as originally used had no derogatory sense. Its 'cruel' association stems from its connection with the French Revolution.

**detergent** (cleansing agent)
Stop to reflect on the word for a moment, and you might suppose that washing powders are so called as they 'deter' dirt. The true origin is a more scholarly one, in Latin *detergere*, 'to wipe away', from *de-* 'off', 'away', and *tergere*, 'to wipe'.

**deuce** (expression of annoyance, as typically 'what the deuce!')

Because of the many curses of religious origin ('My God!', 'What the devil!' and the like), a theory arose that derived 'deuce' in this exclamation from Latin *deus*, 'god'. In fact it probably originated from Old French *deus* (modern *deux*), 'two', and was thus uttered by a player who had thrown only a 'two' at dice. The same origin gave the tennis 'deuce', since when the score is deuce, one of the players needs only two successive points to win the game.

**devil** (chief spirit of evil)
Perhaps because they are not too keen to investigate further, some people apparently feel that the devil is so called because he 'does evil', and that 'devil' and 'evil' are associated words just as 'God' and 'good' are also supposed to be (see **god**). But the devil derives his name ultimately from Greek *diabolos*, meaning 'enemy', 'accuser' (literally 'one who throws across' or slanders), whereas 'evil' is a word of Germanic origin.

**dewlap** (loose fold of skin below throat in cattle, dogs, etc)
A cow's dewlap could well seem to 'lap the dew' when it is standing in long grass in the early morning, but this can hardly be the origin of the word, or at any rate the first half of it. The 'lap' may well relate to the familiar 'lap', with the common link being 'hanging flap', but 'dew' is something of a puzzle. The word as a whole dates from the fourteenth century (when it was recorded as *dewlappe*), and it is just possible that the baffling 'dew' may be an alteration of 'dog' in some Germanic language (not necessarily English). In 'dewclaw', a similar word, the connection with real 'dew' seems much more probable, since this particular (and non-functional) dog's claw touches only the dewy grass, not the ground, like the others.

**diabetic** (related to diabetes)
There is no relation, despite the similarity of spelling, between 'diabetic' and 'diatetic', and therefore 'diabetes' is not etymologically connected with 'diet', although diabetics do have to follow a particular diet. The disorder is so called because of the excessive urination involved (the Greek origin means literally 'passing through', just

as 'diarrhoea' means 'flowing through'), whereas 'diet' comes ultimately from Greek *diaita*, 'way of life'.

**diadem** (jewelled crown)
The rather fine word looks like a blend of 'diamond' and 'gem', but its actual ultimate origin is Greek *diadēma*, 'fillet', i. e. a royal headdress. Greek *diadein* means 'to bind round'. (Moreover, the 'dia-' of 'diamond' is not the Greek word for 'through' as in many other words, but a modification of Latin *adamas*, related to English 'adamant'.)

**dialogue** (conversation between two or more people)
The 'di-' of this word is often popularly understood as meaning 'two', as it does in many other words (such as 'dioxide'), since most conversations are between two people. But 'dia-' actually means 'through', 'across', as it does in most words, and the word derives from Greek *dialogos*, literally 'word across'. Sir Thomas More actually invented a word 'trialogue' on the basis of this misunderstanding, to mean 'conversation between three people'. 'As though it wer a dyalogue', he wrote in 1532, 'or rather a tryalogue betwene himself, the messenger and me'.

**diaper** (linen fabric with diamond pattern)
Many fabrics have names originating from the places where they were first designed or made, such as cambric from Cambrai, damask from Damascus, denim from Nîmes (French *de Nîmes*, 'from Nîmes'), jeans from Genoa, and so on. Doubtless because of this, some lexicographers have tried to see 'diaper' as deriving from French *d'Ypres*, 'from Ypres'. But the true origin of the word is in Old French *diaspre*, itself ultimately from Greek *diaspros*, literally 'shining through white' (*aspros* means 'white', 'shining'). The American use of 'diaper' to mean 'baby's nappy' is of course exactly the same word. For another misassigned fabric, see **dimity**.

**diaphragm** (membrane dividing the thorax from the abdomen)
Despite its obviously Greek origin, as the spelling indicates, it is still sometimes imagined that the word is associated with 'frame', no doubt because of the use of this

word in various contexts to apply to the body. The literal meaning of the word in its Greek original, however, is 'through-fence', i. e. describing the diaphragm as a sort of partition wall.

**diddle** (cheat, fiddle)
'I've been diddled!' The slang word looks like a mixture of 'do' and 'fiddle'. It arose, however, as the name of a swindler called Jeremy Diddler. He was a character in a farce of 1803 called *Raising the Wind* by one James Kenney. His own name was perhaps based on a dialect word 'duddle' meaning 'to trick'. Jeremy Diddler's method of 'raising the wind' (i.e. getting any money he could from whatever source he could) was to keep on borrowing small sums which he never paid back, and otherwise generally 'sponging'.

**dimity** (light strong cotton fabric with woven stripes or squares)
As with '**diaper**' (see above), the name of this fabric has been attributed to a place from which it is supposed to have originated, in this case Damietta, in Egypt. But the word eventually derives from Greek *dimiton*, meaning literally 'double thread'.

**dirge** (chant of lamentation for the dead)
The word is so similar to other 'dismal' words such as 'dreary', 'drudge' and 'dredge' that it is quite a revelation to discover that it comes from Latin *dirige*, 'direct'. This itself is the first word of a line in the Latin office of the dead: 'Dirige, Domine, Deus meus, in conspectu tuo viam meam' ('Direct, O Lord my God, my way in thy sight' – a version of Psalms 5:8).

**dished** (exhausted, 'done for')
Incredibly, some popular reference sources derive this slang word from 'disinherited'. This would be a most unusual corruption. The term almost certainly comes as a metaphor from cooking. A dinner that is 'done' and 'dished up' is one that is finished. There are similar expressions, such as 'cook one's goose' and 'settle one's hash'. See also **gruelling**.

**dismal** (dreary, depressing)
There is no connection between this word

and 'dismay', although the two concepts are similar. Rather interestingly, 'dismal' derives, through Old French, from Medieval Latin *dies mali*, 'bad days'. These days were twenty-four particular ones in the medieval calendar that were regarded as unlucky. In fact, the word is still often associated with 'day' even now, in such phrases as 'dismal day', 'dismal weather', 'dismal scene'.

**ditty bag** (bag for small articles, popularly used by sailors)
Although sailors are well known for their ditties or shanties, there seems to be no connection at all between the song and the bag. The precise origin of 'ditty bag' is uncertain: it may be related to *dhoti*, a type of Indian loincloth. The other 'ditty' comes from Old French, and is related indirectly to 'dictate'.

**Dixieland** (type of jazz music popular in the 1920s)
The jazz is named after its place of origin, the Southern states of the USA, known colloquially as Dixie or Dixieland. There are two rival etymologies here, either of which could be authentic. One traces the name from the $10 bills issued by a Louisiana bank, which carried prominently on the back the word Dix (French for 'ten'). Traders would then say that they were going South to collect some 'Dixies'. The other explanation is that the word derives from the surname of Jeremiah Dixon, who with Charles Mason, drew the boundary, the 'Mason-Dixon Line', between Maryland and Pennsylvania. This line was thus part of the longer line that served as the division between the Northern (free) and Southern (slave) states. Perhaps, as can happen in such cases, the first etymology was reinforced by the second. The name 'Dixie' was first popularized in Daniel D. Emmett's song *Dixie's Land* published in 1859, and this contains the words 'away down South in Dixie'.

**docket** (summary of a document)
There is no relationship between 'docket' and 'document', despite the association of meaning and the link between 'poke' and 'pocket' (the former of these surviving in

dialect and in the phrase 'buy a pig in a poke'). The exact origin of 'docket' is uncertain. It *may* refer to a document that has been 'docked', i. e. shortened, but there is no evidence to support this – nor any to derive it from 'document'.

**dog days** (hottest days in the year)
The phrase does not allude to the 'mad dogs and Englishmen' who 'go out in the midday sun' but to Sirius, the Dog Star (so called as it lies in the constellation Canis Major), which in ancient times was observed to rise when the days were hottest. The English term ultimately derives from Late Latin *dies caniculares*, itself a translation of Greek *hēmerai kunades*.

**doggone** (damned)
The fairly mild American expletive does not derive from 'dog' but as a euphemism for 'God damn' (with a sort of reversal of 'God'). Even so, many expressions relating to 'dog' are unfavourable, such as 'go to the dogs' (from dogracing, admittedly), 'give a dog a bad name', 'in the doghouse', 'dog-end', 'dogsbody', 'like a dog's dinner', 'it's a dog's life', and so on. Even 'doggerel' denotes poor verse.

**dog watch** (in the navy: watch on board ship from 4 to 6 or 6 to 8 pm)
Some sources explain the phrase as being a corruption of 'dodge watch', since the two watches are half the time of all the others, so that the same men are not always on the same watch, and are thus obliged to 'dodge' from one time to another. But this very shortness of time shows the true origin of the expression, since an alternative nautical name for the watch was 'dog sleep', referring to the light or fitful sleep that dogs typically have (and perhaps also alluding to the men off watch who would have a shorter period of sleep than during the other, four-hour watches). (Compare 'catnap' for an even shorter period of sleep.)

**doll** (child's toy baby)
The word is not derived from 'idol', as has been proposed by some, but probably originated from the girl's name Doll, the familiar form of Dorothy. The original

meaning of 'doll' was 'mistress', hence Shakespeare's Doll Tearsheet in *Henry IV*, Part II. (The 'r' in the full name changed to 'l' in the same way that 'Hal' developed from 'Harry', 'Sal' from 'Sarah', and 'Moll' from 'Mary'.)

**dolomite** (type of limestone rock)
The rock is not so called because it is found in the Dolomites, the mountain range in north-east Italy, even though it is (although by no means exclusively), but because it was identified (as a mineral) by the French mineralogist Déodat de Dolomieu (1750-1801), after whom in turn the Dolomites themselves were named.

**Domesday Book** (survey of English lands made by William the Conqueror)
The name has been wrongly explained as representing Latin *Liber domus Dei*, 'book of the house of God', referring to the original copy deposited in Winchester (itself not actually recorded in the book). But the name means what it says, 'Doomsday', since the survey was regarded as a final and irrevocable authority or judgment for legal purposes.

**donkey's years** (very long time)
Why 'donkey'? Is the donkey a notably long-lived animal? The answer is no, of course, and the phrase originated as a pun on 'donkey's ears', which of course *are* long.

**dragoon** (former mounted infantryman)
A dragoon was not so called because he was as fearsome as a dragon, but because he carried a *dragon*, the French name for the kind of musket or carbine that belched out fire and smoke, like a dragon.

**Drambuie** (type of liqueur based on whisky)
The trade name does not derive from the 'dram' or 'wee drappie' that can be drunk of the liqueur, but from Gaelic *dram buidheach*, 'satisfying drink' (or alternatively *dram buidh*, 'golden drink', referring to its colour). 'Dram' in the sense 'small drink' is directly related to 'drachm', the measure. For more 'shorts', see '**whet**'.

**drawing room** (reception room in a private house)
The rather grand-sounding 'drawing room' is not so called since serious or recreational drawing took place there, but because it was originally the 'withdrawing room', the room to which ladies withdrew after dinner, leaving the men in the dining room to get on with the cigars, scandals and general jollity.

**drill** (sow seeds by dropping them into a shallow trench or furrow)
The word is frequently associated with the better known 'drill', in the sense 'bore a hole', so that those unfamiliar with this way of sowing seeds imagine that a hole is specially drilled in the ground before the seed is dropped. (This, of course, is a common way of planting seeds.) But here 'drill' probably derives from an obsolete word *drill* which meant 'rill', that is, was a word meaning 'furrow'. (In modern German *Rille* is the standard word for 'furrow'.)

**dropsy** (medical condition in which widespread swelling of the body occurs)
The swelling in dropsy is caused by an accumulation of excess liquid, and for this reason it is forgivable to link the word with 'drops'. But the original name of the condition (today more usually called 'oedema') was 'hydropsy', or some spelling similar to this, showing the source to be ultimately Greek *hydōr*, 'water'.

**drugget** (kind of coarse, long-lasting cloth)
Since names of fabrics often derive from the place of origin (as already mentioned for **diaper** and **dimity**, which see, above), a derivation for 'drugget' has sometimes been proposed from 'Drogheda', in Ireland. Despite the fame of this town for its linen and damask, however, this is not the source of the name, which in fact comes from French *droguet*, 'useless fabric', itself from *drogue*, 'trash' (not related to English 'drogue' which is probably an alteration of 'drag').

**dryad** (nymph of the trees)
If a naiad is a nymph of the water, then surely a dryad must be one of the dry land? If the word were of Germanic origin, this might be a reasonable assumption, but of course it is Greek, and derives from *drys*, the Greek word for 'tree'. (Some enthusiastic word-chasers have even linked the word with 'Druid', since they also have close associations with trees. There may be a remote connection here just as there is between Greek *drys* and 'tree' itself, but there is certainly no direct correspondence.)

**duel** (fight between two people)
A duel is not so called since it is a 'dual' combat, with two opponents, although the meaning of the word certainly seems to have been affected by Latin *duo* or some other word involving 'two'. It actually derives from Medieval Latin *duellum*, which is itself related to standard Latin *bellum*, 'war'.

**dugong** (large aquatic animal supposed to be the origin of the mermaid)
The whalelike creature is not so named because is has prominent dugs (taking into account its association with mermaids), but because its native Malay name is *duyong*, 'sea cow'.

**dumdum** (kind of bullet that explodes on impact)
Some names of weapons and types of ammunition are onomatopoeic, suggesting the sound they make (such as 'ack-ack', 'pom-pom', 'whizzbang'), and it might be thought that 'dumdum' is in this category. In fact, rather unexpectedly, its name is its place of origin, Dum-Dum, near Calcutta in India, where it was first produced at the arsenal and military base there. See also **howitzer** and **shrapnel**.

**dumps** (in phrase 'down in the dumps': depressed, dispirited)
The word suggests 'dump', of course, as if you fell you have been 'dumped', or are in a place that is a real 'dump'. But the word can be traced back to Middle Dutch *domp*, 'haze', 'mist', which in turn is related to English 'damp'. So if you are 'in the dumps' you are in a sense 'bogged down', or have had your spirits dampened.

**dunce** (stupid person)
Another word for 'dunce' is 'dunderhead', but the two are not related. 'Dunce' has a

surprisingly scholastic origin, since it derives from the name of the thirteenth-century Scottish theologian John Duns Scotus, whose followers were ridiculed by humanists in the sixteenth century as being 'enemies of learning'. His own name comes from the little town of Duns near Berwick-on-Tweed, where he was born. A 'dunder-head' was probably originally a 'thunderhead'.

**earnest** (money given by a buyer to a seller to agree a bargain)
The rarer 'earnest' as defined here is not related to the better known 'earnest', as if the buyer was proving that he was 'in earnest', i. e. wanting to make a serious bargain. The word comes from Old French *erres*, 'pledges', itself ultimately going back through Latin and Greek to Hebrew *ʿērāvōn*, 'a pledge' (from *ʿārav*, 'he pledged'). Clerics have sometimes been known to misinterpret the biblical reference to 'the earnest of the spirit in our hearts' (2 Corinthians 1:22), as if this was a pledge that believers are 'in earnest'. The better known 'earnest' is of Germanic origin.

**earwig** (brown insect with pincers at the end of its body)
The familiar insect is not so called because its thin hindwings are like ears, or because it lives in ears of corn, but from the old belief that it creeps into people's ears, with the 'wig' part of the name perhaps related to 'wiggle'. The earwig has similar names in other languages, such as German *Ohrwurm*, French *perce-oreille* and Russian *ukhovërtka* (literally 'ear-turner').

**easel** (support for artist's canvas or for a blackboard)
The easel is not so called as it eases the work of the painter or teacher, as may well be supposed, but because the word comes from Dutch *ezel*, 'ass', that is, it does the 'donkeywork' of holding the canvas. Some other languages have a similar word relating to a beast of burden, such as French *chevalet* (literally, 'little horse'), and related Italian *cavaletto* and Spanish *caballete*. Compare English 'horse' in similar senses (e.g. 'clothes horse').

**ebony** (kind of hard, dark wood)
The meaning of 'ebony' is sometimes obscured by its false association with 'bony' and by its frequent pairing with 'ivory' (which actually is bony). There is thus 'ivory black', as the name of a black pigment got by grinding charred scraps of ivory, and the colloquial word 'ivories' for the white keys of a piano (by contrast with the black ones). (As a kind of inversion of this, 'ebony' is an American colloquial term for a black person, as distinct from a white.) It is possible that the present spelling of 'ebony' was even influenced by that of 'ivory' since the earlier spelling was 'hebeny' (from Greek *ebenos*, 'ebony tree').

**eclipse** (total or partial obscuring of the sun or moon)
The word does not refer to the way in which one celestial body 'clips' off a portion of another, but derives ultimately from Greek *ekleipsis*, 'a forsaking', from *leipein*, 'to leave'. The idea is that the sun or moon has failed in its regular task of providing light.

**effete** (effeminate)
The two words are not related, and 'effete' is not a kind of contraction of 'effeminate'. The former word comes from Latin *effetus*, meaning 'worn out by bearing young' (i.e. 'ex-fruitful', or 'out of foetuses'); the latter word more obviously derives from *femina*, 'woman'. (However, ultimately, 'effete' and 'effeminate' are from the same source, a root word meaning 'suckle', and thus 'foetus' belongs here, too.)

**egg on** (encourage, urge)
The phrase is not related to the ordinary 'egg', as if encouragement was being given by such exclamations as 'good egg!', but comes from Old Norse *eggja*, 'to urge', itself related to 'edge'. The basic idea is that a person who is being 'egged on' is being 'edged' in the direction of taking some action.

58

**elegy** (kind of sad or reflective poem or song)
An elegy is not so called because it is elegant, nor is it the same thing as a 'eulogy', which is a poem or song of praise. The word comes from Greek *elegos*, 'song of mourning', originally one sung to a flute.

**embargo** (ban)
The word almost looks as if it contains a 'bar', or applied initially to barges (perhaps by some secondary association with 'cargo'). Its actual origin is in the Spanish verb *embargar*, 'to arrest'. This itself, however, may well derive ultimately from a Vulgar Latin word *barra*, meaning 'bar', although this word has not been actually traced.

**ember days** (special days for fasting and prayer)
In the Church of England and the Roman Catholic Church, ember days fall on the Wednesday, Friday or Saturday following a particular day in the church calendar, including the first Sunday in Lent. For this reason, their name is often wrongly associated with the 'embers' or ashes of penitence which Lent marks (beginning on Ash Wednesday). But the term has quite a different origin, and derives from Old English *ymbrene*, 'circuit' (literally, 'about course'), referring to the regular occurrence or appearance of the days. This origin thus rules out the other derivation sometimes proposed, that the phrase is a corruption of Latin *quatuor tempora*, 'four times', relating to the four occasions in the year when ember days are observed.

**enervate** (decrease the energy of)
Because of the similarity between 'enervate' and 'energy', the former word is sometimes misunderstood, so that 'enervating air' is thought of as bracing or exhilarating. There may also be a false link with 'elevating'. In Leonard Michaels' and Christopher Ricks' *The State of the Language* (see Bibliography), Kingsley Amis quotes (in the chapter entitled 'Getting It Wrong') an example noted of this wrong use of the word: 'He brought to his job a style and verve which were refreshing and enervating'. But the word derives from Latin *enervatus*, literally 'having had the nerves removed', and the sense is thus virtually the exact opposite of the misuse quoted here and found elsewhere.

**entail** (involve, imply)
The word is sometimes falsely associated with 'tail', and even understood as a result of mean 'involve afterwards', 'imply a consequence'. A sentence such as 'My work entailed considerable expense' may therefore be wrongly taken to mean that the payment was made after the work was finished, and was a consequence of it in a temporal sense. But the actual base of the word is Old French *taille*, 'division' (as modern French *tailler*, 'to cut') meaning that a 'dividing' or limiting of the action was caused.

**entrails** (internal organs, 'innards')
The word has nothing to do with 'trails', although it may conjure up 'trailing' intestines in a rather grisly manner. 'Intestines' is what the word originally meant in Latin, since *interanea*, the ultimate source, is based on *inter*, 'between', and relates to what is 'internal'. This word then changed to its present English spelling via Medieval Latin *intralia* and Old French (also modern) *entrailles*.

**epicure** (person of discriminating tastes, especially in food)
There is no connection between this word and 'cure', despite the association between 'cure' and various senses involving health and food (if only 'cured ham'). The word actually derives from the name of the Greek philosopher Epicurus, who held that the highest good is pleasure and calmness of mind. (His own name means literally 'helper', 'aider'.)

**equerry** (official in charge of horses)
The title of this royal post would so clearly seem to be derived from Latin *equus*, 'horse', and thus to be related to 'equestrian'. It is in fact, however, an alteration of an earlier spelling 'esquiry', this deriving from the Old French word for 'stable' (modern *écurie*) that also gave English 'squire'. The false derivation from *equus* is also promoted by those

who stress the word on the first syllable (i.e. as '*e*querry', and not 'equ*e*rry'). Both pronunciations are still admissible.

**erl-king** (evil spirit who carries off children)
The name became well known through Schubert's song (called 'The Erl-King' in English) that narrated the legend. The word is not related to 'earl' and in English represents German *Erlkönig*, which actually means 'alder-king'. This itself was a word coined in 1778 by the German folksong collector Johann von Herder as a mistranslation of Danish *ellerkonge*, 'elf-king'. The name thus became established with a false meaning that in turn produced misleading associations in other languages, including English (which could have accepted it simply as 'elf-king' without much difficulty if it had not been for Herder's mistranslation).

**espresso** (kind of coffee)
The coffee is not so called as it is made rapidly (an 'express' coffee), but because it is made in a machine that brews it by forcing steam or boiling water through finely ground coffee beans. The word's Italian origin literally means 'pressed-out coffee' (*caffè espresso*).

**exchequer** (department of state in charge of national revenue)
The title is a misleading one, having no link with 'cheque' or 'exchange' or even with the common prefix 'ex-'. Nor is it somehow linked with the country residence of the Prime Minister, Chequers. The name derives from Old French *eschequier*, 'chessboard', referring to the chequered counting table on which the accounts were originally reckoned. (Compare the American name for

the game of draughts, 'checkers'.) The present spelling of the word is due to wrong association with words starting 'ex-' such as 'exchange' and 'exploit'.

**excise** (type of tax on goods for the home market, especially spirits)
It might well be thought that the tax is so called since an amount is 'excised', or cut off. In fact the two words are not related. The tax so called probably comes, via Dutch, from Old French *assise*, 'session', referring to a panel of assessors passing judgment on the amount to be levied. The other 'excise' of course derives from Latin *excidere*, 'to cut off', 'to cut out'.

**expatriate** (person who has renounced his native land to live abroad)
The comparatively new term is sometimes understood (and even spelt and pronounced) as if it referred to someone who is an 'ex-patriot'. The actual origin is in Latin *ex patria*, 'out of one's native land', through the Medieval Latin verb *expatriare*, 'to leave one's homeland and settle abroad'.

**eyelet** (small hole for a lace in a shoe)
The name does mean 'little eye', as might be supposed. The word is not an English diminutive '-let' such as 'notelet', 'starlet', however, but a French one, since it originates from French *oeillet*, itself from Latin *oculus*. Compare **coverlet** and **cutlet**.

**eyrie** (eagle's nest)
This word can be spelt in a variety of ways, including 'aerie' and 'aery'. For this reason, it is sometimes wrongly connected with 'airy', with reference to its lofty site. In fact it is almost certainly derived from Latin *area*, 'open field', perhaps in the more specialized sense of 'feeding place'.

**fagged** (tired out)
The colloquial word is not derived from 'fatigued', although it may have been influenced by it. Instead it comes from 'fag' in the sense 'work hard' (like a fag in a public school, which is the same word). This itself may somehow be linked with 'flag' in the sense 'droop' (hence perhaps 'fag end').

**fair** (public entertainment or gathering, popularly one with a showground)
A fair is not so called because it is fair (attractive, beautiful). The word ultimately comes, via Old French, from Latin *feriae*, 'holidays', 'days of rest' (with this word also related to 'festival'). The other 'fair' is a word of Germanic origin.

**fairway** (special channel or passage, e. g. for ships or golfers)
There is no link with 'fare' in the sense 'go', despite the fact that the word is or was sometimes spelt 'fareway' and that the German for a nautical fairway is *Fahrwasser* (from *fahren*, 'to go', 'to travel'). The word, for once, therefore seems to mean what it says, describing a way that is 'fair', i. e. obstacle-free.

**fairy** (small kindly creature of folklore and children's tales)
A fairy is not so called because it is 'fair' or beautiful, but because it originated as Old French *faerie*, actually meaning 'fairyland', 'fairy people'. (The English word did not develop as 'fay', as it did in its equivalent form in many other languages.) The French word itself goes back to Latin *Fata*, 'goddess of fate', i. e. as one of the Fates in classical mythology.

**fallow** (of land: ploughed and harrowed but left unsown)
There is almost certainly no connection between fallow land and the fallow deer,

despite the fact that both are (or can be) pale brown in colour. The land can be traced back to Old English *fealga*, and the deer to Old English *fealu*, with the latter word related to Greek *polios*, 'grey'.

**fan** (supporter, devotee)
A fan is not so called because he or she 'blows hot', as has been sometimes popularly (or punningly) explained, but because the word is short for 'fanatic'. This form of the word originated in the nineteenth century in America.

**farthingale** (petticoat with a hooped frame to expand a skirt)
The farthingale was in fashion in Elizabethan times. It is not related to 'farthing', nor is the word a corruption, as has been stated by some, of French *vertugarde*, 'modesty guard'. The term came into English from Old Spanish *verdugado*, itself from *verdugo*, 'rod', 'stick' (in turn from *verde*, 'green'). The English spelling developed, as from many foreign words, in an attempt to make some sort of meaning out of a word that itself had no meaning in English.

**fascia** (front part of a building, or part of it)
The word is not related to 'face' but derives from the identical Italian word meaning 'bandage', with the ultimate source being the Latin *fascis*, 'bundle' that also produced (again via the Italian) the name 'fascism' and 'fascist'. (The political party was so called as its members were 'bundled' or grouped together from an organizational point of view.) The English word 'fascia' is sometimes spelt 'facia', which reinforces the false connection with 'face'.

**fatuous** (stupid, inane)
The suggestion is certainly that of 'fat', since a fatuous remark can well be made by a

fathead. The origin, however, is in Latin *fatuus*, 'foolish'.

**fawn** (young deer)
The animal is so called (as is the colour named after it) since the word ultimately goes back to Latin *fetus*, 'offspring' (English 'foetus'). Its name has no connection with 'fawn', the verb meaning 'show affection' (as of a dog), or with the first word of 'fauna and flora', meaning 'animal life'. The latter comes from the mythological sister or wife of Faunus, identified with Pan. It follows that the animal called 'fawn' in English cannot be related to the mythological creature of Roman mythology called a 'faun' (which had a human body and the horns and legs of a goat). All the 'animal' associations here do sometimes cause a false cross-fertilization of ideas, however.

**feldspar** (name of a group of minerals)
The word is sometimes spelt 'felspar', reinforcing the idea that the derivation is in German *Fels*, 'rock'. The true origin is in obsolete German *Feldspath* (modern *Feldspat*), literally 'field spar'. The group of minerals, however, are nevertheless an ingredient of almost all crystalline rocks.

**fell** (in phrase 'at one fell swoop': all at once)
The word suggests 'fall', like the swoop of a pouncing bird of prey. In this Shakespearean phrase, however, 'fell' has the sense, now poetic in English, of 'evil', and the word is thus related to 'felon'. Probably the wrong association with a bird of prey is strengthened by the mention of particular birds in the extended quotation containing the phrase in the original, where in *Macbeth* the anguished Macbeth, learning of the murder of his wife and children, exclaims:

'All my pretty ones?
Did you say all? O hell-kite! All?
What! all my chickens and their dam
At one fell swoop?'

**female** (relating to a woman or girl)
Those who have strong views about the equality of the sexes – whether 'pro' or 'con' – sometimes like to point out that 'female' contains (or is greater than) 'male', and that a similar relationship exists between the words 'woman' and 'man', and 'she' and 'he'. In fact the present spelling of 'female' did come about because of the assimilation to 'male', but the word's actual origin is in Middle English *femel*, ultimately, via French, from Latin *femella*, a diminutive of *femina*, 'woman'. In this connection, see also **woman** and the similarly relevant **virago**.

**ferrule** (metal ring round a rod or stick to strengthen it)
Although almost certainly influenced by Latin *ferrum* 'iron', the word ultimately comes from Latin *viriola*, a diminutive of *viria*, 'bracelet', with no 'ferrous' connection at all.

**fetlock** (tuft of hair on a horse's leg)
The 'lock' of the word is not a 'lock' of hair, since the word as a whole comes from Middle English *fitlok* or *fitlak*, the latter half of this being simply an addition to a root word that relates to modern 'foot'. A horse's fetlock is on the back of its leg above its hoof. For another false 'lock', see **wedlock**.

**fey** (otherworldly, elated)
This word is not related to 'fay', so is nothing to do with fairies. It derives from Old English *fæge*, meaning 'doomed', 'marked out for death'. This sense still survives in the Scottish use of the word, but generally it has otherwise come to have a number of rather vague 'visionary' meanings.

**fiddle** (move restlessly)
There is no relation between 'fiddle' and 'fidget', despite a similarity of meaning in the sense given here. 'Fiddle' (as also the identical word meaning 'violin') ultimately goes back to Medieval Latin *vitula*, while 'fidget' developed from an older dialect word 'fidge', which may have ultimately come from some Old Norse word.

**field** (expanse of grass or crops)
Some fanciful sources still maintain that this common English word derives from 'felled', referring to the trees that have been cleared by felling to form a field. In fact the word is of Germanic origin, and ultimately related to Greek *platus*, 'broad', which means it is also indirectly linked with English 'flat'. It

is perhaps simply a coincidence that in horseracing 'the field' (the horses in a race) run on 'the flat' (a course without obstacles)

**fieldfare** (kind of thrush)
The bird has a name that looks as if it is a 'field-farer', i. e. one that travels through the fields (just as a wayfarer travels along the ways or roads). But this is clearly a very doubtful origin, since many birds 'fare' over fields, and some other derivation must be sought. The exact source is uncertain. The name has been recorded in Old English as *feldeware*, perhaps meaning 'field dweller', but this is also an unlikely name, and may not even refer to this particular bird. W. B. Lockwood (see Bibliography) suggests that the origin may lie in conjectural Old English *fealu fearh*, meaning literally 'grey piglet', referring to its colour and the distinctive sound of its cry. But this is only one more possibility, and as yet lacks any recorded support. Whatever the ultimate derivation, it is more than likely that the bird's modern name does not mean what it seems to say. See also **wheatear**.

**figwort** (plant of the foxglove family)
The plant is so called not because it in any way resembles a fig or a fig tree, but because it was supposed to be able to cure 'fig', a now obsolete word for piles.

**filibuster** (military adventurer)
The name suggests an origin in a 'buster' of some kind, as a 'blockbuster', 'crimebuster', 'bronco buster', or whatever. But the word's origin is Spanish *filibustero*, 'freebooter', with this word itself probably (as 'freebooter' is) from Dutch *vrijbuiter*. The word later came to be associated in American politics with delaying tactics, which reinforced the wrong 'buster' link.

**fillip** (boost, stimulus)
A literal 'fillip' is a light blow made by releasing a curled finger from the thumb, and this suggests that the word may be based on 'flip'. If anything, it is the other way round, with 'flip' coming from 'fillip'. Ultimately, however, both words are imitative in origin. (Johnson thought it could come from 'fill up'!)

**filly** (young female horse)
In view of the word's development to mean 'fine-looking girl', 'lively young woman', it seems strange that there is no link with French *fille*, Latin *filia*, and similar words meaning 'girl' or 'daughter'. But this is the case, however, and the word actually goes back to Old Norse *fylja*, with the proper association thus with English 'foal'.

**firedog** (one of two metal supports for burning logs in a grate)
It is sometimes suggested that firedogs are so called since, originally, the device was a form of roasting spit which was revolved by real dogs running in a wheel at either end. This is highly unlikely, however, and there is no evidence that the word was ever used in this sense. The use of 'dog' here is probably to refer to a gripping device, whether mechanical or not. Firedogs are also known as **andirons** (which see for their own mythology).

**fishplate** (type of metal plate used to strengthen a joint)
The name does not refer to the resemblance to a fish of some kind, but derives from an old verb 'fish', meaning 'mend', itself probably from French *ficher*, 'to fix'. A fishplate is therefore really a 'fix-plate'.

**fitful** (irregular)
The 'fit' of this word is the sense meaning 'sudden attack' (as in a 'fainting fit' or 'fits and starts'), not the 'fit' meaning 'healthy', and the two words are not directly related. Because of the false association, however, 'fitful' is sometimes misunderstood to mean 'healthy', as if 'fitful sleep' was sound. health-giving sleep, whereas it is actually broken, uneasy sleep. The word is said to exist in English simply because of its single occurrence in Shakespeare's *Macbeth*, where Macbeth, speaking of the dead Duncan, says that 'After life's fitful fever he sleeps well'. The sense of 'irregular', 'spasmodic' was largely popularized by Walter Scott, as in the Prologue to his poem *The Lady of the Lake*, where he writes of a 'fitful breeze'.

**flagstone** (flat stone used for floors, pavements, etc)
A flagstone (properly just a 'flag') is nothing

to do with the 'flag' that is a banner or a kind of iris, but derives from an Old Norse word *flaga* meaning 'slab' and itself indirectly related to English 'flay' and probably 'flake'. The original meaning of 'flag' in this sense in English was 'turf', 'piece cut out of the grass'.

**flak** (fire from anti-aircraft guns)
The word is also spelt 'flack', suggesting that it may be related to 'flake' or 'flap' or some similar word, possibly one of imitative origin such as 'flick'. This appears to be supported by the modern sense of the word to mean 'heavy criticism' ('come in for some flak'), as if someone was being 'torn into strips' or flakes (or was 'flaking out' under the attack). But such associations are all red herrings, however forgivable, and the word actually derives as an abbreviation of German *Fliegerabwehrkanone*, literally 'pilot defence gun'. See also **strafe**.

**flamenco** (vigorous gypsy dance)
The word is not related to 'flame', despite the colourful associations of the dance. The origin lies in the identical Spanish word meaning literally 'Flemish', hence 'gypsy-like'. The name properly applies to the dance of Andalusian gypsies. (The Flemish had a reputation for bright clothes and florid complexions in medieval times.)

**flatulent** (causing accumulation of gas in the body)
There is an apparent suggestion of 'flat' in this word, as if the gas were somehow 'flat' or one's stomach had been 'flat' before the gas built up inside it. But this is a sort of false association of opposites, and the word's origin is in Latin *flatus*, literally 'blowing' (as in the identical English word used to describe the gas itself in this state).

**fleck** (small particle of something)
Both 'fleck' and 'flake' are very likely of Scandinavian origin, but there is no direct link between them, and it cannot be assumed that a 'fleck' is simply a small 'flake'. 'Fleck' developed in English from the adjective 'flecked' meaning 'spotted', while 'flake' is related to Norwegian *flak*, 'disc'.

**flee** (run away, escape)
There is no direct link between 'flee' and 'fly', although both words go back to a common ultimate source and both were already confused in Old English. There is anyway a general basic interconnection between many words starting 'fl-' that express a light or rapid movement, including not only 'flee' and 'fly' but also 'flake', 'flap', 'flea', 'fleet', 'flick', 'flirt', 'flit', 'float', 'fluff' and 'flutter'.

**flock** (tuft of wool, waste wool or fibre used for packing etc)
The word does not related to the other 'flock', despite the common link in 'sheep'. The 'tuft' sense of 'flock' goes back to a Germanic word which may possibly be related to 'flake'. The more common sense of the word, meaning 'group', derives from Old English *flocc*, 'crowd', and probably has Scandinavian connections. Similarly, the English word 'fleece' is unrelated to either word 'flock', and probably has its basic roots in Latin *pluma*, 'feather' (which in turn gave English 'plume').

**flounce** (strip of fabric attached to the hem of a skirt)
The decorative addition is not so called because it enables the wearer to 'flounce' along (or about, or out). The word was originally 'frounce', and comes from Old French *fronce*, 'wrinkle' (modern French *froncer* means 'to gather' in needlework). The other 'flounce' meaning 'move in an exaggerated way' probably derives from some Scandinavian source. See also the stylishly related **furbelow**.

**flush** (drive out, as of game or the enemy)
This sense of 'flush' is probably of imitative origin (not necessarily in English) as if whoever or whatever it was is being 'shooed' out from a place of concealment. The many other senses of 'flush', whether verb ('flush' water), adjective ('ruddy and healthy') or noun ('hand of cards'), all ultimately derive from an origin close to Latin *fluxus*, 'flow', so are not related to 'flush' meaning 'drive out'.

**fly** (smart, knowing)
To say 'He's very fly' suggests 'There are

no flies on him', but there is apparently no connection between the two senses of the word. The second familiar expression qutoed here probably relates to active or alert cattle, who take care, by swishing their tails or tossing their heads, that there are 'no flies' on them.

**fogey** (old-fashioned or aged person)
An 'old fogey' is probably not so called since he is 'foggy', or has obscure or vague notions. The precise origin of the word is itself foggy, but could perhaps be in another word 'foggy' meaning 'fat', 'flabby', with this sense now obsolete.

**foil** (type of fencing sword)
The word is not related in origin to the 'foil' that means 'beat off', 'defeat', as if the weapon were a particularly suitable one for vanquishing an opponent, nor is it apparently derived from 'foil' meaning 'thin sheet of metal'. (This second connection is sometimes explained in a rather far-fetched way with reference to the French word for the sword, which is *fleuret*, literally 'floweret', and the comparison between the button of the sword and a bud; this assumes that 'foil' is somehow connected with French *feuille*, 'leaf' and the Middle English word *foil* that also meant 'leaf' and gave the 'coat of metal' sense.) In short, there is no evidence that the name of the sword is linked with any other 'foil'.

**fold** (pen or enclosure for animals)
This 'fold' is not the same word as the 'fold' that means 'clasp together', as if the enclosure 'folded' the animals within its walls or fences. The first 'fold' comes from Old English *falod*, and the second from Old English *fealdan*. Even any ultimate link has not been conclusively proved.

**folk of peace** (Scottish name for fairy folk)
The name does not refer to the peaceful nature of the fairies, or to their silent movement. Instead, the phrase is a mistranslation of Gaelic *daoine sídhe*, literally 'people of fairy hill', where the second word was taken to be the genitive (*síthe*) of *síth*, 'peace'. (Compare Irish *bean sídhe*, English 'banshee', literally 'woman of the fairy hill'.) The phrase was fairly common in late nine-teenth-century literature, and occurs, for example, in R. L. Stevenson's *Catriona*, which in the opening words of its first chapter has the line: 'I am nameless, like the Folk of Peace'.

**foolhardy** (reckless, foolishly adventurous)
The word does not quite come from 'fool' and 'hardy', since its origin is in Old French *fol hardi*, literally 'foolish-bold'.

**foolscap** (size of paper [13½ x 17 inches] now mainly superseded by A3 [about 11¾ x 16½ inches])
One ingenious etymologist has explained the word as deriving from *folio*, or from Italian *foglio capo*, 'chief sheet', as if it was the main large size of paper. But the true origin is in the English word itself, which is simply 'fool's cap' and refers to a watermark showing a fool's cap and bells that was formerly used on this kind of paper, for both writing and printing.

**footling** (trivial)
There is no reference to 'foot' here, as if describing something that had been kicked about or walked over with the feet. The word comes from a former verb 'footer', meaning 'bungle', itself from French *foutre* (literally 'to copulate').

**footpad** (highwayman)
A footpad was a highwayman who robbed on foot, as distinct from one on horseback. The word looks, therefore, as if it describes a robber who 'pads on foot' to get his victim, or at least one who wears padded shoes. But the real origin is in the cant word 'pad' meaning 'path', and by extension 'highwayman' itself. Put another way, a footpad was a 'path man' as against a 'highway man'.

**forcemeat** (highly seasoned savoury mixture usually containing chopped meat)
The preparation is not so called since the meat or some other ingredient has been 'forced' in some way (as through a mincer or chopper), but because the word is an alteration of 'farcemeat', where 'farce' means 'stuffing'. (The theatrical perform-

ance called a 'farce' has the same origin, since at one time humorous interludes were 'stuffed' into the otherwise serious play.) For another wrong association with 'force', see **forceps** (below).

**forceps** (instrument for grasping or pulling)
It might well be thought that as pincers are used for pinching, and tweezers for 'tweezing', so forceps could be used for forcing (with this association itself reinforced through the 'forceps baby', who has to be delivered with the assistance of forceps). But the ending of the word should give the clue that this is not the proper derivation, and 'forceps' in fact probably comes as a blend of Latin *formus*, 'warm' and *capere*, 'to take', with the original sense being 'smith's tongs' in the Latin.

**foremost** (first)
The origin of the word is not in 'fore' and 'most', as if implying 'most of the fore', but is an alteration of Middle English *formest*, which is the superlative of Old English *forma*, 'first', so that the original sense was 'firstest', so to say. Similar words in English where the final '-most' indicates a superlative, and not 'most', are 'innermost', 'uppermost', 'utmost', 'aftermost' and 'hindmost'.

**foreword** (preface, especially one written by someone other than the author of the main text)
The word looks like an altered spelling of 'forward', and is sometimes misspelt as such (with one such misspelling even found in a publisher's stocklist). But of course the reference is to a 'word beforehand', although the English word originated as a literal translation of German *Vorwort*, 'preface'. Compare **frontispiece** and also **preface** itself.

**forge ahead** (make good progress)
The derivation of the word is not from 'forge', despite the connotation of power and strength, and of 'beating' one's way forward. It is very likely an alteration of 'force', with the sense originally a nautical one, applying to ships moving ahead slowly and steadily through the waves.

**forlorn hope** (desperate or final undertaking or attempt)
This is one of the most famous false etymologies in the English language. The phrase obviously looks like an almost useless hope, one that has been virtually abandoned. The true origin, however, is in Dutch *verloren hoop*, literally 'lost troop'. This was the name given to a storming or attacking party who were the first to go into battle and who were 'written off', alas, as they stood a poor chance of returning alive. The French equivalent for such a body of men was *enfants perdus*, 'lost children'. The expression first came into use in English in the late sixteenth century to apply to any such attacking party, on land or at sea (where sailors were later to call it a 'flowing hope')

**fount** (complete set of printing type)
The semi-technical word is not related to the 'fount' meaning 'fountain', as if the characters were all fully displayed, or as if the set was the source for the characters to be printed, but derives, through Old French, from Latin *fundere*, 'to melt', 'to pour', referring to the casting of the type. The correct association here is thus with 'foundry', not 'fountain'.

**fox** (trick by cunning or ingenuity)
Some attempts have been made to derive the word from French *faux*, 'false', and a few etymologists have even derived the name of the animal itself from this, since the fox is a cunning and crafty creature and will try to set up a false trail for its pursuer. Support for such a link is said to lie in such words as 'foxfire' (the phosphorescent light given out by decaying wood), as if this was really 'false fire'. But all senses of 'fox' relate to the animal – mostly to its nature, appearance or colour – and there is no etymological connection with 'false' in French or any other language. See also **foxglove** (below)

**foxglove** (plant with a flower resembling a finger stall)
The name is admittedly somewhat mysterious, and the allusion to 'foxes' gloves' rather obscure. But there could well be a fanciful idea behind the word of finger stalls or 'thimbles' for foxes, and the plant often grows in woods near foxes' earths. At

all events, the name is certainly not a corruption of 'folks' glove' (i.e. gloves worn by the 'wee folk' or fairies), as has been sometimes proposed.

**foxtrot** (type of ballroom dance)
The dance is so called not because the dancers move with steps like those of a fox trotting, but because the steps are like those of the horse's gait called a 'foxtrot'. This is a pace with short steps that a horse adopts when it is slowing down from trotting to walking. Of course, this term itself does derive from the pace of a fox.

**freemason** (member of a secret fraternity)
The strong association of 'brotherhood' behind the word has led some etymologists to derive the term from a French original *frère-maçon*, 'brother mason'. But the actual origin is what the word implies, that historically there were masons who were 'free' in the sense that they were not bound by guilds and could work where they wanted. (Stonemasons were originally 'free' masons in this sense.)

**frieze** (heavy fabric used for carpets)
There is no connection between 'frieze' in the sense given here and 'frieze' meaning 'decorative band on a wall'. The words are of quite different origin, with the 'decorative band' sense ultimately deriving from the name of Phrygia, the ancient country in Asia Minor that was famous for its embroidery in gold, and the 'fabric' sense going back to its own place of origin, Friesland, famous for its farm animals (including its Frisian cows).

**fritillary** (1 plant of the lily family; 2 butterfly with spotted wings)
Neither plant nor butterfly is so called since it 'flits' or 'flitters' (or 'fritters' away its life in idle showiness), but because its name comes from New Latin *fritillaria*, in turn from Latin *fritillus*, 'dice-box'. The reference is to the mottled markings on the flowers and the spots (usually black on orange) on the wings of the butterfly.

**fritter** (sweet dish, typically an apple fritter)
The dish is so called not because it has been made out of bits and pieces or 'fritters' but because it derives, like all good culinary words, from French, in this case Middle French *friture*, related to 'fry' (and more closely to *pommes frites*).

**Frog** (mainly derogatory nickname for a Frenchman)
Perhaps out of politeness, some word specialists have derived the name from the three toads at one time on the coat of arms of Paris, or as an allusion to the originally 'quaggy' or frog-abounding streets of the capital. But the truth is almost certainly in the fact that the French have a reputation for eating frogs (which the British, although themselves enjoying eels and oysters, find difficult to understand). The alliteration of 'Frog' and 'French' helps, of course.

**frontispiece** (illustration facing the title page of a book)
The word certainly looks as if it refers to the 'front piece' of a book, as if in contrast to a 'tailpiece'. The term came into English from French *frontispice*, however, with this word in turn deriving from Late Latin *frontispicium*, literally 'inspection of the forehead', or 'view of the front'. The association with 'piece' was made early in English, and was almost certainly aided by such words as 'masterpiece'. For other literary red herrings, see **foreword** and **preface**.

**fry** (young of animals)
The word is common in the phrase 'small fry', and is also usually associated with small fishes (which can be either recently hatched or adult). These connotations suggest a link with food (such as sprats) that can be fried, and 'fryers', after all, are young chickens suitable for frying. But the true origin of 'fry' in this 'young' sense is Old French *frier* or *froyer*, 'to spawn'.

**fulsome** (1 abundant; 2 offensive)
The second sense of the word quoted here is still fairly common in such phrases as 'fulsome praise', i.e. praise that is over-complimentary or offensively flattering. For this reason, the origin is sometimes thought to be 'foulsome'. But the word really means what it says, and implies a 'full' or copious amount of something, whether excessively

or not. To complicate matters, too, many people now use 'fulsome' in a sense that is actually quite complimentary, and not at all derogatory, and 'fulsome' praise can mean 'generous' praise, with no hint of undue effusiveness or insincerity.

**funny bone** (point at back of elbow where tingling is felt when it is sharply struck)
The sensation is caused by the striking or jarring of a nerve at this point, which is where it runs over a section of the bone called the 'humerus' (extending from the shoulder to the elbow). Classical or other academic or not so academic wits like to derive the name of the funny bone from this,

since (to spell it out) 'humerus' is 'humorous' or 'funny'. But the more prosaic origin is simply in the sensation itself, which is a 'funny' one (moreover, more 'funny peculiar' than 'funny ha-ha').

**furbelow** (pleated or gathered piece of material)
The word is common in the phrase 'frills and furbelows', and this has to some suggested an origin in 'fur below', since a furbelow is a sort of **flounce** (which see). But it's folk etymology at work again here, and the word comes from French dialect *farbella*, itself of obscure origin.

**gadfly** (kind of fly that annoys livestock)
The fly is not so called because it 'gads about' but because it has a 'gad' or sting (this word is now only in technical or dialect use for a bar or rod). For the sake of accuracy, however, it should be pointed out that gadflies do not sting but bite.

**gaff** (in phrase 'blow the gaff': 'reveal a secret')
This word is usually regarded as nautical, and its origin is normally said to lie in the 'gaffsail' of a sailing ship, although it is hard to see how 'blowing' this could indicate the revelation of a secret. Much more likely, the 'gaff' here is an alteration of 'gab', meaning 'talk', so a person who has blown the gaff has 'shot his mouth' or 'blabbed'.

**gaffer** (old man)
The word is probably not an alteration of 'grandfather', as 'gammer' may be of 'grandmother', but of 'godfather', with the initial 'ga-' by association with 'grandfather', however. This despite the fact that in Britain a 'gaffer' is a foreman, or 'boss'.

**galère** (coterie)
The French word is sometimes rather affectedly or academically used to mean 'exclusive group of people', and is even occasionally offered in a version of the line in which it occurs in Molière's *Les Fourberies de Scapin*, which properly is: 'Que diable allait-il faire dans cette galère?'. This means 'What the devil was he up to in this galley?' Understandably enough, the word is all too frequently taken to mean 'gallery' (which is no doubt more artistic), and translated as such. Such a misinterpretation can occur in quite scholarly works, e. g. Francis West's *Gilbert Murray: A Life*, published in 1983. See also **galley** (below).

**gall** (impudence, audacity)
This sense of the word is often associated with the other senses ('sore on skin' and 'growth on plants'), since such impudence is exasperating or an annoying burden. But although the last two senses of 'gall' are probably related, the 'impudence' sense is a different word, and ultimately relates to Greek *cholē* or *cholos,* which gave the sense 'bile' (as in 'gall bladder') that this particular 'gall' comes from.

**galley** (type of ancient ship)
No sense of 'galley' is related to 'gallery', and even the 'ship's kitchen' sense cannot be connected with the other word, despite the semantic link in 'passageway'. So whatever 'galley' means now, the word derives from Middle Greek *galea,* originally the ship, of course. See also **galère** (above).

**gallowglass** (armed Irish foot soldier)
This historic word, also spelt 'galloglass', has no association with 'gallows' or 'glass', despite the apparent suggestion of some kind of fatal or final drinking bowl (a sort of executioner's stirrup cup). Not surprisingly, the origin turns out to be in Irish Gaelic, so that *gallóglach* derives from *gall,* 'foreigner' and *óglach,* 'servant', 'soldier'. ('Foreigner' since many such mercenaries were originally not Irish.) For another misleading 'glass' word see **isinglass**.

**game** (of leg: crippled)
No conclusive connection with any of the more common senses of 'game' has been proved, although if a person is 'game' (willing) he may show the same determination that someone with a 'game' leg does to walk. The word may have its origin in a dialect expression of some kind, and possibly even derive from French *gambi,* 'crooked'. Certainly 'gammy' seems to be a form of 'game' in this 'crippled' sense.

**ganglion** (mass of nerve cells)
As with some other medical or anatomical terms, several wrong associations suggest themselves, in this case perhaps 'gangling', 'jangle' ('jangling nerves') and even **gangrene** (which see, below). The word is a pure Greek one, originally denoting a tumour under the skin near a tendon or sinew, and today also sometimes used in a similar sense for a small cyst on a membrane round a joint. The term is indirectly related to '**gall**' in the sense 'growth on plants' (see this word).

**gangrene** (death of body tissues, necrosis)
Gangrene can set in when the blood supply to a particular part of the body, such as a hand or foot, has been cut off. The affected part rapidly changes colour. and for this reason it could be supposed that the name means that it has 'gone green'. The true origin is more complex than this, however, and as might be expected the term has a classical derivation, from Greek *gangraina,* literally 'gnawing sore', itself based on Greek *gran,* 'to gnaw'.

**gangway** (passageway)
A gangway is not so called because gangs of people walk along it (or up or down it). Not directly, anyway, since although the first part of the word derives from Old English *gangan,* 'to go', the actual original sense of *gang* as used here was 'way' 'passage'. This in turn came to produce the modern sense of 'gang', implying a group or band of people who are going somewhere for a particular purpose.

**gardenia** (kind of shrub with showy white or yellow flowers)
A gardenia will look and smell good in a garden, but this is not the origin of its name, which comes from the Scottish-American eighteenth-century botanist Dr Alexander Garden. He was Vice-President of the Royal Society, and the name was adopted for this genus in his lifetime.

**gargantuan** (huge, enormous)
The word suggests 'gigantic', and is virtually a synonym in this sense. It also suggests 'gargoyle' and 'gargle', however, and this is closer to the true origin. The term comes from the name of the greedy giant Gargantua, father of Pantagruel in the satirical work by Rabelais (in the original five parts, with the first called *La Vie inestimable du grand Gargantua, père de Pantagruel*). The name of the giant, together with those of his parents, Grandgousier and Gargamelle, were taken by Rabelais from a chapbook called *Grandes et inestimables cronicques,* in turn doubtless under the influence of Old French *gargate,* 'throat'.

**garrotte** (method of execution by strangling with an iron collar)
This unpleasant device, of Spanish origin, suggests a source in some word related to modern English 'gargle', 'gurgle' or 'gargoyle'. The derivation seems to be from Old French *garrot,* 'cudgel', 'stick', this presumably referring to the stick that was turned or twisted to tighten the collar.

**gastric** (relating to the stomach)
This medical word is nothing to do with 'gas', in spite of associated disorders of the stomach and the link with the so called 'gastric juices' or digestive fluids in the stomach. The word is simply derived, as are many anatomical terms, from the Greek for the organ in question, in this case *gastēr,* 'stomach'. ('Gas' is actually an artificial word, deivsed by the sixteenth-century Flemish chemist J. B. van Helmont, who based it on Latin *chaos,* 'space', 'chaos'.)

**gate** (in place-names, especially street names)
In many place-names and street names in the Midlands and North of England, 'gate' does not mean 'gate' but 'street', 'way'. The origin is in Old Norse *gata,* 'path', with the word one that was imported by the Norsemen. One of the best known names containing the word is that of Harrogate, where the first part of the name, also from Old Norse, is a word meaning 'cairn', 'heap of stones'. The word is most often found, however, in street names, such as that of Micklegate in York, where the meaning of the name as a whole is 'big street' (i.e. the same as 'High Street' in the south), and Briggate and Kirkgate, both in Leeds, where the respective meanings are 'Bridge Street' and 'Church Street'. Many southern

'gate' names really are 'gate', however, especially such seaside towns as Ramsgate and Margate, where the 'gate' is a way through to the sea.

**gauntlet** (in phrase 'run the gauntlet')
The phrase means 'submit oneself to an ordeal', 'be subjected to criticism'. Because of other expressions containing 'gauntlet', such as 'throw down the gauntlet' and 'take up the gauntlet' (to indicate respectively offering and accepting a challenge), it is often thought that the 'gauntlet' is the same word ('glove') as in these other two phrases. The origin is quite different, however, and the word was formerly spelt *gantlope*, deriving from Swedish *gatlopp*, itself a compound of *gata*, 'road', 'way' (see **gate**, above) and *lop*, 'course', 'run'. A *gantlope* was thus a double file of men facing each other and armed with clubs or some other weapon with which they would strike at a person made to run between them. The procedure was a form of military (and naval) punishment, and the Swedish etymological origin is probably due to the use of this punishment in the Thirty Years' War, in which Sweden and many other European countries (although not Britain) were involved.

**geezer** (old man, often a slightly eccentric one)
There is no relation between this word and 'geyser', as if the old man so termed were constantly 'spouting' nonsense. The colloquial word is probably an alteration of Scottish *guiser*, related to 'guise', referring to the particular individual's appearance.

**geneva** see **gin**

**genie** (spirit in Arabian folklore)
The word is spelt in various ways, not only as here but also as 'jinn', 'jinni', 'jinnee' and 'djinni', among others. This particular spelling derives from French *génie*, which was the word used for the spirit by French translators of the original *Arabian Nights*. The spelling wrongly suggests a link with 'genius', or more precisely with Latin *genius*, meaning 'attendant spirit', and this certainly seems to have influenced the English word. However, the Arabic word

itself is the true origin, with the meaning simply 'demon'.

**genteel** (aristocratic, elegant)
The word does not derive so much from the popular sense of 'gentle', meaning 'soft', 'kindly', as the basic 'aristocratic' sense still present in such words as 'gentleman' and 'gentry'. The alteration in spelling is due to the word's origin in Middle French *gentil*. See also **Gentile** and **gingerly** (below).

**Gentile** (non-Jewish person)
Gentiles were and are not so called since they are of 'gentle' birth but because they all belong to the same race, Latin *gens, gentis*. Of course, 'gentle' itself also derives from the same Latin word, with associations of 'kinship'. ('Kin' itself is also indirectly related to Latin *gens*.)

**gibbon** (kind of ape)
The name certainly suggests an animal that 'gibbers', but rather disappointingly the actual origin is a native Indian dialect word for the ape which came into English through the French. 'Gibber', as might be expected, is an imitative word, and 'gibberish' is based on it.

**gillyflower** (type of fragrant flower)
The name is properly that of the **clove pink** (see both these words separately), but the 'flower' is a corruption, although an entirely understandable one. In Middle English the word was *gilofre*, and this came from Old French *gilofre* or *girofle*, itself ultimately deriving from Greek *karuophyllon*, 'clove tree' (from *karuon*, 'nut' and *phyllon*, 'leaf'). The flower name is familiar as that of the British television actress Gilly Flower, starring, among other roles, as one of the two sweet old ladies in the BBC comedy series 'Fawlty Towers'.

**gin** (alcoholic spirit)
The name of the drink is a shortening of its 'official' name of 'geneva', which in turn seems to suggest that Geneva is its place of origin. But 'geneva' is actually a variant of Dutch *genever*, 'juniper', referring to the juniper berries with which the spirit is flavoured. 'Geneva' is now sometimes used as an alternative name for the strong ginlike

drink better known as 'Hollands', and this in turn indicates the true provenance of the spirit.

**Ginger** (nickname for a person with red hair)

Those who cannot believe that the name really derives from 'ginger' sometimes like to imagine an origin in the name of Lady Guinevere, the wife of King Arthur, since she was traditionally said to have red hair. But this is a flight of fancy, and the nickname means what it says, referring to the colour ginger that itself came from the root. Lady Guinevere's name is a French version of a Welsh name that also produced the better known English name Jennifer. The Welsh name (Gwenhwyfar) means 'fair and smooth', quite a far cry from the hot, dark 'Ginger'! For more about ginger, see **gingerbread** (below).

**gingerbread** (kind of cake made with treacle and flavoured with ginger)

It may be objected that gingerbread is not 'bread' but cake. This is correct – although for etymological reasons, not culinary! The original English word was *gingebras*, this moreover not meaning 'gingerbread' but 'ginger paste'. This came into English from Old French *gingembraz,* ultimately from the word for 'ginger' itself, *gimgibre.* The word therefore changed its spelling and sense over the centuries, with the modern meaning appearing some time in the fifteenth century.

**gingerly** (very cautiously)

The association is not with 'ginger' here, as if meaning 'hotly' in some way, but from a quite different word. The false link is not helped by the almost exclusive use of the word as an adverb ('He went ahead gingerly'), although it was also formerly widely used as an adjective ('in a gingerly manner'), a usage that has still not died out. The precise derivation is uncertain, but it may well be in Old French *gensor,* the comparative of *gent,* 'well-born', 'delicate' (as for **genteel**, above). For a similar word, see also **jaunty**.

**gingham** (kind of cotton fabric, usually checked or striped)

Many fabrics derive their names from their place of origin (for some examples, see **diaper** and **dimity**), and some source books still maintain that gingham is named after the French town of Guingamp, where it was dyed and made into umbrella covers (with this in turn alleged to have given Dickens the idea for the name of Sarah Gamp in *Martin Chuzzlewit,* in which novel she carries a large untidy cotton umbrella). But although the word came into English from French (where it was *guingan,*) its true origin is Malay *genggang,* 'checkered cloth'.

**glade** (grassy clearing in a wood or forest)

The word is often subconsciously related to 'glad', both because of the resemblance of the two words and because of a natural sense of gladness or happiness arising from a place that is light and bright in a potentially dark and gloomy surrounding. The latter is probably closer to the true origin, since 'glad' formerly meant 'bright', and 'glade' itself thus had a basic sense of 'bright sunny place', with a subsequent poetic contrast made between 'glade' and 'shade'. Hence the gladness.

**glamour** (alluring attraction)

There is no association with 'gleam', however apt this may appear. Instead, the word is a Scottish variation on (unexpectedly) 'grammar', the link between the two being the learning that was popularly supposed to be required to make a magic spell (which last is the original meaning of 'glamour'). The word was introduced into literary language generally by Walter Scott, for example in *The Lay of the Last Minstrel.*

**glass slipper** (shoe worn by Cinderella)

Most debunkers of this attractive fairy tale say that the original French version of the story, as told in the late seventeenth century by Perrault, had *pantoufle de vair,* 'slipper of fur', not *pantoufle de verre,* 'slipper of glass'. But this is not so, and an examination of the original text shows that Perrault did indeed have *pantoufle de verre,* which is in fact much more fitting (as it were) for the story as a whole. Perrault, who told the story in his *Contes de ma mère l'oye* ('Mother Goose

Stories'), was of course narrating, and embellishing, a much older tale, probably of oriental origin.

**gloaming** (twilight, dusk)
The word looks as if it is a variation on 'gloom', but if anything it is related to 'glow', whereas 'gloom' is related to 'glum'. The reference is to the 'glow' that remains after the sun has set, when lovers can go 'roaming in the gloaming'. The word is actually of Scottish origin (first as *gloming*).

**glory hole** (place where objects are thrown or lie in confusion)
The place is not so called since there is a glorious muddle in it, even though there probably is. The origin may well be in Scottish 'glaury', meaning 'muddy', 'miry'. However, by a curious but disconcerting coincidence, the French word for 'summer house', 'arbour', is *gloriette,* and this does actually come from Latin *gloria,* 'glory'. But the original meaning of this word was 'palace', so there is unlikely to be any association with the English glory hole.

**gobble** (of turkey: make characteristic 'gurgling' sound)
Some dictionaries, e. g. *Chambers* (see Bibliography), equate this 'gobble' with the one that means 'swallow food fast'. There may be some influence from this, but the word is most likely to be purely imitative, as are words describing the sounds made by other birds, such as 'cluck', 'cackle' and 'quack'. The 'swallowing' verb is probably based on 'gob' (meaning 'large amount of food' rather than 'mouth').

**god** (supreme deity)
There has long been an almost instinctive association between this word and 'good', if only from the biblical quotation that 'There is none good but one, that is, God' (Mark 10:18). The association is further compounded by the fact that, etymologically, 'goodbye' is derived from 'God be with you', and that 'good gracious', as an exclamation, is probably a variation on 'God gracious'. However, 'god' and 'good', although both very old words, with many

links in other languages, are not related, and their apparent common origin is not a true one. See also **Godhead** (below).

**Godhead, the** (God, especially as regarded as existing in three persons)
The '-head' of the name is really '-hood', so that the basic meaning of the word is 'Godhood', i. e. 'divine nature', 'state of being God', with '-hood' as in 'priesthood' or 'manhood'. There is only one other word in use in current English where '-hood' has similarly become '-head' and that is 'maidenhead'. (There were originally more, so that Chaucer has – in the modern equivalent spelling – 'knighthead', 'manhead' and 'womanhead'.)

**godsend** (blessing, unexpected gift)
The word looks as if it means 'what God sends'. This is not the exact origin, however, as in the seventeenth century the word was 'God's send', with 'send' a noun here meaning 'message'. The two 'sends' are of course closely related.

**godwit** (type of wading bird)
The name of this bird can hardly mean 'God's wit' or anything similar. The exact origin is uncertain, but is likely to have been an onomatopoeic word representing the bird's cry. This then became 'godwit' by the familiar process of folk etymology. Many birds have names based on a representation of their cry or call (e.g. '**chiffchaff**, 'peewit' and, indirectly 'bittern' and 'buzzard'; the second of these has of course the same '-wit' ending as the godwit).

**golliwog** (child's doll representing a black man)
This word has roused, understandably, heated dispute in recent years, not least regarding its precise origin. The name first appeared as that of a doll character in the children's books by the American writer Bertha Upton and illustrator Florence Upton in the nineteenth century, with the latter said to have invented the word. Today it can be said with certainty that it is *not* based on '**wog**' (which see in this connection), that it *may* be based on 'golly' (the exclamation referring to the character's appearance or nature), and that it *could* be

based on the American word for 'tadpole' which is 'polliwog' (literally 'head-wiggler').

**goosander** (kind of duck)
The word suggests a sort of hybrid or hermaphrodite bird, a cross between a goose and a gander. There probably is a blend behind the name, although not this: the original spelling was 'gossander', and this could be based on 'gosling' and 'bergander', the latter being another name for the **sheldrake** (which see separately).

**gooseberry** (prickly green fruit)
It seems unlikely that the berry is so called since it is eaten by geese, or that it has any other connection with this bird. A dialect name for the fruit is 'groser', suggesting a link with the French for 'gooseberry' which is *groseille*. This in turn is probably based on Dutch *croesel*, itself from *kroes*, 'crisp', 'crinkled', an apt enough word to describe it or its leaves. Certainly other berry names related to animals have no direct link with the animal in question, and dogs do not eat dogberries, for example, or (as far as is known) cranes eat cranberries.

**gore** (blood)
Not surprisingly, there is an involuntary association between this sense of 'gore' and the sense 'pierce with a horn or tusk' (as of bulls). The latter action could well result in 'gore'. The two words are not related, however, and the 'blood' gore derives from Old English *gor*, 'dirt', 'dung', while the 'pierce' gore probably comes from Old English *gār*, 'spear'. In turn, neither word is related to the third 'gore' that means 'triangular piece of land or material', as in a 'gored' skirt or the London street called Kensington Gore (from the former wedge of land here). A commercial preparation of fake blood for actors is called 'Kensington Gore'.

**gospel** (one of four books of the New Testament; message sent from God)
Rather surprisingly, the word is not connected with 'God', despite its origin in Old English *godspel* (in turn used to provide the title of the American film *Godspell*, the 'hippie' version of St Matthew's Gospel produced in 1973). This actually means 'good news', or more precisely 'good speech', with the latter half of the Old English word producing the modern 'spell' in the sense 'verbal formula'. The English word arose as a translation of Latin *bona adnuntiatio* or *bonus nuntius*, itself used to explain Latin *evangelium* and Greek *euangelion*.

**gossamer** (fine film of cobwebs floating through the air)
The unusual word has been explained as deriving from 'God's summer', referring to the cobweb's appearance in autumn in fine weather. But it is much more likely to come from 'goose summer', since it appeared (as mentioned, in autumn) at a time when goose was traditionally eaten, or when the bird was being prepared for eating. This theory seems to be supported by the German dialect name for November, *Gänsemonat*, literally 'goose month'.

**gourmand** (person who is excessively fond of food)
There is no direct link between this French word and 'gourmet' (meaning 'connoisseur of food'), oddly enough. The precise origin of 'gourmand' is unknown. 'Gourmet', on the other hand, is a corruption of Old French *gromet*, 'boy servant', with this word in turn related to English '**groom**' (which see). However, the sense of 'gourmet' was almost certainly influenced by 'gourmand', since a serving boy could hardly otherwise have become knowledgeable in food and drink. The two rather specialized words are sometimes confused, understandably enough.

**grass widow** (married woman whose husband is temporarily away)
The expression is a rather strange one, and some have attempted to explain it as an alteration of 'grace widow', as if the woman was a widow 'by grace', so to speak. (Dr Johnson interpreted it in this way.) The original sense of the term, however, was (in the words of the *Oxford English Dictionary*) 'an unmarried woman who has cohabited with one or more men; a discarded mistress', and it seems likely that the expression means what it says, referring to the grass that was used in place of the

proper marital bed. See **bastard** for more in the same vein, and compare such mock lecherous songs as 'Roll me over in the clover'.

**grave** (serious)
The word would seem to be naturally related to the other 'grave' that means 'tomb', from the common association of depth (literally, in the latter case) and seriousness or gravity. But there is no linguistic link, apart from the coincidence in sound and spelling, and the first 'grave' derives ultimately from Latin *gravis*, 'heavy', 'weighty', while the latter word comes from the Old English verb *grafan*, 'to dig' (relating to modern 'engrave' and 'groove'). However, modern English 'grieve' relates to the first 'grave', not the second, since it denotes a heaviness of heart.

**greyhound** (kind of slender dog used for hunting and racing)
Such an obvious name, it would seem. Yet it does not mean what it says, and in any case there are some greyhounds that are not grey. (Indeed, according to *The Observer's Book of Dogs,* edited by Sonia Lampson, their colours are 'black, white, red, blue, fawn, fallow or brindle', or almost anything *but* grey). The first part of the word in fact represents Old English *grig-*, related to Old Norse *grey*, 'bitch', and there is the true origin of the name.

**gridiron** (frame of metal bars used for grilling)
The first part of this word is indeed 'grid', but the latter is not 'iron'. The word as a whole came to be assimilated to its present form from Middle English *gredile* or *gredire,* simply meaning 'griddle'. From 'gridiron' in turn came 'grid' (but not 'grill' which came into English from French). For a similar word with a bogus 'iron' ending, see **andiron**.

**gringo** (nickname for an English-speaking foreigner in Spain or Latin America)
The rather derogatory word is still believed by some to be a corruption of the opening words of the American soldiers' song 'Green Grow the Lilacs'! In actual fact it is almost certainly an alteration of Spanish *griego,*

'Greek', used here to mean 'foreign', 'outlandish'.

**grizzly** (kind of large, powerful bear)
Is the grizzly bear so called as it is grizzled, or grey in colour (as distinct from a standard brown bear, for example)? This *could* be so, although it seems much more likely that the fearsome beast is so called because it is 'grisly'. This seems to be backed up by its scientific name of *Ursus horribilis.*

**groundsel** (type of common weed with yellow flowers)
The groundsel is commonly found in the ground (where else?) of many gardens and plots. Its name does not stop there, however, and in Old English it was called *grundeswelge,* literally 'ground swallower', 'earth swallower'. Even this is hardly original, and is itself probably a corruption of Old English *gundeswilge,* 'pus swallower', since the chopped leaves of the plant were used in poultices on abscesses. Today its use is normally directed towards feeding cage birds.

**grovel** (lie or pretend to lie humbly before someone as a sign of servility)
The word conjures up 'gravel', as if this is or was the accepted place to perform the action. In fact there is no connection between the words, and 'grovel' comes as a formation from the adverb (originally) 'grovelling', meaning 'lying face downwards'. The final '-ling' of this word is thus the equivalent of the '-long' found in similar words denoting position or direction, such as '**headlong**' or '**sidelong**' (see both of these). This implies a former word something like 'grove' to mean 'face' or 'stomach', and this still exists in the Scottish dialect words 'groof' and 'grufe', especially in the phrase 'on grufe', meaning 'prone'. Here is an example of the original use of 'grovelling' from Sir Thomas Malory's fifteenth-century work *Le Morte D'Arthur:* 'Sir launcelot lepte vpon hym, and pulled hym grouelyng doune'.

**gruelling** (exhausting)
The word does not derive from 'gruesome' but from 'gruel', in the obsolete sense 'to punish', 'to exhaust'. There was a popular

expression to 'give someone his gruel', meaning 'punish him', and this was quoted as early as the late eighteenth century by the writer Mary Robinson (better known as 'Perdita', the actress and mistress of the future George IV) in her domestic tale *Walsingham, or the Pupil of Nature*, where she writes: 'My pupil talked of nothing but of returning to Devizes, to "give the ostler his gruel" for having taken him in'. 'Gruel' here refers to the dish, and the expression as a whole seems to be in the same category as 'settle someone's hash', 'cook his goose', and so on. See **dished** (above) in this respect.

**guelder rose** (shrub of honeysuckle family)
The name has been said to be an alteration of 'elder rose' (presumably meaning the flower of the elder), since there is some resemblance between the two. But the name almost certainly derives from that of its native province in Holland, Guelderland (or Gelderland).

**guild** (association of people with similar interests, typically of craftsmen)
Despite the trading or monetary associations of 'guild', there is no direct link with 'gild' or 'gilt' (of 'gilts', as gilt-edged securities). However, there is obviously a common base in 'gold', although 'guild' really came into English from Old Norse (and is seen in another form in 'Danegeld', the tax imposed in tenth-century Britain to buy off the Danes). 'Gild', on the other hand, comes from Old English *gyldan*, 'to cover in gold'. (Guildford in Surrey is so named not since it had a famous guild but because the sands of the river Wey were observed to be golden.)

**gum** ('sticky stuff')
There is no connection between this 'gum' and the gums in one's mouth, in spite of an apparent link in 'chewing gum' (which can stick to your gums). The first 'gum' came into English from Old French *gomme*, ultimately from an Egyptian word, via Latin and Greek. The second 'gum' is from Old English *goma*, 'palate' (interestingly related to Greek *chaos*, 'abyss').

**guppy** (kind of small West Indian fish)
The little fish, also known as 'millions', and frequently found feeding on mosquito larvae in controlled conditions in school 'biolabs', is not so called because it gulps or goes 'glup', as some fish do, but because specimens of it were first presented to the British Museum in the nineteenth century by the Rev. R. J. Lechmere Guppy, President of the Scientific Association of Trinidad.

**gusto** (relish, enthusiasm)
The word does not derive from 'gust', as if such a burst of enthusiasm was like a gust of wind, but is Italian (and Spanish) for 'taste'. The term was in use in English from the seventeenth century.

**gutta-percha** (tough plastic substance derived from latex)
The rather agreeable-sounding term does not derive from Latin *gutta*, 'drop', even though the basic sap is exuded by trees. The word comes from Malay *getah-percha*, where *getah* is 'sap' and *percha* is the name of the tree that produces it.

**guttural** (throaty, pronounced in the throat)
The word is sometimes misspelt 'gutteral', as if it derived from 'gutter' (perhaps from some kind of half-recalled nickname for the throat as 'Gutter Lane', or some sort of 'low' connotation). But the word actually comes from the Latin for 'throat' (*guttur*), whereas 'gutter' is ultimately linked to Latin *gutta*, 'drop'.

**gymkhana** (children's horse-riding contest)
The word has come to have a false association with 'gym', doubtless aided by the athletic skills involved for horse and rider. The origin of the word, however, lies in India, where it developed from Hindi *gendkhāna*, 'ball house', 'racket court', meaning a public place for games. This came to be associated with 'gymnasium', and was altered accordingly. The word was first in use in English in the nineteenth century, but gymkhanas in their present form only really took off in the 1930s.

**gypsy**, **gipsy** (member of a roving or nomadic people)

Gypsies are so called since they are supposed to have come to Europe from Egypt, although their true place of origin is north-west India. From there, they scattered throughout Europe and North America, and in different countries came to acquire different names attributing them to various incorrect regions of origin. In French, for example, they are called *bohémiens*, as if they originated in Bohemia (see **Bohemian**), while the other French name for them, *gitans* (identical with Spanish *gitanos* and Italian *gitani*), also places them in Egypt, like the English. To complicate matters further, the alternative Italian name for gypsies, *zingari*, together with the standard German and Russian words for them (respectively *Zigeuner* and *tsygani*) derives ultimately from Greek *Athinganoi*, the name of an oriental people. For more misplaced gypsies, see **Romany**.

**haberdasher** (dealer in minor articles of clothing)
The word suggests some kind of association with 'habit' or 'dashing', while at the same time looking un-English enough to inspire one enthusiastic etymologist to see it as a corruption of German *habt ihr das?* ('do you have that?'), alluding to the haberdasher's wide range of petty articles! The exact origin is obscure, but the word can with some certainty be traced back to Anglo-French *hapertas*, a word used to denote small items of merchandise, and doubtless the English is a development from this.

**hackney** (breed of horse)
Both riders and non-horsepeople can be forgiven for thinking that the word is derived from 'hack'. In fact it is the other way round: 'hack' is a shortening of 'hackney', and 'hackney' itself probably comes from the name of the London borough of Hackney, where horses were formerly raised and bred (and taken to Smithfield Market along Mare Street). Hackney itself means 'Haca's island'.

**haggard** (drawn and weary in appearance, emaciated)
A haggard person may well look like a thin-faced hag, and it is likely that the 'gaunt' sense of the word may have developed by association with the witch. The ultimate origin is from Old French *hagard*, however, with this word perhaps related to modern English 'hedge'. The word was originally applied to a hawk, especially an untamed or wild one (that presumably lived in a hedge).

**ha-ha** (fence hidden in a ditch as typically found in the grounds of a country house)
Is the origin of this nicely untechnical landscaping term in 'funny ha-ha'? Hardly, since the object itself is not particularly amusing. More likely, the word is meant to represent the exclamation of surprise uttered by the person coming unexpectedly on the fence, in which case it is really 'Ah, Ah', or 'Ah! Ah!', and was indeed spelt in this way formerly in English. (There is a ha-ha in the grounds of the Palace of Versailles, carefully marked on the tourist plan as *Ha! Ha!*.)

**halo** (circle of light round sun or moon or, in religious art, a person's head)
The religious sense of 'halo' suggests a connection with 'holy' or 'hallow' (which two words are themselves related). But this is not the derivation of 'halo', which comes ultimately (through Latin) from Greek *halōs* 'threshing-floor', i. e. where the oxen walked round in a continuous circle. The sense was then extended in Greek to mean 'disc', and in particular that of the sun and moon.

**halt** (lame)
This old-fashioned word, found in the Bible and (as a verb) in Shakespeare, is not related to the 'halt' that means 'stop', as if a halt person were one who constantly had to halt, but derives from an Old English word (*healt*) that is ultimately of the same source as Latin *clades*, 'destruction'. The 'stopping' halt came into English straight from German, with the seventeenth-century phrase 'to make halt' being a translation of German *Halt machen*. The German term itself was a military one, used of soldiers on the march.

**halyard** (rope for hoisting or lowering something)
There is no connection with 'yard' here, in the nautical sense or any other, although the first part of the word certainly links up with 'haul' and even more closely with 'hale' (in the sense 'compel to go', as when someone is 'haled' into court). So as it stands the word, at face value, offers part

true etymology, part false. For another misleading 'yard', see **lanyard**.

**hamburger** (bread roll sandwich containing minced beef)
A hamburger is not so called as it contains ham (it doesn't, anyway), but because it originated as a 'Hamburger steak', in other words, a steak that was cooked as they used to cook them in Hamburg. The culinary phenomenon first appeared in America (where else, as an archetypal fast food?) in the late nineteenth century, and soon came to England. (In the First World War, however, the name was not to the liking of Americans, and the hamburger was renamed the 'Salisbury steak', after the already existing 'nutritious' patty named after the nineteenth-century English dietician, J. H. Salisbury.) The association of 'hamburger' with 'ham' is not helped by the development of such variations as 'beef-burger', 'steakburger' and 'cheeseburger', where the first part of the name does indeed indicate the content of the sandwich.

**handicap** (special 'disadvantage' awarded to a contestant in a sport)
The unusual word, which has passed into many foreign languages, does not indicate a contestant who stands or runs 'cap in hand', but very likely derives from a former gambling game in which either forfeits were held in a cap or money was put into a cap by the players, in both cases a person having to put his 'hand in the cap'. The game was a novelty to Pepys when he first came across it in 1660: 'Here some of us fell to handicap, a sport that I never knew before, which was very good' (*Diary*, 18 September).

**hangar** (large shed where aircraft are housed)
This word did not develop from 'hang', as if it originally denoted some kind of large barn where implements or other equipment would hang, but from the identical French word meaning 'shed'. According to Picoche (see Bibliography), the French word originated as a Picardy place-name, describing a farm where sheds (*angars*) and stables were arranged round a paddock or enclosure. For a similar sort of word, see **penthouse**.

**hangnail** (piece of loose skin hanging by a fingernail)
It might seem that this annoyance is so named since it 'hangs by the nail'. But, since the word is entered here, obviously this assumption must be wrong! Records show that the origin in fact is in Old English *angnægl*, seen clearly in the alternative modern spelling of 'agnail'. This literally means 'tight nail' (with the first part of the word as in 'anguish'), the 'nail' here really being not the fingernail but the 'metal spike' nail, that is, comparing the thing to a small nail digging into the flesh at this point. (In a similar sort of way, French *clou* means both 'metal nail' and 'corn on the foot'.)

**hanker** (long for, desire keenly)
The word is not an alteration of 'hunger', as has been occasionally supposed, but is probably from Flemish *hankeren*, itself related to 'hang' (in the sense that if you are hankering for something you are 'hanging' eagerly in wait for it).

**hanky-panky** (trickery, deception)
The attractive phrase might suggest a sort of conjuring trick done with the aid of a handkerchief ('hanky'), as magicians often do. It is probably, however, an alteration of '**hocus-pocus**' (which see in turn, below). For related word wizardry, see **sleight of hand**.

**hansom** (kind of light cab)
It is too much to hope that the hansom is so called because it is handsome, although it can certainly be quite elegant, with its driver's seat high up at the back. The vehicle is actually named after its patentee, J. A. Hansom (who did not, however, invent it). (There was a former fancy for carriages to be named after their inventors or designers, such as the brougham, after Baron Brougham and Vaux, the tilbury, after John Tilbury, and the stanhope, after the Reverend Fitzroy Stanhope.)

**harass** (worry, actively frustrate or annoy)
The word looks as if it ought to be related to 'harry' and 'harrow' (the latter in the particular sense 'cause distress to'), but the origin lies in Old French *harer*, 'set a dog

on', itself of Germanic origin. See also **harrier** (below).

**harbinger** (person or thing that gives warning of something to come)
The rather poetic and stylish word is sometimes mispronounced and misspelt (as 'harbringer'), by false association with 'bring'. Its true origin can be seen in Old French *herbergere*, from *herberge*, 'lodging' (compare modern French *auberge*, 'inn') so that a 'harbinger' was literally a 'lodger', that is, someone who went ahead of a royal party or an army to obtain lodgings for them (rather in the same way that a courier did subsequently). The English word has acquired an extra 'n', much as similar 'travelling' words have (compare French *passager* and English 'passenger', French *messager* and English 'messenger').

**harebell** (kind of plant with blue bell-shaped flowers and slender stem)
Since associations with 'hare' seem difficult, the word has sometimes been explained as deriving from 'hair-bell', with apparent reference to the flower's very slender or hair-like stem. But the animal association is almost certainly the correct one. The hare was long regarded as a 'magic' animal (see various old folk stories and the allusive illustrations of Kit Williams), and the plant was perhaps regarded as special since it was observed to grow in places where hares lived. (In Shakespeare's *Cymbeline*, the 'azur'd harebell like thy veins' mentioned is actually a bluebell.)

**harlot** (prostitute)
The word almost certainly derives from Old French *herlot*, 'rogue' (which word could also apply to males). But doubtless this is not colourful enough for some etymologizers, who have found an origin for the word in the name of Arlette, the mother of William the Conqueror, who had been known as William the Bastard before coming to the throne. (His father was Robert le Diable.) This, however, is fanciful speculation, and most unlikely to be the ultimate source of the word.

**harridan** (ill-tempered old woman)
A harridan can be something of a hag, but

the two words are not related, nor is a harridan so called since she is hagridden or because she harasses or harries. The word seems to come as an alteration of French *haridelle*, a word for a broken-down old horse, with the reference being to the gaunt appearance of such a woman rather than her actual temperament. It is an interesting paradox that when women age, they are popularly supposed to become 'hard' (compare such words as 'hag', 'harridan', 'shrew', 'witch', 'scold', 'fury', 'battleaxe', 'termagant', 'crone' and 'old trout'), whereas men go 'soft' ('gaffer', 'greybeard', 'old geezer', 'old codger', 'old fogey', 'dotard', 'silly old fool', and so on). Such generalizations are of course very unfair, and there are many exceptions to this principle!

**harrier** (kind of hawk)
The harrier hunts its food just as the hunting dogs called harriers hunt hares. In spite of this common characteristic, however, and the exact identity of the words, the two are not related. The hawk is really a 'harrower', that is it pillages and plunders, which is one of the now obsolete senses of 'harrow'. The dog, on the other hand, is really a 'harer', or a dog that hunts hares (just as a foxhound hunts foxes, a ratter hunts rats, and a **cocker spaniel** goes for woodcock; see the dog for more on this).

**harrow** (plunder, ravage)
The word used in this sense is not derived from 'harrow' the agricultural implement which pulverizes ('harrows') the soil, but from an Old English verb that also gave modern 'harry' (see **harrier** above). The other 'harrow' comes from a quite distinct Old English word. However, the sense of 'harrow' meaning 'cause distress to' (as in 'harrowing experience') *does* come from the farm implement, since a person who is harrowed is 'wounded' as the earth is by the harrow. In the literary or artistic phrase 'Harrowing of Hell' (the spoiling of Hell by Christ), the verb involved is the 'plundering' or 'ravaging' one. Finally, the London borough of Harrow, with its famous school, is nothing to do with any of these, but takes its name from Old English *hearg*,

'heathen temple' (which was once there on the hill).

**hatchet** (small axe)
The word looks as if it is a diminutive of 'axe' (an 'axette', as it were), just as a little kitchen is a 'kitchenette'. This is not exactly so, however, although the word comes into English from French, where *hachette* actually is a diminutive of *hache*, these being the standard words respectively for 'hatchet' and 'axe'. English 'axe', on the other hand, did not come from the French but is a full-blooded Germanic word.

**hatchment** (square panel bearing coat of arms of a deceased person in a church)
The design and appearance of a hatchment suggests an association with 'hatching' (the drawing of fine lines to give an effect of shading), or with 'hachuring' (the drawing of short lines on a map to represent high ground). These words, too, are both suitably specialized. But the term is almost certainly an alteration of 'achievement', its less common alternative name, so called since the arms depict or relate to some notable achievement of the bearer.

**hawker** (pedlar)
A hawker was not so called because he sold hawks, but because he was a 'huckster' (the two words are related), that is, he peddled his goods, or offered them for sale by going from one place to another. (The origin of the word is in an old German verb.) The technical difference between a hawker and a pedlar was that a hawker had a horse and cart, but a pedlar carried his wares himself. Until at least the mid-twentieth century in Britain, many private houses had a notice on the gate requesting 'No hawkers or circulars'. The latter word referred to printed advertisements or handbills, which however continue to arrive, even if the hawkers have given way to the travelling salesman and the Avon lady. See also **pedlar** itself.

**headlong** (headfirst)
As already mentioned under **gravel** (which see, above), the '-long' of this word is really '-ling', which was an adverbial suffix. The association with 'long' is thus a false one, as it is in **sidelong** (which see also). In a few words, the '-ling' has remained unaltered, for example in the poetic word 'darkling', meaning 'in the dark' (as in Keats's 'Darkling I listen' in his *Ode to a Nightingale*). It is interesting to speculate that a verb 'to headle' could have developed, just as 'grovel' did from 'grovelling', 'sidle' from 'sideling', and even 'darkle' from 'darkling' (Byron, in *Don Juan*, wrote the impressive descriptive lines:

> Her cheek began to flush, her eyes to sparkle,
> And her proud brow's blue veins to swell and darkle.)

**hear! hear!** (expression indicating agreement or approval)
Because the expression is spoken much more often than it is written, it is thought by some to be really 'here! here!', as if indicating the person or place where there is approval (while also suggesting the almost synonymous 'same here!'). The phrase is essentially a parliamentary one, and first arose there in the seventeenth century, originally as 'hear him! hear him!'. At one time it could indicate disapproval as well as approval, when it would be a kind of equivalent to 'hark at him!'. It is rather strange to find the phrase in the Bible: 'Then cried a wise woman out of the city, Hear, hear' (2 Samuel 20:16). The sense is not exactly the same here, however.

**Heaviside layer** (region of the earth's atmosphere)
Non-scientists and possibly young budding physicists may be pardoned for imagining that the name somehow refers to the weight or density of the atmosphere. In fact the layer (now usually known as the 'E layer') is named after Oliver Heaviside, the English physicist who predicted its existence in the early part of the present century.

**hecatomb** (ancient Greek and Roman sacrifice)
The word has nothing to do with tombs (or catacombs), despite its sense-association of death and burial. The source is Greek *hekatombē*, literally 'hundred cows', since the sacrifice was properly of a hundred oxen or cattle.

**hector** (bluster, intimidate by loud talk)
This word is not related to 'heckle' or 'hectic', but comes from the name of Hector, the warrior in Greek mythology. In seventeenth-century stage portrayals of him, he was played as a blustering bully.

**hell for leather** (at full speed, fast and furious)
One ingenious explanation for this admittedly unusual expression is that it comes from the famous comic alphabet that begins 'A for 'orses, B for mutton, C for yourself', and so on (or some variation of this), with 'hell for leather' somehow giving 'L for leather'. But in fact it is just the opposite, and the comic alphabet line for 'L' comes from this expression. Another source is needed, therefore, and it is likely to be in 'all of a lather', as jokingly or uncomprehendingly corrupted by someone or some sector of society at some stage. It is first recorded in the *Oxford English Dictionary* only as late as 1889, in a story by Rudyard Kipling, typically enough ('Here, Gaddy, take the note to Bingle and ride hell-for-leather').

**helpmate** (companion and helper)
The word has come to be regarded as applying to someone who is both a 'help' and a 'mate', especially a wife or husband. It is actually a corruption of 'helpmeet', which itself arose as a sort of 'ghost word' from the biblical description of Eve in Genesis 2:18 as 'an help meet for him', i. e. a help suitable for Adam, with 'meet' in the old sense of 'suitable', 'fitting'.

**henchman** (loyal supporter, stout follower)
This word has been frequently explained as being an alteration of 'haunchman', as if it applied to a servant who stood by the 'haunch' or side of his leader (or possibly that of his horse). In fact the derivation is from Middle English *hengestman*, literally 'horse man', 'groom', with this in turn based on Old English *hengest,* 'stallion'. (Hence the name of the early Jutish settler Hengist, who with his brother Horsa, whose name more obviously means 'horse', probably conquered Kent.)

**hen harrier** (kind of hawk)
The bird is not so called because it is female, as if there were also a 'cock harrier' but because it attacks poultry. It is also known as the common harrier, or in the United States as the marsh harrier (or marsh hawk). See also **harrier**, above.

**hermetic** (sealed)
To look at the word, one might suppose that it is related to 'hermit' since he is a man who 'seals himself off' from the world. But it actually comes from the name of Hermes Trismegistus ('Hermes thrice-greatest'), who was an early legendary author of works on alchemy and mysticism and the cunning inventor of a magic seal to keep vessels airtight. (He corresponded to the Egyptian god Thoth.)

**heyday** (time of a person's greatest success, strength, vigour etc)
In an attempt to make this word meaningful, some have derived it from 'high day', with this perhaps even suggested by the alternative spelling of 'heighday'. But the true origin is in an old exclamation of joy or happiness *heyday!*, as a sort of opposite of 'lackaday!'. The first part of this still survives as a similar exclamation today ('Hey!').

**hiccup** (involuntary spasmodic inhalation of air)
The word is also spelt 'hiccough', as if it derives from 'cough', but the origin is purely imitative, as in 'atishoo' for a sneeze (although this has not acquired the status of a noun) or 'burp' for a belch.

**high-falutin'** (pompous, unduly refined)
The strange word has been explained as being a corrupt spelling of 'high-flighting' or 'high-floating' or even 'high-flown', which is really what it means. Its true derivation, however, is probably in 'high-fluting', that is, high pitched like a flute. Early examples of the word, when it first appeared in the United States in the 1830s, relate almost entirely to people, their speech, and their voices (their 'fluting' voices, of course).

**hijack** (steal or commandeer a vehicle or aircraft in transit)

This is a much disputed word, whose true etymology is still uncertain. Not all the theories accounting for it can be true, however, and perhaps one of the most unlikely is that it was the call ('Hi, Jack!') of prostitutes to sailors on the coast of California in its original form. However, it does seem to have been American in origin. Perhaps one of the most likely explanations is that it was the demand of a robber to a driver to 'stick 'em up high, Jack', or some such similar command to a person to give up his arms or weapons. The word is still occasionally spelt 'high-jack'.

**hinny** (offspring of a she-ass and a stallion)
The animal is not so called from its cry (to 'hinny' is to 'whinny'), but because its name comes from the Latin *hinnus*, with the same meaning. In Scotland and the north of England 'hinny' is used as a term of endearment – but although animal names are used for such terms ('my lamb', 'dovey', 'ducky' and so on), this is simply a variation of 'honey'.

**hippie** (unconventional young person, especially a 'social rebel' of the 1960s)
The word does not refer to the person's habit of lying about on his hip, or of wearing hipsters, but simply indicates that he is or was 'hip' or 'hep', that is, aware of current developments and styles and thus 'trendy' (in what was regarded as a new and radical manner in order to reject conventional attitudes and established morality). Hipsters (trendy trousers that hang from the hip rather than the waist) have a clever name that refers to the hips and to their 'hip' style.

**hoarding** (billboard)
The word looks like a kind of alteration of 'boarding', with a suggestion of 'hordes' of advertisements (or even of 'hoarding' them). The derivation is in fact from an obsolete English word *hoard*, meaning 'fence', from Old French *hourd*, 'palisade', and related to modern English 'hurdle'. The American equivalent ('billboard') is much more straightforward.

**hock** (type of dry white wine)
Failing to associate the name with a place or region, as is possible with many wines, one is perhaps tempted to link it somehow with some other 'hock', such as the joint of a leg. But it does derive from a place-name after all, and this is the German town of Hochheim. The English came as the shortening ('hock') of a corruption ('hockamore') of the original German name, *hochheimer Wein*.

**hocus pocus** (sleight of hand, 'mumbo-jumbo')
For many years the curious phrase was explained as deriving from a garbled (or mocking) version of the words *hoc est corpus* ('this is the body') in the Latin mass. But the formula originated as the mock Latin name of an early seventeenth-century conjuror, perhaps itself based on 'hotch-potch'. In turn, the expression led to 'hokey-pokey' for something meaningless or pointless. For another bogus Latin origin, see **hogmanay** (below).

**hogmanay** (Scottish celebration on New Year's Eve)
This is a difficult word to explain, as found by those who cunningly derived it from Latin *hoc in anno*, 'in this year' (as the start of some kind of song or recitation). But this is most unlikely, and the origin *may* perhaps be in Old French *aguillanneuf*, if this actually represents, as is supposed, 'to the mistletoe the new year' (modern French equivalent: *au gui l'an neuf*). But even this lacks the necessary linguistic and historical backing.

**hoity-toity** (flighty, 'stuck up', haughty)
With a term like this, amateur etymologists can have a field day. Among those who have had a fanciful go are the wordmen who have seen a derivation in French *haut toit*, 'high roof' (or *haut comme toit*, 'high as a roof'), while others have equated the word with 'haughty'. Examining past usages, however, it is clear that the expression is one of the famous English rhyming or reduplicative phrases, in this case based on obsolete (sixteenth-century) *hoit*, meaning 'to romp'. At one time the spelling was also 'highty-tighty', under the influence of 'high'.

**hold** (space below a ship's deck where the cargo is stored)

Surely the hold simply holds the cargo? In fact not, and past records show that the word was originally 'hole', in the sense of 'hollow place'. Almost certainly, however, the word was influenced by 'hold' and so acquired its present spelling.

**hollyhock** (kind of tall plant with large leaves and showy flowers)
The name of the plant does not derive from 'holly', despite the rather 'spiky' flowers. It was originally a 'holy hock', with 'hock' meaning 'mallow' and 'holy' pointing to the plant's use as a 'blessed' or healing herb, not indicating its origin in the Holy Land (where it did not come from anyway).

**holm oak** (kind of oak tree)
The tree is not so called because it grows on holms (islands in rivers), but because its name is an alteration of *holin*, 'holly'. It is therefore really a 'holly oak', so named for its holly-like leaves.

**homily** (religious speech, sermon)
A homily is not so called because it is 'homely', i. e. spells out a few home truths, or is delivered in a friendly manner, but because the word comes from the Greek word for 'conversation', 'discourse', in turn from *homilos*, 'crowd', 'assembly'. The English Protestant bishop Hugh Latimer misunderstood the origin of the word, as he wrote in his *Sermons:* 'But howe shall hee read thys booke, as the *Homilies* are read? Some call them *homelies*, and in deed so they may be wel called, for they are *homely* handled'.

**homosexual** (attracted to someone of one's own sex)
Some have tried to see in the word a derivation in Latin *homo*, 'man', since male homosexuals are apparently predominant. However, the origin is not in this, but in Greek *homos*, 'same' (these last two words are in fact related), so that lesbians are homosexuals, too. See also **thespian** for a related misattribution.

**honeymoon** (holiday taken immediately after a wedding)
All etymologists go enthusiastically for this word, which is why it is included here. Why

'honey'? Why 'moon'? Among the most common explanations are those that point to the phases of the moon, or to a period of a month (a 'moon'), saying that affections will wane with the phases of the moon, or that for a month all may be 'honey' but then reality will set in. One theory even maintains that there was once a custom for newly-wed couples to drink mead (which is made from honey) for a month after the marriage. But the truth behind the word is probably not nearly so complex, and the allusion is very likely to be simply to the bliss and happiness, honey and moonlight, 'sweetness and light'. Not for nothing do lovers call each other 'honey'; not for nothing is moonlight romantic.

**hoopoe** (bird with a distinctive down-curving bill and long crest)
The name does not refer to the 'hoop' of the crest, especially when erected, but is imitative of its cry. The bird has similar names in other languages, such as French *huppe*, Italian *upupa*, Spanish *ababilla*, and Russian *udod*. Even its formal scientific name is imitative, *Upupa epops*.

**hopscotch** (children's hopping game)
The name is nothing to do with 'Scotch', and the game did not originate in Scotland. The word is simply a basic description of what happens: the players 'hop' over 'scotches', i. e. lines scotched or scored on the ground.

**horseradish** (kind of coarse radish)
The horseradish is not so called as it is eaten by horses, but because 'horse' here means 'rough', 'course', as in 'horse chestnut', 'horseplay', 'horselaugh'. For a similar concept, see **bulwark**.

**howitzer** (kind of cannon that fires shells at a high elevation)
Some names of guns are virtually onomatopoeic, suggesting the sound they make, such as 'pom-pom', 'ack-ack', 'bazooka', 'whizzbang', and so on, and 'howitzer' might seem at first glance to be in the same category, suggesting an apt blend of 'howl' and 'whizz'. But the word actually comes from Dutch *houwitser*, in turn from German *Haubitze*, itself from Czech *houfnice*, 'cata-

pult', 'ballista'. The Germans had such devices in the Hussite wars of the fourteenth century, and adopted the name then. The French word for 'howitzer' is *obusier*, from the same source, as is the word for 'shell', *obus*. See also **dumdum** and **shrapnel**.

**humble bee** (bumblebee)
The name is simply a variation on 'bumblebee', under the influence of Middle Dutch *hommel* (the bee 'hums' as it flies, just as it 'bumbles', in the sense 'makes a droning and humming sound'). So the word does not suggest that the bee is 'humble' in some way, although Dr Johnson thought so – he said the name meant that the bee had no sting (not true, they do, and sometimes even sting the queen to death).

**humble pie** (pie made of offal)
There really is an edible dish called 'humble pie', originally called 'umble pie' and made from the entrails of a deer (so called 'umbles'). When the form of the word changed (with 'umbles' itself an earlier alteration of 'numbles'), the phrase was used in the familiar saying 'eat humble pie' to mean (punningly) 'be obliged to accept humiliation', 'be very submissive'. The saying was first widely used only as recently as the early nineteenth century, but in time for Thackeray, Charles Reade and other novelists to incorporate it in their writings.

**hurly-burly** (tumult, 'rough and tumble')
The expression suggests a rowdy scrap, with burly men hurling things, but the typically English reduplicative word is almost certainly based on an obsolete verb 'hurl', not in the modern sense but meaning 'make a commotion' (commonly occurring as the verbal noun 'hurling').

**hurricane** (tropical cyclone)
This word has exercised the minds of etymologists wonderfully, with one of the most popular explanations maintaining that the severe wind is so called as it destroyed the sugar plantations, i. e. 'hurried' the 'canes'! So popular was this derivation, that it was taken up by several writers, and even Dante Gabriel Rossetti seems to hint at it in lines from his *Ballads and Sonnets:*

The heavy rain it hurries amain
The heaven and the hurricane.

But the real origin, as we now know, is in a native word, and in the Caribbean language Taino the cyclone is called *hurakán,* based on *hura,* 'wind'. (Compare **tornado**.)

**hurtle** (dash, rush, move speedily and noisily)
There is no connection between this word and 'hurl', which is itself probably imitative in origin. Instead, it derives from 'hurt' with the suffix '-le', in a sense that basically means 'strike against', 'collide with'.

**husband** (married man)
Whether jokingly or not, there are those who like to say that the word is a form of 'housebound', either in the sense 'one who owns the house and is committed to it', or in some more lighthearted concept (as if 'saddled' with a house). In fact the first of these explanations is something like the truth, since 'husband' literally meant 'one who has a house bonded to him', i. e. 'householder'. It is interesting that the English word lacks the expected reference to the householder's sex or marital status, unlike the equivalent in other languages (French *mari,* German *Mann,* Spanish *marido,* and so on).

**husky** (hoarse)
The word does not relate to 'husk' in the sense 'dry outer covering of seed' but derives from an obsolete 'husk', itself of imitative origin, meaning 'have a dry cough'. However, 'husky' in the sense 'big and burly' probably does come from the 'dry seed coat' sense. For another meaning of the word altogether, see the next entry.

**husky** (Eskimo dog)
The dog is well known for its toughness and strength, but this is not the reason it is called 'husky' (as in the second sense in the previous entry). Its name is simply an alteration of 'Eskimo'.

**hybrid** (offspring of two different races, breeds, etc)
Many hybrid plants and animals are those that have been bred to a high degree of

purity, yield, and the like, and this may well suggest that the word is a form of 'high-bred'. The actual source is in Latin *hibrida* meaning (more or less as now) 'offspring of a mixed union' but originally denoting specifically the offspring of a tame sow and a wild boar, then a person born of a Roman father and non-Roman mother (or of a freeman and a slave). The Latin word itself is of uncertain origin. Some have related it to Greek *hybris*, now used in English in the form 'hubris' to mean 'wanton insolence', 'overweening pride'.

**idyll** (short poem about a peaceful pastoral scene)
Because of the pleasant and restful associations of the word, it is frequently associated with (and certainly confused with) 'idol', 'ideal' and even 'idle'. However, as its special spelling suggests, the word is of classical origin, coming into English from Latin *idyllium*, itself from Greek *eidyllion*, which is a diminutive of *eidos*, 'form' (itself in fact related to the English 'idol' just mentioned). Possibly the unstable pronunciation of 'idyll' has not helped to distinguish it from these other similar words, since it can be said as 'eye-dill' or 'id-ill'.

**ignoramus** (ignorant person)
The word looks like a sort of Latin version of 'ignorant'. The true origin is much more interesting, since it comes from a character called Ignoramus in a seventeenth-century play by the English dramatist George Ruggle. The character is an ignorant lawyer, but his name, although Latin, really means 'We do not know', 'We have no knowledge of', 'We take no notice of'. This was a traditional legal term used when evidence in a case was lacking. Ruggle wrote his play 'to expose the ignorance and arrogance of the common lawyers', and the name turned up again soon after in the title of another work by one R. Callis, Serjeant at Law: 'The Case and Arguments against Sir Ignoramus, of Cambridge, in his Readings at Staple's Inn'.

**IHS** (Christian symbol and monogram)
The symbol stands for the name 'Jesus', and is seen on many altar hangings and other church furnishings and vestments. There have been several erroneous attempts to interpret it, with the letters usually taken as an abbreviation for something like 'In Hoc Signo' ('in this sign'), 'In Hac Salus' ('in this [cross] is salvation'), 'Iesus Hominum Salvator' ('Jesus saviour of men'), and so on. In fact it is simply the first three letters of the Greek word for 'Jesus', which is ΊΗΣΟΥΣ, with however the Greek sigma represented by a Roman 'S'. No doubt the false interpretations above are also half suggested by the similar religious abbreviation INRI ('Iesus Nazarenus Rex Iudaeorum', i. e. 'Jesus of Nazareth King of the Jews').

**incentive** (motivating force, stimulus)
The word looks as if it is related to either 'incite' or to words such as 'incense' (meaning 'enrage') or 'incendiary'. Ultimately, however, and rather unexpectedly, it derives from Latin *incinire*, 'to set the tune', 'to sing', so is actually related to 'incantation'. An incentive, therefore, is really a sort of mental 'cantor' or 'lead singer' which gets your music going.

**infantry** (foot soldiers)
The word has been derived in the past from the *infante* who was the heir to the Spanish throne and who raised the infantry for the purpose of rescuing his father from the invading Moors! However, the association with English 'infant' is much nearer the truth, since originally the infantry were boy soldiers, who were thus 'infants' and 'lower' in size, status and actual physical standing (as foot soldiers) than the cavalrymen.

**inkling** (small idea, least notion)
Some words and expressions indicating smallness and minuteness are related to writing, such as 'dot', 'point', 'jot', 'iota' (these two being related), 'tittle' (small sign or accent), and the like, and it almost looks as if 'inkling' means 'little spot of ink'. A person who 'hasn't an inkling', therefore, might seem to be saying that he hasn't the smallest written clue. However, the word almost certainly derives from a Middle English verb *inclen*, meaning 'hint at',

related to Old English *inca,* 'suspicion'. So no ink is involved after all.

**inoculation** (vaccination or similar medical procedure)
The aim of inoculation, of course, is to stimulate the growth of antibodies in order to fight off any disease, or to 'kill the germs', to put it crudely. For this reason, no doubt, the word is thought to be closely connected with 'innocuous' (and is even sometimes misspelt 'innoculation'). But it really means 'implant', from Latin *inoculare* (which literally means 'put a little eye in', 'put a bud in', the reference being to the insertion of a bud in a plant).

**inroads** (sudden incursion, advance)
There is only a very indirect connection with 'roads' in this word, although there is a strong suggestion of advancing or moving in on roads from the coast, for example. The true sense of the word, in its original form, was 'in-riding', or 'in-raiding'. And there is the indirect link, since 'road', 'ride' and 'raid' are all ultimately related.

**instalment** (serial or regular part of something)
The word certainly looks as if it is closely related to 'install', so that the regular payments or whatever have been officially 'set up' (i.e. installed) as a person or thing can be. The original form of the word, however, was *estalment,* coming from Old French *estaler,* 'to place' (modern French *étaler,* 'spread out', 'display'), itself from *estal,* 'place'. This in turn is a word of Germanic origin and actually related to English 'stall'. But 'instalment' is not closely related to 'install', or indeed derived from it.

**interloper** (intruder, interferer)
An interloper is not someone who 'lopes in' but really someone who 'leaps in', since the origin of the word is related to, or even found in, Middle Dutch *lopen,* 'to run', which is itself indirectly related to modern English 'lope'. So although the ultimate Germanic source of 'lope' and 'leap' may be identical, the interloper has no immediate link with the verb 'lope' in its modern sense.

**internecine** (mutually destructive)
The word is used in such contexts as 'internecine strife', 'internecine feud', 'internecine rivalry'. Today the sense implies conflict within a group, as if the original Latin were a combination of *inter-* and *nexus* in some form. But the real Latin origin is *internecinus,* 'deadly' from *necare,* 'to kill', with the prefix *inter-* meaning not 'between' but used as an intensive, in the sense 'down to the last person in the middle'. The modern sense implying 'mutually' appears to have originated because of Dr Johnson's wrong understanding of the word; he defined it in his *Dictionary* as 'endeavouring mutual destruction', taking the 'inter-' as in 'interchange'. The first occurrence of the word in English was in Samuel Butler's *Hudibras* of 1663, where he translated Latin *internecinum bellum:*

> Th'Ægyptians worshipp'd Dogs, and for
> Their Faith made internecine war.

(The 1674 edition of this had 'fierce and zealous' instead of 'internecine', but the damage had been done by then and the word was on its way to being established.)

**inveigle** (win over or persuade by enticement)
The 'in-' of the word is not the usual prefix 'in-', but a spelling of the earlier form *envegle,* which was itself an alteration of Old French *aveugler,* 'to blind' (ultimately from Medieval Latin *ab oculis,* 'without eyes'). The modern spelling, and possibly even meaning, has also been influenced by 'inveigh' (now 'to speak bitterly against').

**invoice** (list of goods sent giving price and terms)
There is no connection with any sort of 'voice' here, as if the document was a sort of dictated statement. The word is really the relic of a former plural, spelt *invoyes,* and actually used as a singular in the way that '**bodice**' came to be (see this word). This previous English word itself came from Old French *envois,* the plural of *envoi,* 'message' (still in use in English as a literary word meaning 'final part of a poem'). The ultimate source of this was Latin *in via,* 'on the way'.

**iron mould** (spot on ironing due to staining)
No doubt the 'mould' developed by association with the steam or dampness used in the actual ironing process. Originally, however, the phrase was 'iron mole', comparing the spot or stain (caused by a rusty iron, for example) to a **mole** on the skin (which see in its own right).

**iron rations** (emergency food pack)
Are iron rations so called because they are full of iron and other essential vitamins, or because they are traditionally iron-hard (as 'hard tack')? The answer is neither, and the term simply refers to the tins or boxes that originally contained the rations.

**isinglass** (kind of gelatine made from fish bladders)
The ending has become '-glass' because of the semi-transparent nature of the gelatine, but the word originated from the obsolete Dutch *huisenblas*, 'sturgeon's bladder'. There is thus also no connection with French *glacé* or English 'icing'.

**island** (land surrounded by water)
Anyone who says that 'island' and 'isle' are not connected will no doubt be regarded with understandable incredulity. Yet this is the case, and in fact 'island' was regularly spelt 'iland' in English down to the seventeenth century. The word originated as Old English *īgland*, which really meant 'island land', since basic *īg* meant 'island'. Later, an 's' came to be inserted under the influence of Old French *isle* (modern *île*), itself derived from Latin *insula*. The Old English word for 'island' can today be seen surviving in the ending '-ey' of many place-names, such as Bardsey, Bermondsey, Hackney, Romsey and Thorney. (In Chichester Harbour, West Sussex, there is an island called Thorney Island, whose name thus means 'thorn island island'.)

**iwis** (certainly)
This old word was used by poets down to the nineteenth century in the form 'I wis', as if it meant 'I know' (or to use another archaic equivalent, 'I wot'). So in 1829 Thomas Hood wrote, 'A well-bred horse he was, I wis', and some thirty years later Swinburne followed with, 'I wis men shall spit at me'. But the word came from Old English *gewiss*, 'certain' (exactly the same word and same meaning in modern German), and the meaning 'I know' was wrongly derived from the Old English verb *witan*, 'to know' (which gave modern 'to wit' and the 'I wot' just mentioned).

**jackal** (kind of wild dog)
The name of the animal has long been associated with 'jack', and even with 'jack call', this latter sense explained as referring to the role of the animal with regard to the lion, whose prey it was supposed to hunt up for it. The jackal was thus a 'jack', or servant (as in 'every man jack' and the name of the playing card), to the 'call' of the lion. Perhaps today the association with 'jack' has been further promoted by the link between the human kind of 'jackal' (a collaborator in evil) and the term 'jack' (and the name Jack) commonly applied to men in various slang or colloquial usages ('jack-in-office', 'jack-of-all-trades', 'Jack Tar' and so on). See also **jackanapes**, below. But the name of the animal in fact comes, through Turkish, from Persian *shagāl*, itself ultimately from Sanskrit. The original source of the name is better preserved in other languages, such as French *chacal*, German *Schakal*, Russian *shakal*, and the like.

**jackanapes** (impudent person)
The word was originally used to mean 'monkey', 'ape', and is first recorded as an unpleasant nickname for William de la Pole, 1st Duke of Suffolk, who lived in the first half of the fifteenth century. (He was popularly regarded – perhaps unfairly – as being responsible for England's defeats in the latter years of the Hundred Years' War and was murdered in mid-English Channel by some of his enemies.) The nickname itself related to the duke's badge, which showed a tame ape wearing a ball and chain. So the word *may* have been 'Jack Ape' or something similar, although it seems likely that the term or phrase as a whole existed before this. An ultimate reference to an ape brought from Italy as a 'Jack of Naples' is only conjectural and has not been substantiated. For other roles of 'Jack', see **jackal** (above).

**jailbird** (prisoner)
The jargon word does not refer to a female prisoner, a 'bird' in jail, but to the concept of a caged bird. In fact the words 'cage' and 'jail' (and 'gaol') are all related, and derive from Latin *cavea*, 'cage' (as 'cave' also does). The slang expression 'do bird', however, meaning 'serve a prison sentence', seems to derive from rhyming slang 'birdlime' = 'time'), although the influence of the last part of 'jailbird' must have had a hand here, too.

**jamb** (upright forming side of a door)
This strange word, baffling small children who see no connection with sandwiches, is sometimes thought even by adults to be somehow related to 'jam', perhaps as in its manufacturing process, jam is 'squeezed' as if caught in a door. And how about the other kind, the 'traffic jam'? These two sorts of 'jam' are certainly related, with the 'squeeze' being the binding factor, but the final letter of 'jamb' indicates the word's different origin. This is in Old French (and modern) *jambe*, 'leg', since the door has two straight side pieces regarded as legs or supports (as for a table). For more about jam, see the next entry.

**jamboree** (large assembly of scouts or guides, noisy meeting or party)
There appear to be several potential references to 'jam' in this un-English-looking word, such as a 'squeeze' or 'crush' of people, or something that is attractive, with 'jam on it', or even a kind of 'jam session', as in 1930s jazz. The word is of American origin, and easily pre-dates the scouting usage, with the *Supplement* to the *Oxford English Dictionary* recorded a first finding of 1868 to apply to a regiment. But no precise derivation for the word has yet been tracked down, and any link with 'jam' is purely speculative. However, Patrick Hanks (see

90

Bibliography) has bravely come up with a possible origin in a blend of 'jabber' and French *soirée* and the last letter of 'jam'!

**jaunty** (cheerful, 'merry and bright')
It is only natural to envisage a jaunty person going on a jaunt. Sad to say, however, the two words are not related. 'Jaunty' comes as a variation on 'genteel' (itself from French *gentil*), hence the 'raffish' overtone to the word, but 'jaunt' is of unknown origin. The kind of carriage known as a 'jaunting car', formerly popular in Ireland, relates to 'jaunt', however, not 'jaunty'.

**Jeep** (type of tough all-purpose vehicle)
The word (technically a registered trademark) is popularly derived from the initials of '*general purpose*', describing the vehicle's versatility. Yet versatile as it certainly is, its name very probably derives from the name of a cartoon character called 'Eugene the Jeep', created by the American cartoonist E. C. Segar in 1936. (The creature made a noise 'jeep' and 'could do almost everything'.) And although the first Jeep proper did not appear until 1941 with its name registered the previous year, it was known by a number of other similar 'cartoon-type' nicknames (such as 'Peep', 'Iron Pony' and 'Leaping Lena'), so the origin in the name of the Segar strip character seems more likely than just in '*g.p.*'.

**jenneting** (kind of early apple)
This name, not to be found in some standard dictionaries, is sometimes popularly explained as being a corruption of 'June-eating', since that is when the apple ripens. But the word probably derives from *Jeannet*, a diminutive or 'pet' form of the French name *Jean* (John), since it is ready for eating round about St John's Day (24 June). Its final '-ing' would thus be modelled on other apple names such as 'sweeting', 'codlin' and the like.

**jerked beef** (beef preserved in long strips dried in the sun)
The phrase looks as if it refers to some vigorous method of preparing the beef, as if the strips or slices had been abruptly rolled or twisted or torn off. But the name was originally just 'jerky', and this was the usual

corruption of a native word, in this case American Spanish *charqui* which itself represented Quechua *ch'arki*. Compare **bully beef** and **corned beef**, and even **hamburger**.

**jerry-built** (poorly constructed, cheaply built)
It should be said at the outset that the precise origin for this term is not finally known. Among the proposed derivations, which cannot all be right, are: 1) built (or bombed) by 'Jerries' (Germans); 2) corruption of 'jury-built', i. e. like a makeshift **jury-mast** (which see, below); 3) tumble-down like the walls of Jericho (!); 4) representing poverty or misery, like a jeremiad (via the prophet of doom, Jeremiah); 5) corruption of French *jour*, 'day', or some form of it, since the building would not last long; 6) built by a person or firm named Jerry (or some similar name). Of all these, the first is impossible and the last the most likely, since the expression was first recorded with regard to houses built in Liverpool in the mid-nineteenth century (in the form 'jerry builder'). Clearly, if this is the case, local research could doubtless produce a more authoritative explanation, with precise dating.

**Jerusalem artichoke** (kind of sunflower grown for its edible tubers)
The flower did not originate in Jerusalem but in Italy, since its corrupt English name derives from the Italian word for 'sunflower', *girasole* (literally 'sun-circler', since the sunflower constantly turns to face the sun). See also **artichoke**, compare **Palestine soup**, and turn finally to **sunflower** itself for more light on the subject.

**Jew's harp** (kind of musical instrument played when held between the teeth)
The name is not an alteration of 'jaw's harp' nor a corruption of French *jeu*, 'playing', and the first part of the term has always been recorded in its present form, even though earlier records show the second word to have been earlier 'trump'. The origin is not at all clear: perhaps Jews sold or imported (or exported) such instruments, or perhaps the association was with the biblical instruments called 'harp' and

'trump'. In fact the instrument is neither of these but is sounded by striking the metal tongue with a finger.

**jo** (sweetheart)
In Robert Burns' famous 'John Anderson, my jo, John', the 'jo' is sometimes understood (mainly by non-Scots, admittedly) to be a pet form of 'John'. In fact it is a Scottish alteration of 'joy', and means 'sweetheart', 'dear one'. If anything, Jo would be a short form of Joseph, not of John, and it is not common as a man's name in any case. See also **tart**.

**John Dory** (kind of edible fish)
The name of the fish is not a corruption of French *jaune dorée*, 'golden yellow', despite its usual yellow to olive colour. The second half of the name may well derive from the French for 'gilded', however, with the 'John' added by association with 'John Doe', an arbitrary name used in legal proceedings. Earlier the fish was simply known as the 'dory'. The French name for the fish also has a 'gold' link, since it is called *saint-pierre*, from the tradition that it is the fish from which St Peter took the tribute money (see Matthew 17:27, where the coin referred to would have been a stater or shekel).

**jolly** (merry, cheery)
This word does not derive from 'jovial' (which itself comes from Latin *jovialis*, referring to the planet Jupiter, or one born under it), but from Old French *jolif* (modern *joli*, 'nice', 'pretty'). This in turn probably came from the Old Norse word that also led to English 'yule'. The final 'f' of the French word could have led to an English ending '-ive', as in 'festive' (which was Old French *festif*), but it disappeared from the standard word. (It has survived, however, in the surname Jolliff or Jolliffe, which developed from the word.) It is quite certain that a 'jolly boat' has no connection with 'jolly', and the term probably relates to some other ship or boat name such as 'yawl'.

**Jordan almond** (large type of Spanish almond used in confectionery)
The almond did not come from Jordan any more than the **Jerusalem artichoke** came from Jerusalem or **Palestine soup** from Palestine (see these names). In Middle English it was a *jardyne almaund*, that is, a common or 'garden almond', with the ultimate derivation from the French.

**journeyman** (worker who has learned a trade and works for another person, usually a day at a time)
The journeyman is or was not so called because he makes journeys, but because he was engaged for a day at a time (Old French *jornee*, modern *journée*, 'day'). However, the English word 'journey' formerly meant 'day's work', 'day's travel', as it did in Old French, and this common link is the source of any modern wrong association.

**Jove** (alternative name for the god Jupiter)
Since the names of supreme gods sometimes overlap ('god' is itself related to 'Jupiter' and thus to 'Jove'), there are some hopeful theolinguists who have tried to link 'Jove' and 'Jehovah'. But the two, although having Latin connections, are actually poles apart. 'Jove' derives from Old Latin *Jovis*; 'Jehovah' is a false reading (through New Latin) of the Hebrew name of God, *Yahweh*. This itself developed from the so called sacred tetragrammaton (literally 'four letter word', with anything but the modern associations) written YHVH. Since this was regarded as too sacred to pronounce, the vowels 'a' and 'o' from *Adonai*, another name of God (literally 'my lord'), were inserted to make a 'substitute' name, i. e. as *Y(A)H(O)V(A)H*. God revealed his personal name Jehovah to Moses on Mount Horeb (see Exodus 6:3). Interestingly, even nowadays, orthodox Jews will not recite the word for God, regarding this as taking his name in vain. In prayers 'Adonai' is used, while another alternative, 'Adoshem', is cited in non-religious contexts. Similarly, when God is written in English, the vowel is always omitted, i. e. 'G-d', for the same reason.

**jubilee** (special anniversary)
The word has come to be associated with 'jubilant', or more precisely with Latin *jubilare*, 'to rejoice', but its actual origin, going back in turn through Old French, Late Latin and Greek, is in Hebrew *yōbhēl*, 'ram's horn', 'jubilee'. The original 'jubilee' was a

year of emancipation and restoration decreed by ancient Hebrew law every fifty years (see Leviticus 25:10, where it is called a 'jubile'), when it would be proclaimed throughout the land by blasts on trumpets made from ram's horns.

**juggernaut** (large irresistible force; heavy articulated lorry)
The modern sense of the word to mean 'heavy lorry' suggests an ending '-naut' (as in 'astronaut', presumably referring to the driver) on a word that seems to link up with something like 'judder', 'juggle', 'jugular' (by association with 'arterial' roads?), or even 'jungle' (again, perhaps the roads, as at Spaghetti Junction). But these are fanciful imaginings, and the word is actually quite venerable, and comes from the Hindi title *Jagannath* (literally 'lord of the world') of the god Vishnu, itself derived from Sanskrit. This title came to mean 'massive irresistible force' from the once held belief that certain devotees of Vishnu threw themselves in ecstasy (or frenzy) under the wheels of a cart that bore his image. The 'lorry' sense of 'juggernaut' relates more specifically to the cart, as an unstoppable vehicle that can cause damage and death.

**July** (seventh month of the year)
There has long been a small but steady fancy that the name is somehow connected with Julia or Julie, if only because down to about the seventeenth century the month was actually pronounced as 'Julie' is today. Even Wordsworth rhymed it thus:

In March, December, and in July,
'Tis all the same with Harry Gill;
The neighbours tell, and tell you truly,
His teeth they chatter, chatter still.

This was as late as 1798. But the month was actually named after Julius Caesar (by Mark Anthony), who was born in it in the year 100 B.C., when it was called *Quintilis*, as it was the fifth month of the Roman calendar. And in any case, who could the Julia or Julie have been? (It is certainly true

that some girls have been named May and June and even April, as they were born in those months, and some may well have been called Julia or Julie because they were born in July. But no Julia gave her name to the month.) Compare **June** (below).

**jumble** (kind of thin usually ring-shaped cake)
The cake or biscuit is not so called because it has been made from a 'jumble' of ingredients, for example, but very likely since it is or was (for the word is now obsolete) a *gimbal*, or ring. Its alternative spelling of 'jumbal' reflects this origin more closely.

**jumper** (knitted garment worn on the top half of the body)
Perhaps by association with 'sweater', which is so called since it is worn by athletes and sportsmen (who sweat), the word may seem to imply that the garment was originally worn by people who jump. However, it was originally called just 'jump', meaning more a loose jacket, and this word was probably an altered spelling of Old French *jupe*, 'coat' (now 'skirt', a shift from top to bottom), itself from Arabic *jubbah*.

**June** (sixth month of the year)
Some classical scholars have liked to derive the name from Latin *juniores*, 'young people', pointing to some connection with the popularity of the month for weddings. But the name is probably from the Roman gens or clan of Junius, to whom it was dedicated. Compare **July** (above).

**jury-mast** (temporary mast on a sailing boat or ship)
There is no connection with 'jury' or 'injury' or even French *jour*, day, as if the mast was one rigged up temporarily for a day (or rigged in a day). The origin is more likely to be in Old French *ajurie*, 'aid', although it must be admitted that the precise origin is still uncertain. For interest, see also **jerry-built**.

**kaput** (finished, 'done for')
The word's German origin does not apparently rule out a seeming derivation from Latin *caput*, 'head', and indeed this is the explanation given by Berlitz (see Bibliography), referring to German burial squads in the Middle Ages counting each corpse as a 'head'. But this is not the true derivation, and records show that the word came into German from French *capot*. This word itself was used, and still is, to mean 'having made no tricks at cards' (*fair capot* means 'to take all the tricks in piquet'), and ultimately comes from a word such as *cape* meaning 'hooded cloak'. (A person who has taken no tricks has been obviously 'tricked' or 'hoodwinked' by the other players.)

**kerseymere** (kind of fine woollen fabric)
Kerseymere did not originally come from Kersey, in Suffolk, although the heavy woollen cloth called 'kersey' probably did. No doubt the present spelling of the word was influenced by the other cloth name, but its true place of origin was Kashmir, in India, which was formerly known in English as 'Cassimere'. Moreover, the influence of 'kersey' came indirectly, through this spelling of the name of the Indian region, rather than straight from the Suffolk village. The words and names here are thus all rather closely interwoven. Compare **worsted**.

**ketch** (type of sailing boat)
If the word is a form of 'catch', which may well be possible, it will be in the sense 'hunt' rather than 'catch fish', since the vessel formerly carried mortars for bombarding the enemy in battle, and was even known as a 'bomb-ketch'. A possible link with some Turkish word should not be altogether ruled out, however, such as the one that gave the French word *caïque* to apply to a small, long, narrow vessel found in the Middle East.

(This was not a sailing boat, however, but was propelled by oars.) The modern French word for 'ketch' is the same as the English.

**ketchup** (kind of sauce, typically tomato)
There are various ways of spelling this word, including also 'catchup' (more common, in fact, in America) and 'catsup'. These all suggest the wrong associations, as if the sauce had been 'caught up' somehow when being prepared, or was eagerly lapped up by cats. Since it is reasonably exotic, at least in its 'proper' form, it is not surprising to find that the name of the sauce is an oriental one, and in fact comes through Malay, from Chinese *kōetsiap*, literally 'seafood sauce' (i.e. a type of pickled fish sauce).

**kidnap** (steal or abduct a person)
The original reference was not to stealing goats but to abducting children ('kid nabbing'), in particular black ones to work on American plantations. The verb derived from the noun 'kidnapper', first recorded in the seventeenth century, but early enough for John Bunyan to use it in *Pilgrim's Progress*: 'Thou practises the craft of a Kidnapper, though gatherest up Women, and Children, and carriest them into a strange Countrey'.

**kittiwake** (kind of gull)
The bird has a name that is nothing to do with 'wake' or 'kitten', and its cry is not a kind of 'kitten mew'. (Nor is the name of the gull called 'mew' or 'seamew', which is a Germanic word related to German *Möwe*, Dutch *meeuw*, Old Norse *már*, and so on, all of which directly represent the cry, not via a mewing kitten.) The kittiwake's name in fact represents its characteristic three-note cry ('kitti-kitti-wake'), rising on the final 'wake', as anyone who has heard it will clearly recognize. Early spellings of the

word show that it was formerly pronounced 'kittiwark', which is even closer to the actual cry.

**knickers** (women's underpants)
The word is not related in any way to 'knick-knack', as has been suggested by some on occasions (presumably as the garment can be small, decorative and cheap, as a knick-knack is). Its origin is actually quite interesting, even literary. It is an abbreviation for 'knickerbockers', referring to the men's trousers that were developed from the knee-breeches worn by Diedrich Knickerbocker, as appearing in the portraits of him by George Cruikshank in Washington Irving's *History of New York* (of which Knickerbocker was the supposed author). The book was published as a satire in America in 1809, and Knickerbocker's own name is though to have been borrowed by Irving from a Dutch family so called who had settled locally a few years earlier. (*Their* own name may originally have meant 'baker of knickers', with the latter being a word for clay marbles.) To mention in passing a derivative expression: the usage of the word as a colloquial exclamation of annoyance or the like ('oh, knickers!') is first recorded by the *Supplement* to the *Oxford English Dictionary* in 1971. It occurs before this, however, in Robert Bolt's children's play *The Thwarting of Baron Bolligrew*, published in 1966, and therefore must have been in use even earlier for him to have included it. 'Knick-knack' is simply one of the much-loved English reduplications (of 'knack').

**knobkerrie** (kind of club)
Those who know that a shillelagh (also a club) is so called because it originated in Shillelagh, in south-east Ireland, might perhaps suppose that a knobkerrie was a 'knobbed' stick of some kind from Kerry. But this would be right off the beaten track,

since the weapon originated in South Africa, where it was used by tribesmen. Its derivation is thus in Afrikaans *knopkierie*, where the first part of the word means 'knobstick', and the latter represents Hottentot *kirri*, 'stick'.

**knot** (kind of sandpiper)
The bird's name is associated with that of King Canute (and even more obviously with his 'proper' name Knut), since the bird itself was said to be a special favourite of his – or according to another account, since it is believed to have come to Britain from Denmark. This link is even reflected in its scientific name, which is *Calidris canutus*. But the name is almost certainly a representation of its 'grunting' cry, and the initial 'k' of the name was pronounced regularly down to the eighteenth century. Whatever the ultimate origin of the name, it is certainly not from 'knot'.

**Ku Klux Klan** (American anti-black secret society)
The admittedly strange name (sometimes mispronounced and even misspelt 'Klu Klux Klan') is said to represent the cocking of a gun. However, it is much more likely to have derived from a combination of Greek *kyklos*, 'circle' and English 'clan'. The original society was founded in 1866, but a new organization of 1915, called 'The Invisible Empire, Knights of the Ku Klux Klan', made much use of the letter 'K' in its titles and general nomenclature, having 'Klonvocations' held by 'Klansmen' in the local 'Klaverns', with these being ruled by an 'Exalted Cyclops', a 'Klaliff', and the like. The substitution of 'K' for 'C' has long attracted several special or 'counter-culture' uses, such as the many brand names (Kleenex, Krooklok and the like) and pop and rock group names (Kenny and the Kasuals, Kool and the Gang, Kleer, Korgis, and so on).

**lama** (Tibetan monk)
Despite the various jokes, quips and puns at the expense of the two words, there is still a lingering suspicion in some minds that the lama and the llama (the animal like a camel) may after all be connected in some way. They are not, however, and the llama is not the sacred animal of the monk. The Buddhist priest derives his title from the Tibetan word *blama*, 'superior one' (in which the 'b' is silent). The llama gets its name, through Spanish (which gave the double 'l' spelling), from Quechua, the language spoken by the American Indian people inhabiting its native Peru. The word is what these people called the animal, and does not derive, as Berlitz (see Bibliography) and others still tell, from the Spanish question directed to a native, *¿Cómo se llama?* ('What is it called?'). In the title of the Dalai Lama, the spiritual head of Tibetan Buddhism, the first word is Mongolian for 'ocean', indicating his domain.

**lampoon** (written attack on a person, satire)
The word looks as if it might derive from 'lamp' in some way, as if the words of ridicule were displayed on a lamp-post. The association of words ending in '-oon' with a French origin, too ('balloon' from *ballon*, 'dragoon' from *dragon*, and so on) perhaps subconsciously recalls 'lamp post' practices of the French Revolution ('À la lanterne!' being the cry to hang an 'enemy of the people' from a lamp-post). And although there is a French word *lampion*, meaning a kind of oil-burning lamp, the origin of 'lampoon' is probably in French *lampons*, 'let us drink', a common refrain in drinking songs.

**landfall** (sighting of land from a ship or aircraft)
The 'fall' here does not mean that one will soon 'fall' on the land, or alight there, but that there is simply an occurrence in the sighting of the land, or in reaching it (as in 'nightfall', which similarly does not imply a 'descending' of the night but the fact that it happens).

**landlubber** (non-sailor, one who knows little or nothing about the sea)
The word is not a jocular nautical corruption of 'land lover', as it might well be, but is simply a combination of 'land' and 'lubber', with the latter word meaning 'lout', 'clumsy fellow', and perhaps originally coming into English from some Scandinavian source.

**landscape** (natural scenery, or a picture of it)
Because of the sense of the word, implying an expanse of land or country that can be seen in a single view, the '-scape' could be taken to be a form of '-scope', as in other 'viewing' words. But the derivation is actually in Dutch *landschap*, literally 'landship' (the '-ship' as in 'township'). This was a technical painting term applied to a picture of natural countryside, as distinct from one of the sea or a portrait. Later, other 'scapes' developed from this, such as 'seascape', 'cloudscape', 'skyscape', 'moonscape' and even just basic 'scapes'. The Dutch were famous for their painting techniques and innovations in the sixteenth century, and other Dutch 'painting' words that have come into English are **'easel'** and **'lay figure'** (see both these).

**lanthorn** (old kind of lantern)
The word is simply an archaic (and corrupt) spelling of 'lantern'. It was taken by many, however, to be related to 'horn', since this was the material from which such lanterns were frequently 'glazed'. This false associ-

ation was made by Samuel Butler in *Hudibras,* when he wrote:

The Moon pull'd off her veil of Light
That hides her Face by Day from
Sight[. . .]
And in the Lanthorn of the Night
With Shining Horns hung out her
Light.

That was in the seventeenth century. Much nearer our own time, a more specific connection between the two words was even made in a late nineteenth-century history book for children: 'When the wind blew and made the candles burn faster, King Alfred put horn round them, and thus made lanthorns or lanterns' (Robert Routledge, *Routledge's British Reading Book*).

**lanyard** (rope or line for fastening something on board ship)
As with the misleading **halyard** (which see), there is no connection with any sort of 'yard' here, whether nautical or not. The word came into English from Middle French *laniere,* ultimately from Old French *lasne,* 'strap'. The alternative spelling 'laniard', in English lessens the false association with 'yard'.

**lapwing** (kind of plover, noted for its slow, erratic, flapping flight)
This is one of the most famous 'wrong' bird names, and does not mean, as it so obviously (and poetically) should, 'flap wing', or even 'lap wing' itself. In Old English the bird was called *hlēapewince,* literally 'leaper winker', with 'wink' here in the sense 'jerk', 'stagger' (as in 'tiddleywinks'), referring to its irregular flight. The 'leap' also very probably refers to this, although it could well describe the way the bird runs or leaps away from its nest to decoy any stranger or unwelcome visitor. The present wrong associations in the name may owe something to a definition of the bird in an early seventeenth-century dictionary: '*Lappe-wing, q.* leapwing, because he lappes or clappes the wings so often' (John Minsheu, *The guide into tongues,* 1617). The lapwing is also known as the peewit, of course, which is a typical 'call-name', imitating its plaintive cry.

**lark** (frolic, play about)
Despite the apparent mutual connection in 'skylark', the verb here is not related to the name of the bird in any way. It is probably a development of a dialect word 'lake', itself from Old English *lācan,* 'to play', 'to sport'. ('Skylark' in this sense originally meant 'lark about in the sky', i. e. in the rigging of a ship. This was in turn, however, a typical nautical pun at the expense of the bird.) See also **wedlock**.

**lash** (bind with rope)
There is no connection between this 'lash' and the one that means 'strike with a whip', as if there was some sort of link in the materials, or in the strong 'subduing' or restraining sense. The 'binding' lash relates to 'lace', and the 'whip' lash is probably ultimately imitative (and perhaps related to 'slash').

**lashings** (lots)
This colloquial word is not connected with 'lavish' or even 'splash', although the latter word may account for the common occurrence of 'lashings' used with a liquid (often, for some reason, 'lashings of hot water'). The derivation is thus from 'lash' in the sense 'strike', the basic concept being of someone who 'strikes out' or breaks out in a fit of extravagance or squandering. (Compare the modern 'lash out'.)

**lass** (girl)
Some rather innocent lexicographers have derived this word as an abbreviation of 'laddess' (as in the still current humorous 'lads and laddesses'). But this is simply a nice idea, and 'lass' is an old word in its own right. Unfortunately, like many similar words (including 'lad' itself), the ultimate origin is uncertain.

**last** (continue, endure, hold out)
It seems strange that there is no common link between this word and the other 'last' meaning 'end', 'final', since if you 'last' long enough you will be the 'last'. But the two words are quite distinct, and the 'holding out' last is actually related to the shoemaker's last, which comes from Old English *last,* 'footprint'. The idea is that of following in someone's steps. The 'final' last comes

from Old English *latost*, which is the superlative of the Old English word for 'late' (so is literally 'latest').

**latchet** (shoe fastening)
This archaic word, found in the Bible, looks as if it means 'little latch'. But it really means simply 'lace', from Old French *lachet*, and is not related to 'latch' at all.

**lath** (thin strip of wood)
Surprising as it may seem, there is no connection between this word and 'lathe', the wood-turning machine (which can also be used for other materials). 'Lath' comes from an Old English word, and may perhaps be related to 'slat'. 'Lathe' probably came into English from Scandinavian, although, somewhat disconcertingly, in Middle English the word was recorded as *lath*.

**launch** (type of boat)
It would be too straightforward to assume that the boat's name is related to the other, common 'launch', meaning 'set a ship afloat'! The word for the boat probably came into English, via Spanish, from Malay *lanchar*, 'swift', while the verb 'launch' derives ultimately from Low Latin, through French, and is related to 'lance'. (Its application to ships is of course only one of a number of senses, with the most basic being 'throw', and originally, 'pierce'.)

**lavender** (herb whose leaves and spikes are used as a perfume)
There is an interesting theory that relates the name of the plant to the basic 'lav-' root that means 'wash' (as in 'lavatory', originally a wash basin, and probably 'lava', which 'washes' down). Certainly the aromatic plant has been long used as a perfume in water and for scenting freshly laundered linen. However, there is no firm proof that this root lies behind the name, and it may be simply the uses of the herb that came to give the association. The name came into English from Old French *lavendre*, itself from Medieval Latin *lavandula*. But the derivation of this earliest word is not precisely known.

**law** (in 'mother-in-law', etc: member of a family)
It is sometimes supposed that all the 'in-laws' of a family are so called since they are 'legally' related to a close member of the family, so that a 'father-in-law', for example, is the father of a person's husband or wife. This is true, of course, but the 'lawful' aspect is not simply the 'law of the land' in a general kind of way but, strictly, Canon Law, i. e. the laws laid down by the Church of England in the 'Table of Kindred and Affinity' found as the final section of the Book of Common Prayer. In common usage, an 'in-law' often means a step-relation, which the Prayer Book Table does not cater for. (For more about such relations, however, see **stepfather**.) Many languages other than English usually have a separate word for an 'in-law', such as French *belle-mère* (originally *marâtre*), Italian *suocera*, German *Schwiegermutter*, Russian *tëshcha* or *svekrov'*, all meaning 'mother-in-law'. (Russian even has two separate words for, respectively, the wife's mother and the husband's mother.)

**lawn** (kind of fine linen)
There is no connection with the familiar garden lawn, despite the pleasant and almost natural association between neat, closely mown and freshly scented grass and fine sheer linen. As with many fabrics (see **diaper** and **dimity**), the word comes from the cloth's place of origin, in this case Laon, the town in northern France.

**layette** (set of clothes for a newborn baby)
The word suggests a 'little lay', that is, a set of clothes in which a tiny person can lie. There is in fact a diminutive behind the name, but this is not it. The word came into English from French as a diminutive of *laye*, 'box', with this itself being a word of Dutch origin, related to English 'load' and 'laden'. The proper sense of the word is therefore 'set of clothes, toilet articles, bedding etc that can be laid in a drawer'.

**lay figure** (artist's dummy)
A lay figure is a model of the human body on which an artist can arrange drapery and which is jointed so that it can be set in different poses. There is no connection with

'lay' in the expected sense, or in fact in any sense. The word was originally *layman* in English, and this came from Dutch *leeman*, literally 'joint man' (from *lid*, 'limb' and *man*, 'man'). For other Dutch artistic importations to English, see **easel** and **landscape**.

**lazy** (idle)
It is tempting to connect this word with a person who 'lays about' (as some say), or who is a 'layabout'. But there is no link with 'lay' or 'lie' in any sense, and the word probably comes from a Low German root meaning 'feeble', itself perhaps related to English 'loose' (but hardly 'lax' or 'leisurely', as has been proposed by some sources). The colloquial Russian word for 'lazybones' is *lezheboka*, which although suggesting a similar and somewhat grosser colloquialism to an English ear (as well as managing to even *look* like 'lazybones'), literally means 'one who lies on his side', so is really a 'layabout' or 'lie-abed'.

**league** (unit of distance)
This word is not related to the more common 'league' meaning 'alliance', as if the distance was a large or 'unified' one (covered in seven-league boots), or by associaiton with the double senses of such words as 'chain' and 'knot'. It derives, through Late Latin *leuga*, from some Gaulish word, whereas the other 'league' is ultimately from Latin *ligare*, 'to bind' (as in English 'ligature').

**leap year** (year with extra day added)
The year is not so called since the calendar 'leaps' over 29 February, or because it has to be adjusted to allow for it, but probably because every fixed festival after 29 February 'leaps' over a day, i. e. does not fall on the next day of the week, as in ordinary years, but the next day but one. For example, Christmas Day 1983 was on a Sunday (as some people wish it always was, like Easter), but in 1984, a leap year, it was on a Tuesday, so had 'leapt' over Monday.

**leave** (permission; holiday)
This sense of 'leave' is not related to the other 'leave' which means 'go off' or 'cause to remain'. It derives from Old English *lēaf*,

related to modern 'believe', 'love' and the second part of 'furlough', with the basic sense being approval resulting from pleasure or satisfaction. The other 'leave' comes from Old English *læfan*, and is related to German *bleiben*, 'to stay'. The expression 'take one's leave' actually contains the 'permission' leave, although is now associated with the other one. This is because it originally meant 'obtain permission to depart', and it occurs in this sense in Shakespeare's *Richard II*, where Bolingbroke says to the Lord Marshal, in the presence of the king:

> Then let us take a ceremonious leave
> And loving farewell of our several
> friends.

**ledger** (book of accounts)
The book is not quite so called since it is kept on a ledge, but because it was originally always laid in the same place, and so 'lay' there as a ledge 'lies' along the edge of something. Both words do come from the same Middle English verb *leggen*, to 'lay', however. Ledger lines in music (short lines added above or below a stave for notes that are too high or too low to be registered on it) are probably so called since they 'lie' (like 'ledges') alongside the stave. The expression certainly does not derive from French *léger*, 'light', 'slight', as is sometimes stated, although the spelling is sometimes 'leger lines'. (In French they are simply called *lignes supplémentaires*.)

**leech** (former term for a doctor or physician)
The 'leech' of old was not so called since he used leeches in his treatment and cures, even though he did, and despite the fact that the two Old English words were identical (*lēce*). This can be shown by comparing the words in different obsolete Germanic languages, with the worm recorded as *lieke* in Middle Dutch and *liche* in Middle English (whereas the other 'leech' always had *a* or *e* for its middle vowel). However, any original difference was soon lost and the form of the 'worm' word was assimilated early to the other one.

**leghorn** (breed of chicken)
The distinctive domestic fowl, famous for its high production rate of fine white eggs, does not have a name that points to prominent portions or features of its anatomy, but is so called because it originally came from Leghorn, in Italy (now almost always called by its Italian name *Livorno*).

**leitmotiv** (musical phrase or theme representing a particular idea or person)
The recurring leitmotiv (sometimes spelt 'leitmotif') has a name that certainly sounds as if it is a sort of 'light motif', as if representing a less serious note in an otherwise 'heavy' or tragic work. This is not the case, and as can be seen by the spelling is German in origin, meaning literally 'leading theme'. The word is particularly associated with the dramatic operas of Wagner.

**lemon sole** (type of edible flatfish)
The lemon sole is a red herring! It is not so called since, like some fish, it is eaten with lemon, or because of its lemon-yellow colour, although this shade is apt, but because its name derives from French *limande*, a word that is perhaps related to French *lime*, 'rasp', referring to its rough skin.

**Lenten** (relating to Lent)
Today, 'Lenten' is naturally understood as the adjective of 'Lent'. Originally, however, in Old English, it was the standard noun meaning 'spring' (i.e. the season), *lencten*, with this word probably referring to the gradually lengthening day. Later, the shorter form of this, 'Lent', took over to mean the religious fasting season, although also meaning 'spring' initially for a time. This is just one minor point of interest. Also interesting is the fact that the word for 'spring' is not used in any other language to mean 'Lent'. French *carême*, for example, literally means 'fortieth day' (from Latin *quadragesima dies*), and German *Fasten* obviously means 'fasting time'.

**leopard** (kind of 'big cat')
The leopard is not so called because it 'leaps', even though the name has been recorded in such spellings as *lepard* and *lippard* in the past, and even though it is still sometimes misspelt 'leapard' today (including a private advertisement in *The Times* in August 1984, where a 'tiger or leapard skin rug' was urgently required). The leopard (also known as 'panther') has a name actually coming from Late Greek *leopardos*, a hybrid of *leon*, 'lion' and *pardos*, 'pard' (this being its earlier name in English), and the animal was thought to be the result of cross-breeding. Originally this new name applied to what is now called the cheetah (which is also known as a 'hunting leopard'). Eventually 'leopard' replaced 'pard' altogether, while 'panther' today is usually limited to the so called 'black leopard'.

**leotard** (close-fitting garment worn by dancers and some gymnasts)
The word looks as if it relates to 'leopard', with perhaps a subconscious association with the 'catlike' or 'slinky' movements of a dancer or gymnast wearing the garment. It could also suggest 'leonine', with a similar concept. It actually takes its name, however, from the French acrobat who first wore it, Jules Léotard. As a trapeze artist, he found that conventional clothes hampered his movements, and the garment was thus the result of his practical and sartorial protest. He lived entirely in the nineteenth century, but the word itself did not catch on in English until the 1920s at the earliest.

**let** (in tennis: serve that does not count)
It often seems strange that this sense of the word, which implies a fault or hold-up in play, is the same as the much more common 'let' that means 'allow'. Or could it be that the player is allowed to serve again, that the umpire (or a particular rule) 'lets' him do so? The answer, of course, is that the two words are not related, and have different origins. The tennis 'let' comes from a verb that formerly meant 'hinder' (and is still found in this sense in the Prayer Book) for example ('sore let and hindered in running the race'), with its Old English form *lettan*. The other 'let', meaning 'allow' comes from Old English *lǣtan*. Modern English 'late' is related to the tennis 'let', the common link being the obstructing or delaying involved.

**limbo** (West Indian acrobatic dance)
The name of this dance where the performer passes under a gradually lowered pole is nothing to do with 'limb', even though getting limbs under the pole is the hardest part of the dance. Nor of course is there any connection with the other 'limbo' that means 'place of oblivion' (properly in a religious sense). The word is a West Indian one, although *Chambers* (see Bibliography) does suggest a possible influence from 'limber'.

**lime** (kind of tree)
There are two kinds of lime tree, with each having a name of different origin. The one that gives the fruit (which in turn gives lime juice) has an ultimate origin, through French, in Arabic *līm*, and the word is related to 'lemon' (as the fruit is, since they are both citrus). The other lime, called properly and poetically 'linden' (also the German word, as in the famous Berlin street *Unter den Linden*), derives from Old English *lind*, and was originally known in English as the 'line'. The two confusing English place-names Newcastle-under-Lyme and Ashton-under-Lyne are nothing to do with either tree, although by coincidence the respective 'Lyme' and 'Lyne' *does* denote a tree, since it means 'elm place'. (The word is of Celtic origin.)

**limerick** (humorous and often indecent five-line verse)
One of the more extraordinary explanations of this verse (containing the best and worst of English humour), is that its present name, relating to Limerick in Ireland, was influenced, at least partly, by an earlier similar type of verse called a 'learic'. This word, which seems to have died a fairly rapid death, was coined by a Jesuit priest, Father Matthew Russell, to refer to Edward Lear, who of course popularized the limerick. The earliest reference we have to the use of the word (according to the *Supplement* to the *Oxford English Dictionary*) is in a quotation of 1896 by Aubrey Beardsley (who had been trying to amuse himself by writing limericks on his troubles). It seems unlikely that the shortlived 'learic' (half suggesting 'lyric', perhaps intentionally)

had a significant influence, or any at all, on the name of the limerick.

**lingerie** (women's underwear and nightclothes)
A number of English words ending in '-erie' taken directly from the French have a closely corresponding shorter word with which they can be directly related. For example, 'camaraderie' can be linked with 'comrade', 'menagerie' with 'ménage' and even (less directly) 'manage', 'rotisserie' with 'roast', 'patisserie' with 'pastry'; and so on. Perhaps because of this, 'lingerie' is sometimes wrongly connected with a similar-looking English word such as 'linger' or 'lounge' (the first of these exploited by advertisers in marketing the garments). But the true association, of course, should be with 'linen', and the misleading 'g' comes from the French word for this which is *linge*. Unfortunately, we have no word directly resembling this for the correct association to be made, and we got our word 'linen' from Germanic sources, not the Romance ones that gave the French equivalent.

**lingua franca** (kind of 'common language' made from a mixture of existing languages)
Why 'lingua franca'? This does not mean 'free language' or even 'French language', as is sometimes imagined. It is in fact Italian for 'Frankish language', i. e. literally, 'language of the Germanic people called the Franks (who occupied Gaul among other countries)'. The reason for the choice of this particular language seems to have been the Arabic use of the expression to mean any language other than their own. As originally understood, lingua franca was the mixture of Italian Arabic and other languages spoken mainly in the Middle East by merchants, seamen, and others who needed to communicate. A form of lingua franca is **Pidgin English** (which see).

**links** (golf course)
The word does not refer to the way in which the different holes are 'linked' by fairways, and so on, but is from Old English *hlincas*, 'ridges', denoting the undulations or sandhills of the course, typically one by the sea (which is why 'links' occurs in the names of

many Scottish seaside places, even where there is no golf course).

**liquorice** (kind of black-coloured confectionery)
The word does not relate to, or derive from, 'liquor', despite its frequent pronunciation as 'lickerish', suggesting 'liquor-like'. The name actually goes back ultimately to Greek *glykyrrhiza*, literally 'sweet root', and the English word 'lickerish' (also spelt 'liquorish') meaning 'fond of good food', not 'fond of good liquor', relates to 'lecherous'!

**lists** (tournament, place of competition)
This historic word, still used in such modern phrases as 'entering the lists', is not directly related to the 'list' that means 'run of names in order', as if relating to a competitor whose name had been officially entered in a list. Instead, it belongs to the 'list' that means 'edge', in the sense 'band of material', 'selvage' (hence the initially puzzling 'list slippers', made of such material). However, ultimately the two words are related, with the common denominator being the sense 'row', 'line'. The tournament or jousting 'lists' referred to the palisades or other barriers that lined or surrounded the area of combat.

**livelong** (whole, entire)
This poetic word ('the livelong day') does not mean 'life-long', or 'lasting as long as you live', or even 'living' (perhaps half suggested by 'living daylights'), but literally 'as long as you want it to be'. The first half of the word is from Middle English *lefe*, meaning 'dear' and related to the archaic word 'lief' (as in 'I'd as lief go as stay'). It is thus indirectly related to 'love' (almost as in 'I'd love to'). Here it is in its typical poetic context, as used by the nineteenth-century American poet Ralph Waldo Emerson, in his poem 'Good-bye':

Where arches green, the live-long day,
Echo the blackbird's roundelay.

And here is the same phrase semi-inverted, by Robert Burns in his 'Mother's Lament':

So I, for my lost darling's sake,
Lament the live-day long.

**loadstone, lodestone** (form of magnetic iron ore)
The first spelling here suggests a stone that is somehow 'loaded' (with magnetism?). But the true connection is with 'lead', since the stone was used as a magnet by early sailors. There is a similar use of the word in 'lodestar' (or 'loadstar'), which was a star (especially the Pole Star) that similarly guided travellers. The basic 'lode', now used as a word to designate an ore deposit, comes from an Old English word that means 'course', and it should in all fairness be pointed out that it is itself indirectly linked to both 'lead' (in the sense 'conduct') and 'load'. A 'course', after all, is a route along which you can lead something and along which loads can be carried.

**loafer** (idler)
This word is not derived from 'loaf' in any sense, as if a loafer was too idle to work for his bread but begged for it, or (much less seriously) as if he couldn't use his loaf. The true origin seems to be in German *Landläufer*, literally 'land-runner' but actually meaning 'tramp', 'vagabond' (with the sense first current in America). The type of shoes called 'loafers' get their name from the trade mark of the company marketing them, 'Loafer' (with this name being first registered in 1939 by Fortnum and Mason of London, although the shoes, and their name, have strong American connections).

**locket** (small case containing a lock of hair or other memento)
The locket and the lock of hair are not connected (except in their actual use as objects), and 'locket' comes from French *loquet*, 'latch', as a diminutive of an earlier word meaning 'lock' in the 'doorlock' sense. It is possible, however, that the two kinds of 'lock' may be ultimately related. Both words come from the Germanic, and 'lock' or its equivalent has many different meanings in these languages.

**log** (record of a ship's progress or the flight of an aircraft)
The 'record' sense of the word has led one or two word fanciers (mainly nineteenth century clergymen) to derive it from Greek *logos*, 'word', 'account'. But alas, the true

origin is not so academic or classical, and the word means what it says, referring to the former wooden float tied to a line that indicated the rate of progress of a ship through the water. Here is a sixteenth-century account of the procedure: 'They hale in the logge or piece of wood again, and looke how many fadome the shippe hath gone in that time'.

**loo** (lavatory, toilet)
It's a brave person who claims to state categorically what the origin of this word is since this is still not precisely known. It is *probably* a fanciful (or even serious) development from French *l'eau,* 'the water'. Whatever it is, one or more of the following are false origins, and so should be recorded here: (1) a pun of some kind on 'Waterloo'; (2) a corruption of French *lieux d'aisance,* 'water closet' (literally 'places of easement'); (3) from Scottish 'gardyloo', a cry made in a town when slops were about to be emptied from an upstairs window, itself perhaps from French *garde à l'eau!,* 'watch out for the water!'; (4) a distorted or 'mincing' pronunciation of 'lavatory', on the lines of 'lav'. These are only half a dozen of the many etymologies proposed (some linguists have penned whole theses on the word). The unique advantage of the colloquialism is that it is equally acceptable to people who call it 'lavatory' (or 'bathroom', in the United States) and those (now the majority) who automatically say 'toilet'. It first gained general usage in Britain in the Second World War.

**loony** (mad, 'batty')
This is not the adjective of 'loon', meaning 'crazy or eccentric person', which itself comes from Middle English *loun,* 'rogue'. However, the sense of 'loon' itself was influenced by 'loony', which in fact is a shortened and altered form of 'lunatic' (deriving ultimately from Latin *luna,* 'moon', from the once held belief that lunacy or madness depended on the phases of the moon).

**loophole** (small opening in wall, etc; way of escape)
The apparent link with 'loop' is a false one, that is, with the ordinary sort of 'loop'.

There was, however, an old word 'loop' which actually meant 'loophole' (in the sense 'vertical opening in a castle wall'), and this is the word to which 'hole' was added. The historic word could link up with modern English 'louvre' or else be related to some Germanic word meaning 'watch', 'peer'. It was in use by some rather specialized writers until quite recently. A nineteenth-century guidebook describes a church tower near Oxford as having windows that are 'plain Norman loops'.

**loosestrife** (plant of the primrose family)
This plant name is a curious jumble. It does not itself 'loose strife' (i.e. end conflict), but derives from a sort of translation of the name of its reputed Greek discoverer, Lysimachos (living in the third century B. C. and a companion of Alexander). In this Greek name the first part means 'loosing' and the second 'strife', as in the learned 'logomachy' or 'war of words'.

**lovage** (kind of herb used for flavouring)
Hardly surprisingly, many people have linked the name with 'love', and some have even derived it as a corruption of 'love-ache'! After all, there are other plant names like this, such as 'love-in-a-mist', 'love-in-idleness', 'love-lies-bleeding', and similar sentimental references. But the word is nothing to do with love or lovers, and can be traced back like this: Middle English *lovache,* Old French *luvesche,* Late Latin *levisticum,* Latin *ligusticum.* This final word means 'Ligurian', i. e. relates to the ancient country, now part of Italy, called Liguria. And that is where the plant is supposed to have come from originally, although there is some evidence that it never grew there.

**love** (in tennis: zero, no score)
The derivation here is not the same as the 'duck' in cricket which comes from the 'duck's egg' or round zero (as if 'lovey' were like 'ducky'), nor does it come from the 'O' symbol that represents 'love' in letter-writing (where it stands for a hug, while 'X' is a kiss). It in fact comes from the expression 'play for love', i. e. play for nothing, or without any stakes (as in a 'labour of love' which is done without any financial reward). While on the subject, it is

worth pointing out, perhaps, that the saying 'There is no love lost between them' used to mean either 'Their love is mutual' (they keep all their love for each other), or 'They do not love each other' (they do not waste any love on each other). Today only the latter sense is understood.

**lump** (in phrase 'like it or lump it')
The phrase means, of course, 'accept it willingly or put up with it', suggesting that the 'lump' relates to a burden or 'lump' of something disagreeable. There is no evidence, however, that the two sorts of 'lump' are related, and in the expression here the word may be simply imitative, and a kind of verbal representation of something undesirable. Many similar 'sour' words exist, such as 'bump', 'hump', 'sump', 'stump', 'mump'. Doubtless the 'l' of 'like' seemed to require the same letter for the other verb, to make a satisfactory jingle of opposites (as in 'love me or leave me'), or the 'lump' may actually be an emotive alteration of 'leave'.

**lurcher** (kind of hunting dog)
The dog is not so called because it 'lurches' after its prey, but probably because it 'lurks' hidden waiting for it. The 'lurcher' is thus really a 'lurker'.

**luscious** (delicious)
The word is not related to 'lush' but is very likely a shortening of an early form of 'delicious'. Words of 'drooling' approval like this are often rather overblown, such as 'scrumptious' (probably from 'sumptuous') and 'yummy' (from the lip-smacking verbalization 'yum-yum').

**lutestring** (kind of glossy silk once used for dresses)
The word is the familar attempt to see some English sense in a non-English word, in this case Italian lustrino, the name of the fabric, itself related to English 'lustre'. (It is surprising that the word assumed the distorted form when a perfectly good and comprehensible base already existed. This is used more readily, however, for the alternative spelling 'lustring').

**lymph** (watery liquid in body containing white blood cells)
The word looks like 'nymph', and was probably influenced by this since the Greek mythological nymphs were the goddesses of water. Its true origin is new Latin lympha, 'water'.

**lynch** (kill by the action of a mob)
There are many unpleasant or 'violent' words ending in '-nch', such as 'clench', 'drench', 'wrench', 'clinch', 'pinch', 'punch' and 'crunch'. 'Lynch', however, is not one of them, but derives as the surname of a Charles Lynch (died 1796) or a William Lynch (died 1820), who organized such punishments outside the law in Virginia. The term originated as 'lynch law', or more precisely 'Lynch's law'.

**madding** (in title of Hardy's novel: *Far From the Madding Crowd*)
The word is often popularly misunderstood in this famous title to mean 'maddening' 'driving one mad'. It actually means 'behaving as if mad', 'raving'. Hardy took the quotation that forms the title from Gray's well known *Elegy*, where the complete line runs: 'Far from the madding crowd's ignoble strife'. Gray himself probably based his words in turn on a poem ('Dear Wood') written in 1614 by William Drummond of Hawthornden, where the line runs: 'Far from the madding worldling's hoarse discords'.

**madrigal** (old love poem set to music: part-song)
It was Christopher Marlowe who wrote the magic words, 'Melodious birds sing madrigals', and the word itself is so evocative that it conjures up a whole host of agreeable but unfortunately wrong associations, among them 'magical', 'magnify' 'melodical', 'Magnificat', 'musical', 'canticle' or some sort of heady blend of these. And the charm of the word is just as potent today as the songs themselves were in historic times (enough, for example, to move Paul Jennings to write in the *Radio Times* of 12-18 May 1984: 'The word madrigal is somehow as lovely as the thing it describes'). So what it the actual origin? The word came into English from Italian *madrigale*, itself deriving from Medieval Latin *matricale*, meaning 'simple', 'primitive'. This apparently came from Late Latin *matricalis*, 'of the womb' (*matrix*, 'womb'), perhaps referring to a 'maternal' poem or song, one that was sung in the mother tongue. This at any rate seems the most likely origin, although others have proposed a source in Italian *madre*, 'mother', implying a poem dedicated to the 'Mother of God' or the 'Mother Church', or suggesting a

mother's song to her children. But the origin is far earlier than just Italian, and the Late Latin derivation above is the most promising.

**malinger** (pretend to be sick so as to avoid work)
The word suggests an origin in 'linger'. The true source, however, is in French *malingre*, 'sickly (person)', probably from *mal*, 'bad', 'sick' and Old French *haingre*, 'feeble', 'weak'. The word was chiefly used in English of soldiers and sailors, who would even wound themselves and leave the wound untreated in order to be spared duties.

**mammon** (personification of wealth of possessions)
The word is sometimes wrongly associated with 'mammoth', perhaps accompanied by a link with 'Ammon' (the name of the ancestor of the Ammonites in the Bible, as well as the classical name of the Egyptian god Amen identified with Zeus and Jupiter) Mammon himself appears in the Bible, of course, and memorably in the words 'Ye cannot serve God and mammon' (Matthew 6:24). But there is no connection between this word and the fearsome former large-sized elephants. Their name can be traced back to an Old Russian word, but that of 'mammon' ultimately derives from Aramaic *māmōnā*, 'riches'. In medieval times the word was regarded as a name of the devil ('God and Mammon'), which may partly explain the half-association with the ancient and no doubt frightening mammoth.

**mandarin** (Chinese public official)
The title is on occasions falsely associated with 'mandate', Latin *mandare*, 'to entrust', and other related words. The mandarin did have status and influence, of course, but his title is ultimately from Sanskrit *mantra*,

'counsel', and came into English through Malay and Portuguese. The only connection between mandarins and mandarin oranges, incidentally, is their colour, since mandarins wore yellow robes.

**mandrake** (plant with a forked root seen as representing a human figure)
There is much vintage folk etymology at work in this word, since the 'man' has come to refer to the root and 'drake' probably represents 'dragon', with reference to the root's supposed magical powers as an aphrodisiac. (This features in the Bible in the story about Jacob and Leah in Genesis 30:14-21.) But the word itself is probably an alteration of Middle English *mandragora* (still an alternative name today), which itself goes back to Latin and Greek, where its ultimate origin is uncertain (it may even have been the name of a Greek physician). A kind of modern equivalent of the mandrake is ginseng, whether in the form of a medicinal preparation from the root of this plant, or the root itself, which similarly resembles a forked human figure. (The first half of its name is Chinese for 'man' for this reason.)

**mangelwurzel** (coarse kind of beet used as animal fodder)
The attractive rural name, seized on by children's writers and pop groups alike, does not relate to 'mangle' (as if the beet were 'mangled' in the course of its preparation), but 'mangold', in turn from German *Mangoldwurzel*, literally (hardly surprisingly) 'beet root'. The first half of the word seems to have been altered by association with German *Mangel*, 'dearth', 'lack', as though it were a kind of famine food. See also **mangle** (below).

**mangle** (pass clothes through rollers to squeeze out the water)
There is no connection between this 'mangle' and the one that means 'crush', 'wreck' (as in 'mangled bodies', 'mangled cars' in accidents). The 'wringer' ultimately goes back, through Dutch, to a Greek and Latin word equivalent to English 'mangonel', the name used for the historic type of large catapult employed for hurling rocks at the enemy. (Early mangles had a handle that moved backwards and forwards like the 'firing' arm of the mangonel.) The 'crush' word probably comes from an Old French word that is related to English 'maim'. It is the sense similarities that cause the false association between the identical words.

**mangosteen** (edible dark-coloured fruit with thick rind and luscious taste)
The mango is a similarly exotic and juicy fruit, but the two words are not related, and the mangosteen is not a kind of derivative of the mango. The mango's name comes (via Portuguese) from Tamil, while the mangosteen has a Malay origin. It is true, however, that the mango's name passed from Tamil to Portuguese via Malay.

**mangrove** (tree or shrub whose trunks and branches produce many roots)
This is a complex word rather like 'mandrake', with which it is even sometimes confused. The complicating factor is that in a sense it does grow in groves, too, which explains the influence of this word on the present spelling. Originally, however, it was known in English as *mangrow*, with this developing probably from Portuguese *mangue*, itself representing a Taino word. The Taino people formerly lived in the West Indies, the mangrove's native habitat.

**manner** (in phrase 'to the manner born')
The phrase is commonly used as if it meant 'naturally suited to (whatever it is)', in such sentences as 'He took to water-skiing as to the manner born', as if he had been born to water-ski, or as if he had done it all his life (since he was born). But the phrase, which comes from Shakespeare, did not originally mean this, but 'destined to be subject to (whatever it is)', which is not quite the same thing. Here is the original, in which Hamlet refers to the king's habit of revelling at midnight:

But to my mind, – though I am native here
And to the manner born, – it is a custom
More honour'd in the breach than the observance.

He means, 'Although I was born here, and

so have been obliged to accept the native way of doing things'.

**maroon** (strand on island)
If you are marooned, you will do your best to attract the attention of a passing ship. If you had a gun you would probably fire it when a ship was passing. This suggests that the 'maroon' defined above may be related to the other 'maroon' that means 'distress signal'. But the two words are of quite different origins. The 'stranding' maroon comes from American Spanish *cimarrón*, 'wild' (literally 'peak dwellers'). This was the name given to runaway West Indian slaves who lived 'wild' in the mountains and forests. A 'marooned' person has to live in similar conditions. The 'signal' maroon comes from French *marron*, 'chestnut', so is the same as the dark brownish-red colour. When a maroon is fired as a distress signal, it goes off like a chestnut popping in the fire! These respective origins look highly fanciful, but they are the actual ones. Thus do words and their various senses develop.

**marry** (former exclamation)
This famous Shakespearean word is nothing to do with the word that means 'get married'. It was used mainly for emphasis, and also to express agreement. So when someone said something like 'Marry, I could have eaten a horse', this is not the same sort of usage as 'Laugh, I could have died'. Instead, it is simply a version of 'By Mary', i. e. 'By the Virgin Mary', a religious oath.

**marshal** (high military rank)
The word was, and still is, the title of a high official in the royal household. Despite the military connections, it is nothing to do with 'martial'. It actually derives, through French, from a Germanic word related to Old High German *marahscalc* that literally means 'horse servant'. Originally, a marshal was a farrier, then the word became the title of the man who was in charge of the cavalry, and from this developed the modern sense. Something similar happened with 'constable', which originally meant 'companion of the stable'. (See also the falsely associated **martinet**, below.)

**Martello tower** (kind of circular fort built for coastal defence in Britain)
Many military structures are named after their designers, or the engineers who built them, such as the Bailey bridge and the Nissen hut. The Martello tower is not in this category, however, and its name is not even derived from a person. It comes as an altered form of the name of Cape Mortella, on Corsica, where the British captured a tower of this type in 1794. The alteration in spelling may have come about by association with Italian *martello*, 'hammer'. Most of the British Martello towers are in southeast England, where they were built in the early 1800s against a possible invasion from the French.

**martinet** (strict disciplinarian)
This is a good word for conjuring up all the wrong associations, such as '**marshal**' (which see, above), 'martial', 'martyr' or some specialized word such as 'martingale' (equestrianism) or 'martlet' (heraldry). So what is its actual source? The original sense of the word was 'military tyrant', and especially one like the infamous French drillmaster of the seventeenth century, General Jean Martinet. So the present word is the memorial to him, for what it is worth. Coincidentally, the French word *martinet*, apart from meaning 'martin' (the bird) means 'strap', 'tawse' (i.e. for chastising a child) as well as 'tilt-hammer'. But the latter two meanings seem to have derived, as does the bird name, from the forename *Martin*, and not from the punishing drillmaster. (In the case of the 'tilt-hammer', too, there was probably an influence from the standard French word for 'hammer', *marteau*.)

**marzipan** (kind of almond paste used for coating cakes)
The word was formerly spelt 'marchpane', and this doubtless produced the idea that the last part of the word represents 'bread', as either French *pain* or Latin *panis*. The modern French word *massepain*, meaning 'marzipan cake', seems to support this. But the true origin is almost certainly nothing to do with this, and the word may ultimately come from Arabic *mauthabān*, 'seated king', this being the name of a coin showing Christ seated, as struck by crusaders in the Holy

Land. The sense development from this unlikely source might thus be: 'coin', 'coin worth a certain weight or capacity', 'box of this weight or capacity', 'box containing confectionery', 'confectionery itself from this box'. This all seems farfetched, but it is more than possible. And at least it rules out the spurious 'bread'.

**mass** (celebration of the Eucharist in a Roman Catholic or Anglican church)
The mass (or 'Mass', as many Catholics prefer to spell it) does not take its name from the 'mass' of people in the congregation attending it, but from Late Latin *missa*, itself from the verb *mittere*, 'to send'. This is probably a reference to the words occurring near the end of the Latin mass, *Ite, missa est*, literally, 'Go, it is a dismissal' (corresponding to the Anglican Prayer Book 'Depart in peace'). The precise logic of naming an important service by its *ending*, however, and not its opening words, is not clear. It is rather like calling the 'Our Father' the 'World without end'.

**massacre** (mass murder)
There is no connection between this word and 'mass' or any related word (such as 'massive' or 'massed'). The origin is in Old French (same word), with however the ultimate derivation uncertain. Perhaps it goes back eventually to an Arabic word meaning 'shambles', 'slaughterhouse'.

**masterpiece** (outstanding work)
It seems strange that this word does not mean what it says, 'masterly piece', 'work executed by a master'. Yet this is really so, since originally the word was used in a technical or even academic sense to apply to a work that had been presented to a guild in the Middle Ages for qualification of the executor of the piece as 'master'. In other words, it was a kind of entitlement to a 'master of arts' (or more exactly 'crafts'). The term was probably borrowed into English from Dutch *meesterstuk* or German *Meisterstück*.

**mastiff** (breed of large, powerful dog)
This imposing name, suggesting simultaneously both 'massive' and 'master' (and even 'stiff'), is quite misleading, and in fact

means the virtual opposite of such fearsome words. It came into English from Old French, itself deriving from Latin *mansuetus*, which means 'tame' (literally 'hand-accustomed')! This is also the origin of the now rare English word 'mansuetude' meaning 'meekness', 'gentleness'. The implication is, of course, that the large, strong dog has been tamed by man.

**masturbate** (stimulate genital organs)
Classicists considering the origin of the word have sometimes derived it from Latin *manus*, 'hand' and a verb *stirpare* or *stuprare*, 'to defile'. There is no linguistic evidence to support this, however, and the ultimate source of Latin *masturbari* is actually unknown.

**matchboard** (kind of long, thin board)
Those who are not DIY experts may perhaps be forgiven for relating this word to 'matchwood'. But here the 'match' is a different one, meaning 'correspond', and refers to the fact that the groove along one edge of the board can take a 'matching' ridge along the other edge of a similar board. So all such boards will have a groove down one side and a ridge down the other, and can be fitted into one another to line walls, ceilings and the like, thus making a perfect multiple match with one another.

**matt** (not glossy, dull)
The word is also spelt 'mat', suggesting that a 'matt' surface is one that has had a 'mat' or layer of something coated over it to mask its glossiness or shininess. But the true origin is in French *mat*, which via Latin *mattus*, 'inebriated', 'dead drunk', goes back to the Arabic word that means 'dead' and that is the second half of '**checkmate**' (which see).

**mattress** (basis of a bed)
There is no link between this word and 'mat', despite the fact that 'mattress' ultimately derives from the Arabic *almatrah* meaning 'place where something is thrown down' – which almost *is* a mat. However, there is a fairly close correspondence of meaning between the two words as used by civil engineers, since both 'mat' and 'mattress' can mean 'concrete slab used as

a foundation'. But the origins of the words are still different, of course.

**Maundy Thursday** (Thursday before Easter, when maundy money is distributed)
The word 'Maundy' is often associated with 'day', and sometimes even mispronounced 'Maunday' (no doubt to rhyme conveniently with 'Thursday'). But the name does not indicate a 'mourning day' or indeed any sort of 'day' at all. It comes from Old French *mandé*, meaning 'something commanded', and represents the first word of the Latin text of Jesus' words in John 13:34: *Mandatum novum do vobis*, 'A new commandment I give unto you' (which was 'that ye love one another'). Jesus said this after he had washed the apostles' feet, and the modern name thus arose from the custom of princes, senior churchmen and other 'high' dignitaries doing likewise on this day, and washing the feet of the poor. (The tradition is occasionally observed in some parishes even today.) So Maundy Thursday is really, to use a more meaningful related word, 'Mandate Thursday'. The distribution of maundy money by the sovereign to specially selected pensioners is an extension of the 'loving one another' that was symbolized by the feet-washing.

**Maxim gun** (former type of automatic gun)
The gun was not so called because it fired the maximum number of rounds or achieved some other highest rate, but because (as the capital 'M' correctly indicates) it was invented by a man called Maxim. This was Sir Hiram Stevens Maxim, an American-born Englishman, who evolved the concept of a gun of this particular type in 1884.

**mead** (alcoholic drink made of honey and other natural ingredients)
The name of the drink, with its 'health food' ingredients of honey, malt, yeast and other good natural things, suggests that it might be related to 'meadow', which is also sometimes called 'mead', if only poetically. But the word for the drink goes back ultimately to Greek *methu*, 'wine', while 'meadow' and its poetic variant are related to the Old English verb 'to mow'. However, all is not

quite as disappointing as it looks, since the name of the plant 'meadowsweet' *is* related to the drink, and it was originally called 'meadsweet'. The flower was used in sweetening or flavouring mead, as also was meadwort.

**meal** (grain that has been ground to powder)
This kind of meal is not related to the common 'meal' meaning 'food taken at a regular time'. It is a word of Germanic origin, ultimately related to Latin *molere*, 'to grind' and thus to English 'mill'. The 'food-time' meal comes from an Old English word that meant 'measure', 'set time', and is related thus to German *Mahlzeit* which means 'mealtime' or just 'meal'. In this respect, see also **piecemeal**. For more wrong associations with the 'grain' meal, see the next entry.

**mealie** (in South Africa: maize)
This word is not connected with either 'meal' in the previous entry. It comes from Afrikaans *mielie*, itself deriving, through Portuguese, from Latin *milium*, 'millet'. See also **mealy-mouthed**, below.

**mealy-mouthed** ('soft-spoken', unwilling to speak the truth)
Which 'meal' or related word is involved here? Or perhaps there is some quite different origin? Many etymologists have thought so in the past, and have linked the 'mealy' with the basic *mel-* root that is seen in the Latin and Greek for 'honey', since a person who is mealy-mouthed is 'honey-tongued'. But the actual source is likely to be in 'meal', in the sense 'powdered grain', with perhaps an adaptation of some non-English saying, such as the German expression *Mehl im Maule behalten*, 'to carry meal in the mouth', i. e. to be indirect in what one says, to 'flannel'.

**meat** (in phrase 'meat and drink')
It is worth remembering that the original sense of 'meat' was 'food', and that only later did the word come to mean 'flesh'. 'Meat and drink', therefore, means 'food and drink', and the 'food' sense exists in other words such as 'sweetmeat' and 'mincemeat' (although what we now call

'mince' is 'minced meat' in the 'flesh' sense). A similar sense development occurred in French, so that the precursor of modern French *viande* meant just 'food', and was related to English 'victuals' and the rarer 'viands' meaning 'provisions'.

**membrane** (soft pliable sheet, especially as in the body)
The word is not connected with 'brain' although the brain does actually have membranes enveloping it (called the 'meninges', inflammation of which gives meningitis). 'Membrane' comes ultimately from Latin *membrum*, 'member', 'limb', itself related to 'meninges' as just mentioned, with the basic etymological concept being 'skin that covers the members or organs of the body'.

**menial** (servile, lowly)
A menial task can be a poor, dull or mean one, yet there is no common ground between 'menial' and 'mean'. 'Menial' derives from Old French *mesnie*, 'household' and so is related to English 'mansion' (but not to 'demesne' where the 's' was inserted in an alteration of 'domain'). 'Mean' is indirectly related to English 'common', and is of Germanic origin. See also **demeanour**.

**mercerize** (give a fabric a lustre and added strength)
It would be not at all surprising to find that this verb is based on 'mercer', since this is the word for a dealer in fine fabrics. But the word actually derives from the name of John Mercer, a nineteenth-century English dyer and maker of fabrics, who is said to have invented the process now called mercerizing or mercerization.

**metal** (road surface consisting of broken stones)
The covering known as 'road metal' and also 'metalling' is often thought to be a different word to the 'metal' that means 'iron' and the like. But both meanings have developed from the same word, which comes from Latin *metallum*, 'mine', 'what is got out of a mine', this being the common factor that unites the two materials. From 'metal', too, came the word now spelt 'mettle'. This version was used to refer to

the pluck or 'stuff' of a person, his stamina and staying power. So for once we have here not two apparently related words with quite different origins (as in the senses of '**meal**' above), but no less than *three* words of distinct meanings with actually one common derivation and origin!

**methinks** (it seems to me)
This archaic word is still sometimes used humorously (as in 'Methinks 'tis time for a wee drappie' – users of archaisms often confuse their non-standard English), and is probably regarded as a form of 'me thinks', in other words 'I think'. In fact the word has a meaning as given in the definition above, that is, in the obsolete impersonal sense of 'seem', 'appear'. The correct form of this formula in Middle English was *me thinketh*, with 'me' grammatically in the dative case and 'thinketh' with 'it' understood. Here is a genuine example of its use from a late fourteenth-century text, when it had virtually died out in this obsolete sense:

> With such gladnesse I daunce and skippe,
> Me thenkth I touche noght the flor.
> (John Gower, *Confessio Amantis*, 1390)

**microbe** (germ)
The word looks as if it is a shortening or derivative of some such word as 'microscopic', since it is very small. In which case, where does the 'b' come from? In fact it is an artificially devised word from Greek *mikros*, 'small' and *bios*, 'life'. The word came into English from French, in which language it was created in 1878 by the surgeon Charles Sédillot. It is not actually a very good word, since he meant it to mean 'small living thing', but *mikrobios* in Greek would mean 'short-lived'.

**midwife** (woman who assists at the birth of a child)
There have been several speculative accounts to explain this word, and in particular the baffling 'mid-'. Does this mean she is a sort of 'go-between', in the middle between child and mother? That is a popular explanation. Another is that the first half of the word derives from Middle English *mede*, 'reward', either as she is rewarded for her labour (and the mother's),

or because she delivers the mother's own 'reward' into her arms. However, attractive though these theories may be, neither is true, and the 'mid-' actually comes from Old English *mid*, 'with' (compare modern German *mit*). The midwife is thus a woman ('wife') who stays *with* the mother to assist her.

**mildew** (coating of fungi, as on rotting leather or diseased plants)
The word is not related to 'mould', 'mild' or 'milled'. It is, however, related to 'dew' and the first part of the word comes from an obsolete word for 'honey', related to Latin *mel*, French *miel*, English 'mellifluous' and so on. In other words, mildew is really 'honey dew'! This was its original meaning in Old English (as *meledēaw*). Later, from the resemblance of honey dew (the sugary substance deposited on plants by aphids) to mildew, the meaning changed. At the same time, the first half of the word was influenced by the word that is now 'meal' in the sense 'grain ground to powder' (see **meal** and **mealy-mouthed**, above), and this finally pushed the 'honey' sense into the background.

**millboard** (kind of strong cardboard)
There can be an inaccurate impression behind the word, as if it referred to board that was somehow connected with, or actually manufactured in, a mill. The present form of the word is in fact an alteration of 'milled board', this meaning cardboard that has been flattened by being rolled, as in a milling machine.

**milliner** (manufacturer or seller of women's hats)
But are hats made in a mill? Not in this case, since there is no connection with the word. A milliner was originally called a 'Milaner', since in the sixteenth century Milan in Italy was famous for its fancy finery. And that was where the milliner got his (or more often, her) hats from, typically the famous 'Milan bonnet'.

**millipede** ('insect' with lots of legs)
The millipede doesn't have 1000 legs any more than the **centipede** (which see) always has a hundred. 'Milli-' here simply

means 'many' (the creature in fact has up to two hundred pairs of legs). Perhaps it would be better to call it a 'multipede'. This, at any rate, is what the Russian name for it means (*mnogonozhka*).

**milt** (soft roe)
It looks as if there could be an alteration of 'milk' here. There isn't, but there is a confused connection all the same, since a now obsolete word for male fish roe was actually 'milk'. 'Soft roe' and 'hard roe' are really euphemisms, since what we are properly talking about are, respectively, the testes of male fish when they are filled with sperm, and the ovaries of female fish when they are filled with mature eggs. Remember that when you next have some for supper!

**miniature** (very small)
Such a clear association here with 'mini-' or 'minute'! Yet the true origin is nothing to do with this. The word, through Italian, goes back to Medieval Latin *miniatura*, which itself ultimately comes from Latin *minium*, 'red lead', 'minium'. This produced a verb *miniare*, 'to paint in a red colour', and was the word used for illuminating manuscripts. These, of course, had to be done on a very small scale – hence 'miniature'. For another misascribed 'mini-', see the next entry.

**minion** (servile worker or attendant, petty official)
Because the connotation of 'minion' is 'small and insignificant', a connection with 'mini-' might be imagined. But the word actually comes from French *mignon*, which means 'darling', 'delicately small person'. The sense alteration went roughly: 'lady-love', 'loved one', 'favourite', 'fawning servant', 'servile attendant'. For two more supposed 'mini-' words, see **miniature** (above) and **minnow** (below).

**minnow** (kind of small fish)
The minnow is not called a tiddler for nothing. But its name does not relate to the diminutive 'mini-' prefix, although it was almost certainly influenced by it. In Old English its name was recorded as *myne*,

although it cannot be substantiated that this was actually a minnow and not some other fish.

**misogynist** (woman hater)
The word is sometimes wrongly understood, as if the '-ogynist' meant 'hater' (even a 'miss-ogynist'?), just as the '-ophile' of words like 'Francophile' means the opposite, 'lover'. But the actual opposite of '-ophile' in words of Greek or pseudo-Greek origin like this is '-ophobe' (so, 'Francophobe'). (Greek -*phobos* means literally 'fearing', 'dreading', hence the English 'hating' sense.) What has happened in this word is that the thing hated (or loved, as the case may be) has come second, so that the 'mis-' means 'hatred', from Greek *misein*, 'to hate', and the other half is based on *gynē*, 'woman' (as in 'gynaecology'). The 'mis-' here, it will be noticed, is not the common prefix 'mis-' that begins many other words, such as 'mistrust', 'misunderstand', despite this element's unfavourable or negative sense. So what is the opposite of a 'misogynist'? The word would be 'philogynist'. But this is a rare word, or used only humorously, since the phenomenon itself is unremarkable. In his larger *Etymological Dictionary*, Ernest Weekley (see Bibliography) quotes a temperance orator who declared himself to be an 'uncompromising beerogynist'.

**mistletoe** (plant with thick leaves and small white berries)
Is the parasitic plant so called because its leaves (or some other feature) resemble the toes of a mistle-thrush? No, although the 'mistle-thrush' reference is correct, since this bird feeds on the berries of the plant. The apparent 'toe' is in fact an alteration of Old English *tān*, 'twig'.

**mob cap** (former type of women's large cotton cap)
The cap, popular in the eighteenth century, was not so called as it was worn by the 'mob', but because it was typically worn by a 'mob', this being a nickname (perhaps from the name 'Mab' or 'Mabel') of a slatternly woman or slut. The word 'mob', meaning 'crowd', derived as a seventeenth-century shortening of Latin *mobile vulgus*,

'excitable crowd'. (Perhaps see, in this respect, **madding**.)

**mohair** (fabric made from the long silky hair of the Angora goat)
This is a trick word, both displaying and meaning 'hair', and actually deriving from a word that meant 'hair', yet having no connection with the English word 'hair'! Earlier in English the word was *mocayere*, this ultimately coming, via Italian, from Arabic *mukhayyar*. This meant literally 'choice', 'select', but was used to describe and designate a cloth that was made of goats' hair. Hence the rather twisted strands of 'hair' that came to produce the modern word.

**mole** (dark-coloured spot on skin)
There is no connection here with the animal, despite the possible apparent link with 'moleskin'. This sort of mole comes from an Old English word that is related to Old High German *meil*, 'spot'. The medical term for a mole is 'naevus', which is related to Latin *natus*, 'born', since moles occur naturally, as birthmarks.

**mongoose** (small animal related to the civet cat that feeds on smaller animals)
Because of its name, this animal is on occasions thought to be some kind of bird. But although it may feed on birds, the creature is no goose. Its native name, of which this is the typical English corruption, was *mangūs*, from the language spoken in its home state of Maharashtra, in India.

**moquette** (thick velvety fabric used for carpets, etc)
The origin of this word is not in 'mock', although it is hard to say for sure what its ultimate source is. It came into English from French, where it may perhaps have been an alteration of some word like *mocade* that was itself a corruption of Italian *mocaiardo*, 'mohair' (which see, above).

**moratorium** (officially authorized postponement of some action)
The word has rather disagreeable connotations of 'mortal' (as if the action has been temporarily 'killed') and 'mortuary' and 'crematorium', as a sort of similar deathly

blend word. More cheerfully, it actually derives from a New Latin word that ultimately comes from Latin *morari*, 'to delay', with Late Latin, used for legal documents, developing as *moratorius*, 'dilatory'. When the term was first used in English in the nineteenth century, it meant 'legal authorisation to a debtor to delay payment'. For a word with similar associations, see the next entry.

**morgue** (mortuary)
This is a word with several funereal associations, including such words as 'mortuary', 'mortal', 'morbid' and the like. The title of Edgar Allan Poe's story, *The Murders in the Rue Morgue*, does not help much, either, although it does at least point to the true origin of the word as a French proper name. The street of the story has a name based on a building there called *le Morgue*. This was in effect a mortuary (to reinforce the false word association even more) where the bodies of people found dead were exposed for identification purposes. But we now need to know how the building got its name. It seems to derive from the original sense of French *morgue* which was 'haughtiness'. This was in the fifteenth century. The sense development then seems to have gone something like this: 'prison area where newly arrived prisoners were searched' (and where they expressed their disdain for the procedure), 'place where dead bodies were laid out for identification'. The original French word may derive from a conjectural Latin word *murrum*, 'nose', 'muzzle'. Admittedly the actual origin seems rather unlikely, but any derivation from the 'death' element *mort-* can be almost certainly ruled out.

**Mormon** (member of the Church of Jesus Christ of Latter-Day Saints)
How did the Mormons get their name? It sounds vaguely moral or biblical, suggesting perhaps 'mortal' or even '**Mammon**' (which see, above). The resemblance to 'moron', too, cannot go unnoticed. It actually derives from the name of their sacred text, the 'Book of Mormon', with Mormon the name of the book's alleged fourth-century editor. The 'Book of Mormon' was claimed to have been discovered by the nineteenth-century founder of the sect, the American Joseph

Smith, and he apparently explained the name as being a combination of English 'more' and Egyptian *mon*, 'good'! Mormons originally called themselves 'Mormonites'.

**morris dance** (traditional English folk dance)
The name of the dance suggests the personal name 'Morris' or a link with some other traditional pastime such as 'nine men's morris'. The true origin is that the apparently native English dance is historically a 'Moorish dance', that is, was imported to England from Spain or some other country where in turn it was a dance (perhaps a military one) performed by the Moors. But the whole background to the development of the dance is rather confused, and its precise manner of reaching England still not very clear. The derivation in 'Moorish', however, is certain enough. (Nine men's morris, however, is of quite a different origin, deriving from a French word of uncertain meaning.)

**mosaic** (artistically arranged pattern of pieces of glass, stone, etc)
The word (with a capital 'M') also happens to mean 'relating to Moses', and for this reason some etymologists have attempted to derive modern 'mosaic' from the Bible, and in particular from the passage in Exodus 28 where Moses orders the breastplate of the high priest to be divided (symbolically) into twelve squares, each of a different colour. But the word actually derives from a classical and artistic source, and can be traced back through French and Italian to Latin and Greek, and ultimately to Latin *Musa*, 'muse'. A mosaic is thus artistically inspired, and influenced by the Muses.

**Mosquito Coast** (region along the coast of eastern Nicaragua)
The Ivory Coast is so named for its ivory, the former Gold Coast (now Ghana) for its gold, the historic Slave Coast of West Africa for its slaves, so obviously there is no need to question the origin of the Mosquito Coast. But there is! The name does not relate to mosquitoes at all, however apt this might be to apply to this hot and rainy part of Central America. Instead, it relates to the Indian Miskito tribe who lived here, and

who are now still here in reservation. Their name was popularly corrupted to the more meaningful 'Mosquito' (and also 'Mostique').

**motley** (multicoloured, composed of different elements)
Early philologists derived this word from 'medley'. It is now fairly certain, however, that the real origin is in Middle English *mot*, 'mote', 'speck'. The reference is to the 'speckled' connotation of 'motley'. 'Medley' comes from Middle French *medler*, 'to mix', from which also came English 'meddle'.

**moulder** (crumble into dust or decay)
Research into early uses of the word show that it was certainly influenced by 'mould' in the sense 'fungal growth', but that its actual source is the other sort of 'mould' meaning 'crumbling soft soil'.

**mouldwarp, mouldywarp** (mole)
This archaic or dialect name for a mole does not derive from 'mole' itself. In Middle English it was spelt *moldewarpe*, and the origin is ultimately in a Germanic word (not actually traced) something like *moldewarpon*, meaning literally 'earth thrower'. The 'mould' of the name is the same as the modern English word that means 'crumbling soft soil' (see last entry).

**mound** (hill, raised heap)
There is no connection between 'mound' and 'mount', despite the similarity of spelling and meaning. The precise origin of 'mound' is uncertain. The word's initial sense was 'earthwork', in the sixteenth century, and a link with Old English *mund*, 'hand', 'guardianship' has been suggested, implying a protective or defensive position. 'Mount', on the other hand, clearly derives from the basic word seen in Latin *mons*, *montis*, French *mont* and English 'mountain'.

**mugwump** (politically independent person)
The strange word, more familiar to an American than a Briton, suggests someone who is somehow a 'mug', and this association has been reinforced by the classic humorous definition of such a person as 'an animal that sits on the fence, with its mug on one side and its wump on the other'. But the word is actually a native Indian one, meaning 'captain', 'great chief', implying a person who stands aloof from politics. Even so, and despite knowing this, one is strongly tempted to conjure up some sort of picture of a disdainful 'fence-sitter' with a smug mug!

**mulled** (of wine, beer etc: heated, sweetened, and flavoured with spices)
This word is not related to the 'mull' of 'mull it over', as if in an alcoholic haze, nor is it a form of 'mould', as has been ingeniously explained, referring to the ale served at funerals, when the body was buried in the 'mould' or earth. The actual derivation of the word is still unknown, and it does not appear to be related to any of the other English 'mulls'.

**mulligatawny** (kind of rich meat soup)
The soup is not so called because it is tawny-coloured, nor does the name derive from the American 'mulligan' that is a kind of mixed stew. The soup is of Indian origin, and so is its name, therefore, which in Tamil means literally 'pepper water'. This refers to the 'hot' nature of the soup, which is highly seasoned (usually with curry).

**mummer** (kind of masked actor, mime artist)
Although a mummer mimes, the two words are of different origins. 'Mummer' derives from Old French *momer*, 'to go masked', 'to mime', while 'mime' goes back ultimately to Latin *mimus* and Greek *mimos*, 'imitator'. In the expression 'mum's the word', however, the first word is probably imitative, and does not relate to 'mummer'.

**Muscovy duck** (kind of large duck native to South America)
The name of this duck is an alteration of 'musk duck', which in turn alludes to its slightly musky odour. So it has no connection with Moscow at all. At least, however, it is a duck, which is more than a **Bombay duck** is (see this name).

**muse** (be absorbed in thought, ponder)
The classical Muses inspired people to produce great thoughts and artistic achieve-

ments. They are not behind this word, however, which goes back to Middle French *muse*, 'animal's mouth', 'muzzle'. The reference is probably to an animal projecting or raising its muzzle, such as a pointer when it 'points' (scents game and stands with taut, rigid body), or a stag when it scents a possible pursuer and lifts its muzzle. The imagery is not as lofty as being inspired by a Muse, but it is quite picturesque, all the same.

**muslin** (kind of cotton fabric)
The derivation of fabric names from proper names has already been mentioned (often from places, as quoted with reference to **diaper**). For this particular fabric, an association has sometimes been made between 'muslin' and 'Muslim', since Muslim dress is traditionally made of it, or a light fabric resembling it. But for once here the origin actually is in a place name, in this case Mosul, in Iraq, where muslin was first produced. The word came into English from Arabic, via first Italian (*mussolina*), then French (*mousseline*). (This last word is also used in English for the name of a fabric that resembles muslin.)

**mustard** (seasoning made from seeds of common mustard plant)
No doubt this word will not raise too many false associations. For some philologists of the past it did, however, and there was a high-flown tale about how mustard originally came from Dijon, in Southern France,

since this town was famous for its mustard and had a city motto which was *Moult me tarde*. The word 'mustard' was said to derive from this motto, itself alleged to be a corruption of Latin *multum ardeo*, 'I desire much' (a maxim that could equally well have applied to the classical scholar who concocted this particular etymology). The true source of the word is in Old French *moustarde* or *mostarde*, itself coming from Latin *mustum*, 'must', referring to the fermenting grape juice ('must') that was added to the seasoning in its original form.

**mystery** (something unclear or not understood)
Words such as 'mystery', 'mystify', 'mysterious' and so on can sound as if they are connected with 'misty', since mist can obscure clarity, and a 'mysterious island', for example, may be so because it is shrouded in mist. But the two words are actually quite distinct in origin, with all the 'mystery' words ultimately deriving from a Greek word *mystos*, 'remaining silent', and 'mist' being an Old English word. Perhaps the two were confused more in the past, when spelling was more fluid, and when 'mystify', for example, was often spelt 'mistify', and when even 'mystify' could mean 'covered in mist', as in these lines from Byron's *Don Juan:*

When gazing on them, mystified by distance,
We enter on our nautical existence.

**namby-pamby** (weak and sentimental, 'sloppy')

The phrase looks like a fairly random jingle suggesting undue sentimentality, as well as hinting at such 'effeminate' adjectives as 'pansy', 'niminy-piminy' and the like, or even some child's toy or puppet called 'Andy Pandy'. This last brings us closer to the truth, since the phrase was based on the name of the eighteenth-century poet Ambrose Philips. His odes addressed to young lords and ladies, often when they were mere babes in arms, prompted the derision of much 'loftier' poets such as Pope and his associates, and it was one of the latter, Henry Carey, who devised the nickname, incorporating it in a mocking verse that ran:

> Namby-Pamby is your guide,
> Albion's joy, Hibernia's pride,
> Namby-Pamby Pilly-pis,
> Rhimy-pim'd on missy-mis.

This seems to be rather overdoing it, but when some of Ambrose Philips' actual odes are seen, one feels that Carey had some justification. Here, for example, is what he wrote for the baby daughter of the M. P. Daniel Pulteney, under the title 'To Mistress Charlotte Pulteney':

> Timely blossom, infant fair,
> Fondling of a happy pair,
> Every morn, and every night,
> Their solicitous delight,
> Sleeping, waking, still at ease,
> Pleasing without skill to please.
> Little gossip, blithe and hale,
> Tattling many a broken tale.

There were poems even more twee than this, including one that began, 'Dimply damsel, sweetly smiling'. Whatever one's views on such craft ('yummy' or 'yucky', according to taste), that is the true origin of 'namby pamby', and it was this nickname that in turn produced the closely related 'niminy-piminy'.

**nautch-girl** (dancing girl)

Owing to such false associations as 'naughty', 'raunchy' and even 'nautical' in some undesirable sense (perhaps connected with visiting sailors), this word has coloured the actual meaning, or rather, discoloured it. A nautch-girl is a professional Indian dancing girl who performs the intricate traditional dance known in Hindi as the *nāc*, with this word ultimately deriving from a Sanskrit word meaning simply 'dancing'. A similar slur, although without such English word associations, has come to apply to the geisha girl in Japan, where she is a professional entertainer and conversational companion (with arguably greater intimacy than the Indian dancer).

**navvy** (unskilled labourer)

Not surprisingly, this word has frequently been associated with 'navy'. This is only half the truth, however, and the word originated as an abbreviation of 'navigator', with its eighteenth-century sense of someone who builds a 'navigation or artificial waterway'. (This older word is preserved in the names of pubs that today are still called 'Navigation Inn' and that stand near a canal, even a disused one.) Of course, both 'navigator' and 'navy' ultimately derive from Latin *navis*, 'ship', and to that extent the association can be justified. 'Navy' is not the direct origin of 'navvy', however.

**navy blue** (dark blue)

The shade so called does not refer to the 'deep blue' of the sea, but to the traditional colour of naval uniform (as romantically worn by 'the sailor with the navy blue eyes'). Compare **ultramarine**.

**neat's-foot oil** (kind of oil made from the bones of cattle and used to dress leather)
The oil is made properly by boiling the feet of cattle, and the 'neat' does not refer to the property of the oil but derives from Old English *nēat*, 'cattle'.

**net, nett** (not gross; free of additional charges or deductions)
This word, commonly used with prices, payments, wages, salaries and so on, is nothing to do with 'net' in its basic sense or even in its meaning of 'make a profit' ('I managed to net two hundred quid last week'). It is in fact an alteration of 'neat', deriving from French *net*, with this in the sense seen in 'neat spirits', i. e. with nothing added or subtracted.

**news** (recent information)
The hoary old story about news being so called because it comes from all quarters of the world (N, E, W, S) is still told by some rather unoriginal jokers or leg-pulling uncles (who may once have half believed it). Of course the word, which originally meant 'novelties', derives directly from the Old English equivalent for 'new' which itself can be traced back to Latin *novus* and Greek *neos* and which has near-equivalents in many European languages, such as French *nouveau* and *neuf*, German *neu*, Italian *nuovo*, Swedish, Danish and Norwegian *ny*, Russian *novyy* and so on and so forth. (It is also worth noting that the French word for news, *les nouvelles*, is exactly equivalent to the English, i. e. a plural of the word for 'new'.)

**nickname** (extra name given to a person, often a descriptive one)
Here is one popular explanation of the name: it derives from the verb 'nick' meaning 'catch', since a nickname is an apt one, and 'hits home'. Here is another more abstruse: it derives from French *nique*, since *faire la nique* means 'make fun of', 'cock a snook at', and that is what a nickname does. Here now is the true origin: the word was originally not 'a nickname' but 'an ekename', where 'eke' means 'extra', 'something added' (like its modern German equivalent *auch*, 'also'). The word was thus wrongly divided when 'an' before a vowel

was taken to be 'a'. (This also happened with other words, so that 'a newt' was originally 'an ewt'; it happened the other way round, too, so that 'an apron' was really 'a napron' – hence related words such as 'napkin' and 'nappy'.) The word 'eke' is still occasionally encountered in poetry today, perhaps one of the best known examples being the opening lines of Cowper's *John Gilpin:*

John Gilpin was a citizen
Of credit and renown,
A train-band captain eke was he
Of famous London town.

**nicotine** (poisonous chemical compound found in tobacco)
The word is not related to 'narcotic', despite the disturbing effect that both have on the normal functions of the body, but derives from the name of Jacques Nicot, the French ambassador at Lisbon in the sixteenth century, who introduced tobacco to France.

**Nigeria** (African country)
The name of the country in no way relates to 'nigger' or 'negro', or to Latin *niger*, 'black', but comes from its chief river, the Niger, whose native name is *gher n-ghrea*, 'river among rivers'.

**nightingale** (bird famous for its song)
The bird is not so called since it sings 'at night in a gale' (which it would be unlikely to do anyway, although a storm **petrel** might – see this word). Its name literally means 'night singer', with the latter half of the name representing Old English *galan*, 'to sing' (related to modern English 'yell').

**nightmare** (bad dream)
The latter half of this word is not related to 'mare', as if the dreamer were being taken on a mad and frightening ride on a runaway mare, but derives from the obsolete *mare* meaning 'evil spirit'. The same basic word lies behind the French word for 'nightmare', *cauchemar* (where the first half represents *caucher*, 'to press'). For a related concept, see **succubus**.

**nightshade** (kind of poisonous plant, typically the 'deadly nightshade')
The sinister-sounding 'shade' does not

relate to the damp, shady woods where the plant is often found but to its narcotic (more precisely, soporific) qualities: it will make you become unconscious, or 'black out'. (The 'night-' probably refers to its black berries and perhaps its frequency in dark places, as mentioned.)

**nincompoop** (idiot)
The precise origin of this word is unknown, but it is almost certainly not a corruption of Latin *non compos mentis*, 'not of sound mind', as has been proposed by some writers. It may be based on the name Nicholas or Nicodemus, with an addition of the now obsolete word 'poop', meaning 'cheat', and the first part of the word altered by association with '**ninny**' (see next entry).

**ninny** (idiot)
It is hardly likely that this is a corruption of Spanish *niño*, 'child', as has been sometimes suggested. More probably, it could simply be an abbreviation of 'an innocent', with perhaps half a hint at the personal name Innocent.

**nipper** (small boy)
This colloquial word does not refer to the way in which a small boy can 'nip about' or be 'nippy', but derives from the slang 'nip' meaning 'steal' (with its modern equivalent 'nab'). In the sixteenth century, pickpockets and cutpurses were usually small boys. Later, the word came to be used of a costermonger or street hawker's boy assistant. From this, the word came to mean simply 'boy'.

**nob** (rich or important person, 'toff')
The colloquial word is sometimes said to be a shortening of 'nobleman'. Very likely, however, it is simply a usage of 'nob' in the sense 'head' (i.e. a sort of 'bighead'). People whose surname is Clark are sometimes nicknamed 'Nobby' since clerks were 'superior' in some way – either because they wore top hats (called 'nobby hats') or because their level of literacy was higher than that of many of their associates.

**nog** (eggnog)
No link has been proved between this word and 'noggin', meaning 'small measure of spirits'. Both have been recorded from the seventeenth century, but the precise derivation of neither is known.

**noisome** (offensive, repellent)
This word is nothing to do with 'noise', even though that, too, can be offensive and repellent. In Middle English it was spelt *noysome*, and this derived from *noy*, 'annoying'. So that is the origin of the word, which is now used mainly of unpleasant smells, and not at all (except wrongly) of unpleasant sounds.

**nondescript** (insignificant, of no interest)
The rather unusual word looks as if it implies that the noun it accompanies is not easy to describe, or not worth describing. It originated in the seventeenth century as a natural history term to mean 'not hitherto described', that is, to apply to a creature that had not yet been officially classified. For example, a text of 1772 talks of a 'fine non-descript owl' and one of 1812 notes that a particular botanist has discovered 'nearly one hundred and fifty non-descript plants'. The word itself arose as a negative or opposite (with 'non-') of a plant or animal that was 'descript', that is, classified as belonging to a particular species, with 'descript' coming from Latin *descriptus*, 'described'.

**noon** (midday)
One ingenious theory derives this word as a variation on 'none', that is zero, since when the clock says twelve o'clock it has to start off counting the hours again from 0 (i.e., when the clock has struck twelve there are no more hours left to count – at the end of the next hour it will strike one). But despite the mathematical or logical attractions of this, the true origin of 'noon' is in Latin *nona hora*, 'ninth hour'. This is not as crazy as it looks, since 'noon' was the name given to the ninth hour after sunrise, in other words what is now three o'clock. The sense altered to 'twelve o'clock' when this time became associated with a regular daily event, probably either the church office of nones or, more simply, a mealtime. (Nones was, or still is, one of the seven so called 'canonical hours' reckoned from 6 a. m. when Divine Office was appointed to be

said in the Roman Catholic church, with matins very early, prime ('first hour') at 6, tierce ('third') at 9, sext ('sixth') at 12 midday and, apart from nones, vespers in the evening and compline ('complete') as the final office at about 8 or 9 p. m. Later, many of these times were altered, but the actual names of the offices were retained.)

**nosegay** (posy, small bunch of flowers)
The word looks as if it indicates something 'gay for the nose to smell'. This is not quite the origin, however, since 'gay' here is used in its obsolete sense of 'ornament', 'toy', as in these lines from a late sixteenth-century poem by Nicholas Breton:

Though (perhaps) most commonly
    each youth
Is giuen in deede, to follow euery gaye.

**nubile** (marriageable)
The descriptive word, often used humorously or semi-lasciviously of an attractive girl, may suggest 'Nubian', with visions of Nubian slaves or some similar 'haremic' scene. But the correct association should be 'nuptial', since the word ultimately derives from Latin *nubere*, 'to marry'. So 'marriageable', as stated above, is the true sense.

However, as perhaps some Englishmen or Americans who have Italian girl friends may have discovered, if an Italian girl is unmarried, her passport, under the equivalent heading 'marital status', will have the word (Italian, of course) *nubile*. This means not so much that she seeks marriage, but that she is at present 'single' and so potentially available for marriage. Whether she is 'nubile' in the English sense or not will largely lie in the eye of the beholder, like beauty itself.

**nuthatch** (kind of small tree-climbing bird)
This name does not mean that the bird hatches out among nuts, but that it cracks or 'hacks' nuts to eat, i. e. it is essentially a 'nutcracker'. The 'hatch' is related to both English '**hatchet**' (which see) and French *hache*, 'axe'.

**nuzzle** (push with the nose; lie close to)
The word is directly related to 'nose', but in its various senses has come to be influenced by 'nurse' and 'nestle', although not linguistically linked to either of these. Originally 'nuzzle up' meant 'rear', 'train', 'bring up'.

**oakum** (loosely twisted strands of rope used for caulking seams in wooden ships)
There is no connection with 'oak', here, in spite of the association of wood and doubtless 'Heart of oak'. The word comes from Old English *ācumba*, literally 'off-combings'.

**obscene** (arousing disgust)
In its time, the word has been fancifully derived from Latin *ob scena*, 'against the stage', that is, 'bad theatre'. But the true origin is much more straight-forward, coming from Latin *obscenus*, 'ill-omened', 'indecent'. The ultimate source of this is still uncertain, but it is not likely to be as first stated here.

**oh dear!** (exclamation of annoyance or sympathy)
It is highly unlikely that, as sometimes stated, the expression derives from Italian *O Dio mio*, 'O my God'. It is probably short for 'O dear God' or 'O dear Lord'. Admittedly, the variations 'Dear, dear!' and 'Dear me!' seem harder to justify as English in origin, but there is no evidence to support any theory that they are not.

**O.K.** (all correct, everything's all right)
There have been a number of complex explanations to account for the origin of this common abbreviation, one of the favourites being that it originated in the initials of the 'O.K. Club' which was founded in America in 1840 by Democratic supporters of the presidential candidate, Martin Van Buren, who was born at Old *K*inderhook, New York. However, the *Supplement* to the *Oxford English Dictionary*, quoting articles published in the language journal *American Speech*, notes that 'O.K.' was understood as '*orl korrect*' (the common explanation) in 1839 and has five instances of it in this year, in three of which it is actually spelt out (as 'all correct'). There seems no reason to doubt,

therefore, that after all 'orl korrect' really is the origin. Doubt still remains, however, as to why precisely this misspelt version of 'all correct' was adopted for the abbreviation, and not the initials of 'all correct' itself. Perhaps it was due to the current vogue for humorous phonetic spellings in American literature of the day.

**Orangemen** (members of Irish loyalist society)
It is true that when Orangemen go on parade they wear orange sashes, but this is not the origin of the name. They are so called since historically the first such loyalists were dedicated followers of William III of England, otherwise known as Prince of Orange ('William of Orange'), who finally deposed the Roman Catholic king James II in 1690 at the Battle of the Boyne. The Orangemen as we know them today did not exist then, although several so called 'Orange Lodges' or clubs of militant Protestants sprang up, and from one of these, the Orange Lodge of Freemasons, in Belfast, the present Order of Orangemen was founded in 1795. William's own title came from the French town of Orange, near Avignon, since this town has previously passed to the House of Nassau from which the king came. (Needless to say, some hopeful etymologists have tried to link the ordinary orange with this town, saying that the fruit is so called since it was imported to France through it from North Africa!)

**orison** (prayer)
This archaic or poetic word has long been specifically understood to mean 'morning prayer', as if by association with 'orient', 'Orion' or some other word suggesting the east where the sun rises (perhaps even 'horizon' had an influence). Similarly, it seems to have been somehow taken to be the opposite of a 'benison', which was

thought of as an evening blessing or prayer (presumably on departing or going to bed). For example, in *Paradise Lost*, Milton says that, 'the sun scarce uprisen', our first parents began

Their orisons, each morning duly paid,

and in *Rokeby*, Walter Scott says the summer sun was wont in Matilda's bower to

Rouse her with his matin ray
Her duteous orisons to pay.

But there is nothing in the origin of the word to imply 'morning' or 'sunrise', since it derives from Late Latin *oratio*, 'speech', 'oration'. No doubt the tradition of saying prayers at the start of day and at its close also prompted the 'polarization' of the two words into 'orison' for the morning and 'benison' for the evening.

**orrery** (mechanical model of the solar system)
Since many people have vaguely heard of an orrery, and may even know that it was something mechanical, there is a temptation to link the word with something apparently similar or related, such as 'horology', or 'orbit', or even 'horary' ('relating to the hours'). Possibly, too, some of the false associations mentioned for **orison** in the previous entry may suggest themselves. But the true source is in the name, or rather the title, of Charles Boyce, 4th Earl of Orrery, who had such a device made for him in about 1700. Orrery is in Ireland, in Co. Cork.

**osprey** (large kind of hawk that dives into the water to catch fish)
Is the bird so called from its method of seizing its *prey*? Is it even because of the *spray* it makes as it dives? Or does the name somehow link up with the feather 'spray' or trimming for hats that was also called an 'osprey'? The answer, as no doubt you will have guessed, is none of these. The name has been traced back to Latin *ossifraga*, literally 'bone breaker'. This, however, was not the name of the osprey but of the sea eagle, itself a rather vague name for an eagle that dives for fish. Whatever the exact identification, the Latin name, anglicized as 'ossi-

frage', either refers to the bird's ability to break the bones of the fish it catches, or may even be a folk etymology of some other name. But at least the osprey is not named for 'prey' or 'spray'.

**ostler** (stableman at an inn)
This historic or at any rate Dickensian word seems to suggest that the man is so called since he looks after the 'osses! But this, of course, is just a pleasantry, and a closer look at the word and its meaning should bring the right connection with 'hostler', that is 'innkeeper', with this related to 'hostel' and 'hotel' (which are really one and the same word). The 'hostler' lost its initial 'h' since this was not pronounced, just as there are still some people who don't pronounce the 'h' in 'hotel' today (and who call it 'an hotel').

**outcaste** (Hindu who has been ejected from his or her social class)
This word should not be confused with 'outcast', even though it in a sense denotes one. As the final 'e' shows, it applies to someone who has been thrown out of a **caste** (see this word).

**outrage** (great sense of anger or injury)
Unexpectedly, there is no connection here with 'rage', although the sense has certainly been influenced by both 'out' and 'rage'. An outrage in its basic meaning is an act of violence, and the word comes from French *outre*, 'beyond', implying something that is excessive, or has 'gone too far'. The same French word lies more obviously behind 'outré', meaning 'violating convention', 'beyond what is normal'. See also **utterance**.

**outrigger** (projecting framework etc on a boat or aircraft)
This nautical word has certainly been influenced by and even based on 'out' and 'rigged', but there is good evidence that originally it was something like an 'outligger', that is, an 'outlier'. This can be seen in other languages, where the word for 'outrigger' is so based, such as Dutch *uitlegger*, German *Ausleger* and even Russian (based on the Dutch) *utlegar*.

**overweening** (presumptuous, arrogant)
There is no connection here with 'wean', as if implying an excessive degree of nourishment ('like the cat that got the cream'). The word is based on the old verb 'to ween', meaning 'to be of the opinion,', 'to imagine'. The implication is thus that more than is reasonable is expected.

**oyez** (cry of a town crier)
The word is pronounced either 'o-yes' or 'o-yea', which may suggest that it actually means 'Oh yes!' or 'Oh yea!'. The origin of the strange cry is in Old French *oiez!*, 'hear', itself derived from Latin *audire*, 'to hear'. English 'yes', however, is of quite a different origin, from Old English *gese*.

**pack** (influence composition of)
When this word is used in such phrases as 'pack a jury' or 'pack a meeting', meaning that the particular body or assembly is filled with one's own supporters so as to achieve some desired vote, the origin is not in the common 'pack' that means simply 'fill'. Instead, the verb is a now obsolete form of 'pack' that means 'make a secret agreement' and that is probably an alteration of 'pact'. The verb is mostly used in a specifically legal or political context. Macaulay uses it in this special sense in his *History of England* published in 1849: 'Having determined to pack a parliament, James set himself energetically and methodically to the work'.

**paddock** (small field where horses are kept)
The word 'pad' can be used of a horse, particularly one that moves along gently and easily, but 'paddock' is not based on this, nor does it have any sense of 'dock', as if the word meant a 'horse enclosure', or 'pad dock'. However, Old English *pearroc* did actually mean 'enclosure', and that is the origin of 'paddock' (and also in fact of 'park').

**paddy field** (wet field where rice is sown)
The name certainly suggests a field where rice planters have to 'pad' or 'paddle'. But the actual origin, as can be appreciated, is not in an English word at all but in Malay *pādī*, which is simply the word for rice in the straw or husk. Rice is grown widely in Far Eastern countries, of course.

**page boy** (boy messenger in hotel etc)
The page boy is not so called because he carries or delivers pages of messages, as a paper boy delivers papers, or because when he 'pages' someone he finds their name or number on a page. Nor is there any historic connection with 'pageant', in which page boys appeared as royal attendants. In short, there is no connection with the ordinary 'page' of a book. The word came into English, via Old French, from Italian *paggio*, in turn probably (although not certainly) from Greek *paidion*, 'boy', itself a diminutive of *pais*, *paidos*, 'child' (as in modern English 'pediatrics' and 'orthopaedics', both of which relate to the medical or surgical treatment of children).

**Palestine soup** (cream soup made of Jerusalem artichokes)
This soup did not originate in Palestine, and its name arose as a pun (what *Chambers* calls a 'quibble') on '**Jerusalem artichoke**' (which see), similarly not from Jerusalem. The name seems to have arisen only in the nineteenth century, and the earliest reference to it in the *Supplement* to the *Oxford English Dictionary* is dated 1834. This was early enough, however, for it to be included in Mrs Beeton's famous cookery book of 1861, where she recommends it as a good first course for a 'Dinner for 6 persons'. Compare **Bombay duck**.

**palliasse** (type of straw mattress)
This word is sometimes regarded suspiciously as a possible joke name, no doubt with a pun on 'pally ass' and the 'donkey's breakfast' that was nautical slang for a straw mattress. The true origin is in French *paillasse*, which itself derives from *paille*, 'straw'.

**palmyra** (kind of tall tropical palm found in Asia)
The name of this tree has no connection with the ancient Syrian city of Palmyra, but comes, obviously enough, from the basic word that gave English 'palm' (in this case, Portuguese *palmeira*).

**pamphlet** (small publication, booklet)
This common but interesting word has baffled many etymologists in the past. Does its final '-let' indicate a diminutive of some kind, as for 'booklet'? Perhaps it is a blend of French *paume,* 'palm of the hand' and *feuille,* 'leaf'? Could it be from Spanish *papeleta,* 'slip', 'card'? Or how about Latin *pagina filata,* 'threaded page'? Or even French *par un filet,* 'by a thread' (referring to its stitching)? Can we consider a link with 'papyrus'? The great Professor Skeat does not consider any of these (quite rightly, as they are all speculative or fanciful), and goes instead for the name of an early author Pamphilus. This is almost it, but the actual origin is not in the name of a writer but in that of a literary work. This was a twelfth-century love poem called in Latin *Pamphilus, seu de Amore* ('Pamphilus, or On Love'), with the name of the central character deriving from Greek to mean 'all-loving' (i.e. 'loving all'). The popular work was a satire on the machinations of an old procuress, and was thus the archetypal pamphlet.

**panama hat** (type of lightweight straw hat worn by men)
The panama hat was not so called since it originated in Panama, although it was exported or distributed from there. It in fact came from Ecuador, where it was made from the palmlike plant called the 'jipijapa' (which word is also sometimes used to mean a panama hat, especially in Latin America). The name of the actual tree (which should be pronounced something like 'heepee-harper') derives from that of the town of Jipijapa in Ecuador. For another product named after the place where it was not made, see **Stilton**.

**panel** (group of doctors etc)
Some doctors' surgeries are in old houses where the walls and doors have wooden panelling. This association may arise for a 'panel' of doctors, but it is not the source of this sense of the word. The original meaning of 'panel' was 'piece of cloth'. This then came to be a piece of material or parchment on which names of jurors were written. Later came a modern sense to mean first 'jury schedule', then 'list of doctors' with the latter meaning first developing just before the First World War. (The 'door' sense of panel is fairly late, and is first recorded only in the seventeenth century, whereas 'panel' itself goes back to the thirteenth century, when it came into English from Old French.)

**pansy** (garden plant related to the violet)
The name of this well known flower has been derived in the past from 'Pan's eye', with reference to its heart-shaped 'eye', as well as from 'panacea', since the plant was regarded as a 'cure for all diseases and sorrows'. But it actually came into English from Old French (and modern) *pensée,* 'thought', since the flower was regarded as a token of personal concern, and a memento of the giver. This tradition is referred to in poor, deranged Ophelia's words in *Hamlet,* when she says: 'There's rosemary, that's for remembrance; pray, love, remember: and there is pansies, that's for thoughts'. (See **rosemary** for more on this.) The debased and derogatory sense of the word to mean 'effeminate man', 'homosexual', first developed only as recently as the 1920s.

**pantry** (room for storing food, larder)
The pantry is not so called since it is or was used for storing pots and pans, but because it was originally a bread store (Old French *paneterie*). However, a larder is so called since it originally stored 'lard', i. e. in the French sense of bacon and pork. Compare **buttery**.

**papier-mâché** (kind of modelling material made from pulped waste paper)
The name sounds as if it means 'mashed paper', which is a fairly good basic description of it. But the French words mean, rather unappetizingly, 'chewed paper' (French *mâcher* is related to English 'masticate'). However, this is not genuine French – the French themselves call it *carton pâte –* and the term was probably invented by an Englishman as a sort of 'trade' name in the belief that it actually *did* mean 'mashed paper'. It is first recorded in the eighteenth century, and various other types of artistic 'papiers' have arisen since, also with French names, such as 'papier collé', 'papier déchiré' and 'papier poudré'.

**parasol** (type of umbrella to protect a person from the sun)
This word is sometimes wrongly interpreted, even in 'origin books', as meaning 'beyond the sun', from the Greek, as if a person under a parasol will be beyond the sun's reach, or out of the sun. But this is incorrect, since there are two popular 'para-' prefixes, and this is the wrong one. In some words, 'para-' literally means 'beyond', as in 'paranormal' and 'paradox' (literally 'beyond opinion'). This 'para-' is Greek. The other one comes from Italian (through French), where it represents the verb *parare*, 'to ward off', itself from Latin *parare*, 'to prepare'. This 'warding off' 'para-' is the one in 'parasol', and also in 'parachute' (warding off a fall) and the French word for 'umbrella', *parapluie* (warding off the rain).

**parboil** (boil until partially cooked)
The meaning of the verb has been influenced by 'part', but this is not in its origin which is in Old French *parboillir*, 'to boil thoroughly' (with the *par-* representing Latin *per-*, 'through'). The Old French meaning was originally that of the English, which then altered as in the definition above.

**parchment** (animal skin dried and prepared for writing)
There is no connection with English 'parch' in this word, which comes from Old French *parchemin*. This ultimately derives from Greek *Pergamenos*, 'of Pergamum', the ancient city of Asia Minor (now Bergama, Turkey) where parchment was first adopted in the second century B.C. In its gradual development from Greek to French, the word was probably influenced by Latin *Parthica pellis*, the name of a special scarlet-dyed leather (literally 'Parthian leather') and by Old French *parche*, 'leather', itself coming from the Latin phrase.

**parsimony** (thriftiness; meanness)
This word is in no way connected with 'parson' or 'money', from subconscious associations, perhaps, with church collections, but derives from Latin *parsimonia*, itself based on the verb *parcere*, 'to spare'. The English sense was originally 'thrift',

although today the word is mostly used in its sense of 'stinginess'.

**partner** (one who shares; associate)
A partner is not so called since he or she takes 'part' in something with another although the spelling and meaning have been influenced by 'part'. The original form of the word was *parcener*, which meant 'a person who takes an equal share with another', or legally a 'joint heir'. This itself came from Old French *parçonier*, derived from *parçon*, 'distribution', ultimately from Latin *partire*, 'to divide'. The former English word, as well as 'coparcener', is still in strictly legal use today.

**partridge** (kind of game bird)
A folk etymology for the name of this bird has explained it as being so called because as it rises into the air it 'parts the ridges'! Even the French name for it (and also the Latin), *perdrix*, has been said to derive from the verb *perdre*, 'to lose', since it 'loses' its brood. The present English word goes back through Middle English *partrich* to Old French *perdris* to Latin *perdrix* to Greek *perdrix*, which ultimately may come from the Greek verb *perdomai*, 'to break wind', referring either to the bird's hoarse, rasping cry or to its noisy, 'spluttering' flight, especially when startled.

**passbook** (building society account book)
The book is not so called since it enables money or funds to 'pass' from the holder to the society, or the other way round, nor does the word refer to the role of the book as a sort of 'pass' or proof of the holder's identity. It is apparently so called since it simply passes between the holder and the society, and there is some evidence that originally it was called a 'passage book'. The word formerly also applied to what is now called a 'bankbook' (a book held by a bank customer who has a deposit account).

**passing** (more than, in phrases such as 'passing strange')
In phrases such as 'passing fair', 'passing rich' and so on, the 'passing' is sometimes misunderstood to mean 'temporarily', 'briefly'. The word really means 'very much', or even 'exceedingly', and in its

present sense is a survival of the old sense of 'surpass'. Expressions with 'passing' like this are now found mainly in older literary works, such as those of Goldsmith and Hardy.

**passion fruit** (fruit of the passion flower)
The fruit, which is otherwise known as 'granadilla', is actually so called since the passion flower, from which it comes, has parts that bear a fanciful resemblance to the Crown of Thorns and other instruments of the Crucifixion. In popular usage, however, the fruit has been associated with the other 'passion' that is 'sexual attraction' (or just 'love'), and so has now become a sort of traditional dish or present for Valentine's Day. (Some restaurants lay on a special Valentine's Day dinner for lovers and spouses and serve passion fruit up for the sweet.)

**Passover** (Jewish festival commemorating the delivery of the Hebrews from slavery)
Although the word is familiar enough to most people, there is often some doubt regarding who passed over what (or what passed over whom). Additionally, some older or more amateur etymological sources claim that the word does not mean what it says, and that 'Passover' is a corruption of some foreign word, whether Hebrew or German or otherwise. The truth of the matter is, as a glance at Exodus 12:23-27 will show, that God spared or 'passed over' the Israelites when all the first-born in Egypt were slaughtered. The English word is a translation of Hebrew *pesach*, from the root *pāsach*, 'he passed over'. It is simply a coincidence that the English resembles this. The Passover subsequently became the Christian festival of Easter, and the word for this festival in several European languages derives from the Hebrew quoted here, so that one finds French *Pâques*, Spanish *Pascua*, Italian *Pasqua* and Russian *paskha*, for example.

**pasteurized** (of milk: partially sterilized)
The term may suggest milk that has come from 'fresh fields and pastures new' (to quote the popularly misquoted quotation), but the word has its origin in the name of Louis Pasteur, the nineteenth-century French chemist who invented a method for sterilizing milk.

**patter** (rapid talk, empty chatter, magician's 'word spell')
This would seem to be a straightforward word, perhaps half imitative, and half suggesting the patter of feet or rain or of words that come out 'pat'. But the verb was originally used of prayers that were spoken or recited rapidly and mechanically, and the actual source is thus in Latin *paternoster*, 'Our Father'. This itself looks like a folk etymology, but past records of the word and its uses show it to be the true one.

**pea-jacket** (kind of heavy jacket worn by sailors)
The jacket is not pea-green in colour, and has nothing to do with peas. Like several nautical words, it came into English from Dutch, where it was *pijjekker*, with *pij* being the name of a kind of cloth, and *jekker* meaning 'jacket' (to which English word it was assimilated). The English word in turn gave what is now the standard Russian word for 'jacket', *pidzhak*. Since many Russians feel this is rather a 'foreign' word, some of them contrive to make it meaningful by altering it to *spindzhak*, from *spina*, 'back'. This shows that folk etymology is by no means confined to English!

**pearl barley** (kind of barley used in cooking, especially in soups and stews)
The term is not an alteration of 'peeled barley', as has been sometimes stated, but means what it says. When the barley is ground into small round grains, these resemble pearls.

**pearmain** (kind of eating apple)
It seems unlikely that a common variety of apple should be called by a name that suggests 'pear'. The word came into English from Old French *permain*, and this in turn probably derived from Latin *Parmensis*, 'of Parma', referring to the origin of the apple in or near this northern city of Italy (which also gave the world Parmesan cheese).

**pedantic** (presenting knowledge in an unduly detailed or 'plodding' way)
The word is the adjective of 'pedant', of

course, and it might be supposed that the 'ped-' of these refers to the 'foot' or plodding course of a pedant, as in other words starting thus ('pedal', 'pedestrian' and so on). There is good evidence, however, that this element does not form the basis of the word, and that the Italian word (*pedante*) which gave the English itself derives from, or at least relates specifically to, Latin *paedagogus*, 'pedagogue'. The link could have been reinforced by the 'teaching' concept of both words, and by the fact that there was an Italian term *pedagogo pedante*, referring to a sort of peripatetic teacher, or a 'pedagogue who accompanied on foot'. The important thing in all this, however, is that the 'ped-' of 'pedagogue' does not mean 'foot' but derives from Greek *paidos*, 'boy' (see also **page boy**), since the Greek *paidagogos* was literally a 'boy leader', or a slave who looked after his master's son and took him to school and back. In modern English, 'pedant' and 'pedagogue' are in a sense synonymous, and both are used in a derogatory way for a dull or unimaginative teacher or 'imparter of knowledge'.

**pedigree** (register of a person's or animal's ancestry)
The word has for some time been wrongly associated with 'degree', and indeed its present spelling owes something to this false link. The term originated in Old French *pie de grue*, literally 'crane's foot', referring to the shape made by the lines of a genealogical chart (typically in the symbol ∧ ). The suggestion of 'degree' is understandable, of course, since it contains the idea of 'rank' that is all important in determining a person's ancestral standing.

**pediment** (triangular piece of wall under roof in classical architecture)
This rather technical term has undoubtedly been influenced by the Latin *ped-* element that means 'foot', although this is hardly suitable for a feature far from the ground at the top of a building. The original word was *periment*, which itself appears to be a sort of 'artisan' version of 'pyramid'. The influence of Latin *ped-* is more obvious and rational in the other meaning of 'pediment' to apply to a gently sloping surface of bedrock at the base of a steeper slope. For another 'ped-'

word that is nothing to do with feet, see the next entry.

**pedlar, peddler** (person who travels about selling goods)
The person is not so called since he 'pedals' along on a bicycle, or even because he uses his feet, as a pedestrian does (see **pedantic**, above). The first part of the word here actually comes from Middle English *ped*, 'basket', 'panier', since that is what the pedlar (or American peddler) carried his wares in.

**pekoe** (type of high-quality tea)
The tea is not so called since it come from Peking. It is a real China tea, however, and derives its name from *pek-ho*, 'white down'. This refers to its downy tips when it is picked. (Peking is now 'officially' called (and spelt) Beijing.)

**pemmican** (dried meat used for emergency rations)
The name of this food, traditionally made by North American Indians, is nothing to do with 'can', but comes from a native (Cree) word *pimikân* based on *pimii*, 'fat', 'grease'.

**pencil** (writing implement)
Because the two go commonly together, it might be supposed that 'pen' and 'pencil' are words of related origin. They are not, though, and 'pencil' comes, via Old French, from Latin *penicillus*, 'painter's brush' (literally 'little tail'), while 'pen' goes back to Late Latin *penna*, 'quill pen' (literally 'feather'). 'Penicillin' is related to 'pencil', and has more obviously the same origin. The reference is to the 'tufted' appearance of the fungus spores. It is interesting that the modern concept of 'pencilled eyebrows' directly reflects the Latin 'brush' origin of 'pencil', as does the 'pencil' that is a set of light rays.

**penknife** (pocket knife with folding blade)
Some penknives do contain other gadgets besides a blade, although one that also incorporated a pen would be a real rarity. The knife is so called since its blade was originally used for mending or paring quill pens.

**pennyroyal** (plant of the mint family with blue or pink flowers)
The plant is not so called because it is a 'sovereign remedy' for various disorders, but because its name has been corrupted (and folk etymologized) from Latin *pulegium*, which is actually fleabane. It is likely, however, that the plant's name was influenced by that of the pennywort, and that it may even have been confused with it. (The latter plant is so called because of its round leaves shaped like pennies.)

**penthouse** (structure attached to another)
The penthouse is interesting not only for its quite opposite meanings (either a mere lean-to shed against a wall or a luxury apartment on a roof), but because of its false associations. The word is nothing to do with 'house', and although obviously influenced by this, derives, via Middle English *pentis*, from Old French *apentis*, which is itself probably from Medieval Latin *appendicium*, 'appendage'. It is possible, though, that another influence on the word, as it developed in different languages, was French *pente*, 'slope'.

**perform** (carry out, enact)
This word looks as if it belongs to the great 'form' family that includes 'conform', 'reform', 'deform', 'inform' and the like, where the last part derives from basic Latin *forma*, 'shape'. 'Reform', for example, is from Latin *reformare* 'to form again'. But 'perform' is not from some Latin verb *performare*, meaning 'form completely'. Its origin is in Anglo-French *performer*, which in altered form comes from Old French *parfournir*, itself comprising the prefix *par-* that means 'thoroughly' (from Latin *per-* in this sense) and *fournir*, 'to provide' (modern French 'to furnish'). To perform, therefore, is literally to provide or furnish completely. Compare the related **parboil**.

**periwig** (kind of long curly wig)
Unfortunately, this word does not derive from 'wig', as it so obviously should, but is an alteration of the alternative word 'peruke', which itself comes from French *perruque*. It seems that the '-wi-' of 'periwig' arose as an attempt to render the thin 'u'

sound in this French word. For another non-wig word, see **whig**.

**periwinkle** (kind of trailing evergreen plant)
What can the relationship be between this name and the 'periwinkle' that is a kind of sea snail? What does the name actually mean? There are a number of tangles to be sorted out here. In the first place, although it is possible that the spelling of the plant name may have been influenced by that of the mollusc, the two words are of quite distinct origin. The plant was called *perwince* in Old English, with this deriving from Latin *pervinca*, itself probably a combination of *per-*, 'through' and the base of *vincire*, 'to bind', referring to a climbing variety. (Many kinds of periwinkle are not climbing or trailing plants at all, of course.) The snail has a more difficult name, which may be an alteration of Old English *pīnewincle* and be based on Latin *pina*, the name of a kind of mussel, and an Old English word that meant perhaps 'shell'. ('Winkle' is simply a short form for 'periwinkle'.) And just as the plant name may have been influenced by that of the sea snail, so the opposite could have happened. The names were in fact both recorded as *perwinke* as early as the sixteenth century. But the snail's name is almost certainly not a corruption of 'pettywinkle' or 'pennywinkle', as has been proposed by some.

**perk** (of coffee: percolate)
When the coffee is perking this is not because it is 'perking up' and nearly ready, but simply because the word is short for 'percolate'! Compare the next entry.

**perks** (special privileges or rights)
What perks do you have in your job? Do they help you to perk up when routine is boring, or make you perky when you are beginning to feel tired? These words are not related, alas, and 'perks' is simply short for 'perquisites', an admittedly rather pompous-sounding word that derives from Medieval Latin *perquisitum*, 'something acquired'. Compare the **perk** of the previous entry.

**pester** (annoy, harass)
It is a surprise to discover that this word is

not related to 'pest', although it has probably been influenced by it. It actually comes from Middle French *empestrer*, 'to hobble (a horse)', itself ultimately related to Latin *pastor*, 'herdsman'. 'Pest', on the other hand, can be taken back to Latin *pestis*, 'plague'.

**peter out** (give out, come to an end)
Although the expression seems to have been first used in connection with mining in the United States, there is no proof that its origin is in Greek *petros*, 'stone' or *petra*, 'rock'. Nor has any precise reference to saltpetre been substantiated. Until further evidence is provided, we will therefore have to say of this term, 'origin unknown'.

**petrel** (kind of seabird, especially the storm petrel)
Is the bird so called since, like St Peter, it can 'walk on the water' (see Matthew 14:29), or because it 'patters' through the waves? The temptation to link the name with that of the saint is strong, and the English round-the-world sailor and writer William Dampier first made the connection in 1703 when he wrote that as the birds fly, 'they pat the Water alternately with their Feet, as if they walkt upon it; tho' still upon the Wing. And from hence the Seamen give them the name of Petrels, in allusion to St. Peter's walking upon the Lake of Gennesareth'. But in giving his account, Dampier had altered the original spelling of *pitteral*, and the derivation of this is still obscure. Unless further evidence is forthcoming, therefore, we should treat the 'Peter' connection with suspicion. The link with 'patter' seems most unlikely, too.

**pettifogger** (person who quibbles or fusses)
There does not seem to be any connection with 'fog', though there perhaps is with 'petty'. The second half of the word may well derive from a fifteenth– and sixteenth-century German family of financiers and merchants in Augsburg called Fugger.

**pettitoes** (feet of pigs used as food; trotters)
The true origin of this word is not 'petty toes', which would be quite suitable, but the rather surprising obsolete word *pettytoe*,

which meant 'offal', 'giblets' and itself derived from Old French *petite oye*, literally 'little goose'. The sense development from 'giblets of a goose' to 'trotters of a pig' seems rather far-fetched, but the common link is probably 'animal parts cut off for food'.

**petulant** (peevish)
A petulant person may often get into a pet, but there is no known link between these two words. 'Petulant' ultimately goes back to Latin *petere*, 'to seek', 'to go to' (as in English 'petition'), since a petulant person seeks attention, but the origin of 'pet' in the sense 'fit of peevishness' is unknown. It does not seem to be related to the 'pet' that means 'spoilt child' (which is probably related to 'petty').

**petunia** (kind of tropical plant with large, bright flowers)
This flower name conjures up 'petal' and 'tune', but this is not its true derivation. Nor does the name come from that of its first grower or the botanist who introduced it, as often happens. The New Latin name is based on obsolete French *petun*, 'tobacco', itself from a native word, since the petunia is closely related to the tobacco plant. The name was devised in 1789 by the French botanist Antoine Laurent de Jussieu, who founded the National History Museum in Paris.

**phantasmagoria** (optical effect in which figures on a screen change size and shape)
This impressive word is related to 'phantasm', as is apparent, but the last part is nothing to do with 'gory', despite the association of the word as a whole with feverish or frightening visions. The word was coined in 1802 by an exhibitor of optical illusions in London, one Baron Philipstal. His device, basically a special kind of magic lantern, produced an effect whereby 'the figures were made rapidly to increase and decrease in size, to advance and retreat, dissolve, vanish, and pass into each other, in a manner then considered marvellous' (*Oxford English Dictionary*). The origin of the word, as mentioned, was 'phantasm' (or perhaps the French form of it, *fantasme*), with the final section apparently based on the Greek verb *ageirein*, 'to gather', 'to assemble', as

seen in the modern English 'agoraphobia' (fear of open spaces, or literally of the 'gathering place'). But no doubt Philipstal really wanted to find a word that was as exciting as his exhibition, and the Greek ending may have been chosen more by good fortune than good linguistics.

**piccaninny** (small black child)
This word, now regarded as a derogatory term, is not based on 'ninny' but very likely comes from Portuguese *pequenino*, 'little one', in turn from *pequeno*, 'small'. The American spelling of the word is usually 'picaninny' or 'pickaninny', and in its original use it was a term of affection, not of disparagement, as now.

**pickaxe** (heavy tool used for breaking up hard road surfaces etc)
The 'axe' in the name is a delusion, since the implement is simply a 'pick'. In Middle English, however, it was called a *pikois*, from Old French *picois*, and the second half of this became altered by wrong association with 'axe'.

**Picts** (ancient people who once occupied Britain and settled in Scotland)
The name of this race is usually interpreted to mean 'painted people', from Latin *picti*, related to the verb *pingere*, 'to paint', with this allegedly referring to the people's habit of tattooing themselves. But this 'pseudo-learned etymology', as one modern linguist and place-name expert has called it (W.F.H. Nicolaisen in *Scottish Place-Names*), is now not regarded as acceptable by many, and the true origin seems to be in some earlier name for the race. What this itself was, is not precisely known, but it is believed to be represented in the first part of many Scottish place-names beginning 'Pit-' (e.g. Pitlochry, Pitsligo, Pittenweem, etc), since these are the places where the Picts are known to have settled (mainly in eastern Scotland). Little has been learned about the language that the Picts spoke, but it is known that this 'Pit-' means 'share' (i.e. share of land), and that it is almost certainly related to English 'piece'. Perhaps the Picts are therefore really the 'piece-of-land people'.

**picturesque** (attractively pretty)
The derivation of this word is not exactly 'picture', the English word, but Italian *pittore*, 'painter'. The Italian adjective *pittoresco*, based on this, gave French *pittoresque*, and this in turn produced the present English word. So the true original meaning was really 'in the style of a painter'. The word was first recorded in English in the early eighteenth century.

**Pidgin English** (kind of mixed language based on English and used for trade)
It is possible to communicate and send messages by means of pigeons, but these birds are not behind this name, which is simply a corruption of 'business English'. Pidgin English was originally used in Chinese ports, but then became more widespread. The present form of the expression explains the saying, 'That's your pigeon', which thus really means, 'That's your business'. (The phrase seems at times to be half-associated with 'pigeon-hole', so that if I say 'That's your pigeon' I seem to be saying 'That's something that's been passed on to you to deal with'.) Kipling caught the expression early, as he often did (compare **hell for leather**), and in *Traffics and Discoveries*, published in 1904, he has the exchange: '"What about their musketry average?" I went on. "Not my pidgin," said Dayley'. Later, 'pidgin' in this type of saying became 'pigeon', as it is today.

**piebald** (of horse: spotted or blotched with black and white markings)
The sense of 'bald' here is not 'hairless' but 'marked with white', the common link between these meanings being something like 'shining area'. The 'pie' of the word is the same as for 'magpie', with a basic sense 'of more than one colour', and specifically black and white. (The 'Pied Piper' of Browning's famous poem, however, was 'Half of yellow and half of red'.) Compare **skewbald** and also see, out of interest, **bald**.

**piecemeal** (gradually)
This word is sometimes wrongly used to mean 'in pieces', as if subconsciously regarded as a sort of opposite of 'wholemeal'. Almost certainly, too, there is an association with 'meal'. But 'meal' here is

not the common 'foodtime' one but means 'measure', 'amount taken at a time' (see **meal** itself for more on this). 'Piecemeal' thus really means 'a piece taken one portion at a time'. There were once similar formations in English, such as (in their modernized spellings) 'dropmeal', meaning 'drop by drop', and 'limbmeal', meaning 'limb by limb'. 'Piecemeal' is now the only word left like this.

**piggyback** (carried on a person's back and shoulders)
The origin of this familiar childhood word is not 'carried on the back of a pig', although it is not unknown for these beasts to have been used for human transportation, if only as a rustic romp. The word is known to be an alteration of an earlier form 'pick-a-pack', or 'pick-a-back' (or even 'a pick back' or 'a pick pack' in the earliest form recorded). It is not quite clear what the references are here, or whether even the 'back' is what it seems to be There is a modern alternative in 'pickaback', although 'piggyback' is now the more popular form, either because of the false (or agreeable) association with pigs, or even because of the influence of similar words, such as 'piggy bank' and 'piggywig'.

**pikestaff** (in phrase 'plain as a pikestaff')
What is a pikestaff? A sort of weapon or walking stick, half pike, half staff? In what sense is it plain? There *is* a word 'pikestaff', meaning a spiked walking stick for use over slippery ground, but this is not the one here. The phrase is an alteration of 'plain as a packstaff', with the latter word being the smooth or plain staff used by a **pedlar** (whom see, for another false association). The packstaff was the stick or staff on which the pedlar supported his pack when he stopped to rest but remained standing.

**pile** (soft raised surface on carpet)
This pile is not the same word as the pile that means 'heap', 'mound', as if referring to the raised surface of the carpet. It ultimately comes from Latin *pilus*, 'hair', whereas the 'mound' pile derives from Latin *pila*, 'pillar' (and the other pile that means 'post' comes ultimately from Latin *pilum*, 'javelin'). So there are three quite unrelated 'piles', and to complete the pack we should include the painful plural one, whose origin is in Latin *pila*, 'ball' (which is not the same as the 'pillar' *pila* just mentioned).

**pillar to post** (from one place to another)
The familar phrase today suggests a dash to post a late letter, as if the post has been collected from your nearby *pillar* box and you have to hurry to the *post* office. The origin of the expression, however, is in the game of real tennis, where the ball could be sent 'from post to pillar' in the court, and the opposing player would be kept on his toes. The phrase was mostly used with the word 'tossed' (or 'tost' as it was often spelt in the sixteenth century), and probably the order of the words was changed round in order to rhyme with this. This true origin will thus settle the hash of another false etymology of the expression, which is that it evolved from 'pillory to whipping post'. Ingenious, but incorrect.

**pinchbeck** (counterfeit, sham)
The word is often used of imitation gold, in jewellery, and itself suggests a derivation in some sense of 'pinch', as if the metal had been thinned or flattened, or had been applied in a mean quantity, or had even been used in place of genuine gold that had been 'pinched'. But the original alloy so called was invented by an English watchmaker called Christopher Pinchbeck, and that is the source of the term. (The inventor, who died in 1732, almost certainly derived his surname from the village of Pinchbeck, in Lincolnshire.)

**pineapple** (large yellow-fleshed fruit)
How did it come about that a fruit, which is clearly not an apple and does not grow on pine trees, finished up with such a misleading name? The answer is that 'apple' was originally used quite generally to mean any fruit, and that 'pineapple' formerly meant 'pinecone', referring to the shape and appearance of the fruit. (Compare French *pomme de pin* to mean 'pinecone', with *pomme*, which now means 'apple', also formerly used to mean just 'fruit'.) Archbishop Trench (see Bibliography) mentions that in the mid-nineteenth century the famous French daily paper, Le Journal des Débats,

'made some uncomplimentary observations on the voracity of the English, who could wind up a Lord Mayor's dinner with fir-cones for dessert'.

**pink** (flower related to the carnation)
Why is the pink so called since it can also be white or red (or variegated)? The answer is that the colour pink was named after the flower, not the other way round. The name of the flower thus has another origin. This is still uncertain, although it was perhaps formerly called 'pink-eye', as the flower has small 'eyes' (see next entry), or possibly the open flowers were regarded as resembling 'pinks', the word used for ornamental openings in Elizabethan dresses. (The former of these seems to be supported by the French name of the plant, which is *œillet*.) Such phrases as 'in the pink' and 'pink of condition' and even 'tickled pink' all derive indirectly from the plant, which was seen as a sort of 'flower of perfection'. The first recorded use of its name in this metaphorical sense comes in Shakespeare, where in *Romeo and Juliet* there is a nice little interchange:

*Mercutio.* Nay, I am the very pink of courtesy.
*Romeo.* Pink for flower.
*Mercutio.* Right.

**pinkeye** (conjunctivitis)
Although pink eyes are an obvious result of conjunctivitis (inflammation of the membrane lining the eyeball and eyelid), there is some evidence that the term is at least partially a translation of obsolete Dutch *pinck oogen*, 'small eyed', alluding to another consequence of the condition. One of the former meanings of 'pink' in English was 'small', and this sense still survives in the American (and British dialect) word 'pinkie', meaning 'little finger'. See also **pink** (above).

**pip** (depression)
'That really gives me the pip'. What sort of pip is this? It could mean that you feel you are beaten, that you have been 'pipped', or perhaps there is some obscure allusion to dominoes? The 'pip' here is actually the name of a poultry disease, in which a scale or crust forms on the tongue of the bird and

it consequently becomes sickly and 'down in the mouth'. The ultimate origin of the word in this meaning is probably in Latin *pituata*, 'phlegm', referring to the secretion of mucus in the bird's mouth and throat that forms the crust.

**piping hot** (very hot)
The reference in this phrase is not to hot water pipes, but to frying food, which when really hot can make a hissing or piping sound. An example of this, if doing it properly, is bubble and squeak – hence its name.

**pistol** (firearm)
Although early types of pistol were certainly made at Pistoia, in Italy, the word does not come from this place but from French *pistole*, which itself goes back through German to Czech *pištal*, literally 'pipe', this word being related to Russian *pishchal'*, 'arquebus'.

**pitchblende** (black mineral composed of uranium oxides)
The name of the mineral suggests that it is somehow a 'blend of pitch' or a 'blended pitch'. It originated as a partial translation of German *Pechblende*, in which *Pech* is 'pitch' but *Blende* derives from the verb *blenden*, 'to blind', 'to deceive'. This latter is a separate word (also 'blende' in English) to serve as the name for a number of similar minerals (especially sphalerite), and itself is intended to indicate that the mineral designated is deceptively like galena (native lead sulphide), although does not actually yield any lead.

**pitcher** (kind of large jug or similar vessel)
The vessel is not so called since water or whatever can be easily 'pitched' out of it, but because the word came into English from Old French *pichier*, in turn from Medieval Latin *picarium*, a variation of *bicarium*, meaning '**beaker**' (see this word).

**pitchfork** (type of long-handled fork used for pitching hay etc)
A pitchfork is certainly used for pitching or throwing hay or sheaves up to a trailer or rick, but its name actually originated as a 'pickfork' (Middle English *pikfork*), that is, as a fork that is used as much for turning sheaves as for lifting and 'pitching' them.

**pitfall** (trap, snare)
The image of this word is certainly that of falling into a pit. In origin, however, the two Old English elements that comprise it were *pytt*, 'pit' and *fealle*, 'trap'. The basic sense was thus one of trapping animals by means of a pit, rather than just digging a pit and hoping they would fall into it. Dr Johnson quotes one contemporary account of the process in his *Dictionary* (under 'elephant'): 'Wild elephants are taken with the help of a female ready for the male: she is confined to a narrow place, round which pits are dug; and these being covered with a little earth scattered over hurdles, the male elephants easily fall into the snare'.

**pittance** (small amount, meagre wage or allowance)
The word suggests 'pit' in some 'mean' or unpleasant sense, as well as a sum of money that is 'pitiful' (or that is given out of pity). The term came into English from Old French *pitance*, where it meant 'piety', 'pity', ultimately from Latin *pietas*, 'dutifulness'. 'Pity' does lie behind the concept, therefore, but not so much in a personal way as out of a sense of pious duty, as an act of charity. The pittance was thus the original historic 'dole', as established by pious request, and human nature being what it is, the donors were not as generous as they were supposed to be – hence the present 'meagre' sense of the word.

**placard** (notice, displayed advertisement)
This word is not related to 'card', but came from Old French *plaquart*, derived from the verb *plaquier*, 'to plate'. It is thus related to 'plaque', and the Old French verb itself came from Middle Dutch *placken*, 'to patch', 'to stick on', itself probably imitative in origin.

**plain sailing** (good, uninterrupted progress)
The phrase is a nautical one in origin, and although the sense has always been 'straightforward sailing', the term was formerly somewhat different, as 'plane sailing'. This meant sailing by means of a plane chart, which operated as if the earth was flat and had lines of latitude and longitude that were straight and parallel. Such a system worked well for short distances, of course, but not for longer hauls. Obviously, such a navigation system would have been much simpler and 'plainer', since no allowance would need to be made for the curvature of the earth.

**plainsong** (type of early church music, in particular Gregorian chant)
The term suggests singing that is 'plain' or ordinary in some way, perhaps because it is unaccompanied or unadorned. It usually *is* unaccompanied, although can be quite complex, with various embellishments, so is hardly 'unadorned'. The English word is a translation of French *plain chant*, which itself translates Medieval Latin *cantus planus*. This means 'clear singing', 'distinct chanting' and refers to the fact that the singing is monophonic, that is, all the singers sing in unison, with a single melodic line. That is why it is 'plain'.

**plankton** (minute organisms found in the sea)
The association with 'plank', whether 'ship's plank' or any other kind, is misleading. The term came into English from German, and ultimately derives from Greek *planktos*, 'wandering', 'drifting', referring to the way in which the organisms slowly make their way through the water.

**platelayer** (workman who lays and repairs railway lines, 'track chargeman')
A platelayer doesn't lay plates, but (technically) 'plate-rails'. This is the historic name for the flat wheeltrack that was formerly used in mines as an early form of railway. The word came to be transferred to ordinary railway lines, and survives in the 'platelayer' appearing here.

**plight** (sorry state)
This is not the same word as the other 'plight' that means 'make a pledge' (as in 'plight one's troth'), although it could perhaps be thought that someone who found himself in a 'plight' had got into it because of some promise he had made, a pledge that had to be kept at all cost. The 'sorry state' plight comes ultimately from a Latin word meaning 'fold', and so is related to 'plait'. (The concept is that of being in a 'fold', or a

'complicated' condition.) The other 'plight', now an archaic word, is of Germanic origin and so related to modern German *Pflicht*, 'duty'. In Old English it had developed as *plihtan*, 'to endanger', and this undesirable sense may have already linked it with the the other word.

**plimsoll** (type of gym shoe or sports shoe) The word is sometimes spelt (or misspelt) 'plimsole', reinforcing the association with 'sole'. But the first spelling here is the correct one to provide the actual origin, which is in the Plimsoll line, the load-marking line on the side of a ship. If the shoe is regarded as a 'boat', then this line can be seen as the upper edge of the rubber as it runs along the side. Fanciful, of course, but this does appear to be the true explanation. The fact that plimsolls are some-times worn for deck games on board ship may have prompted this particular comparison. The Plimsoll line itself is named after the Member of Parliament who advocated its adoption in the nineteenth century, Samuel Plimsoll.

**plonk** (cheap wine) The *Supplement* to the *Oxford English Dictionary* notes that 'various popular and humorous etymologies' for this word 'are without foundation'. It thus rules out the explanation proposed in the *Daily Telegraph* for 15 November 1967 where the writer maintained: 'Surely the word "plonk" is onomatopoeic, being the noise made when a cork is withdrawn from the bottle?'. Most authorities now agree with the *OED's* judg-ment, and hold that the word is most likely to be a semi-humorous alteration of French *vin blanc* – this despite the fact that most plonk is actually red wine. In 1970 there was even a cheapish wine called 'Vin Plonque' on sale.

**plump** (fall down heavily) This verb is almost certainly imitative, suggesting the heavy 'flop' or 'plunk' of something landing on a soft surface, such as a stout person in an armchair. It is not therefore related to the other 'plump' that means 'stout', 'fat', but which originally meant 'dull', 'blockish' and probably came into English from Middle Dutch. The verb

'plump for', meaning 'choose', comes from the first 'plump'; the verb 'plump up' (meaning 'make fuller and rounder', as of cushions) comes from the second.

**plum pudding** (kind of rich steamed or boiled pudding containing dried fruit and spices) What goes into a plum pudding? As most recipes or cookery books will reveal, some-thing like: flour or bread crumbs, raisins, currants, suet, eggs, spices and other flavou-rings. But not plums, although other dried fruits may be added. The explanation for this apparent misnomer is that originally, in the 'good old days', there *were* plums in the pudding. Later, however, and from about the seventeenth century, dried grapes or raisins were substituted for the plums. The word 'plum' itself is related to 'prune', which is a dried plum, just as a raisin is a dried grape (compare those two French confusibles, *raisin*, 'grape' and *raisin sec*, 'raisin', and while we're about it, French *prune*, 'plum' and *pruneau*, 'prune'). There are now really two sorts of plum pudding: the one usually called 'Christmas pudding', which is the richest one, with raisins, currants, dried fruit, and so on, and the ordinary 'suet pudding' with just raisins.

**ply** (of a boat etc: travel to and from a place regularly) It would not be surprising to find that this 'ply' is the same as the one that means 'strand', 'twist', referring to the regular 'strands' of the boat's course between the places. But the words have different origins. The first 'ply' (which is the same as the verb in 'ply one's trade') is short for Middle English *applien*, 'to apply'. The other 'ply' has its links in French *plier* and Latin *plicare*, 'to fold', and so is related to English 'pliable' and 'pliers'. However, it must be added that 'apply', as just mentioned, is also related to the second 'ply' here, so there is something of an indirect link.

**poached egg** (egg cooked in simmering liquid such as water) Poached eggs are not so called since they were originally stolen or taken by poachers, as has been sometimes half-humorously (and therefore half-seriously) suggested.

The word comes from Old French (and modern) *poche*, 'bag', 'pocket', which gave the 'poke' of 'a pig in a poke' and the ordinary English 'pocket' itself. The reference is not to the bag or container in which the eggs are poached, but the yolk of the egg appearing inside the 'pocket' of white when the egg has been cooked. See also **poke** (below).

**poetaster** (poor poet)
The word looks like a 'poem taster', in other words a poet who simply 'tastes' a poem without producing a proper one. But there is no link with 'taste' here and the ending '-aster' is simply one sometimes used to denote a person or thing that is inferior in some way. Another example is the rarish 'policaster' (defined by Dr Johnson in his *Dictionary* as 'A petty ignorant pretender to politicks'). This '-aster' suffix is the same as the French *-âtre* on the names of colours, usually working out in English as '-ish' (*bleuâtre*, 'bluish', *rougeâtre*, 'reddish'). Such colours are poor imitations of the real thing.

**point blank** (of a bullet etc: so close to the target that it flies straight)
This expression is not related to the 'dummy' bullet called a 'blank', nor is it a version of French *point blanc*, as is sometimes said, since no such French term exists. The true source is probably in the idea of a weapon that is pointed at the 'blank', that is, the white spot in the centre of a target (as formerly in archery). A missile fired 'point blank' is one where no allowance need be made for a trajectory, as would be needed at a more distant range.

**poke** (in expression 'pig in a poke')
If you buy 'a pig in a poke' you are buying something without the chance to see it and assess its value beforehand. The 'poke' does not mean 'poky place' but (as mentioned above under **poached egg**) 'bag'. Other languages have equivalent expressions, such as French *acheter chat en poche*, German *die Katze im Sack kaufen*, Russian *kupit' kota v meshke* (all identically 'buy a cat in a bag').

**pole** (as in 'North Pole', 'magnetic pole', etc)
This geographical and scientific pole is

nothing to do with the ordinary pole such as a telegraph pole or barber's pole. In the North 'Pole' and similar poles, the derivation is from Latin *polus*, 'end of an axis' and Greek *polos*, 'pivot', 'axis' (itself related to Greek *kyklos*, 'wheel'). The other 'pole' comes, via Old English, from Latin *palus*, 'stake', 'prop', which is related to English 'pale', 'paling', 'palisade' and so on. The old land measure 'rod, pole or perch' is obviously the second of these. So the two words are quite distinct, and their origins are really poles apart.

**poleaxe** (kind of battle-axe)
This historic weapon is not so called since it consisted of an axe on the end of a pole, but because originally it was a 'poll axe', with 'poll' meaning 'head' (as in the modern 'poll' or election, where the idea is of counting heads). This meant either that the axe had a special sort of head or that it was literally used for cutting off or splitting open an enemy's head. Perhaps the latter is more likely, although the word 'poll' still survives in a technical sense to mean 'flat end of the head of a hammer' (the other end is called the 'peen'). For more about poles that are not what they seem, see the next entry.

**polecat** (kind of small animal related to the ferret)
The animal is not so called since it is a sort of cat that climbs poles, but probably because it was a 'poultry cat', i. e. it preyed on poultry. The first part of the name thus represents Old French *pol*, 'cock' (compare modern French *poule*, 'hen'). See also **catchpole**.

**policy** (insurance document)
This sort of policy is not related to the more general 'policy' that means 'plan of action', although the association seems sensible enough. It was originally *police* (rhyming with 'Hollis'), representing the identical Middle French word that meant 'certificate' and that evolved, through Italian *polizza* and Latin *apodixis*, from Greek *apodeixis*, 'demonstration'. The other 'policy', which is related to modern 'police', goes back through Old French to Latin *politia*, 'administration', which is ultimately related to Greek *polis*, 'city'.

**polony** (kind of pork sausage)
The polony did not originate in Poland, whose Medieval Latin name was *Polonia* (although the dance called the polonaise did). The word is actually an alteration of 'Bologna sausage', and this Italian city is thus its true place of origin. Compare **Hamburger** and **chipolata**.

**Pommy** (Australian term for a British person)
As may be imagined, there have been several attempts to explain this not always friendly name (also occurring in shorter form as 'Pom' or in expanded version as 'Pommy bastard'). One of the most unlikely origins is that it referred to convicts who were designated P.O.M.E. ('Prisoner of Mother England') or P.O.H.M. ('Prisoner of His Majesty'). Probably something like the true origin is given by D. H. Lawrence in *Kangaroo*, where he suggests that the word is based on 'pomegranate', alluding to the redness of the fruit and the traditional florid complexions of the British, with this word in turn used as a sort of humorous substitution for 'immigrant'. This seems borne out or at least supported by the fact that the rhyming slang term for 'immigrant' (or 'emigrant') was 'Jimmy Grant', and 'pomegranate' could have been partially based on this.

**pool** (combined stakes in a gambling game; common fund)
It comes as something of a revelation to discover that this is not the ordinary 'pool' that is a deep body of water. The sense development seems quite natural: a pool holds a supply of water just as a common fund holds a supply of money, which is moreover 'liquid' in the sense that it can be readily channelled or converted as required. But the 'gambling' pool (and therefore the football pools) actually comes from French *poule*, 'hen', since originally this bird was the prize and target in various card games. (Compare the 'cockshy' in which the prize was a cockerel.) Some etymologists suggest, in a rather far-fetched way, that the two words may have become associated with each other by the use of 'fiches' (counters) in gambling games, which suggested the 'fish' in a pool!

**popinjay** (supercilious person)
A popinjay struts along haughtily, and so might be thought to be a sort of 'jay' or dandy. The present form of the word was probably influenced by this, but it actually derives from Old French *papegai*, 'parrot', ultimately coming from Arabic *babaghā*.

**poplin** (kind of strong cotton fabric)
As already mentioned (see **diaper**, for example), many names of fabrics come from the town where they were first produced. In the case of poplin, there are two rival sources. The favourite one is usually given as Avignon, in France, since the French for 'poplin' is *popeline,* coming from Italian *papalina* meaning 'papal', and Avignon was the seat of the pope from 1309 to 1408 and was regarded as a papal town down to 1791. This seems rather contrived, however, and the true origin is likely to be in another town, as follows: French *popeline* is actually an adoption of English 'poplin' which came from French *papeline* which itself is an (admittedly unexplained) alteration of *drap de poperinge,* 'cloth of Poperinge', a famous textile centre in Flanders. The matter is still not finally settled, but the second origin seems more convincing.

**pore** (read studiously)
'The student sat pouring over a book'. Similar sentences have appeared in various written texts at different times, suggesting that there is a link between the two words (as if someone 'poring' over a book were 'pouring' all his or her attention into it, or as if the person was sweating over it, as a despairing student might). The latter association is encouraged by the link with the 'pores' of the skin. But there is no linguistic link between any of these, and the two kinds of 'pore' are quite unrelated – the 'opening in the skin' is from Latin *porus* (so related to English 'porous'), and the 'study' verb is a purely English word perhaps related to 'peer' (look closely).

**porringer** (kind of small bowl or dish)
It is quite likely that a porringer could contain porridge as well as soup, but the link between the two is indirect. The rather old fashioned word came into English from Old French *potager*, which itself comes from

*potage.* And as everyone knows, that means 'pottage' or soup, not porridge! (In all fairness, it should be pointed out, though, that 'porridge' is an alteration of 'pottage', hence there is some justification for the association of 'porringer' with the former word.)

**porter** (kind of dark sweet ale)
Is porter a sort of 'beery' port? Are the two names connected? The answer is 'no', and the two drinks are included here for the benefit of those who don't indulge in either or who are not quite sure what porter is anyway. (Many overseas visitors have heard of the drink, but do not realise that it is now almost a thing of the past. Instances have thus been known where a non-English guest, dining in a London hotel, has ordered 'porter, please', and has been baffled when a young man in uniform has been produced.) The beer so called was originally known as 'porter's beer' or 'porter's ale', probably because it was the favourite brew of street porters. Port, on the other hand, although a dark sweet wine, properly comes from Oporto, in Portugal.

**Portland cement** (type of cement capable of setting under water)
Portland cement does not come from Portland, the peninsula in Dorset, but is made of lime and clay from several sources (the clay originally from the mud of the Thames). Its name arises from the fact that it resembles the colour of Portland stone, which of course is quarried on the Isle of Portland.

**posh** (fine, superior)
The word is popularly supposed to derive from the abbreviation P.O.S.H. (standing for '*p*ort *o*ut, *s*tarboard *h*ome'), said to be the most desirable location of a cabin on ships sailing to the Far East, since they would be on the shaded or north-facing side. But this seems over-ingenious, and it is much more likely that the colloquial word is simply a slang term meaning 'money', 'dandy', and perhaps at least for one of these, originally a Romany word.

**poster** (public advertisement, often one on a hoarding)
There is no connection between 'poster' and

'post' meaning 'mail', in spite of the apparent common 'communication' link. A poster is so called since it is or was fastened to a post. The 'mail' post goes back to the days when royal mail was sent by means of men 'posted' (i.e. stationed) at intervals along the road to pass on the messages. Hence the phrase 'post haste' and the more modern 'I'll keep you posted'. But see also the next entry for more on the first of these.

**post haste** (as speedily as possible)
The term seems to mean 'with the haste of the post'. More interestingly, it in fact comes from the former direction on letters in the sixteenth century, 'Haste, post, haste', meaning 'Hurry, courier, hurry'. That was the way to get first class delivery in those days.

**posthumous** (occurring after a person's death)
The 'h' of the word has been inserted by false association with a former incorrect etymology, which explained the origin as Latin *post humus*, literally 'after the earth', i.e. after the burial. The word actually derives from Latin *postumus*, 'late-born' (i.e. born after the death of a child's father), which itself was used as a superlative of *posterus*, 'coming after' (the comparative of this being *posterior*, as the English word today).

**posy** (small bouquet of flowers)
The attractive little word may suggest a 'pose' of flowers or even a sort of nosegay of roses (a 'rosy posy'). But its earlier meaning was 'motto', 'line of verse', and its origin is thus in the word 'poesy', meaning simply 'poem' or 'art of poetry'. The original posies were inscribed on knives, in rings, and in other suitably 'memorable' places. In an issue of the *London Gazette* in 1675, mention was made of a wedding ring which had this posy inside it: 'In thee my Choice, I do rejoyce'.

**pram** (type of flat-bottomed boat)
The name of this boat has nothing to do with the baby carriage (that itself is a shortening of 'perambulator'). The boat is Dutch in origin, and its name is simply the Dutch

word for it (*praam*). This word itself is a remotish cousin of English 'fare'.

**preface** (foreword or introduction to a book)
There is a suggestion of 'face' in this word, as if it 'faced' the reader as he starts to read the book, or as if the author were 'facing' the reader for the first time. This same association arises when a speaker 'prefaces' his speech with some opening remarks: the audience will see his face for the first time as he stands up and faces them. But there is no 'face' behind the word, which ultimately comes from Latin *prefatio*, 'foreword' (literally, 'a saying beforehand'), with this also giving the adjective of 'preface' which is 'prefatory'. See also **frontispiece** and **foreword** itself. (Although several dictionaries define 'foreword' as 'preface', and 'preface' as 'foreword', many careful writers and publishers like to distinguish between the two, because a 'foreword' is usually written by someone other than the author of the book.)

**pregnant** (meaningful)
In such expressions as 'pregnant silence', 'pregnant pause', the meaning of 'pregnant', while related to the 'about-to-be-born' sense, may well owe something to a now obsolete word 'pregnant' of different origin. This was frequently used of an argument, and meant 'compelling', 'well-reasoned', even simply 'obvious'. Shakespeare used it in this sense in *Othello*, when Iago, seeking to discredit Cassio, Othello's lieutenant, says to Roderigo: 'Now, sir, this granted, as it is a most pregnant and unforced position, who stands so eminently in the degree of this fortune as Cassio does?'. This 'pregnant' came into English from Old French *preignant*, ultimately from Latin *premere*, 'to press'. The more common current 'pregnant' derives from Latin *prae-*, 'before' and the base of the verb *nasci*, 'to be born'.

**press** (compel to enlist, as formerly in the navy)
This verb 'press', familiar from the former 'press-gangs' who rounded up men in order to force them to join the navy, is not related to the ordinary 'press' that means 'put pressure on'. The word was originally 'prest', this meaning 'enlist by paying wages in advance', and deriving from the identical word in Old French (corresponding to modern French *prêt*, 'loan'), which ultimately came from Latin *praestare*, 'to supply', 'to provide'. The sense was undoubtedly influenced by the other, more common 'press', however, which derives ultimately from Latin *premere* (see **pregnant**, above).

**Pretender** (historical nickname)
There was an 'Old Pretender' and a 'Young Pretender', of course, the former being the Scottish claimant to the British throne, James Francis Edward Stuart, and the latter his son, Charles Edward Stuart, otherwise 'Bonnie Prince Charlie'. The modern sense of 'pretend' suggests that the two eighteenth-century would-be kings were impostors in some way, especially as in the event neither succeeded in his claim. But 'pretender' here means simply 'claimant', 'one who maintains he has a right to something', and there is no sense of false representation at all. This is because 'pretend' changed its meaning over the years. Its original sense was 'put forward', 'claim', from Latin (through French) *praetendere*. In about the sixteenth century, perhaps under the influence of 'pretext', the verb took on a new meaning of 'claim under false pretences', 'feign'. For two other sometimes misunderstood historical titles, see **Confessor** and **Unready.**

**prevent** (go before, satisfy in advance)
The older sense of 'prevent' is sometimes encountered in literature and the Prayer Book, and is misunderstood to have its current popular sense of 'keep from happening', 'hold back from'. Those who rarely go to church but sometimes, in spring-time mood, attend an Easter Day communion service, are thus somewhat baffled to hear a prayer (the Collect for the Day) referring to God's 'special grace preventing us', and then in the next breath, asking for his help. Regular churchgoers encounter a similar usage in one of the six prayers at the end of this same service which begins 'Prevent us, O Lord, in all our doings...' (Modern versions of the Prayer Book avoid this by substituting

something like 'Go before'.) Both senses come from one and the same word, which derives in the long run from Latin *praevenire*, 'to come before', 'anticipate'. The modern 'stop from happening' sense only really became fixed in the eighteenth century.

**prime** (apply first coat of paint)
It has still not been definitely or conclusively proved that this use of 'prime' relates to the 'first' sense of the word, as in 'primary', and there may have been an influence of some French word such as *imprimer*, 'to imprint'. The word 'prime' is an unusual one in English anyway, since it can have virtually opposite meanings: 'preliminary' (and so 'most basic', 'lowest'), as in 'prime rate' (the lowest commercial interest rate available), and 'finest' (so really 'highest'), as in 'Prime Minister'. Related words reflect this polarization, too, so that 'primitive', 'primordial', 'primer' and 'primary school' are at the lowest or bottom end of the scale, while 'prima donna', 'prime of life', 'prime time' (the peak time) and 'prime rib' (best beef) are at the top, as is the Primate of All England, the grand official title of the Archbishop of Canterbury. See also **primrose** (below).

**primrose** (spring-flowering plant)
Since the flower is obviously not a rose, some word specialists have endeavoured to find some other suitable explanation for the name. The favourite theory is that the name was originally French *prime rôle*, 'first place', as the flower is one of the first to appear in the spring. But this is only half correct, and there is no need to abandon the 'rose'. The name actually means 'first rose', with 'first' as already explained, and 'rose' simply in a general sense to mean 'flower'. (The 'prim' is thus not the adjective meaning 'demure', however aptly this might seem to accompany the modest 'rose'.) A related name is that of the primula, which in Medieval Latin was called *primula veris*, 'firstling of spring'. So 'first rose' and 'little first one' are the pleasant names of these two harbingers of spring.

**privet** (type of ornamental shrub)
Unfortunately, the precise origin of this name is unknown. It is *possible* that it may

somehow relate to 'private', since the shrub or hedge is often planted to make parts of the garden private, or to conceal compost heaps, dustbins, and so on, but there is no firm evidence that this is the correct derivation. Early forms of the name were *prim*, *print* and *prinne-print*, whatever this means, and this may have been altered to 'privet' by association with 'private'. The oldest record we have of the word in its present form is in the name of the village of Privett, near Petersfield in Hampshire.

**prize** (ship captured in battle)
Although the capture of an enemy ship in war can result in a kind of 'prize' or reward to the victor, the word 'prize' used to denote such a ship has quite a different origin. When 'prize' means 'reward' it is really an alternative spelling of 'price'; when it means 'booty of war', however, the derivation is in Old French *prise*, 'act of taking', from the verb *prendre*, 'to take'. (This same source also gives modern English 'prize' in the sense 'move with a lever', 'obtain with difficulty', since 'taking' is involved here, too.)

**probang** (surgical instrument used for removing obstacles from the oesophagus)
This is something of a mystery word, which appears to have been influenced by 'probe' (but not by 'bang'!). The device is basically a flexible rod with a sponge on the end, and this was invented in the seventeenth century by a Welsh judge named Walter Rumsey. He actually called it, for reasons that are now not known, a 'provang'. This looks like some artificial word, but whether based on any standard English (or Welsh) word or not, is not clear. Later, under the influence mentioned, the 'v' became 'b'.

**proboscis** (elongated mouthparts of some insects; elephant's trunk)
In the first sense here, some ambitious etymologists have traced the quite clearly Greek word back to an original Latin *promuscis*, allegedly meaning 'fly flapper'. True, there actually *is* a word 'promuscis', meaning 'proboscis', but it is simply an alteration of the other word. 'Proboscis' literally means 'front feeder', from Greek (through Latin) *pro-*, 'before' and *boskein*, 'to

feed'. So modern English 'promuscis' is a popular perversion of 'proboscis', and 'proboscis' does not derive from this in some spurious Latin form.

**prodigal** (recklessly extravagant)
Many people's experience of this word is virtually limited to its use for the biblical 'Prodigal Son'. And even knowing the story (or parable) about him will not prevent the word's false association with 'prodigy' (and even 'progeny'. 'Prodigal' comes from Latin *prodigere*, 'to squander' (literally 'to drive forth', with the idea of dissipating one's wealth or 'spending money like water'). 'Prodigy', meaning 'very gifted child', comes from Latin *prodigium*, 'monster', 'unnatural happening'. (The Prodigal Son was hardly that.) 'Progeny', meaning 'offspring', comes from Latin *progignere*, 'to beget' (to use a somewhat biblical word). So here are three different types of children: one bad, one good, and several plural.

**protagonist** (one who plays the leading role in a play)
The word is often used in the sense 'supporter', in sentences like 'He's one of the main protagonists of the new bypass'. This sense has presumably developed by contrast with an 'antagonist', who is 'against' something, so that a 'protagonist' must be 'for'. But the actual origin of the word is quite different, since it comes from Greek *prōtagōnistēs*, from *prōtos*, 'first' and *agōnistēs*, 'actor', 'competitor (in sport)'.

**Protestant** (member of non-Roman Catholic church)
One ingenious explanation of the name claims that the word comes from Latin *Pro Te stant, Jesu*, 'They stand for you, Jesus'. But perhaps this was simply intended as an agreeable ecclesiastical conundrum. Protestants, of course, are so called since they historically 'protested' against the Church of Rome, specifically when they dissented from an anti-Lutheran edict of the so called 'Diet of Spires' in Germany in 1529 (when a *Protestation* was issued by them).

**provost marshal** (officer in charge of military police)
The rank or office has come to be wrongly associated by some with 'court martial'. This is because there are really two kinds of provost marshal. The first is the one in the British Army who is in charge of the police generally in a camp or base. The second is the so called 'Master-at-Arms' (in the Royal Navy, the Chief Petty Officer responsible for discipline in a ship or base) who is specially appointed 'Provost Marshal' for the occasion when a court-martial is to be held in that ship or base. The title is probably derived from Old French *prévost des mareschaux de France*. This French origin has influenced the pronunciation of the 'Provost', which is like 'provoke' without the final 'k' sound. In other senses, such as for religious and academic heads, 'provost' is pronounced in the normal way.

**prude** (person who is unduly modest or 'pure', especially in sexual matters)
It might be thought that a prude is so called because he or she is being extra prudent. The words are not related, however, and 'prude' comes from the French, where it means 'good woman', 'prudish woman', and is a shortening of *prudefemme* in this sense. (This happened because the first part of the word was misunderstood as an adjective, but the whole word actually was the feminine equivalent of masculine *prud'homme*, 'good man and true', which was itself evolved from the earlier word *prodome*, a form of the phrase *pro de ome*, 'fine thing of a man'.) 'Prudent', on the other hand, comes from Latin *prudens*, which is a contraction of *providens*, 'acting with foresight'. Thus 'prude' is ultimately related to English 'proud', and 'prudent' to 'provident'.

**public school** (independent fee-paying school at secondary level)
The sense of 'public' is notoriously misleading here. Such schools are not called 'public' in the sense of this word in such a phrase as 'public figure', that is, because they are famous or well-known. Nor are they because they are kept in business by the fee-paying British public, or because the people in them, staff and/or students, have a common interest (in the sense of 'racing public', for example). Nor again are they so called as they are maintained at the expense of the public, since they are not – although

state schools are, and, confusingly, so are the so called 'public schools' in Scotland and the United States (which thus really justify their name). These are some of the usual explanations put forward to account for the name. The true origin of the designation is a historic one: unlike private schools, with which they were originally contrasted, such schools did not serve a local area but were open to pupils from anywhere in the country and increasingly so from the nineteenth century. In other words, they were like a private commercial company that had 'gone public', and offered its shares for sale to anyone who could afford to buy them. However before the eighteenth century a 'public' school was implicitly contrasted with a 'private' one, and education at such a school was similarly compared with 'private' education at home by a tutor.

**puffin** (kind of seabird with short neck and plump body)
Despite all kinds of learned attempts to derive the name of this homely-looking bird from some Latin or Cornish word (Latin as its name is first recorded in latinised spellings, Cornish since it is particularly associated with Cornwall and the Scilly Isles, as well as with other Celtic-speaking islands such as the Isle of Man), the word really does seem to mean more or less what it says, and so alludes to its 'puffed-out-ness' or plumpness, and young puffins are visibly globular. This origin is supported by the traditional simile 'as plump as a puffin', which although not so widely used now was once quite popular.

**pulley** (grooved wheel over which rope passes, used for raising, lowering etc)
A pulley is not so called since you pull on the rope round it to raise an object. The word goes back to Old French *polie*, which is probably ultimately derived from Greek *polos*, 'axis', 'pivot' (see **pole**).

**Pullman train** (kind of express train with extra facilities and comfort)
The train is not so called since it 'pulls' you along rapidly, nor because you need special 'pull' to travel on it! The name, which properly applies to a single carriage, not the

whole train, comes from that of its inventor, the American designer George M. Pullman. (He lived in Chicago, which now has a district named after him there.) British Rail use the term rather loosely of their so called 'InterCity' trains, especially those on which businessmen holding first-class tickets travel between London and Leeds, Manchester and Liverpool (*British Rail Passenger Timetable*, 1985). In Italian, *pullman* is now the standard word for 'coach' (i.e. the road vehicle).

**pumpernickel** (kind of black bread, rather coarse and sour-tasting)
The bread is wholesome, but not noticeably 'refined', and whatever the name means, it is probably not too complimentary. The explanation that derives the word from the remark of the French country soldier, who said the bread was only *bon pour Nicolas* (i.e. for his horse), can be enjoyed but confidently ignored for authenticity. The name is clearly German in origin, and had an earlier sense 'lout', 'stinker'. Perhaps the name actually means something like 'stinking Nicholas', with the *pumpen* the German verb for 'fart', and the second half of the word this personal name. Or perhaps the *pumpen* is simply suggestive of the hollow 'pump' sound heard when the loaf is struck? Even though the final derivation is still uncertain, at least the French one proposed here can be ruled out.

**pumpkin** (kind of large, round fruit)
The name of this marrow-like fruit is not related to 'pump' in any sense (as if it was a 'pumped up' marrow), or to 'plump'. The final '-kin', too, can hardly denote a diminutive. The word is in fact an alteration of the fruit's earlier name of *pumpion*. This came from Old French *pompon* and ultimately derives from Greek *pepōn*, 'ripe'. The pumpkin is thus a fruit that is basically ready to be eaten.

**pumps** (kind of light shoes used for dancing, gymnastics etc)
Pumps are not so called since they were worn in a pump room, where the waters of the local spa were drunk and where dances were held. Nor does there appear to be any other reference to 'pump' in any sense, and

it seems unlikely that the word derives from the idea that the foot fits as closely in the shoes as a piston in a pump, as suggested by the *Oxford Dictionary of English Etymology*. Perhaps the name is simply imitative of the sound the shoes make (i.e. is 'echoic', as linguists say), since a person running or jumping in pumps will make a a 'flumping' sound. (Compare **plump** and **pumper-nickel**, above.)

**punch** (kind of draught horse, typically the Suffolk punch)
The Suffolk punch (or any other) is a powerful horse, but it is not so called because of its 'punch' or forcefulness. Its name is almost certainly a dialect word for a short, fat animal (or person), and is thus the same as that of the little hook-nosed humpbacked hero of the Punch and Judy show (whose own name comes from the similar character called Punchinello in Italian puppet shows). See also the next entry.

**punch** (alcoholic drink, typically served hot and spiced and with a base of wine or spirits)
The party drink is not so designated because it 'packs a punch', although it undoubtedly does. Nor is it so called as it comes out of a puncheon (a large cask). The name very likely relates to its original five ingredients, and so derives from Hindi *pāc*, 'five' (which word also lies behind the name of the Punjab, which means 'five rivers'). One traditional recipe says the five ingredients are: arrack (an Asian spirit based on rice and molasses and fermented coconut sap), lemon, tea, sugar and water.

**pundit** (learned man)
No doubt associations of 'pun' and 'punch' and 'pungent' arise for this word, and even French *dit* or some learned English derived word. But the word simply comes from Sanskrit *paṇḍita*, 'learned'.

**pupil** (part of eye that varies in size according to the light)

This word is not a corruption of 'apple', referring to the 'apple of the eye', as has been sometimes stated. It in fact derives, through French, from Latin *pupilla*, 'little doll', referring to the minute reflection of oneself that can be seen in the pupil of someone else's eye. (This actually works. Make sure that the other person stands with his or her back to the light, however. If no one is handy, face a light source and look into a mirror. You will then see yourself quite literally 'in your own eyes'.) The 'apple of the eye' phrase is said to have been first used by Alfred the Great, and refers to the 'solid' appearance of this part of the eye. While we are about it, the other sense of 'pupil', meaning 'school student', has something of a similar origin. Latin *pupilla* meant not only 'little doll' but 'female ward', as a diminutive of *pupa*, 'girl' (also 'doll'), while the masculine equivalent of this was *pupillus*, 'male ward', the diminutive of *pupus*, 'boy'.

**pursue** (follow)
The word is sometimes misspelt 'persue', and is perhaps even understood in this way, as if it meant 'follow through', with the 'per-' prefix of such words as 'pervade', 'perambulate'. And in fact it was regularly spelt like this quite commonly as late as the eighteenth century, as in Dr Johnson's *Rasselas* of 1759, where he writes, 'Rasselas prepared to persue the robbers'. The word goes back through Old French *poursuir* (modern *poursuivre*) to Latin *prosequi*, 'to follow after'. This also gave 'prosecute', which by association with 'sue' may have also clouded the true origin.

**pustule** (small spot on the skin containing pus)
However annoyingly, this word is not actually related to 'pus' at all. It came into English from Latin *pustula*, 'blister', 'pimple', which is based on an element that is related to Greek *physan*, 'to blow' and (unexpectedly) English 'fog'. 'Pus', on the other hand, has a Latin origin that relates to such modern English words as 'suppurate', 'purulent' and 'putrid'.

**quadrille** (card game; square dance)
Unlike many words beginning 'quad-' ('quadrangle', 'quadrant', 'quadruplet' and so on), this word does not derive from a root word meaning 'four', despite the fact that the card game is a four-handed one played with a pack of forty cards and that the square dance is for four couples. Both senses come from Spanish (via French) *cuadrilla*, 'little square', in turn from Italian *quadriglia*, 'band', 'troop', ultimately from *quadra* (Spanish *cuadra*), 'square'. However, it must be allowed that this ultimate source is related to Spanish *cuarto*, Italian *quarto* etc meaning 'fourth', as is English 'square' itself in the long run.

**quail** (kind of game bird resembling a small partridge)
The bird is not so called since it is timid or 'quails' from strangers, although this popular explanation of the name is still current in country lore (and even in some 'word origin' books). In Medieval Latin the name of the bird was recorded as *quaccula*, and this (suggesting 'quack') gives a good clue regarding the actual source of the word, which is imitative of the cry, as with many birds. The cry of the quail consists of three sharp notes, and these are also represented in some of the popular names for the bird, such as 'but-for-but', 'wet-my-lip', 'wet-my-feet' and (perhaps the best known) 'quick-me-dick'. The call is made by the cock over a wide area, which may explain the further nickname of 'wandering quail' for the bird.

**quandary** (state of doubt, dilemma)
This fairly common word is not derived from 'hypochondria', as some sources say, and it is certainly not a corruption of French *qu'en dirai-je?* ('what shall I say about it?'), as also proposed by one enthusiastic etymologist. Its actual origin is still uncertain, but it may have derived from a semi-humorous use of Latin *quando?* ('when?'), with the ending similar to that of now obsolete terms and jocular words such as *backare!* ('back!'), *vagare*, ('vagary') and *jocundare* ('merry mood'). This ending was meant to suggest that of a Latin verb, and was accented (so that *backare* sounded like 'Bacari'). Tying in with this is the fact that 'quandary' was formerly also stressed on the '-ary' ending (like 'dairy'). Its present pronunciation sometimes leads to the spelling 'quandry', as for words like 'foundry' and 'laundry'.

**quarterdeck** (stern area of upper deck of a ship)
The origin of this word does not lie in French *écarter*, 'to set aside', as has been explained by some authorities, presumably referring to the fact that the quarterdeck is 'set aside' for the use of the officers only. It is in fact so called since originally it was a smaller deck above the halfdeck, which in old ships extended aft from the mainmast, for half the length of the ship.

**quiz** (test of knowledge)
This unlikely word has been explained in all sorts of entertaining ways, one of the best known telling how it was invented as the result of a bet undertaken by an Irishman called Daly in about 1780, who had it chalked up on several walls in Dublin overnight and so introduced a new word into the language in twenty-four hours (and won his bet that he could find a way of doing this). It originally meant 'eccentric person', and the first record we have of it is in the *Early Diary* of the novelist Madame d'Arblay (otherwise Fanny Burney), published in 1782, where in the entry dated 24 June she writes; 'He's a droll quiz, and I rather like him'. But the true origin of the word is still unknown, and the 'Irish' story is, alas, almost certainly a piece of fiction. Perhaps it somehow comes from Latin *quis?*, 'who?'

This could link up with the original 'oddball' sense and account for the modern development of meaning, since many quizzes involve the correct identification of an unknown or 'mystery' person, and even 'quizzical' implies a desire to identify a person or find out more about him (or her).

**rack and ruin** (destruction and devastation)
There is frequent confusion of spelling, sense and etymology between the various words 'rack' and 'wrack'. The one in this phrase (which can also be spelt 'wrack and ruin') is not related to the 'rack' that means 'torture' (as in 'on the rack'). As the second spelling indicates, it is in the 'wrack' family that is related to 'wreck', 'wreak' and 'wretch'. The spelling is thus optional, but the etymology is fixed in Old English *wrecan*, 'to punish', 'drive', 'urge'. See also **racket** (below).

**racket** (implement for playing tennis)
The word may look as though it has an origin in a 'little rack', perhaps referring to the framework of the implement. Or could it be somehow related to the other 'racket' that means 'noise', 'scheme', 'easy occupation'? Anyone for tennis? As its former spelling of 'raquet' hints, however, the word came into English from French (*raquette*), and it entered that language, via Italian, from Arabic *rāḥah*, 'palm of the hand'. So that is the much travelled true origin of this English-looking word.

**racy** (vigorous, piquant, risqué)
This sense of the word might suggest that it developed from 'race', the contest in speed, with the idea of being 'fast' or of being carried away by zeal and over-enthusiasm. But the actual origin is in the 'race' that means 'set of people of the same stock', when this is used in its derivative narrow sense of 'distinctive flavour of wine'. (This usage attributes the flavour of the wine to the soil, as if this were its particular 'stock'.) However, 'racy' can also mean 'long-bodied and lean', i. e. really 'suitable for racing', and here the influence of the speed contest 'race' is clearly present.

**rake** (dissolute person)
This rather archaic word should not be directly associated with 'rake' in the sense 'scrape together' (and the garden implement), nor is it a corruption of 'reckless' as has been suggested in the past. The word is actually a contraction of 'rakehell', a word in use for about two hundred years from the sixteenth century to mean 'scoundrel', 'rascal', one who 'rakes through hell'.

**rampart** (fortification or protective barrier)
There is no link between this word and 'ramp' or 'rampant', even though certain apparently apt associations may spring to mind (such as the ramp that is a kind of stairway or upward slope, as if leading to a rampart, or the militant connotation of 'rampant', meaning 'advancing threateningly'). The word in fact comes from French *rempart*, which is a form of the verb *remparer*, 'to fortify' (literally 'to re-protect', itself based on Latin *parare,* 'to prepare'). However, 'rampage' *is* based on 'ramp', referring to an animal that 'ramps and rages'.

**rankle** (cause bitterness)
There could so easily be a link here with 'rank' meaning 'coarse', 'rancid' and the like, but the two words are actually of quite distinct origins. 'Rankle' gradually changes shape and meaning as it is traced back through the various languages: directly from Middle English *ranclen*, 'to fester', from Old French *draoncler* with the same meaning, from *draoncle*, 'festering sore', from Latin *dracunculus*, 'little serpent', ultimately from *draco*, 'serpent', with this word also producing English 'dragon'. The basic concept in the modern word is thus one of a lingering, poisonous sting. 'Rank', on the other hand, ultimately relates to English 'right', since the word has changed its

meaning over the centuries, and originally meant 'proud', 'strong'.

**ransack** (rob, plunder)
This word did not develop from 'sack', also meaning 'plunder', which itself came via French from Latin *saccus*, 'bag'. For once, we have an Old Norse word here (suitably enough for the Vikings, no doubt), and in that language *rannsaka* came as a combination of *rann*, 'house' and *saka*, 'to seek' (which is related to the Norse word). 'Ransacking' thus was originally 'house-searching', and the Old Norse word that gave the source also produced English 'ramshackle', since a ramshackle building may well look as if it has been ransacked.

**rap** (in phrase, 'not to care a rap')
'I don't care *that* much', we might say, with a contemptuous snap of the fingers, and it could look as if the 'rap' here was a similar 'knock' to accompany the words, a forceful rap with the knuckles on the table, perhaps. But the origin of the word is not in aggression but diminutiveness, since the 'rap' of the phrase is an archaic name for a former small counterfeit Irish coin, a sham halfpenny, with its own name of Irish origin. Other names of small coins are used similarly, as in 'not worth a brass farthing', and 'hadn't a sou to his name'. And with 'not to care' itself we have a wide variety of similar small coins and sums to choose from to express our contempt, among them 'I couldn't care twopence' and the rather nice 'I don't care a continental' (this originating in the worthless Continental paper currency that circulated in America during the Revolution, because 'Continental' was the name used to apply to the colonies that later formed the United States).

**rare** (of meat: not fully cooked)
A 'rare' steak is something of an acquired taste, and some gourmets (and even gourmands) maintain that this is the best way to have them, rather than 'medium rare' or 'well done'. But such meat is not so called because of its 'rarity' or excellence, or because of the 'rare' skill needed to cook it to just the right degree of 'bloodiness', and the word is actually an alteration of earlier 'rear' or 'rere'. This was a term meaning

'half-cooked', used chiefly of eggs, and was an Old English word that is also perhaps related to 'raw'. A seventeenth-century book on medical practice thus recommends that in certain conditions the patient should abstain 'from Wine, Flesh, and Rear Eggs' (Nicholas Culpepper and William Rowland, *The Practice of Physick*, 1655).

**rarebit** (melted cheese on toast, typically the 'Welsh rarebit')
This dish is a favourite with children and tyro etymologists, who maintain that it should 'really' be 'Welsh rabbit'. Well, in a sense they are right, since it was certainly called 'Welsh rabbit' originally. However, this was clearly no real rabbit dish, but simply a fanciful or humorously presumptuous name for it, like 'Scotch woodcock' (which is really anchovies and scrambled egg on toast). But popularly the 'rabbit' was taken to be 'rarebit', since there was obviously no literal rabbit involved, and this is the form and spelling of the dish that is the standard one today. See also **Bombay duck**.

**ratline** (type of rope used on ship to form steps of a rope ladder)
Is the rope so called since rats used it when they deserted the proverbial sinking ship? Hardly. (In any case, ratlines run up to the mast, and the rats would need to go over the side of the ship.) The precise origin of the word is not known, although we do have alternative spellings such as *raddelyne* and *radelyng*, and the much more common alternatives *ratlin* and *ratling* in more recent times. Whatever the ultimate origin, it is nothing to do with rats!

**rear admiral** (senior naval rank and officer)
The rear admiral is not so called since in the rank table he follows just behind an admiral. He is so called since originally he was the admiral appointed to command the rear of the fleet in battle. And the top naval ranks actually go in this order (starting at the top and going down): admiral of the fleet, admiral, vice admiral, rear admiral, commodore etc. A rear admiral is thus the equivalent of a major general in the army

and an air vice marshal (rather confusingly) in the RAF. See also **admiral** itself.

**recoil** (spring back)
There are several shades of meaning for this verb, but the association with the firing of a gun (when a firearm moves back sharply as it is fired) may suggest a link with 'coil', as of a spring. But the word in fact comes from Old French (also modern) *reculer*, 'to draw back' (literally, 'to take one's backside back again'), whereas 'coil' is related to modern French *cueillir*, 'to gather', and so to English 'cull'.

**refrain** (recurring phrase in a poem or song, chorus)
This sort of refrain is not so called since it 'stops' the flow of the poem or song, or 'refrains' it (in the archaic sense of 'restrain'). The musical refrain does, however, come ultimately from Latin *refringere*, 'to break up', so in a sense the 'hold up' or 'cutting in' sense is almost right. But the other 'refrain', meaning 'hold oneself in check', comes from Latin *refrenare*, 'to bridle', 'hold back', and this means that the two words are not etymologically related. However, this does not stop the two senses of the word serving to be exploited for punning anecdotes, like this one, recounted in rather mannered English (in English) in Félix Boillot's *Le Vrai Ami du traducteur anglais-français et français-anglais* (Paris, 1930):

The tale is told of two women who attended musical events rather because it was 'the thing' than through any love or knowledge of music. At a certain concert they were sitting near the back of the hall, and began to argue about the identity of a certain composition that the orchestra was rendering.

Giving a suggestion of authority, they argued about the works of various composers and each decided upon what it was. Neither could convince the other to her way of thinking, so one suggested that she should go up and read what it said on the signboard by the platform.

She toddled up the aisle in the interval between the items and returned quickly to her companion.

'Well', said the one who had remained in her seat, 'I was right, wasn't I?'

'No', said the investigator, 'we were both wrong: it was the "Refrain from Spitting"'.

(To which one can hardly refrain from a time-honoured 'Oi!')

**regale** (entertain lavishly)
If you regale someone you give them a 'right royal treat'. The word is not related to 'regal', however, but comes from French *régaler*, which is in itself based on *gale*, 'pleasure', 'merrymaking' (a word related to English 'gala'). 'Regalia', however, is certainly related to 'regal' since it pertains to the emblems of royalty. See also **regatta** (below), for further false associations.

**regatta** (sailing or rowing race or contest)
A regatta can be rather a grand thing, such as the annual Royal Regatta at Henley. In spite of this, the word does not have any connections with such 'royal' words as 'regal', 'regent' and 'regalia' or with such 'grand' words as **'regale'** and 'gala' (see previous entry). It comes from an Italian Venetian dialect word *regatta* or *rigatta* meaning basically 'contest', 'strife', and is said to have originally been used in that language to refer to boat contests on the Grand Canal in Venice.

**reindeer** (type of deer commonly domesticated)
The deer is not so called because, as in Lapland, it can be harnessed for pulling sleds and so wear reins. In fact, it is the 'rein' that actually means 'reindeer', from Old Norse *hreinn*, with the 'deer' thus representing Old Norse *dyr*, 'animal'. This origin can be seen also in the German word for 'reindeer', *Renntier*. See also **wilderness** for more 'deer'.

**rest** (in well known carol: 'God rest you merry, gentlemen')
The familiar line is often mispunctuated (as 'God rest you, merry gentlemen', or without the comma altogether), resulting in the sense being taken to be 'May God give you rest, merry gentlemen', as if applied to Christmastide carousers who are in danger

of overdoing it. But taken as punctuated in the heading above, the actual meaning is 'May God grant that you remain happy, Sirs', or more basically, 'Enjoy yourselves, gentlemen'. 'Merry' here is used in its older sense of 'happy', as in 'Merry England' and 'the merry month of May'. The greeting or wish expressed in the line was a standard one in Shakespeare's day, and in fact occurs in As You Like It, for example, where the 'country fellow' William takes his leave of Touchstone with the words, 'God rest you merry, sir'.

**rest-harrow** (kind of shrub with tough roots, commonly found in fields)
The plant is not so called since it 'rests the harrow' in some way, but because its sturdy roots make harrowing difficult, as they 'arrest the harrow' in its progress. Both 'rest' and 'arrest' are related words, with the basic sense common to both being 'cease from action'.

**retch** (make an effort to vomit)
This unpleasant verb is often pronounced (and even spelt, as it formerly used to be) 'reach'. However, there is no connection between the two words; and the first here is imitative in origin (as are similar verbs such as 'hawk' and 'keck' and even 'cough'). In the alternative form, however, there could be ambiguity in such a statement as 'I reached over the side of the boat'.

**rhapsody** (lyrical or emotionally charged poem, song or piece of music)
The word is sometimes misspelt or mentally envisaged as 'rapsody', just as 'rhyme' was formerly 'rime', and this can lead to a false association with 'rapt', through the 'emotionally transported' sense implied in both words. The word actually comes from the Greek, as the correct spelling suggests, where the ultimate source is a combination of *rhaptein*, 'to sew', 'to stitch' and *ōidē*, 'song' (giving English 'ode'). A rhapsody is thus literally a 'poem consisting of songs that have been stitched together'. A colourful origin, but the real one. In French, incidentally, the equivalent word can be properly spelt with or without its 'h', as *rhapsodie* or *rapsodie*. Compare also English doublets

'rumba' and 'rhumba', and see **rhythm** (below).

**rhumb** (one of 32 points of mariner's compass)
This rather technical word has almost certainly been influenced by the equally technical 'rhombus', but the two words are not really related in any way. 'Rhumb' comes from Spanish *rumbo*, which probably itself derives from Middle Dutch *ruum*, 'space', 'ship's hold' (the link being the 'rhumbline' or straight course followed by a ship). 'Rhombus', on the other hand, comes from Greek *rhombos*, literally 'spinning top', since formerly tops had square sides, and a rhombus is a four-sided figure (actually an oblique-angled parallelogram).

**rhythm** (metre, regular occurrence of stress or sound)
The link with 'rhyme' in sense and spelling is not coincidental. 'Rhythm', which ultimately derives from Greek *rhein*, 'to flow', originally meant 'piece of rhyming verse' and itself rhymed with 'time', as it does in this piece of seventeenth-century verse:

> And what were crime
> In prose, would be no injury in
> rhythm.
> (Joshua Poole, *The English Parnassus*, 1677)

At the same time, the modern meaning began to develop. 'Rhyme', on the other hand was formerly also spelt 'rime' – but probably derived from Latin *rhythmus*, 'rhythm'! So the two words are interrelated in a complex way, with varying senses and spellings. But you must admit that most rhymes have got rhythm.

**riding** (former administrative area of Yorkshire)
Since the change in local government boundaries of 1974, there have no longer been any any ridings in Yorkshire. Formerly, there were three: East, West and North Riding. Yorkshire, with its spacious dales and rolling country is a fine county for riding. But this is not the origin of the word, to which a clue has just been given. The clue is in their number, since 'riding' is really 'thirding', that is, one of three equally

important areas. The word is of Old Norse origin (where it was *thrithjung*), and came about simply because the Scandinavians who had settled in this part of England regarded Yorkshire as too large for a single administration. The modern spelling came about since the initial 'th' of the Old Norse word (or rather of its Old English equivalent) blended with the final 't' of the original words for 'east' and 'west' (as *Estreding*, for example, the spelling in the eleventh-century 'Domesday Book'), and this produced the 'riding', without its initial 'th', that evolved as the modern word. (The Yorkshire novelist Winifred Holtby wrote a book in the 1930s called *South Riding*, but this was just a fictional name to describe an area of her native county.)

**righteous** (morally right)
This word looks as if it is formed on the same basis as 'piteous', 'nauseous', and so on, that is, with an '-eous' ending added to its corresponding noun. Originally, however, it was *rightwise*, meaning 'in a right way', 'in a virtuous manner', but this Middle English word altered its spelling in the sixteenth century to resemble adjectives such as 'beauteous' and 'plenteous'.

**rigmarole** (confused talk, convoluted procedure)
An association here with 'rig' is an understandable one, since the word almost implies an elaborate or deliberately 'rigged' enterprise. The actual origin lies in the unexpected 'ragman roll'. This was the name of a list of characters in some medieval game, where the first character was called *Ragemon le bon* (perhaps meaning 'Ragman the Good' or 'Ragged Man the Good'), and where the players drew a verse with an attached string at random to see what luck they could get, as a sort of gambling game. Doing this was obviously quite a rigmarole in itself.

**ringleader** (leader of a gang or group of 'baddies')
The 'ring' here was originally not the 'ring' that today means 'people working together for a corrupt purpose', since this sense arose only in the nineteenth century. The word as a whole comes from the phrase 'to lead the ring', which in its basic sense means 'people standing in a ring', as for a dance. The earliest date we have for this phrase is in the fourteenth century, where it is found in the words, 'Woman the ryng leduth for joye', almost certainly referring to a dance. Subsequently, the 'ring' began to denote more sinister groups, until it evolved in the specialized sense the word now has.

**ritzy** (unduly 'smart', 'jazzy')
This word in its sound and spelling has all the right associations for its sense, conjuring up such suitable synonyms as 'rich', 'chintz', 'de luxe' and even offering a suggestion of opulent Biarritz. But of course the true reference is to the Ritz Hotel, with its connotation of wealth and luxury, and ultimately we owe the word to the name of the founder, the Swiss hotelier César Ritz. How fortunate it was, though, that (in English, at any rate) he had such an apt glitzy, kitschy name!

**rivulet** (small stream)
It seems strange, but there is no actual connection between this word and 'river'. It came into English from Italian *rivoletto*, which itself derived from Latin *rivulus*, a diminutive of *rivus*, 'stream'. 'River', on the other hand, comes (via French) from Latin *ripa*, 'bank'. On the other hand, there was a word 'riveret', now obsolete, but common in the seventeenth century, that was a diminutive of 'river', and this formed a sort of bridge between the two.

**roam** (wander, travel 'far and wide')
There is a persistent tale that 'roam' derives from 'Rome', with reference to the pilgrims who used to travel (or 'roam') there. Support for this theory is said to be provided by such foreign words for 'pilgrim' as Old French *romier*, Spanish *romero*, Italian *romeo*, and so on. Shakespeare, too, puns on the two words, as in *Henry VI*, Part I, where the following exchange occurs:

> *Bishop of Winchester*. Rome shall
>   remedy this.
> *Earl of Warwick*.   Roam thither then.

But this is a relatively late pun by linguistic standards, and there is no real evidence that the two words have a common link. The exact origin of 'roam', therefore, is still unknown.

**Romany** (gypsy, or gypsy language)
The name romantically suggests associations with Rome or even Romania. However, Romany is not even a Romance language (like French, Italian, Spanish, and so on), and the word is actually a Romany word (an adjective) meaning 'gypsy', deriving from *rom*, 'male gypsy', itself ultimately from a Sanskrit word *domba* denoting a male low caste musician. The word was popularized by George Borrow in his attractive novel *The Romany Rye*, whose title means 'The Gypsy Gentleman', the nickname bestowed on Borrow when he was young by a Norfolk gypsy, Ambrose Smith. ('Rye' is related to 'rajah' and 'royal'.) See also **gypsy** itself.

**rookie** (raw recruit)
This chiefly American word may wrongly suggest that the recruit has been 'rooked' or swindled into enlisting. But it is probably just a version of 'recruit'. Kipling used the word in his *Barrack-Room Ballads* of 1892, which is just about the first written record we have of it:

So 'ark an' 'eed, you rookies, which is
  always grumblin' sore.

**root** (of pigs: to turn up the earth with the snout)
This sense of the word is not related to the ordinary 'root' of plants, as if that was what the pigs grubbed up or were even looking for. The origin is in the Old English verb *wrōtan* in this sense, which later resulted in a spelling 'wroot', itself at least partially influenced by Old English *wrōt*, 'snout'.

**rosemary** (fragrant shrub of the mint family)
This agreeable plant name is probably so pleasant since it conjures up 'rose' and 'Mary'. But it is actually nothing to do with either, since it comes from Latin *rosmarinus*, itself based on *ros*, 'dew' and *marinus*, 'marine'. The plant is thus a sort of 'seadew', apparently so called since it is often found growing by the sea. The 'Mary' would have been taken to be a reference to

the Virgin Mary. See **pansy** for a relevant quotation concerning the shrub.

**rote** (in phrase 'by rote': using the memory automatically, without thought)
There is no evidence to confirm a connection here with 'rotation' or 'rota', nor is there any evidence that the word links up with 'route' or 'routine'. The word may derive from Latin *rota* in its medieval Latin sense of 'public way', thus denoting a regular course. 'Route', on the other hand, comes from Vulgar Latin *rupta via*, literally 'broken way', i. e. a well-beaten one.

**roundelay** (song with a refrain)
'Lay' is an old word for a song or poem, but there is no evidence that this word is connected with it, even though it may well have been influenced by it. It in fact derives from Old French *rondelet*, literally 'little circle', itself a diminutive of *rondel* (producing English 'rondel' and 'roundel'). The basic idea is a poem in which certain lines 'do the rounds' and keep turning up as a refrain.

**rover** (pirate)
A rover is not so called since he roves the seas, but because his name comes from Middle Dutch *roven*, 'to rob'.

**rowlock** (device to hold oar on side of rowing boat)
The word obviously suggests a kind of *lock* in which the oar can be held for *rowing*. This is not quite the origin, however, since the word was formerly 'oarlock', as the device is still normally called today in North America. The 'oar' of this became 'row', and the original form of the word became further disguised in the pronunciation 'rollock'.

**ruffian** (violent criminal)
There is a clear suggestion of 'rough' in this word, and also of such words as 'scruffy' and 'ruffle'. Of course, 'rough' also exists in its own right to mean 'ruffian', 'hooligan', which only serves to strengthen the association. Charles Dickens commented on the similarity of the two words in his weekly periodical *All the Year Round*, where in the issue for 10 October 1868 he writes: 'I enter-

tain so strong an objection to the euphonious softening of ruffian into rough, which has lately become popular, that I restore the right reading to the heading of this paper'. (The paper in question was 'The Ruffian, by the Uncommercial Traveller'.) Dickens was wrong to link the two words etymologically, however, since they are not connected, and neither is a 'softening' or alteration of the other. The word came into English from Italian *ruffiano*, where its origin, although not certain, may be in a dialect word *rofia*, 'scurf', 'scabbiness'.

**runagate** (runaway, fugitive)
This rather dated word picturesquely conjures up someone running away through a gate, which of course is the most convenient way if it is open. However, the derivation of the word is in the now obsolete 'renegate', related to 'renegade', both these coming ultimately from Medieval Latin *renegatus*, a verbal form of *renegare*, itself based on *negare*, to deny'. This same source gave the modern English verb 'to renegue' (or 'renege'), meaning 'deny', 'revoke'. There must have been an influence from 'run', however, to give the present spelling of 'runagate'.

**ryegrass** (kind of grass used for animal fodder)
This is a misleading name, falsely suggesting 'rye'. The word was originally 'raygrass', where even 'ray' is not what it seems, since it is an old word for 'darnel', which is a grass related to ryegrass.

**Sabaoth** (in title of God: 'Lord of Sabaoth')
This religious word looks very like 'Sabbath', but is in fact quite distinct from it. In the original Hebrew, where it is the plural of *ṣābā*, it means 'armed hosts', and the title as a whole is translated 'Lord of Hosts' in the English Old Testament. In the New Testament, however, as well as in the *Te Deum* in the *Book of Common Prayer* and also in a number of hymns, 'Sabaoth' is left untranslated. 'Sabbath', however, although also deriving from Hebrew, has another original sense altogether, since *shabbāth* means 'rest'. The two words or names have been confused and wrongly associated with each other by more than a few writers, including even Spenser in *The Faerie Queene*, where he has the lines:

All that moveth doth in change
   delight:
But thenceforth all shall rest eternally
With him that is the God of Sabaoth
   hight:
O! that great Sabaoth God, grant me
   that Sabaoth's sight!

**sack** (type of dry white wine)
The wine is not so called since bottles of it were sold in sacks, nor because the name derives from Spanish *sacar*, 'to draw out', referring to its export from Spain, but because it is properly a *dry* wine (French *sec*, 'dry'). The wrong association has been further promoted, alas, by a brand of sherry called 'Dry Sack', with the bottles actually being marketed in a little decorative sack. This trade name also suggests, of course, that 'Sack' cannot itself mean 'dry' since it is actually preceded by the word 'Dry'. (Logically, too, to call any wine 'dry' seems a contradiction in terms, although French also uses *sec* in the same senses: 'opposite of wet' and 'opposite of sweet'. And to think that a 'dry' country is one where alcohol is forbidden!)

**sacrilegious** (irreverent)
This word is sometimes misspelt 'sacreligious', as if it was associated with or even derived from 'religious'. It is not, however, and in fact means almost the opposite (i.e. 'irreligious'), so that its origin is actually in Latin *sacrilegus*, 'temple-robber', from *sacra*, 'sacred things' and the verb *legere*, 'to take', 'to steal'.

**safe** (type of strongbox for money and other valuables)
A safe is not so called since things are kept safe in it, but because it was originally a 'save', or place mainly for keeping something for future use. Admittedly, the senses are quite close, and if you 'save' something you will almost certainly keep it 'safe'. It is still worth recording here, however, that the present noun originated in a slightly different verb (and noun) that was assimilated to an adjective ('safe') that became the noun it now is!

**sainfoin** (pink-flowered plant of pea family grown for fodder)
The name is explained by some nature lovers as deriving from the French for 'holy hay'. The derivation is indeed from the French, but not quite in this sense, since French *sain*, 'healthy' is involved, not *saint*, 'holy'. The ultimate origin is in Medieval Latin *sanum faenum*, literally 'wholesome hay'. The plant is so called since it is good fodder for cattle and also has uses in medicine. The second half of the word is basically the same as 'fennel'.

**salmonella** (type of bacteria causing food poisoning)
This word suggests that the disease can be caused by eating unwholesome tinned salmon, for example. But the name owes its origin to the American veterinary surgeon who initially identified the particular

bacteria genus, Daniel Elmer Salmon (1850-
1914). The genus was first so designated in
1900 in the French professional *Bulletin de
la Société centrale de Médecine Vétérinaire*.

**saltcellar** (container for salt)
If you can keep coal and wine in a cellar,
then presumably you can keep salt likewise.
But this is not the origin of the word, which
in the fifteenth century was *salt saler*. The
second word here comes from Old French
*saliere*, 'salt container'. This derivation was
not understood, however, so an extra 'salt'
was added to it, and the second word, also
subsequently not seen as meaningful, was
altered to 'cellar' by association with this
word and its household 'container' sense.
French does things much more neatly here,
and modern *salière* means 'saltcellar' just as
*poivrière* means 'pepper pot' and *saucière*
means 'sauce boat'. All much more
economical.

**salver** (type of ornamental tray)
Because literature, children's stories and the
like often involve a 'silver salver', the latter
word is also sometimes taken to be
connected with 'silver'. This is because in
many similar jingling or rhyming phrases
the two words are often mutually meaningful (as in 'teeny-weeny' suggesting simultaneously and synonymously both 'tiny' and
'wee', and 'eager beaver' connoting
someone who is both keen to work and a
keen worker). However, there is no trace
of 'silver' behind 'salver'. The word comes
(through French) from Spanish *salva*, itself
based on the verb *salvar*, 'to save'. A *salva*
was a tray from which the king's taster
sampled food just to ensure that it was not
poisoned (deliberately, that is). The tray
was thus basically a 'safeguard'.

**sandblind** (having poor eyesight)
This now archaic word would seem to
suggest inability to see properly through
having sand thrown or blown in one's eyes.
In Old English, however, the word
(although not found recorded as such) was
probably *samblind*, where the *sam-* (related
to 'semi-') means 'half'. The meaning is thus
'half-blind', and so also 'purblind' (which
originally, however, meant 'totally blind',
since the 'pur-' means 'pure').

**sangreal** (the holy grail)
The word is sometimes said to derive from
French *sang real*, and so mean 'holy blood'.
It is actually a variant spelling of 'sangrail',
however, which shows it to be based on
'grail' itself. This derives, through French,
from Medieval Latin *gradalis*, 'dish', 'bowl'.
'Sangreal' therefore means 'holy bowl'.
According to medieval legend, the holy grail
was the cup used by Christ at the Last
Supper and later sought for by the Knights
of the Round Table.

**sapper** (mining engineer)
The soldier who digs trenches and lays
mines is not so called because he 'under-
mines' the strength of the enemy, in other
words 'saps' it. He doesn't sap anything, in
fact, not even morale, since the word that
gives his special role comes ultimately from
Italian *zappa*, 'spade', 'hoe'. It must be
allowed, however, that the two different
kinds of 'sap' (relating to the sap of a tree
and the more technical 'sap' that means
'underground trench') produce senses that
are quite close to each other. If you thus
'sap' someone's energy, you could say you
are draining it away, like sap from a tree,
or that you are weakening it, like digging a
sap under the enemy defences. Dictionaries
themselves vary in the 'sap' that they cite
for this metaphorical usage.

**Saracen** (member of nomadic tribe,
especially Muslim in the Crusades)
Word-hunters and trackers have wondered
for some time about this name, and have
derived it from several sources, mainly
Arabic words, but also from the name of
Abraham's wife in the Bible, Sarah! It is
still something of a mystery, and although
it can be traced back fairly confidently to
Late Latin and Late Greek, its ultimate
origin is rather misty. One of the more sensible suggestions is that it relates to Arabic
*sharq*, 'sunrise', 'east wind'. But it can
hardly be attributed to Sarah.

**sardine** (small fish used for food)
All that need be said here is that any direct
link with 'Sardinia' is unlikely, even though
sardines are caught there and exported from
there. The original Latin *sardina* that gave
the present English word (and also the

name of the fish in many other languages) could be a diminutive of *sarda* that itself is the name of some other fish, presumably an edible one. Many dictionaries, even specifically etymological ones, relate the fish name to the island, but on the other hand many do not. For the sardine's provenance, therefore, we will have to pass the verdict 'not proven'.

**sash window** (window whose upper and lower parts open vertically)
The name of this type of window is sometimes misunderstood to derive from the cords (sashcords) used to open and close it. No doubt there is a connection between 'sash' and a word such as 'band', thinking of the length of material. But this is quite a different sash (from an Arabic word meaning 'muslin'), and 'sash' in the case of the window is a semi-technical word for the frame in which the window is housed and in which it slides up and down. This sense probably comes from French *châssis*, with this word wrongly taken to be a plural. So a sash window is so called not from its sashcords but directly from the two sashes themselves.

**satyr** (minor woodland god in classical mythology)
This god has a name that suggests an association with 'satire', all the more as there was a type of bawdy comic play in ancient Greece called a 'satyr play' or 'satyric drama'. However, the god's name is simply a version of what he was called in Greek, *satyros*, while 'satire' goes back through French to Latin *satira* or *satura*, 'mixture', ultimately based on *satis*, 'enough'.

**savvy** (know)
This colloquial word is obviously not English, and is often taken to be a rather wilful spelling of French *savez*, 'you know'. It is actually, however, a corruption of Spanish *sabe* in this meaning (with *usted*, 'you' understood). The word evolved to its present form and usage through Black English and **Pidgin English** (which see).

**scalpel** (surgeon's or scientist's thin-bladed knife)
No doubt a scalpel could be used for

scalping, since it is used for both dissection and surgery, but its name has nothing to do with this but derives from Latin *scalpellus* or *scalpellum*, the diminutive of *scalprum*, 'knife', which itself comes from the verb *scalpere*, 'to scrape', 'to carve'. The same Latin origin lies behind English 'shelf', the basic concept being of something that has been carved out, like a shelf of rock.

**scarify** (make scratches or cuts on, injure feelings of)
As can be seen from these two definitions, the verb has nothing to do with 'scare', although it is surprisingly often used in this sense. It even occurs in the works of such reputable modern writers as Mary Webb and Noel Coward. The former has it in her novel *The Golden Arrow* ('Fixing a scarifying gaze on the truant'), and the latter uses it in his play *The Rat Trap* ('I suppose it's silly nerves, but to be on the brink of a great happiness is a scarifying feeling'). This use or misuse of the word seems to be a sort of blend of 'scare' and 'terrify'. 'Scarify' (which is also not related to 'scar') derives ultimately, through French and Latin, from Greek *skariphasthai*, 'to scratch an outline'. The word is perhaps most commonly found in its sense of 'break up the surface of' (e.g. a road or field).

**school** (large group of fish, whales, etc swimming together)
There are several interesting or even esoteric 'group' names in English (such as the grand 'convocation of eagles'), and it could be thought that this one is a tribute to the 'disciplined' way in which the creatures swim together, change course all together, and so on. Disappointingly, the word is simply a variation of 'shoal', with both words deriving directly or indirectly from Old English *scolu*, 'multitude'. (This 'shoal' is in turn not related to the other 'shoal' that means 'shallow', 'sandbank', which comes from Old English *sceald* and is indirectly related to English 'skeleton'.) Some schoolteachers are fond of happily pointing out to their charges that their own 'school' comes from a Greek word (*scholē*) meaning 'leisure'. Perhaps they do not always add that this is not quite such a paradox as it may seem, since the sense is 'leisure to

dispute in search of knowledge'. See also **charm**.

**scissors** (cutting implement with two pivoted blades)
If one sets out in pursuit of the undoubted classical origin of this word, one may well take the wrong turning and end up with Latin *scindere* (past participle *scissus*), 'to cut', 'to split', with this related to such English words as 'scission' and the Greek-based 'schism' and 'schizophrenia'. And indeed because of this very association a letter 'c' was added to a word that was previously spelt without it (as Middle English *sisoures*). So another origin is needed, and it is actually Old French *cisoires*, which itself comes from Latin *caedere*, 'to cut' (also giving Late Latin *cisorium*, 'cutting instrument'). The spelling with 'sc-' first appeared in the sixteenth century. Early forms of the word were spelt in a variety of ways (one common one was *sizars*), and even as late as 1719 Daniel Defoe, in *Robinson Crusoe*, wrote that his hero, looking for implements on his desert island, managed to find 'one Pair of large Sizzers'.

**scone** (kind of small light cake cooked in an oven or on a griddle)
The fact that this is essentially a Scottish comestible can lead to a false connection with the village called Scone, near Perth, and also with the 'Stone of Scone' (where Scottish kings were crowned) that was formerly there. But the scone is not related to this place, and probably gets its name from Dutch *schoonbrood*, 'fine bread'. There is actually a difference of pronunciation between the different words, too, so that the Scottish village is pronounced 'Scoon' and the scone is pronounced to rhyme either with 'cone' (mainly in the south of England) or 'con' (elsewhere, and certainly in Scotland itself).

**scot free** (without incurring any payment, penalty or other 'damage')
The phrase is nothing to do with the Scots or Scotland, despite the popular association between this people and their alleged reluctance to spend more than can be avoided. It comes from the old or at least rare word 'scot' meaning 'money paid as a tax' (prob-ably itself from Old Norse), and was first in general use in the sixteenth century, with the sense gradually extended to apply to freedom from any imposition or injury, not just the payment of money.

**scour** (search widely but rapidly)
The verb is typically used in such phrases as 'scour the country'. It is not the same word as the 'scour' that means 'clean', 'clear', as if a vigorous 'sweep' or 'clean-up' were being made to find someone or something. In this special sense, 'scour' is probably of Scandinavian origin, while the 'rub clean' verb ultimately comes from Late Latin *excurare*, 'to cleanse', 'to clean off', so is thus indirectly related to modern 'cure'.

**scrip** (brief writing, certificate)
Most senses of 'scrip' derive from 'script', but the financial 'scrip', meaning a certificate entitling the holder to a particular number of shares etc, is probably an abbreviation of 'sub*scrip*tion receipt'.

**scrumpy** (rough cider, especially the kind made in the West Country)
This famous strong, dry cider may well be scrumptious, but that is not the origin of its name. Nor even is it made from apples that have been 'scrumped', i.e. stolen from gardens and orchards. The source of the name lies in the dialect word 'scrump' used of the small, shrivelled apples from which it is made. The 'scrump' that means 'steal apples' is also a dialect word, deriving not from the cider apples just mentioned, but as an alteration of 'scrimp'. Finally, 'scrumptious' is probably an alteration of 'sumptuous'.

**scullion** (kitchen servant)
This old word did not arise from the fact that a scullion worked in the scullery, but referred to the implements, since it derives from Old French *escouillon*, 'dishcloth', itself an alteration of *escouve*, 'broom' and ultimately from Latin *scopa*, literally 'twig'. The scullion was thus a rather basic washer-upper. 'Scullery', where admittedly the washing-up was done (and perhaps in some houses still is), comes from Anglo-Norman *squillerie*, ultimately from Old French *escuele*, 'bowl'.

**sect** (breakaway religious body)
Because in many words the element '-sect-' means 'cut' or 'cut off' (as in 'section', 'dissect', 'sector' and so on), it might be thought that a sect is so called since, logically enough,' it has cut itself off from the main body. But this is surprisingly not the case, and the word derives from Late Latin *secta*, 'organised body', 'faction', 'following', itself based on the root of the verb *sequi*, 'to follow' (which has a past participle *secutus*).

**sedan chair** (type of portable chair, in use in the seventeenth and eighteenth centuries)
Did the original sedan chair come from Sedan, in France, as has been sometimes stated? Almost certainly not. And although the precise provenance of the chair is not certain, the word could well derive ultimately from Latin *sella*, 'saddle', 'stool', which in turn is based on the verb *sedere*, 'to sit'. Even the identical Italian verb *sedere* may lie somewhere behind the name.

**seersucker** (kind of light fabric used for summer wear)
Seersucker is usually striped and slightly puckered, which may suggest some sort of association with 'suck' (such as a sweet, especially a striped one intended for sucking). Oddly enough, although this is not the origin, the actual derivation is somewhat on these lines, since the name comes, through Hindi, from Persian *shīr-o-shakar*, 'milk and sugar', with this actually referring to the appearance of the stripes. We have a sort of English parallel for this in the cloth for coats and so on that is called 'pepper and salt', meaning basically black and white or dark and white but mixed together in small flecks.

**sentry** (soldier standing guard or on watch)
A sentry and a sentinel perform more or less the same duties, and although the first word is now much more common than the second, one would expect to find a common origin for the two similar-looking words. However, it is probable that 'sentry' derives from an identical obsolete word meaning 'sanctuary', and that it is itself an alteration or corruption of this. 'Sentinel', on the other

hand, comes from Old French *sentinelle* which in turn derives from Old Italian *sentinella*, and this is based on *sentina*, 'watchfulness', from the verb *sentire*, 'to notice'. Nevertheless, despite these diverse beginnings, one of the two may well have had an influence on the meaning and spelling of the other.

**serenade** (song or instrumental work, especially one performed in the evening as a compliment to a woman)
The Italian for 'evening' is *sera* (compare French *soir*), and this seems to be the basis for the word, especially in view of its particular meaning. But the actual origin (through the French) is Italian *serenata*, from *sereno*, 'calm', 'peaceful' (as of weather), although it is likely that *sera* also had its influence.

**setter** (type of gun dog)
Why is a setter so called? Does it set track for the game, or set its ears back (or its tail up) when it scents or spots game? There are so many meanings of 'set' that the true origin is easily obscured. In the seventeenth century it was called a 'setting dog', and its name refers to the way in which it 'sets' or remains rigid to indicate that it has detected the quarry. Originally, too, it sat or crouched, as distinct from a **pointer** that remained standing, but today a setter is usually trained to point as well. See also **terrier** and **lurcher**.

**sexton** (church official who looks after church property and carries out certain regular duties, such as ringing the bell, digging graves, and so on)
The duties of a sexton, where he exists, have modified and been simplified over the years, but he is not so called, as some like to believe, since he works on six days a week to prepare the church for Sunday! (Admittedly, many words beginning 'sext-' do relate to 'six', such as 'sextant', 'sextet' and 'sextuplets'; but he is not one of them.) The word is simply an English alteration of the Latin-derived 'sacristan' (so called because he looks after the sacristy, where the sacred church vessels are kept).

**shagreen** (kind of untanned leather; sharkskin)
The word has come to be spelt in this way by false association with 'shag' (in the 'coarse fibre' sense as for a carpet) and 'green'. However, its true origin is French *chagrin*, ultimately from Turkish. (See this word itself for more background.)

**shako** (kind of military hat with a tall crown and a plume)
Such an agreeable and aptly descriptive name for this distinctive hat with its shaky plume. But this is not the origin after all, and the word is the English attempt to represent the Hungarian name for it, which is *csákó*, 'peaked' (with *süveg*, 'cap' understood). Hungary is the home of the shako.

**Shalott** (in title of Tennyson's poem: *The Lady of Shalott*)
This quite well known title is popularly misspelt with the last word the same as the 'shallot' that is the plant related to the onion (although to name a lady after this would be bizarre!). So who or what is this Shalott? Having quickly ruled out the plant, we must look in the direction of Arthurian legend. There we will find that the Lady of Shalott was Elaine, the 'Fair Maid of Astolat' who fell in love with the famous Launcelot of the Lake (otherwise Sir Lancelot). This, at any rate, is the story as retold in English in the fourteenth century, in a version based on the French. (King Arthur has roots in many lands, as do the characters associated with him.) So 'Shalott' is Tennyson's rendering of 'Astolat' (which also appears in the early English version as 'Ascolot'). The origin of the name is obscure, but its location was stated to be Guildford, at any rate by Thomas Malory in his account of the story entitled *Le Morte d'Arthur*. However, the Lady of Shalott belongs wholly to Tennyson:

> But Lancelot mused a little space;
> He said 'She has a lovely face;
> God in his mercy lend her grace,
>     The Lady of Shalott'.

**shambles** (scene of disorder or destruction)
The term does not refer to people who are shambling about, causing chaos, but relates to its original sense, 'meat market', so called from the 'shambles' that were the tables on which meat was displayed. The word itself comes from Old English *scamul*, 'counter', 'stool', ultimately from Latin *scamnum* in this latter sense. The verb 'shamble' probably came from the meat table, alluding to its trestles, since a shambling person walks with bent or bowed legs. Some towns still hold a regular weekly market in a building called 'The Shambles', such as at Devizes, and the word is also found in street names, as at York.

**shamefaced** (showing shame)
A shamefaced person has a face which shows he's ashamed. Yet the word is in fact an alteration of 'shamefast', meaning 'held fast by shame'. The origin is thus similar to other words ending in '-fast', such as 'steadfast'.

**shammy leather** (type of leather or other cleaning cloth)
The name is a corruption of 'chamois', in fact, since the cleaning cloth is properly made from the skin of this small goatlike antelope. However, many proprietary brands of 'chamois' are not made from leather at all, so really are 'shammy'.

**shamrock** (small plant having three leaflets and serving as a floral emblem for Ireland)
The name does not relate to either 'sham' or 'rock', as if referring to the plant's deceptive appearance or its preferred habitat, despite the fact that 'rock' occurs in plant names (such as the rockrose or the rock plants themselves). But not for nothing is the shamrock the symbol of Ireland, since its name is Irish, and thus *seamróg* simply means 'trefoil' (this word itself being a diminutive of *seamar*, 'clover').

**shark** (greedy exploiter, 'crook')
The shark seems very clearly to be so called since he 'preys' on people. However, despite the undoubted influence of the other, sea beast word, this sense of 'shark' has its likely origin in a corruption of German *Schurke*, 'rogue', which word also gave English 'shirk'.

**sheen** (lustre, shine, bright surface)
This word does not derive directly from 'shine', but comes from an older word (Middle English *shene*) that meant 'beautiful', 'shining' and that is related to modern German *schön*, 'beautiful'. This means that the word is related to English 'show', whereas 'shine' is not.

**sheldrake** (kind of duck)
The name of this bird is not related to 'shell', any more than the feminine 'shelduck' is. It derives from a combination of the dialect word *sheld*, 'variegated', 'particoloured' and 'drake' or 'duck'. This refers to the boldly contrasting colours of the plumage (black, white and chestnut), which is common to both sexes.

**shemozzle** (scene of confusion, 'to-do')
This is a strange enough word anyway, but has occasionally been given some even stranger etymologies, one of the most curious being the supposed origin in the name of the Polish town of Przemyśl, allegedly referring to the five-month-long siege here in the First World War! However, the word existed some time before this, and is almost certainly a London East End slang word that was adapted from the Yiddish, with the source thus being *shlimazel*, 'bad luck' (from *shlim*, 'bad' and *mazel*, 'luck').

**sherry** (type of fortified wine)
The name of the agreeable and cheering drink, associated with parties and various festive seasons, could so easily derive as a combination or blend of 'sheer' and 'cheery' or 'merry' or similar uplifting words. It even serves as a girls' name (although here probably based on French *chérie* – another pleasant association!) But in fact, as no doubt most sherry tasters will know, the origin in fact lies in Spanish *Xeres*, the name of the city in south-west Spain (now Jerez) from which it has long been exported and near which it was originally made. This Spanish name came into English as *sherris*, which was taken to be a plural and so lost its final 's'. (Compare **sash window** for a similar phenomenon.)

**shire** (county)
The word that corresponds to 'county', and ends many actual county names, is often popularly explained as deriving from some form of 'shear', as if the region had been 'shorn off', or 'sheared up' for administrative purposes. The true origin of the word is in Old English *scīr*, 'office', 'care', itself of unknown derivation but possibly related (if only remotely) to 'care'. The allusion is to an administrative area that is under the care of a single officer, today rather more generally represented by a county's Lord Lieutenant (who acts on behalf of the sovereign) or, more directly, by a sherriff (literally a 'shire reeve').

**shiver** (break into fragments, as of glass)
This sense of 'shiver' is not related to the more common word that means 'tremble with fear or cold', although a violent 'trembling' of a glass window, for example, may well cause it to shatter or shiver. The derivation is in a Germanic source, from a root element *skif-* that is also present behind 'shed' (in the 'cast off' sense) and modern German *Schiefer*, 'slate', 'shale'. The other 'trembling' shiver was formerly *chiveren* and may well be imitative in origin, representing the chattering of teeth of a shivering person. (Old English *ceafl* meant 'jaw', 'jowl'.)

**shock-headed** (with bushy or tousled hair)
The descriptive word suggests someone who has had a shock, and whose hair is on end (although some shock-headed people have such a profusion of shaggy, bushy locks that they themselves shock). The origin is not in this 'shock', however. It *may* be in the other 'shock' that means 'stook of sheaves', alluding to the resemblance, or otherwise derive from some other word. One possibility is in the obsolete 'shough', 'shock' or 'shock-dog' that is mentioned in *Macbeth*, where Macbeth lists a variety of dog breeds and types:

As hounds and greyhounds, mongrels, spaniels, curs,
Shoughs, water-rugs, and demi-wolves, are clept [i.e. called]
All by the name of dogs.

The shough here is said to have been a kind of dog from Iceland. So perhaps a shock-headed person resembled a hairy or woolly dog, just as person who is said to have a 'mane' of hair looks like a lion.

**shrapnel** (bomb or shell fragments)
This word readily suggests similar-sounding warfare words, such as 'scrap', 'grapnel', 'star shell' and semi-imitative words such as 'shriek', 'shrill', 'snap' and 'zap'. But it is not imitative, and is not a naturally evolving common noun, since it derives from the name of the British soldier who invented this type of bomb or shell in the Peninsular War, General Henry Shrapnel (originally under the name of 'spherical shot').

**shuttlecock** (object serving as 'ball' in game of badminton)
The name of the shuttlecock is sometimes explained as being an alteration of 'shuttle cork', since it is made of cork. Although this is so, the word has never been recorded with this spelling, and the 'cock' probably refers allusively or half imaginatively to the flying motion of the object, and to its feathers. It was first used in the game of 'shuttlecock and battledore' (or 'battledore and shuttlecock'), with the 'battledore' the name of the racket. From this badminton developed, sometimes pronounced 'badmington' by those who are learning to play it – but not those who first played it in the grounds of Badminton House, in Gloucestershire).

**sideburns** (sideboards, whiskers on the side of the face)
This word is not an attempt at a picturesque description of the whiskers, as if they resembled a 'burned' area on the side of the face, nor is it an alteration of 'sideboards', although it was probably influenced by this. Its actual origin is in the 'burnsides', or side-whiskers that became the fashion in America when they were first sported in the United States Civil War by General Ambrose E. Burnside. This documented etymology proves that there are sometimes occasions when a true word origin is stranger than the fanciful fictions also found.

**sidelong** (towards the side, slanting)
This word is in the small but interesting 'headlong' category (see that word), where 'long' is not what it seems but is a develop-

ment of -*ling*. In Middle English the word was thus *sideling*. Later, the verb 'to sidle' developed from this. See also **grovel** for related background on these words.

**sidesman** (churchwarden's assistant)
This title has been explained as being an alteration of 'synod's man', as if the bearer originally attended church synods. But it is nothing so complex, and is more or less what it says, implying a man who stands 'at the side of' the churchwarden (which he can do quite literally when taking the collection, for example).

**siesta** (noontime or early afternoon nap or rest)
The word is obviously not English, but nevertheless suggests a derivation from a basis meaning 'sit' or 'session', perhaps implying a time for a 'sit-down'. But the Spanish word actually means 'sixth', i. e. 'sixth hour' (from Latin *sexta hora*), meaning 'noon'. That is the time when the sun can be hottest and when it is best to take a break for a rest. See also **noon**.

**silhouette** (portrait in profile, usually all dark or black against a white or light background)
What does the word suggest to you? Perhaps something like one or more of the following: 'stiletto', 'solitary', 'style', 'statuette', 'stylolite', 'storiette', 'pirouette'. But although these may spring to mind, some fairly aptly (a profile portrait can look something like a solitary statuette), the actual origin is in no common word but the name of the French politician Étienne de Silhouette, who lived in the eighteenth century. There is some uncertainty as to *why* the distinctive portraits were named after him. One theory is that as they are 'partial' portraits, the name refers to his brief career as controller general (less than a year). Another maintains that the word is a punning reference to his policy as minister of finance, from his petty economies. (The portraits are slight, and can be executed quite cheaply.) Yet another says that the minister enjoyed decorating his château at Bry-sur-Marne with designs made by tracing round the shadow of a face. While this last is an attractive suggestion, the 'petty economies' expla-

nation seems the most likely, since this would have been the most widely known. His actual name is of Basque origin, meaning 'hole', 'ditch', and is related to English 'silo'. This would have originally meant 'one who lives in a hollow place'.

**singlet** (vest, light garment worn by athletes)
The garment is not so called since it is the sole or single one, often, to be worn on the top half of the body, but because originally it was unlined, and so was in contrast to the 'doublet', which was lined. The word first became widely used in English in the eighteenth century.

**sirloin** (cut of beef)
This is one of the elder statesmen of false etymologies, whose various origins and attributions are quoted by the *Oxford English Dictionary*. Let us repeat one of them to get the substance of the explanation, which has its roots in the seventeenth century: 'This joint is said to owe its name to King Charles the Second, who dining upon a Loin of Beef . . . said for its merit it should be knighted, and henceforth called Sir-Loin' (*Cook's oracle*, 1822). This is one of the later variations, with the earlier tales naming the king as Henry VIII. Even Dr Johnson refers to the story, in the fourth entry under 'sir' in his *Dictionary,* where he says: 'A title given to the loin of beef, which one of our kings knighted in a fit of good humour'. However, Johnson was one of the first to spell the word with an 'i' where formerly it had been spelt with a 'u'. The earlier spelling points more accurately to the true origin, which is in Middle French *surlonge,* referring to the location of this particular cut, 'above the loin', or more exactly, from the upper part of the hind loin. Of course, there is no reason to suppose that a monarch did not make this pun and act out the burlesque scene – but that is not the origin of the word! Compare **baron of beef**, and see also **surname**.

**skewbald** (of a horse: marked with spots and blotches of white and brown)
The other colour is not always brown, but properly it is never black. There is no connection with 'bald', except as for **piebald** (which see), and the 'skew' does not mean that the spots and patches run 'askew' or diagonally in any way. The 'skew' is the uncertain element here. It can hardly derive from Old French *escu,* 'shield', as has been suggested. Perhaps it is from an obsolete word 'skew' meaning 'heaven', 'sky' (to which second word it may be related). The image would thus be of patchy or blotchy clouds in a bright sky. See also **bald** itself.

**skewer** (wooden or metal rod used to pin a piece of meat together)
The skewer is not so called because it runs 'askew' through the meat, but is probably an alteration of a dialect word *skiver,* of unknown origin. 'Skew' itself is of Germanic origin, and is related to 'eschew' and, less directly, 'shy'.

**skivvy** (female servant)
This derogatory or at least unflattering term is not related to 'skive', which originally (if the same word) meant 'cut leather or rubber into slices'. Its origin is somewhat obscure, although it could perhaps be a form of 'slavey', which was earlier used for a female domestic servant or 'maid of all work'. But all words mentioned here are quite recent, none recorded before the nineteenth century, and more research is needed to establish proper sources.

**slam** (in phrase 'grand slam')
The phrase properly belongs to the card game bridge, where a grand slam is the winning of all the tricks, and the little slam winning all the tricks except one. Whichever it is, the 'slam' does not relate to the word that means 'bang', which is probably of Scandinavian origin. Perhaps there was an earlier card game with this term, or even called by this name. There were formerly words such as *slampain* and *slampery* that meant 'trick' or 'trickery', and one or other of these may lie behind it.

**sledgehammer** (kind of large heavy hammer)
The implement is not so called since it was used for breaking up (or making) sledges, or because it was transported by them or made out of them. It was simply called a

'sledge' (Old English *slecg*), with this word related to 'slay'. Later, when the Old English word was no longer understood, 'hammer' was added.

**sleight of hand** (manual skill or dexterity)
The first word is pronounced 'slight', suggesting that it could be an altered spelling of this, perhaps to refer to a small but deceptive movement, or to the ability of a 'slight' or delicate hand to deceive more skilfully than a large and clumsy one. But it in fact comes from the same Old Norse word that gave 'sly', so that is the actual origin and connection.

**slowworm** (kind of legless lizard)
This creature is not noticeably slow, nor is it a worm in the general understanding of the word. The first half of the word probably derives from a Scandinavian word meaning 'earthworm', while 'worm' is used here in its former wide sense of 'reptile'. Another name for the slowworm is the blindworm, although, equally, it is not blind.

**slughorn** (slogan)
Many modern dictionaries eschew this word, which is a pity as it has an interesting if corrupt background. As indicated above, it is simply an old alteration of 'slogan' (in the proper sense of 'war cry', 'rallying cry', especially as applied to a Scottish clan in battle with another). Its origin is thus in Gaelic *sluagh-ghairm*, literally 'host shout'. In its spelling here, it of course suggests 'horn', and because of its association with battles was taken by some to be a sort of war trumpet. Poets writing of 'deeds of derring-do' therefore seized on it, and incorporated it in their works. One of the first to do so was Chatterton, and the word comes in his poem 'The Tournament', written in mock Old English:

Methynckes I heare yer slugghornes
    dynn.

Later, Browning used it in his famous 'Childe Roland to the Dark Tower Came':

Dauntless the slug-horn to my lips I
    set,
And Blew.

**smack** (taste, flavour)
This 'smack' is not related to the one that means 'open lips with sudden sharp sound in anticipation of food and drink', despite the sense association. It comes from Germanic, where it has its modern related words today (as in German *schmecken*, 'to taste', and *Geschmack*, 'a taste'). The other 'smack', which is the same as the 'slap' word, is probably imitative. The fishing 'smack' is related to neither, but is probably a Dutch word in origin, while slang 'smack' meaning 'heroin' is probably of Yiddish derivation.

**smallpox** (infectious disease)
For such an acute disease, formerly often fatal, the term 'small' seems quite inappropriate. The explanation is that it was regarded as relatively 'small', or at any rate at least potentially curable, when compared to the 'great' pox, which was the pox proper, i. e. syphilis. Compare **chickenpox**.

**smithereens** (bits)
'Smashed to smithereens' – by Smithers, the butter-fingered 'tweeny' of 'Upstairs, Downstairs' days, perhaps? If not, then what? The rather strange word is actually Irish in origin, where as *smidirín* ('little fragment') it is a diminutive of *smiodar*, 'fragment'. Compare other 'little' Irish words ending in '-een', such as 'colleen' ('little girl'), 'poteen' ('little pot') and the affectionate 'Kathleen Mavourneen' of Julia Crawford's poem, who is thus really 'Kathleen my little love'. (Even Kathleen, or its Irish equivalent Caitlín, would suggest a diminutive to a native Irish speaker.)

**sola topi** (kind of lightweight helmet-like hat worn in the tropics)
This name is sometimes misspelt 'solar topi', thus reinforcing the incorrect association with 'solar', since after all the hat is designed to give protection from the heat of the sun. But 'sola' is simply the native (Bengali) name of the plant whose pithlike stem is used for making the hat, while 'topi' is the similar native word for the hat. Perhaps the travelling Englishman would have done better to stick to 'pith helmet' after all.

**somersault** (athletic 'head over heels' turn)
The word is also spelt 'summerset', which one way or the other suggests some kind of seasonal sport or rustic frolic (in Somerset?), akin to the gambolling of lambs in spring. But the true derivation is in Old French *soubresault*, ultimately based in Latin *super*, 'over' and *saltus*, the past participle of *salire*, 'to jump'. So a somersault is an 'overleap'.

**sorry** (regretful)
It is strange to find that this word is not related to 'sorrow', although it has certainly been influenced by it. It comes from Old English *sārig*, which is related to 'sore'. 'Sorrow', by contrast, derives from Old English *sorg*, related to modern German *Sorge*. The two words seem to have been mutually associated fairly early, however.

**SOS** (distress signal)
This internationally known signal, represented in morse by the familiar three-fold groupings of dots and dashes ( . . . – – – . . . ), is almost always popularly understood in English to stand for 'save our souls'. There have been other interpretations, however, such as 'save our ship', 'save or starve', 'stop other signals', 'sink or swim', 'send our succour' (or 'send our saviour'), and so on. There have even been 'meanings' in other languages, too, such as the Russian *spasite ot smerti* ('save from death'). Which is right? The English 'save our souls' is perhaps the most apt, since it means not only 'save the souls on board' but also has the religious sense which could be urgently felt in an hour of distress. But the true origin is in none of these! The signal arose as a combination of morse dots and dashes that would be distinctive and easy to recognize. In the early years of the twentieth century it replaced the former distress signal CQD, where CQ (representing spoken 'seek you', of course, although also interpreted as 'call to quarters' or 'come quickly') was the agreed code for 'message coming', while D stood for 'danger' (or 'distress'). This signal in turn had been agreed at an international radiotelegraphy conference in Germany, where some countries had proposed a distress call SSSDDD. This was opposed by Britain and Italy, however, and it was these two countries who had suggested the alternative CQD. Finally, however, SOS was eventually accepted as the agreed international signal. (In the Second World War the signal was modified to SSS to apply to a submarine in distress.) 'Mayday', the other well-known international distress signal, comes from French *m'aider*, 'help me' (implying in full, *Venez m'aider*, 'come and help me').

**sovereign** (royal ruler)
Despite the spelling, this word is not related to 'reign' but derives from Old French *soverain*, in turn from an assumed Vulgar Latin *superanus*, from Latin *super*, 'above'.

**spade** (playing card figure)
The figure may *look* something like a spade, but that is not the origin of the name, which actually derives from Italian *spada* (or perhaps Spanish *espada*), 'sword'. However, the appearance of the card figure called 'club' is even less appropriate, since the trefoil hardly resembles a club. But here this is the same word as for the weapon. In the tarot pack or deck, the numeral cards, added (perhaps by the Venetians) to the original picture cards, were divided into four suits, one of which was 'swords'.

**spanner** (tool for tightening nuts)
Perhaps the word looks as if the implement was originally intended to 'span' in some way, or was devised for building bridges and tightening the nuts and bolts that held the components together. It is actually a pure German word, meaning 'stretcher', and was originally a tool for winding up the spring in the wheel-lock of a firearm.

**sparerib** (pork rib with most of spare meat taken off to make bacon)
A sparerib certainly is rather 'spare', but this is not the origin of the name. The word comes from Low German *ribbesper*, a term used for pork ribs roasted on a spit · or 'spear', so the literal meaning is 'rib spear', or 'speared rib'.

**spatchcock** (chicken that is split and grilled as soon as it is slaughtered)
Popular etymology maintains that such a bird is a 'despatched cock', with even a pun

on the two senses of 'despatch' ('kill' and 'carry out quickly'). But the word is in fact an alteration of 'spitchcock', a term used for a way of cutting up and frying an eel, itself of unknown origin.

**spendthrift** (person who squanders money)
The word looks as if it means something like 'person who has saved in the past but who then decides to squander all his savings'. But this is too involved, and the 'thrift' here has the earlier sense of 'substance', 'wealth' (shades of which survive in modern 'thrive'). The word replaced an earlier term for such a person as a 'scattergood'.

**sperm whale** (kind of large whale)
The sperm whale has a large, blunt head in the front of which is a cavity containing a mixture of so called 'spermaceti' and oil. This substance, which gives the name of the whale, was formerly thought to be sperm (in the head, of all places!), but is actually a white waxy substance used for making candles, ointments and cosmetics. 'Spermaceti' derives from Medieval Latin to mean simply 'sperm of whale' (*sperma ceti*).

**spinet** (type of harpsichord or early piano)
The word seems to suggest some sense of 'spin', as if the instrument had strings that were 'spun' in some special way, or as if it could 'spin out' a melody. Or perhaps it was a suitable instrument for spinsters to play, as the closely related **virginals** could be for modest young maidens? However attractive such fancies may be, the word almost certainly derives from the name of its early sixteenth-century inventor, the Italian instrument maker Giovanni Spinetti. The name 'caught on' since his own name would have been inscribed on the instrument, just as today, for the same reason, we talk of a 'Bechstein'.

**spinnaker** (kind of large triangular sail)
The name of the sail seems to suggest some association with 'spin'. Perhaps it helps the boat to 'spin' along, or protects it from spindrift. It even suggests the name of another sail, the spanker. But it is not likely to be any of these and may be either a combination of 'spin' in some unspecified sense and 'moniker' (meaning 'name' or 'nickname'), or else be a corruption of 'Sphinx', traditionally said to be the name of the first yacht to adopt this type of sail.

**spiv** (black marketeer)
This now rather dated word, which was all the rage at the end of the Second World War, is sometimes explained as being an inversion (suggesting a corrupt or 'back-to-front' practice) of 'VIPs', just as a 'yob' is an inverted 'boy'. But the word is almost certainly a dialect one, deriving from 'spiff', meaning 'smart', 'well-dressed' (compare 'spiffing'), and there is the origin of the slick and slippery fellow.

**spoke** (in expression: 'put a spoke in someone's wheel')
Considered logically, this expression is a nonsense, since the spokes are already in the wheel, and putting another one in can hardly be a hindrance, which is what the phrase implies. The saying seems to be a mistranslation of Dutch *een spaak in het wiel stekken,* where *spaak* actually means 'bar', 'pole' (and so related to English 'spike'). If you put a bar in someone's wheel while he is moving you will certainly upset him and thwart him, and this sense of the metaphor can be seen clearly in its equivalents in other languages, such as French *mettre des bâtons dans les roues,* Italian *mettere un bastone nelle ruote,* and even Russian *vstavlyat' palki v kolësa.* All these relate to sticks being thrust into a wheel, not spokes.

**spooning** ('courting or love-making of a sentimental kind' [*Oxford English Dictionary*])
This now out-moded word, whose meaning so intrigued the young hero of L. P. Hartley's *The Go-Between,* is sometimes imagined to have a direct derivation from the eating utensil, with the usual semi-bawdy explanation being that lovers lie close together like spoons in a drawer. True, the verb was used in this sense in colloquial nineteenth-century English, but the verb came from the 'amatory' activity, not the other way round. The true source of the word goes back, via the 'wooden spoon' that was awarded to the student who came bottom in an examin-

ation, to the eighteenth-century meaning of 'spoon' as 'simpleton'. The inspiration for this vogue use was probably the fact that a spoon is open and shallow, or that it is generally the most 'basic' of the eating implements, with which we eat before progressing to a more sophisticated knife and fork. The word has not really had an exact successor, since 'canoodling' is too affected a word, and 'billing and cooing' not quite 'physical' enough, as well as being somewhat mannered. Perhaps modern 'snogging' or 'smooching' come nearest, although they lack the visual punning etymology that 'spooning' had. They lack the 'flirting' aspect implicit in the older word, too.

**spray** (flowering branch of tree, arrangement of flowers and leaves)
This kind of spray is not related to the water spray, as if the flowers or leaves were regarded as a 'fountain' or 'shower', however picturesque this might be. The original sense of the ward was 'small twigs', 'fine brushwood', and this is preserved in the names of some places in Devon, such as Spreyton between Okehampton and Crediton, and the little hamlet of Sprytown east of Launceston, with both these meaning 'farm in brushwood country'. The 'water' spray, on the other hand, is probably of Dutch origin, and is indirectly related to 'sprout'.

**spree** (bout of unrestrained indulgence)
There are a number of words beginning 'spr-' that suggest an enjoyable activity, such as 'spry', 'sprightly' (not related), 'sprite', 'spring' and so on. But 'spree' is not really in this group, since it is probably of Scottish origin, perhaps deriving from *spreath*, 'cattle raid' (and so ultimately related to 'prey'). Q. Why do people living or working in Berlin have such a good time? A. Because they're always on the Spree.

**spruce** (neat and smart)
The adjective does not relate to the tree so called, as if it was a specially 'neat' or smart-looking tree. The word probably derives from so called 'Spruce leather', which was a fashionable leather from 'Pruce', i. e. Prussia. The present sense would have

evolved from the use of the word to describe a garment, such as a 'spruce leather jerkin'. However, the tree called the spruce (spruce fir or spruce pine) also got its name from Prussia, since this country had many such trees and was the source of many objects made from their wood.

**stalemate** ('draw' in chess, in which king can move only into check)
The term suggests that for the lone king, battling against uneven odds right at the end of the game, time has run out, and he is now in a 'stale' situation, where there is no hope of a revival or comeback. But the word, originally just 'stale', comes from Old French *estal*, 'fixed position' (literally 'stall'), and simply describes his inability to move. (See also **instalment**.) The 'mate' is misleading, too, and was added on the basis of '**checkmate**' (which also see).

**stalk** (track silently, pursue stealthily)
This 'stalk' is not related to the plant one, as if the stalker kept close to the ground, or worked at 'grass roots' level. Both words have Old English origins, with the 'tracking' sense coming from a verb related to modern 'steal' and 'stealthy', and the 'plant' word perhaps deriving from an Old English word *stalu* that meant 'upright piece of wood'.

**standard** (banner, criterion, etc)
The many senses of this word do not derive directly from 'stand', since the Middle French *estandard*, 'rallying point', from which it comes, is related more to 'extend'. However, the many 'upright' meanings of 'standard', such as 'standard lamp', 'standard rose' (with an erect main stalk), and so on, are obviously influenced by 'stand', and even if there is no direct link between the words, there is a common linguistic association.

**stark naked** (completely naked)
Some etymologists have endeavoured to derive this special use of 'stark' from Old English *steort*, 'tail', and have pointed out that early records of the phrase show it in such forms as *stert naket*, as if to prove this. The phrase thus originally meant 'tail naked', 'naked even to the tail', they claim. But this earlier spelling was itself the result

of folk etymology, and the 'stark' here is the same as the main one that means 'strong', 'sheer', 'absolute' (even in such colloquial phrases as 'stark raving bonkers'). But there certainly was a word 'start' meaning 'tail', and this still survives in the name of the bird called the redstart, literally 'red tail'.

**stationer** (bookseller)
The word is sometimes wrongly associated with 'station', that is, with 'railway station', perhaps because of the bookstalls usually found there. The derivation *is* from 'station', but not in this sense. The word comes from Medieval Latin *stationarius*, which was the word for a person having a regular 'station', that is, a tradesman, and specifically a bookseller, who had a fixed selling point, unlike an itinerant vendor. The direct adoption of the word from Medieval Latin into English was due to the fact that such 'fixed' booksellers set up their stations at universities in the Middle Ages.

**stay** (kind of strong rope used to support tall object)
This word is not the same as the other 'stay' that means 'remain', as if the rope was used to make the object it supported 'stay put' in position. It has its derivation in Germanic sources such as Middle Low German *stach* and Dutch *stag*, whereas the 'remain' word came into English from French, ultimately from Latin *stare*, 'to stand'. It is likely, though, that the 'support' sense of 'stay' apart from the rope, such as the 'stays' that once stiffened (still stiffen?) corsets, was influenced early on by the rope word.

**stem** (1 make headway; 2 check or stop)
This is a rather awkward word, with two apparently opposite meanings. If a ship 'stems the tide', for example, it makes progress against it. But if you 'stem' a river or a flow of blood, you stop it. This disparity of meaning stems from (that's actually the first one) their different origins. The ship that stems the tide does so with its stem (as distinct from its stern), and this word is the same as the ordinary stem of a plant, with their common origin in an Old English word that is related to modern 'stand'. The other 'checking' stem comes ultimately from Old

Norse *stemma*, which is related to modern English 'stammer'.

**stepfather** (person's mother's second or subsequent husband)
All the 'step-' relations have titles that are in fact nothing to do with 'step' in the ordinary sense, as if there were a 'step' in the family tree, or a different degree of relationship. The word comes from Old English *steop-* which itself derives from a Germanic root meaning 'bereave'. That is, the 'stepfather' (or other relative) has acquired his family status because of the bereavement of a parent – or more precisely, because a parent has been 'bereft' of his or her spouse. In his *Dictionary* published in the mid-eighteenth century, Dr Johnson stated that 'stepmother' was the only 'step-' relation word surviving in common use. Since then, of course, it has come to be applied to most other direct family members, including the more general 'stepparent' and 'stepchild'. Perhaps here English has the advantages over some other languages, where the 'step-' relationship is not always clearly expressed. In French, for example, *beau-fils* can mean either 'stepson' or 'son-in-law', even though there is another existing word for the latter (*gendre*). See also **law** for the 'in-laws'.

**steppe** (vast treeless plain in south-east Europe or Asia)
The word suggests 'step', of course, or 'stepping stones', perhaps especially when it occurs in highflown prose or verse, or literary or musical titles (such as Borodin's *In the Steppes of Central Asia*). But there is no connection between the two, and 'steppe' is simply the Russian word for the plain, *step'*.

**sterling** (British currency)
There have been several attempts to find a satisfactory explanation for this apparently 'easy' word. Some punsters have seen a connection in the Scottish town of Stirling, near which, they are quick to point out, is the town of Dollar! Others have gone for a derivation in some such word as 'easterling', claiming that the term was originally used to apply to money from eastern Germany, which was greatly valued for its purity. But the first meaning of the word was as the

name of an early silver penny, and it is likely that the origin is thus in Old English *steorling*, 'coin with a star on it', to refer to this coin. This is not finally proved, however, and the Old English word is an 'assumed' or conjectural one, not actually traced anywhere.

**stickler** (person who insists on detail or accuracy)
It might be thought that this word is related to 'stick', since a stickler holds fast to his ideals – or 'wields a big stick' (metaphorically, of course) to get the high standard he requires. But the word has a different origin, from the former sense of 'stickle', which was 'arbitrate', 'contend'. This itself came from an Old English verb *stihtan*, 'to arrange', 'set in order'.

**Stilton** (type of blue-veined cheese)
Stilton is a village in Cambridgeshire (formerly in Huntingdonshire), where it is south of Peterborough on the A1, formerly the 'Great North Road' and before *that* the famous Roman road called Ermine Street. The cheese was formerly sold and distributed from the Bell Inn here, where it would be sent by coach down the Great North Road to London. The cheese was not actually made here, however, but came originally from the Vale of Belvoir in Leicestershire and the region of the Dore Valley in Derbyshire. So unlike many other cheeses, which are named after their original place of manufacture (such as Cheddar and Caerphilly), Stilton had a different initial source. Compare **panama hat** for a similar sort of name origin.

**stirrup** (metal frame for horse rider's foot)
There is no connection with 'stir up' here, even though a stirrup cup or farewell drink may have been 'stirred up' before the rider drank it! Nor in fact is there any link with 'up', although the stirrups aid the rider to climb up onto his horse. In Old English, the word for 'stirrup' was *stigrāp*, with *stig* here meaning 'step' (up or down) and *rāp* being 'rope'. The first of these elements is related to German *Steig*, 'path' and *steigen*, 'to go up', as well as to modern English 'stair'.

**stocks** (in phrase 'on the stocks')
The phrase means 'in preparation', of course, as when a writer has a new novel 'on the stocks', and this particular sense of 'stock' does not refer to the 'stores' (as when goods are 'in stock') but to the yard where a ship is built. When a ship is 'on the stocks' it is on the frame that holds it while it is being built. It is therefore at a stage when it is nearing completion and can be launched. (This is nothing to do with a 'stockyard', however, which is a yard where livestock are kept for marketing, slaughter, and so on). The word 'stock' has so many diverse meanings in English, from the general to the specific, that phrases based on it may lose their original connotation. The source of all the senses is Old English *stocc*, 'treetrunk', 'stump'.

**stony broke** (absolutely without money)
The phrase almost seems to imply that the person has to live on stone pavements or that he has nothing but stones in his pockets. The origin is not quite so literal as this, but comes from a use of 'stone' as an intensive, such as 'stone blind', 'stone deaf', and the like. The first such phrase to be recorded was 'stone dead'. German uses the equivalent word in much the same way, so that *steinalt* means 'old as the hills', and *steinreich* means 'enormously rich'.

**strafe** (rake with machine-gun fire, spray with bullets)
There are several words beginning 'str-' that denote a violent or sudden action, such as 'strap', 'strop', 'strike', 'strive', 'strain', 'streak', 'strangle', 'strip', etc. The word 'strafe' seems to belong to this group, while also suggesting its actual meaning of 'rake'. But it is pure German, and comes from the German 'hate' slogan of the First World War, *Gott strafe England*, literally 'God punish England' (but often popularly translated as 'God hate England'). The Germans gave English three modern 'attacking' words from warfare use, the other two being **flak** (which see) and 'blitz' (short for 'blitzkrieg', 'lightning war').

**strait** (narrow channel)
A strait is not so called because it is straight, although it quite frequently is, but because

it is narrow, from Old French *estreit* in this meaning, in turn from Latin *strictus*, 'constrained' (which also gave modern English 'strict'). What even more confuses the issue here is that a 'straitjacket' can also be spelt 'straightjacket', and the two spellings are also possible for 'straitlaced'. The two basic words were associated quite early in English, in the days when spelling was much more flexible than it is now.

**strappado** (kind of torture, or the instrument used for it)
The word suggests 'strap', but this is not the basis of the term or even of the torture itself, which consists of hoisting the victim by a rope tied to the wrists and then allowing him to drop suddenly. The word came into English via French *strapade*, itself from Italian *strappata*, 'sudden tug', 'snatch' (from the verb *strappare*, 'to pull sharply'). The torture was familiar enough for the word to be used in English as early as the sixteenth century, although when Dr Johnson included it in his *Dictionary* he defined it wrongly as 'Chastisement by blows'.

**strawberry** (kind of juicy red fruit)
The name is unusual enough for various tentative etymologies to have appeared for it. These fall into two camps: those that say the name is an alteration of some other word, and those that concentrate on explaining the 'straw'. Of the former, two possible alternatives are said to be 'stray-berry' or 'strewberry', both these referring to the plant's runners. As for the 'straw', the general favourite (which is in fact the most likely origin) says that the reference is to the straw-like appearance of the seeds on the fruit's surface, while others point to the straw-like runners, the use of straw to protect the plants, and their frequent location under mown grass. Most other Germanic languages have a name meaning 'earthberry' for it, as German *Erdbeere*. And although the plant does propagate by extending or 'strewing' its runners, it seems more likely that the name has a more immediate origin, referring to its appearance, as mentioned.

**stucco** (material used to form coating for outside walls)
Although stucco is applied to a wall when soft, and so is in a sense 'stuck' on to it, this is not the origin of the word, which although itself Italian, is of Germanic stock with a basic meaning 'piece' (related to modern German *Stück*).

**stud** (group of animals used for breeding; studhorse)
This 'stud' is not connected with the identical word that means 'rivet', 'projecting piece', as if there was some concealed or blurred basic allusion to the act of breeding. The word (in the 'horse' sense) comes from an Old English source that is itself related to 'steed' and 'stand' (this verb being actually used technically of a stallion that is available as a stud). The other 'stud' comes from the Old English word that means 'post', 'prop' and that is related to German *stützen*, 'to prop'. Out of interest, the name of the German city of Stuttgart relates to the first 'stud' here, since the literal meaning is 'stud garden', referring to the stud farm there in the twelfth century.

**succubus** (female incubus)
The succubus is not so called because it sucks blood or anything else, but because it (or she) literally 'lies under' a person while he sleeps (Latin *sub-*, 'under' and *cubare*, 'to lie). An incubus is so called, by contrast, because he 'lies on' his victim while she sleeps. The purpose of the demonic visit in either case is to 'consort' (as *Chambers* delicately puts it). It is rather strange that grammatically the succubus, though female, has a masculine ending, and that the alternative 'succuba' did not prevail. See also **nightmare** for another evil spirit.

**suffragette** (woman who agitated for 'votes for women')
The word is based on 'suffrage', of course, but neither of these has anything to do with 'suffer', although undoubtedly suffragettes *did* suffer. The basic origin is Latin *suffragium*, 'support', 'the vote', itself of uncertain derivation. The same source gave the 'suffragan' who is a subordinate or assistant bishop. The word is first recorded in English in 1906, and many other feminine '-ette'

designations stem from this period, including 'usherette' and the now obsolete 'munitionette', or female munition worker in the First World War (headline in *Daily Sketch* of 9 November 1915: 'Munitionettes Who Receive Threepence An Hour').

**sunflower** (plant of the daisy family with large yellow flower)
This word has already been dealt with under **Jerusalem artichoke** (which see). It is entered here only to record that some nineteenth-century wordologists actually explained the name as an alteration of 'sun follower'. This would be fair enough if the name had been found recorded somewhere in this form, but it hasn't. (Interestingly, however, the French for 'sunflower', and also the Italian as mentioned in the other entry, actually do mean this, respectively *tournesol* and *girasole*.) Perhaps the English name is more subtle than it first appears: it not only refers to the way in which the flower follows the sun, but alludes to its appearance, since the large yellow flower actually looks like the sun. The sunflower has an exact doublet in the heliotrope, which although unrelated to it botanically, has a name of Greek origin that means 'sun turner', 'flower that turns to the sun'.

**surcease** (desist from, come to an end)
Surprisingly, this word is not based on 'cease'. In Middle English it was *sursesen,* which comes from the past participle (*sursis*) of Old French *surseoir,* itself from Latin *supersedere,* literally 'to sit over'. This Latin verb also more directly gave modern English 'supersede'. Compare **surround**.

**surname** (family name)
Over the centuries, this word has been both popularly and seriously explained as being 'sir name', or 'sire name', as if it referred to the name of the father or 'sire'. But like most words beinning 'sur-', the sense is 'over', since the family name is 'over and above' a person's individual Christian name or forename. Formerly, it was enough for a person to have just one name. Later, when various Jacks and Jills began to proliferate, and there was a need to distinguish between them, an extra name was added, this relating usually to the father. (Hence the

many names ending in '-son', such as Johnson, Jackson, Williamson, and so on.)

**surplice** (white top garment worn by clergymen, choirboys, etc)
The garment is usually worn over a cassock, and it is not so called because it is a 'surplus' or extra garment, nor is the '-plice' the 'fold' (Latin *-plic-*) element seen in such words as 'duplicate'. The origin is in Old French *surpliz,* from Medieval Latin *superpellicium,* itself comprising *super-,* 'over' and *pellicium,* 'coat of skins' (from *pellis,* 'skin'). How cold those churches must have been in medieval times!

**surround** (enclose, go round)
Like **surcease** (above), this word is something of a surprise, since it does not derive from 'round'. The origin, through French, is in Late Latin *superundare,* 'to overflow' (based on *super-,* 'over' and *unda,* 'wave'). This is because the original meaning was 'overflow', 'flood'. Later, this idea of surrounding by water became applied more generally to any kind of enclosure. The association with 'round', however, had fixed the present spelling by the sixteenth century.

**swallow** (kind of bird with graceful flight and distinctive forked tail)
The forked tail is not the only distinctive feature of a swallow, since they also feed on insects while in flight. Could this therefore be the origin of the name? Disappointingly, the answer is no, and the Old English form of the name, *swealwe,* is probably based on a root word that means 'swirl', 'flash', referring to its crazy, mazy flight, now up high, now swooping down low and skimming over water.

**swingeing** (very great, powerful)
This word ('swingeing cuts' and so on) is also spelt (or misspelt) 'swinging', which suggests that these are really one and the same word. No doubt the image of a swinging 'axe' to make the cuts prompts the association. However, the words have different origins, and 'swingeing' (from the verb 'swinge', rarely used in any other form than this) comes from an Old English verb *swengan,* 'to shake' which may in turn be

related to *swingan*, 'to beat'. This latter verb is thus the origin of 'swing'.

**switchback** (roller coaster)

The name does not denote the many 'backs' of the amusement ride, which keep 'switching' or changing. The word originally applied to the coaches or carriages of a railway on a steep slope that zigzagged up a hill. Where required, the coaches could be 'switched back' or reversed on stretches of the line, i. e. at the bottom or top end of each stretch of the zigzag there would be a 'switch'.

**syllabus** (summary of course of study)

The learned-looking word would seem to derive from Greek *syllabe*, from the same Greek verb *syllambanein*, 'to put together', that gave English 'syllable'. However, the actual origin is in a fifteenth-century misprint (*syllabos*) for *sittybas*. This occurred in an edition of Cicero's *Epistolae ad Atticum* ('Letters to Atticus'), where it is grammatically the accusative plural of *sittyba*, a Latin version of Greek *sittyba*, meaning 'label for a book'. This misprint was later wrongly related to the Greek verb mentioned above, and the English word derived from it, through Latin, accordingly.

**tabby cat** (cat with striped or mottled coat)
The cat's name has long been agreeably but erroneously associated with the first name Tabitha, largely because 'Tabby' is a short form of this name (just as Abby is for Abigail), and also since 'tabby' was a nickname for an old maid, being used as what the *Oxford English Dictionary* calls a 'dyslogistic appellation' (or uncomplimentary name!). The latter association relates not so much to witches and their cats but to the supposed 'cattiness' of elderly spinsters. Grose (see Bibliography) makes the specific connection under 'Tabby', which he defines as: 'An old maid; either from Tabitha, a formal antiquated name; or else from a tabby cat, old maids being often compared to cats'. Of course, in more recent times, the association between the cat's name and the girl's (or old maid's) has been revived by the popularity of Beatrix Potter's cat character Tabitha Twitchit, who with her children Tom Kitten, Moppet and Mittens features in *The Tale of Tom Kitten*, and elsewhere. But neither name is based on the other. 'Tabby' came into English, as the name of a silk taffeta with a wavy finish, from Old French *tabis*, itself from Arabic *'attabi*. This original name of the fabric came from the place where it was made, the district of Baghdad called *Al-'Attabiya*, meaning 'the quarter of 'Attab', the prince who was the great-grandson of Omayya or Umayyah, an ancestor of the founder of the Ommiads (Umayyads), the great Arab dynasty of caliphs. The cat was thus named after the cloth, since its stripes suggested the wavy design (technically, moiré) of the fabric. The name Tabitha, on the other hand, actually means 'gazelle' (from the Aramaic).

**table d'hôte** ('set meal')
This is one of the most familiar French menu terms, together with its 'opposite number', 'à la carte'. It is sometimes popularly understood to mean 'table at a hotel', since it is frequently encountered by guests staying at or visiting a hotel. It in fact means 'host's table', implying that the hotel manager or chef has already selected the courses of the meal and has decided at what time it will be served, usually at a fixed price. 'À la carte', on the other hand, gives the diner a wide choice of dishes (and prices) from the menu, since what he eats is literally 'by the bill of fare'. 'Table d'hôte' is usually pronounced in an entirely anglicized way, as 'tarble dote', with perhaps a slight concession to the French in an alternative 'tarbler dote'. In many popular chain restaurants and steak bars, both French terms have long gone by the board, if they ever existed.

**tacky** (shabby, vulgar)
This colloquial word, of nineteenth-century American origin, was initially used of an inferior horse, and it has no connection with 'tacky' meaning 'sticky', as if something were 'stuck on', or as if one were 'stuck' with an inferior alternative to the real thing. Nor is it related to 'tack' in the sense 'saddlery', 'equipment for horses', as this is a modern shortening of 'tackle'. The source of the word is not known. (As used of the horse, it was a noun.)

**taffrail** (rail at stern of sailing ship)
The nautical term is not derived from 'rail'. Formerly, the word was 'tafferel', coming from Dutch *taffereel*. This meant 'panel' and referred to the decorated panels often found on the upper flat section of the stern. However, there is no doubt that English 'rail' influenced the spelling of the word.

**taiga** (area of marshy pine forest bordering the Arctic)
If the term is heard before it is seen, it could

well conjure up 'tiger', since the two words are pronounced identically in English. And who knows what beasts lurk in those dark Russian forests? But the word is simply a Russian one, itself of Turkic origin, and although there are wolves and bears in the taiga, there are no tigers.

**talisman** (kind of magic charm)
Because the word ends in '-man', it is often wrongly associated with a person, and is perhaps even sometimes actually misunderstood as the name of some oriental or other magician (perhaps a sort of 'charismatic tallyman'). Moreover, the word occasionally appears in the plural as 'talismen', even in the writing of educated people. Thus *The Times* has fallen under the corrupting spell of the word, so that a first leader in this great newspaper's issue for 28 April 1984 referred to coalminers as 'talismen of a particular type of society and culture which has great symbolic appeal to the Left'. However, the true origin of the word, which came into English via French or Spanish (or even Italian), is in Arabic *ṭilsam*, from Medieval Greek *telesma*, 'ritual'. (The 'tele-' here is not the Greek 'far off' element of 'telephone', etc, but *telos*, 'end', implying a completion of the ritual, a final initiation into the mysteries). There are one or two other misleading '-man' words in English that do not refer to persons and that have a plural in '-mans', among them 'cayman' (reptile like the crocodile), 'dolman' (Turkish robe) and 'ottoman' (upholstered seat).

**tank** (armoured combat vehicle running on caterpillar tracks)
The tank is not so called because it looks like a tank, i. e. a large vessel for storing water or some other liquid, but because this was the 'codeword' used for the vehicle when it was first manufactured in World War I in order to conceal its existence from the enemy. The word was adopted in December 1915, and of course originally applied to the rather spectacular early rhomboid tanks that had tracks running right round the whole body of the vehicle. The name was therefore not derived, as some people have alternatively claimed, from that of a tractor designer called Thomas Tank Burall.

**tankard** (large drinking vessel)
However strange it may seem, this word is of unknown origin and does not appear to be related to 'tank'. Its original fourteenth-century sense was 'large tub' (usually a wooden one hooped with iron). It is just possible that the word was some sort of ultimate rearrangement of Latin *cantharus*, which was a large, wide-bellied drinking vessel with handles. But whatever the etymology, no link between 'tankard' and 'tank' has been proved.

**taper** (slender candle, long waxed wick used for lighting candles)
This word is not related to 'tape', but probably derives ultimately from Latin *papyrus*, 'paper', referring to the original use of the object simply as a wick. The Latin source of the name is seen more clearly in the modern word for 'wick' in some Romance languages, such as Spanish *pabilo*.

**tart** (prostitute)
The origin of this word is often explained as simply being a reference to the designated person's 'sweetness'. Supporters of this derivation point to similar names for a 'scrumptious' woman or girl (not necessarily an immoral one), such as 'honey', 'honey bun', 'sugar', 'sweetie pie', 'cupcake' and possibly 'crumpet'. But these are mainly 'eulogistic appellations' (compare **tabby cat**), and 'tart' does not really belong to this category. But 'sweet' does seem to lie behind the word if two other possibilities are considered: first, that the term is a shortening of 'sweetheart'; second, that it is the latter half of 'jam tart', which itself is rhyming slang for 'sweetheart', This last seems quite likely, given the subject range catered for by cockney slang and the association of prostitutes and London. The word would thus have started in a 'good' sense and finished up in its present 'bad' one, although it seems that 'tart' was used in a non-derogatory sense (if not a positively good one) as recently as the Second World War. For other 'sweet' names, see **hinny** and **jo**.

**tattoo** (1 outdoor military display or parade; 2 coloured figure etched on skin)
Perhaps because of the linking association of soldiers (many tattooed men must participate in tattoos), it could appear that one of the two words derives from the other, with simply a sense development. But this is not so, and the words are quite distinct. The 'military parade' word (well known from the annual Edinburgh Tattoo) comes from Dutch *taptoe*, this representing the command *tap toe!*, 'turn off the taps!' (i.e. stop drinking and get back to barracks). The other 'skin effect' tattoo is a word of Polynesian origin (probably Tahitian *tatau*).

**teapoy** (small table containing receptacles to hold tea)
The word has been assimilated to 'tea', but actually derives from the language of its country of origin, so is from Hindi *tipai*. This in turn is based on Sanskrit *tri*, 'three' and *pada*, 'foot', since the table is properly a tripod one.

**teetotal** (abstaining from alcohol)
This word does not mean that the drinker is totally committed to tea, nor does it relate to the kind of top called a 'teetotum' in any sense or imagined allusion (as if a teetotaller were someone who had given the top a spin and it had decreed his abstemious future by displaying the letter 'T', which it had displayed on one of its sides). The rather strange word is said to be a representation of 'total' (i.e. 'total abstinence'), with a repeated letter 't'. It is said to have been coined in 1833 by a keen promoter of such abstinence, Richard Turner, who may or may not have stammered (and thus have said 't-total abstinence'). In its early existence, the word was usually spelt 'tee-total'.

**template** (thin plate cut to shape required)
When it first appeared, in the seventeenth century, the word was spelt 'templet', with this probably deriving from the identical French word that was the diminutive of *temple*, meaning the temple of a loom (a device for keeping the cloth stretched). It does not therefore derive from 'plate', although this word must have influenced the spelling.

**terrapin** (kind of freshwater reptile resembling a tortoise)
The terrapin goes on land and in water, but the first part of its name does not come from Latin *terra*, 'land'. In fact, its other name is 'water tortoise', showing that land would not be its most usual habitat. Its name is thus a word of Algonquian origin, related to Delaware *torope*, 'turtle'.

**terrier** (breed of dog formerly used for driving or digging out small animals from their burrows)
If a **pointer** 'points' and a **setter** 'sets', perhaps a terrier . . . 'terrifies'? No doubt it does (or did), when unearthing its prey, but here we have the Latin *terra* that the **terrapin** (above) lacked, and the terrier's name comes from French *chien terrier*, literally 'earth dog'. (Members of the Territorial Army are also nicknamed 'Terriers', but this is simply a handy pun on their shortened title – they 'dig out' the enemy when required.) See also **lurcher**.

**thespian** (actor)
The word is sometimes used humorously, even semi-equivocally, for an actor or actress, with the jocular use no doubt arising from the 'mincing' initial 'th-' and the resemblance to 'lesbian', allied to the popular (mis)conception that acting is an affected or 'pansy' profession. Yet it has even found currency among actors themselves, who frequently shorten it to 'thesp'. This colloquial use of a once formal and 'grand' word is quite recent, and lest it be thought that its origin actually is in some corruption or other, it might be timely to mention its true derivation here. The word comes from the name of the reputed founder of Greek drama, Thespis, who lived in the sixth century B.C. (as coincidentally did Sappho, the Greek poetess and alleged homosexual who lived on the island, Lesbos, that gave its name to lesbianism). See also **homosexual**.

**thug** (tough criminal)
The word seems just right for the person it denotes, suggesting a blend of a word such as 'thick', 'thief' or 'thud' (or even 'ugly') with one of the many unpleasant words ending in '-ug', such as 'bug', 'slug', 'mug',

'pug', or 'plug' (i.e. 'shoot'). Its actual source is in Hindi *thag*, literally 'thief', since the original Thugs were members of an organization of assassins and robbers in India. They could be negotiated with on civilized terms, however, provided the circumstances were favourable or even flattering, and as the *Daily News* reported in its issue of 22 September 1897: 'When the Prince of Wales was in India, a Thug criminal showed him how victims were strangled'.

**tick** (in phrase 'on tick')
To get something 'on tick' is to get it on credit, with a chance to pay for it later. This does not refer to the traditional 'tick' of correctness in school exercises, as if the credit had been approved by the vendor, but is short for 'on ticket', with this being a reference to the official note or bill made by the vendor or moneylender (or possibly the equivalent 'IOU' signed by the purchaser or borrower).

**tipstaff** (lawcourt official)
This official is not so designated since he tipped his staff in some way, but because he originally carried a 'tipped staff', that is, a staff with a metal tip.

**tipsy** (slightly drunk)
Is a tipsy person so called since he or she has been tippling? Almost certainly not, since the word implies that the drinker is likely to 'tip over', whereas the verb 'tipple' comes from an old word *tippler*, meaning 'seller of drink', of uncertain origin.

**titchy** (very small)
This common if colloquial word has been curiously absent from standard dictionaries until very recently (post-1980), so not surprisingly its origin has been mainly speculative, at any rate at a popular level. Perhaps it is semi-imitative, such as 'teeny' or 'itsy-bitsy'? It certainly sounds just right for a tiny 'mingy' thing. Its actual derivation is in the nickname, 'Little Tich', given to the small but rotund music-hall comedian Harry Relph who died in 1928. He gained it as a child, when it was based on the corpulent so called 'Tichborne Claimant' who was then in the news. This

was one Arthur Orton, who claimed to be Roger Tichborne, the heir to the considerable inheritance due to the Tichborne family. So that is the genuinely 'popular' etymology of 'titchy'! See also **titmouse** (below).

**titmouse** (kind of small bird)
Why is this bird called 'mouse'? Does it eat them, or scuttle about like a mouse? On the contrary, it eats insects, and is otherwise simply a 'tit', the family name for the species. The 'mouse' comes from an older name for it, *mose*, still found in the modern German word for the bird, which is *Meise*. This was assimilated to 'mouse' and added to 'tit', which itself was a general word for any small thing or creature. And although not really a mouse, the plural of 'titmouse' is 'titmice', unlike the **mongoose**, for example (which see) where the plural is 'mongooses'. For a coincidental 'titty' word, see **titchy**.

**tobacco** (leaves of plant *Nicotiana tabacum* prepared for smoking)
Tobacco has long been popularly connected with the island of Tobago, but it is unlikely that the word derived from this name. It probably originated as a native Taino word of the West Indies, used for the rolled tobacco leaves that were smoked like a sort of primitive cigar. The Spanish then came to the West Indies, and assumed it to be the name of the plant itself. Through them, and Spanish *tabaco*, the word spread to other languages (including English), where it still has a form close to its native origin, such as French *tabac*, German *Tabak*, Russian *tabak*, and so on. If anything, it is likely that the Spanish, or even Columbus himself, named Tobago after this word, from the distinctive use of the plant leaves, which must have impressed the Spanish in the late fifteenth century.

**toff** (upper-class or 'snooty' person)
This now outmoded nickname does not derive from 'toffee-nosed', as has been sometimes suggested (perhaps not too seriously), despite a sort of implicit pun on 'stuck up'. The word is probably an alteration of 'tuft', the slang term for a titled undergraduate at Oxford or Cambridge who had a gold tassel

('tuft') on his cap. For more about tufts, see
**tuffet**.

**toils** (in phrase 'toils of fortune')
This is not the same 'toil' that means
'labour'. Its basic sense is 'snare', 'trap',
deriving from Middle French (and modern)
*toile*, 'cloth', 'net'. Today the word is used
only in the plural.

**tomboy** ('a wench that skippeth as a boy'
[Richard Verstegen, né Rowlands,
*Restitution of Decayed Intelligence in Antiquities
concerning the English Nation*])
In giving the definition above, in his fasci-
nating book on the history, languages and
surnames of Britain, published in Antwerp
in 1605, Verstegen derived the word
'tomboy' from 'tumbler', that is, based it on
Old English *tumbian*, 'to dance'. But this is
a misplaced deduction, alas, and the word
comes much more simply from a combination of 'Tom' and 'boy'. 'Tom' is
frequently used as a name or word to denote
a male, as in 'tomcat', 'tomtit' and so on
(not forgetting 'Tom, Dick and Harry', for
three random males). Originally 'tomboy'
was used of both bold boys and women;
later, it came to apply to a girl who acted
like a boy – boisterously, in fact.

**top** (in phrase 'sleep like a top')
This is an apparently meaningless
expression, since how can a top sleep? Word
analysts, seeking a way out of this difficulty,
have declared in the past that the 'top' here
is actually a corruption of French *taupe*,
'mole'. But the word really is 'top', and the
expression comes from the apparent stillness
of a top when it is spinning vertically. Moreover, when a top spins upright like this, it
is said to 'sleep'.

**topsy-turvy** (upside down)
What is the origin of this jingling
expression? Some have said that it relates
to turves of grass, which are always laid
'wrong' side up. Others have decided that
the phrase is a corruption of 'topside t'other
way'. But the true origin is very likely in a
simple combination of 'tops' and an old verb
'terve', meaning 'turn upside down'. See

also **upside-down** itself, for more linguistic
inversion.

**tornado** (violent whirlwind)
This word is not based on 'turn', at least,
not in English. It is really the result of a
Spanish folk etymology, and is probably an
alteration of Spanish *tronada*, 'thunderstorm'
(from *tronar*, 'to thunder'), influenced by
*tornar*, 'to turn'. Compare **hurricane**.

**trade wind** (wind blowing towards the
equator)
The wind is so called not because it blows
'trade' or commerce along in ships, but
because it blows on a regular 'trade', in
the old sense of the word meaning 'track',
'course' (hence its relation to 'tread'). Even
the eminent scientist T. H. Huxley got the
derivation wrong when in *Physiography*,
published in 1877, he wrote: 'Such steady
winds were of so much importance to navigation that much of the world's commerce
depended on them, and they were therefore
called trade winds'.

**train oil** (oil from a whale used in various
manufacturing processes)
So why 'train' oil? There is clearly nothing
to do with trains here. The term was originally just 'train' or 'trane', deriving from
some German related word that probably
meant 'tear' (as in modern German *Träne*).
This could have referred to the drops that
emerge when whale blubber is boiled.
(Notice that 'blubber', too, has a link with
the meaning.)

**tram** (passenger vehicle running on rails)
The word has long been popularly associated with the name of Benjamin Outram,
who ran experimental vehicles on stone rails
in Derbyshire in about the year 1800. But
this is not the source of the word, which
originated as a dialect term for the shaft
of a cart or wheelbarrow, itself probably
deriving from Low German *traam*, 'beam'.
The sense then developed something as
follows: 'shaft' → 'truck' → 'track' → 'road
where a track is laid' → 'vehicle that runs
on this'.

**trappings** (coverings over a horse's harness)
There is no reference here to the 'trap' or carriage that a horse draws, or in fact to any kind of other trap. The word comes from Middle English trappe, 'cloth', in turn from Middle French *drap* also meaning this. The sense is now often widened to mean 'obvious accessories', as 'all the trappings of success'.

**Trappist** (Cistercian monk who keeps a vow of silence)
Certainly the name suggests that the monks so called are isolated in a 'trap', far from other human company, or even that their words and voices are 'trapped' (they keep their 'trap' shut!). Officially, they are the Reformed Cistercians of the Strict Observance, whose order was originally formed at La Trappe in France – on the map today as Soligny-la-Trappe in Normandy.

**treacle** (golden syrup)
The rich, sugary substance is not so called as it 'trickles' from the spoon or knife, but because the word derives from Old French *triacle*. This comes from Latin *theriaca*, 'antidote for a poisonous bite', from the Greek equivalent which ultimately comes from *thērion*, 'wild beast'. This unexpected origin can be explained by the fact that formerly treacle was used as a sort of general-purpose 'salve' or remedy for venomous bites, various poisons, and diseases generally. A well known reference to this occurs in the so called 'Treacle Bible', where in some early English translations of the Bible, such as the one by Miles Coverdale, the word 'treacle' is used instead of 'balm', notably in Jeremiah 8:22 (which in the Authorized Version runs, 'Is there no balm in Gilead?').

**trellis** (wooden or other framework for plants to climb up)
The device is not so called since it can be used for 'trailing' plants. The word comes from Middle French *treliz*, the name of a coarsely woven fabric, itself from an assumed Late Latin word *trilicius*, 'woven with a triple thread' (from *tri-*, 'three' and *licium*, 'thread'). It is likely that the modern sense of the term, however, has been influenced by French *treille*, 'vine-arbour'.

**tribulation** (suffering, distress)
This word is sometimes misunderstood to mean almost the exact opposite, i. e. 'rejoicing', either because the phrase 'toil and tribulation' or 'trials and tribulations' is itself thought to refer to opposites, or because the word is itself wrongly associated with 'rejoicing' words such as 'tribute', 'tribune', 'triumph' and so on. The rather unexpected origin is in fact in Latin *tribulare*, 'to afflict', which itself is based on *tribulum*, 'threshing board'. The metaphor implicit in this is the separating of the corn from the husks, so that the 'chaff' of a person's sorrows and distress are 'threshed out' from the 'wheat' of the wholesome or acceptable side of life.

**trifle** (insignificant matter or object; kind of dessert or 'pudding')
A trifle is not so called because it is trivial, and the two words have quite different origins. 'Trifle' comes from Old French *trufle*, 'mockery' (from the verb *trufler*, 'to cheat'). 'Trivial', more interestingly, comes from Latin *trivium*, 'crossroads' (literally 'three-way place'), implying something that is public knowledge and belongs to the street. ('Trifle' in the 'pudding' sense gets its name from being a 'light' confection – compare 'gooseberry fool', equally enjoyable.)

**trog** (walk along aimlessly or heavily)
This fairly recent colloquial word might seem to derive from some popular sense of 'troglodyte', properly meaning 'caveman' but also used (often in the short form 'trog') to mean a solitary, unsociable or rather eccentrically outmoded person. But the verb 'trog' is more likely to be a blend of 'trudge' and 'slog', since the other word indicates a person's nature and character rather than his method of walking. Even so, one is reminded of both words in certain situations or contexts, such as the 'mindless masses', 'common herd' and so on ('trogs') who 'trog' round their daily business or routine tasks (e.g. the Saturday shopping chore).

**troy weight** (measures based on the pound of 12 ounces)
Troy weight, whose measures include not only pounds and ounces but grains and

pennyweights, does not derive from the ancient Greek city of Troy in any way. It was first used in the fourteenth century at the great annual fair held in Troyes, in north-east France, and the units originating there were subsequently adopted by other medieval fairs.

**truck** (in phrase 'have no truck with')
Which 'truck' is this? Is it the vehicle, implying an unwillingness to do trade with someone, or to deal commercially with them? Or does the word relate to 'truculent' in some way? The answer is coincidentally quite close to the first of these, although there is no linguistic connection with the vehicle. The word derives from Old French *troquer*, 'to barter', and still exists in this basic sense in the American 'truck farm' that corresponds to the British market garden. The vehicle called a 'truck', however, probably gets its name from some link with 'truckle', or even an ultimate source in Greek *trochos*, 'wheel'.

**trudgen** (swimming stroke)
Most swimming strokes have names that describe the position of the body or method of progression through the water, such as 'breaststroke', 'backstroke', 'sidestroke', 'crawl', 'butterfly', 'dog paddle' and the like. For this reason, it would be quite logical to assume that the 'trudgen' indicated some kind of 'trudging' motion in the water. But the name in fact derives from the English swimmer who introduced the style in about 1865, John Trudgen. And far from resembling a 'trudge', the stroke is a fairly fast one, combining the overarm action of the crawl and the scissors kick.

**trump card** (card of a suit whose cards will win over all cards of other suits)
The word suggests 'trumpet', or even some sort of punning allusion to the 'last trump', as if a player with such cards had the final victory over all others. Or could it on the other hand relate to 'trumpery', with some sort of reference to 'trickery' and card tricks? The answer is in fact neither, and the word is actually an alteration of 'triumph'. Shakespeare uses the word in this sense, although metaphorically, in *Anthony and Cleopatra*,

where Anthony says to his friend Eros, talking of Cleopatra:

'she, Eros, has
Pack'd cards with Caesar, and false-play'd my glory
Unto an enemy's triumph'.

**tuberose** (plant of daffodil family with fragrant white flowers)
This plant is not a rose, and the 'tube' of the name is also misleading. The origin of the words is in Latin *tuberosus*, 'tuberous', 'knobby', referring to the roots of the plant. The name is pronounced 'tube-rose' in two syllables by some, no doubt on the basis of this popular interpretation.

**tuffet** (kind of low seat)
First, what *is* a tuffet, such as the one that Miss Muffet sat on? Was she indoors or outdoors at the time? The *Oxford English Dictionary* assigns Miss Muffet's tuffet to the sense 'low stool', but adds that the word may have actually been intended in the original nursery rhyme to mean 'mound', 'hillock'. (In one version of the rhyme, too, she sat on a 'buffet', which is definitely a kind of stool.) So, with both these meanings in mind, what is the derivation of the word? It does not relate to 'tussock', even in the 'hillock' sense. Most likely, it is simply an alteration of 'tuft'. Not that the word is at all commonly used today, but it is at least familiar from the famous rhyme, which according to one source specifically related to a Miss Patience Muffet, the daughter of a sixteenth-century entomologist who was a particular authority on spiders.

**tumble** (understand, catch on)
'I soon tumbled to his plan.' The word looks like a sort of simplified version of 'undercon-stumble'. But it means what it says, and is the basic 'tumble' that means 'fall'. The usage is thus similar to occasions when 'the penny drops'.

**tummy** (stomach)
This children's and family doctors' word could be assumed by some classically minded word fanciers to be based on the Latin *tum-* root that occurs in words such as 'tumour', 'tumulus', 'tumid' and so on, where the source is Latin *tumere*, 'to swell'.

But the actual origin is in the child's alteration of 'stomach' itself. The word seems to have first emerged in the mid-nineteenth century.

**tureen** (deep bowl for serving soup)
One popular etymology derives this word from the name of the Italian city Turin, claiming that tureens originated there. And one more colourful account (retold by Rosie Boycott, see Bibliography) says that the dish was named after a seventeenth-century French marshal, Vicomte de Turenne, who one day hit on the device of using his helmet as a soup bowl. (When out in the field, the true professional soldier has to be resourceful.) But the real origin lies in French *terrine*, 'earthenware bowl', itself ultimately from Latin *terra*, 'earth'. (In modern English use, 'terrine' is not just the word for a type of earthenware dish, but for a pâté served in one.)

**turkey** (large bird fattened for Christmas dinners)
The bird has been landed with a misnomer, since it does not and did not come from Turkey. The name was first used of the African guinea fowl, apparently since it was originally brought from New Guinea through Turkish territory by the Portuguese. Later, the name came to apply to the North American bird, to which it subsequently became exclusive. However, the ordinary turkey was given the genus name *Meleagris* by Linnaeus, since this was the name by which the guinea fowl was known to the Greeks and Romans. So the wretched creature has finished up with names that indicate not only the wrong country but even the wrong bird!

**turtledove** (kind of wild pigeon)
The association with 'turtle' seems rather bizarre for a bird that is not remotely connected with this animal. And of course this is simply the usual wrong connection of etymological wires. The bird was originally just called the 'turtle', with this name coming ultimately from Latin *turtur*, where it is imitative of the characteristic 'purring' call made by the pigeon. This earlier English word is thus the one occurring in the famous line in the biblical Song of Solomon, where, as a harbinger of spring, 'the voice of the turtle is heard in our land'. However, it is likely that the 'real' (shell-backed) turtle has a name that was influenced by that of the bird, and that it is thus a corruption of French *tortue*, 'tortoise'.

**tweed** (type of rough woollen fabric)
As already mentioned, many fabrics are named after their place of origin (see **diaper**). In the case of woollen cloths, there are thus Harris tweeds from the island so named in the Outer Hebrides, Fair Isle garments from this island in Shetland, and of course the famous jersey worsted from the Channel Islands. (Where would Britain's textile industry be without her islands?) But tweed is the odd man out here, since although the word has undoubtedly been influenced by this river name, the actual derivation is from Scottish *tweel*, 'twill', itself coming from Old English *twilic* meaning literally 'having a double thread' (compare **trellis**, where there is a close parallel).

**ultramarine** (vivid blue)
The name seems to suggest a colour that is darker than navy blue, since it literally means 'beyond the sea'. But the explanation here is in the fact that lapis lazuli, from which the colour was originally produced, was itself brought from Asia, from 'over the sea'. (Lapis lazuli in turn has a name that links up with 'azure'.) Compare **navy blue** itself.

**Unready** (nickname of King Ethelred)
The nickname or title of this tenth-century English king is usually taken to mean 'unprepared', 'not ready', as if he had been a weak ruler or a badly organized one. He was hardly weak, however, and was in fact a cruel and passionate man, who among other orders commanded the massacre of all the Danes in the country. 'Unready' literally means 'lacking counsel', 'rash', from the obsolete word *rede*, 'counsel', related to modern 'read', the common link being the transmission of information. So far from being slow off the mark, Ethelred was the reverse – over-hasty and ill-advised. In its Old English form, his full name would have appeared as *Æthelred Unred*, and including his own personal name as well, this interestingly translates as 'noble counsel, bad counsel', since 'Ethelred' also contains the 'counsel' element ('-red').

**uproar** (commotion, noisy disturbance)
The word has become associated with 'roar', but did not originate with this element. The derivation is from Dutch *oproer*, literally 'up motion', with the original sense of 'insurrection', 'tumult'. The English word was first used in the sixteenth century by Tindale and Coverdale for their translations of the Bible from Luther's German translation (where the word was *aufruhr*, as it still is in modern German), with the Dutch word mentioned occurring

in a Dutch Bible of the same century, where it translated the word that is now 'treason' in II Kings 11:14. Coverdale's version of the last part of this verse thus ran: 'Athalia rente hir clothes, & sayde vproure, vproure'. The adjective 'uproarious' developed from 'uproar' in the nineteenth century, with a much 'jollier' connotation, however, than the noun has.

**upside down** (topsy turvy; wrong side up)
How can this expression be best explained? Perhaps it really means that the 'up' side is 'down'? Originally, the wording was *up so doun*, meaning 'set up so that the upper part is underneath, or down'. The present spelling came about because 'so' did not seem to make good sense in the original expression, and it was therefore altered to a more meaningful 'side'. Compare **topsy turvy**.

**utterance** (in phrase 'to the utterance')
The now archaic phrase means 'to the bitter end', 'to the utmost limit', with one of its best known occurrences in Shakespeare's *Macbeth*, where Macbeth, defying Banquo, says:

Rather than so, come fate into the list,
And champion me to the utterance!

The word is nothing to do with 'utter' (in either of its senses, 'absolute' or 'speak'), nor is it therefore related to 'utmost'. It derives from Middle French *outrance*, from the verb *outrer*, 'to pass beyond', ultimately (what else) from Latin *ultra*, 'beyond'. The word *is* therefore related to the French *outré* used in English to mean 'carried to excess', and also to the French phrase *à outrance*, used in English (sometimes in the inaccurate form 'à l'outrance') to mean virtually what 'to the utterance' meant, i. e. 'to the bitter end'. See also **outrage**.

**vagrant** (person who is 'of no fixed address' and often almost destitute)
Because of the similarity of the actual words, and their nearness of meaning, there might seem to be a direct connection between 'vagrant' and 'vagabond'. There is not, however, since although 'vagrant' is immediately of French origin, its ultimate derivation is Germanic, with the word generally related to 'walk'. 'Vagabond', on the other hand, is primarily of Latin origin, from *vagari*, 'to wander'. The Latin *vag-* root must have had some fairly early influence on 'vagrant', however, for the word to have arrived in English from Old or Middle French (where it was *waucrant*).

**valance** (piece of drapery along edge of bed, etc; pelmet)
As with many fabrics and cloths, the origin here looks like a place name, and this could actually be Valence, the town in south-east France that is noted for its textiles. At any rate this place appears to have preference over the lace-making town of Valenciennes and the textile centre of Valencia, the Spanish city whose name is actually *Valence* in French. But while perhaps half-admitting the French town name, it is quite likely that the true origin may be in some derived form of Old French *avaler,* 'to descend' (see **avalanche** in this respect), with reference to the function of a valance, which is to hang down as a border from a height. The word has been in use in English since the fifteenth century.

**van** (motor vehicle used to transport goods; railway goods wagon)
By muddled association with 'vanguard' and 'guard's van' (on a train), the basic 'van' is sometimes believed to derive from one or other of these. However, 'vanguard' is quite a different word (from Middle French *avant-garde*, literally 'fore-guard', i. e.

the opposite of 'rearguard'), while 'guard's van', although incoroporating the same word as van, derived from it, not the other way round. There are two complicating factors here, of course, to add to the false association: 'vanguard' and 'guard's van' are 'attractive opposites', so to speak (a vanguard leads the way at the front, a guard's van brings up the rear of a train), and also 'van' can be an acceptable abbreviation for 'vanguard' in certain contexts (mainly historical, in a military sense, or in such modern artistic and literary usages as 'in the van of haute couture'). So, after all this, the true origin of 'van' is as an abbreviation – not of 'vanguard', however, but 'caravan'. In its modern sense of 'motor vehicle', the word is first recorded in 1829, in Lord Bulwer-Lytton's novel *The Disowned* ('Yes, Sir, we have some luggage – came last night by the van'). The guard's van followed some forty years later when the railways and their new jargon were beginning to become established. (To cloud the issue still further, however, the term 'vanguard' appeared for a while in the 1920s and 1930s to mean the guard of a mail van, so that to modern readers this report from the issue of the *Daily Express* dated 22 September 1931 is rather puzzling; 'A vanguard [. . .] was accused of being concerned with another man [ . . . ] in stealing a motor-car'.)

**vaudeville** (type of light entertainment for the stage)
The final '-ville' of this word suggests not only French *ville*, 'town' but also the American use of the element as a suffix to mean 'place where this happens' (or ' . . . these people live'), with the first part of such a word supplying the definition, as e. g. 'squaresville', 'dragsville' and the like. But we can rule this latter possibility out, since the usage is too recent, and vaudeville dates

from the eighteenth century. So what about the actual French *ville*? Perhaps 'Vaudeville' is the place where the entertainment was born? Well, no – yet yes, it was, although not a town! The present word is in fact a corruption of Middle French *vaude-vire*, this representing *vau-de-Vire*, that is, 'valley of the Vire'. The expression applies to a popular satirical song that originated in this part of Normandy in the valley of the river Vire. Such songs were themselves said to have developed from the drinking songs of a fifteenth-century fuller who lived in this valley, named Olivier Basselin. Later, in the seventeenth and eighteenth centuries, the songs, in the form of couplets, were introduced into the light comedies of French theatres. And thus modern vaudeville was born!

**vent** (slit in garment, such as at back of jacket)
This 'vent' is fortunately not the same one that means 'outlet', 'opening for the escape of a gas or liquid or for the relief of pressure' (*Longman Dictionary of the English Language*, see Bibliography). This second 'vent' comes from Middle French *vent*, wind' (from Latin *ventus* in the same meaning). The first 'vent' is also from Middle French, but from *fente*, 'slit', from the verb *fendre*, 'to split', ultimately from Latin *findere* in the same sense.

**verdigris** (greenish chemical deposit on copper, brass etc)
The obviously French word looks as if it means something like 'green of grey'. 'Green' is right, but not 'grey'. In Old French the term was *vert de Grice*, literally 'green of Greece'. The precise sense of this is not certain, but perhaps the reference was to some colour or pigment that came from Greece or was believed to have come from there. In modern French, the word is *vert-de-gris* where the false influence of *gris*, 'grey' is much more apparent. (In German, 'verdigris' is *Grünspan*, literally 'Spanish green'!)

**verge** (edge)
This sense of 'verge' is not related to the verb that means 'move', as when one 'verges towards' something (such as a cliff edge). It comes from the identical Middle French word that itself derives from Latin *virga*,

'rod'. This means 'rod of office' (compare the English church official called a 'verger'), so that a former phrase 'within the verge' developed in English to refer to the area subject to the Lord High Steward, who was the 'verge-bearer'. The other 'verge' comes from Latin *vergere*, 'to bend', 'incline', indirectly related to English 'wrench'.

**veronica** (kind of plant with small flowers)
The flower of this name, better known as the speedwell, is not so called since it came originally from Verona, just as japonica is connected with Japan (rightly since it is of Japanese origin). The name instead derives from the identical Christian name, presumably that of St Veronica, although the ultimate reference here is uncertain. The flower (or herb) name is first recorded in English in the sixteenth century ('A dragma of pouder of ye same herbe Veronica'). Even the saint and her name have a cloudy and rather mysterious background, both historically and linguistically, since although the original Veronica is said to have been the name of the pious woman who wiped the face of Christ as he fell when carrying his cross to Calvary, the word itself is somehow linked with the Latin words for 'true icon', i. e. as if *vera icon*. Whether this links up with the biblical story or the other way round is hard to say. Whatever the origin of the personal name, the modern girl's name almost certainly derives from that of the saint, not the flower, which runs contrary to the general principle, so that most girls called Pansy, Poppy, Heather, Holly, Rose and the like are named after these plants. But whether word or name, flower or saint, Veronica has inspired artistic and poetic compositions in both sublime painters and vernacular versesmiths. And for more about verses, see the next entry.

**versed** (well informed or experienced)
This word, usually found in the phrase 'well versed in', appears to imply a person who has 'learnt his lines' well, and so can produce the required quotation or relevant phrase for the matter in hand. However, the actual derivation is in Latin *versari*, 'to be turned', 'be engaged in', and not in English 'verse' at all. It is true that 'verse' itself ultimately comes from the same Latin root,

but the connection between the two words is more remote than it might at first appear.

**vicious circle** ('a process by which an evil is aggravated by its own consequences' [*Chambers*])
The term does not relate to the modern popular sense of 'vicious' meaning 'fierce', as if the circle, whatever it is, is one that will retaliate and 'strike back'. Both words have their origin in a formal sense as applied to logic, with 'circle' meaning 'instance of circular reasoning' (that is, a false one, where a proposition is made to lead to a conclusion, and is afterwards proved by means of the very same conclusion that it had been posed to establish), and 'vicious' added to this term to emphasize how faulty such reasoning is, since it goes round and ends up where it began, like a circle. The English term arose as a translation of the French *cercle vicieux*, used by Descartes in the seventeenth century. The expression also has a formal medical use, implied by the *Chambers* definition above, meaning that one disease or disorder leads to a second, which in turn aggravates the first. After such rarefaction, perhaps the following illustration of a proper vicious circle in logic may help:
'The Compton St Denis Cricket Club is the best in West Anglia; they are the best because of their unique batting potential; they have this potential because of the great skill of Chas, Dave, and Fearless Fred at the wicket.'
'But how do you know that Chas, Dave, and Fearless Fred are such good batsmen?'
'How do I know? Because these three are the real driving force behind the best cricket club in West Anglia.'

**Viking** (Norse 'sea rover' and invader of Britain)
The word can be traced back confidently to Old Norse *víkingr*, which certainly suggests 'king'. However, this does not form a basis of origin for the name, which almost certainly derives from Old Norse *vík*, 'sea inlet', 'creek', with the *-ingr* ending meaning 'people of'. If this is so, the Vikings were the 'sea inlet men', or the ones experienced in travelling quite literally 'up the creek' in their specially designed long, narrow boats.

The coastal town of Wick in northern Scotland has a name that is directly based on this Norse 'sea inlet' word, with the actual inlet there being Wick Bay. The resemblance of 'Viking' to 'king', however, has led in the past to the coining of the expression 'sea king' for a great Viking pirate chief, and even, heaven help us, 'viqueen' for a 'vice-queen' (not a 'vice queen'!). This latter word appears in Horace Marryat's *One Year in Sweden* (1862): 'There Lina lies like a vi-queen in her grave'. (This is not the better known Frederick Marryat, author of *Midshipman Easy* and other stirring Victorian novels of sea life.)

**villain of the piece** (main evil character in play, film, novel etc)
The expression has sometimes been wrongly understood, and consequently wrongly used, to mean 'villain of the peace', as if referring to a person who disturbs the peace, as some kind of mischiefmaker or rowdy. This wrong use may be partly due to an incorrect accentuating of the words in the phrase, with both 'villain' and 'piece' stressed equally ('*villain* of the *piece*'), instead of just the word 'villain'. Other factors leading to the miscomprehension are probably the substitution of literary 'piece' for 'play', and an association with such more familiar terms as 'justice of the peace', 'keeper of the peace', and so on. The expression seems to have arisen in the nineteenth century as a semi-humorous term for the 'baddy' in a play, the opposite to the hero, and the *Oxford English Dictionary* has a first noting of it in 1867 (in a work on history). Since then it has been widely used by writers such as Theodore Dreiser and Iris Murdoch and by people generally in everyday speech, usually fairly playfully ('So he's the villain of the piece after all!').

**virago** (loud overbearing woman)
This word is not related to 'virgin', as is sometimes supposed, perhaps because of the recent use of both words in the names of commercial organizations (Virago Press, Virgin Books, Virgin Airlines) as well as the common 'feministic' or at any rate feminine or female bond between the two, with however a sort of 'polarisation' of 'virago'

and 'virgin' to represent, in popular imagery, 'hard' or 'tough' womanliness on the one hand, and 'soft' or 'unsullied' femininity on the other. However, 'virago' is based on Latin *vir*, 'man', while 'virgin' is ultimately of somewhat obscure origin (earlier than Latin *virgo* in the same sense), although Eric Partridge has a good go in *Origins* (see Bibliography) at deriving it likewise from *vir* with the '-ago' ending possibly representing Latin *egere*, 'to lack', so that the whole ultimate etymology suggests 'woman who lacks a man'. This seems somewhat academic, however (in both senses of the word), and certainly there is no immediate link between the two words. It should be added, perhaps, as an interesting footnote, that 'virago' itself originated in the Vulgate (the Latin version of the Bible in use from the thirteenth century in England) as the word now appearing in the Authorized Version as 'Woman' in Genesis 2:23, i. e. it is the name given by Adam to Eve. The relevant part of this verse thus runs in Latin: 'Haec vocabitur virago, quoniam de viro sumpta est' ('She shall be called Woman, because she was taken out of Man'). For more on this concept, see **woman**.

**virginals** (kind of harpsichord popular in the sixteenth and seventeenth centuries) The name of this musical instrument is undoubtedly based on 'virgin', but in what particular respect? There have been a number of suggestions, such as those that intimate a reference to hymns sung to the Virgin Mary, which could have been accompanied on the virginals, or that declare the instrument to have been a favourite with Queen Elizabeth I, the 'Virgin Queen'. But the most likely origin is simply that this particular sort of harpsichord, rather an artistic and delicate variety, was designed to be played by suitably inclined chaste young ladies. This seems to be borne out by the title of the first music for it published in England, which was entitled *Parthenia* (literally 'maidens' songs') and first appeared in 1611. (The title page of this work, which depicts a rather cloyingly soulful-looking maiden seated at the instrument, eyes closed in rapture, ran: 'PARTHENIA or THE MAYDENHEAD of the first musicke that ever was printed for the VIRGINALLS'.)

**wag** (joker)
This brief semi-colloquial word does not point to a person who is good at 'wagging' his tongue, but apparently comes as a shortening of an obsolete word *waghalter*, meaning 'one about to be hanged', 'gallows bird' (i.e. someone who 'wags' or swings in a 'halter', as a hanging rope was called). The sense link here is 'mischievous person', i. e. someone who could hang for his mischief.

**wainscot** (lining of wall inside a room)
The word looks like a rather fanciful respelling of 'waistcoat', perhaps from the resemblance of a wainscot to a garment that goes right round, serves as a 'lining' etc. The precise origin is a little unclear, but it is certainly not this. In Middle Dutch the word was *wagenschot*, this perhaps meaning 'wagon planking', referring to the boards or planks that formed the sides of a cart. The ultimate source is still not known. There may also have been an influence of the word that in modern German is *Wand*, 'wall'.

**waive** (refrain from demanding, postpone)
There is enough similarity of sound, spelling and sense here to suggest a direct link with 'wave'. A person who 'waives' or dismisses something may well give a dismissive 'wave' of the hand. There are also uses of 'wave' that suggest a sense of 'waive' or allowing to pass, as 'waving through' a bill in parliament, or even 'waving on' a car, as by a policeman (who does not require the driver to stop). There even seems to be a mutual influence of 'waft' somehow, as well. But the two words have different origins, with 'waive' ultimately related to 'waif', in the 'abandoned' sense, and 'wave' related to 'waver' and 'weave'. 'Waft', however, is a word of Germanic origin, related to neither 'waive' nor 'wave'. The two basic meanings of 'wave' (movement of the hand, water at

sea) are in one and the same family, however.

**walleye** (eye with opaque cornea; squint)
The 'wall' can perhaps be explained if the opaque covering is seen as a 'wall' that prevents the eye from seeing properly, or if the squint results in one eye looking towards the wall when it should be straight ahead. The actual source of the word (which itself comes from the adjective 'walleyed') is in Old Norse *vagl-eygr*, where the first part here apparently means 'film', 'obstruction', and the latter is 'eyed'.

**wallop** (thrash, punch)
The word is not derived, as is sometimes colourfully proposed, from the name of Admiral Sir John Wallop, who thrashed ('walloped') the French in 1514, although this professional sailor did give his name to the village of Farleigh Wallop, near Basingstoke in Hampshire. So 'wallop' in fact comes from Old North French *waloper*, 'to gallop', and this is what the word originally meant in English. Here it is, for example, in a late fifteenth-century text by William Caxton, the first English printer: 'Cam there kyng charlemagn, as fast as his horse myghte walop'. Later, 'wallop' was superseded by 'gallop' in English in this sense, while 'wallop' was retained for a number of less steady uses, such as those it has today (including the one that means 'beer', which is the most recent, and dates only from the 1930s).

**walnut** (kind of nut from tree with richly grained wood used for fine furniture)
The walnut tree is not so called because it grows by walls. In Old English the word for 'walnut' was *wealh-hnutu*, literally 'foreign nut', since the tree was brought to Britain from overseas, probably by the Romans. (In this Old English word, the first element is

the same word that gave the name of Wales, since the Welsh were 'foreigners' to the Anglo-Saxons when these came to settle in Britain in the fifth century A. D. The Welsh themselves referred to their own race as *Cymri*, 'fellow countrymen'.)

**waxy** (angry, irritated)
This rather dated colloquial word, smacking of school stories, might seem to derive from 'wax' with some reference to getting 'heated' as candle wax. But the probable source is in some such phrase as 'wax angry', where 'wax' means 'grow', as in the 'waxing and waning' of the moon, with this word related to modern German *wachsen*, 'grow'.

**wayward** (capricious, 'stroppy')
The word looks as if it means something like 'getting in the way', or 'following one's own way'. The second of these is nearer than the first, since the present spelling is an alteration of earlier 'awayward'. The original meaning was thus 'turning away', 'turned away'.

**wedlock** (marriage)
How about being 'locked' in marriage? Is this what the word means? The answer is no, since it derives from Old English *wedlāc*, 'marriage bond', from *wedd*, meaning 'pledge' and the *-lāc* ending meaning 'action', 'what is carried out', perhaps related to the old word that produced modern English '**lark**' (which see).

**weever** (kind of fish with sharp poisonous spines)
Most people know of the seaside danger lurking in the weever fish, whose sting can be very painful. Perhaps they are so called since they 'weave' their way inshore, or because their spines can 'weave' into unsuspecting feet and legs? In fact the word is nothing to do with 'weave', but comes from Old North French *wivre*, 'viper', ultimately from the Latin (*vipera*).

**werewolf** (person who has been changed into a wolf)
The most cunning sort of werewolf, in the best tradition of stories and films involving them, is the one that can change *back* when required, usually in the daytime. For this reason, perhaps, the word looks as if it denotes a person who by day is a normal human being, but at night is quite different, as if he 'were a wolf'. The word has also been explained as indicating that you must 'beware' of the creatures. But the true origin lies in Old English *were*, 'man', and *wulf*, 'wolf'. The werewolf is thus a 'man-wolf', part human, part wolf.

**wheatear** (kind of bird related to the thrush)
This is quite a nice rustic name for a bird, suggesting, perhaps, that it feeds on ears of wheat, or that it lives in wheatfields. But earlier its name was 'wheatears', and the present name was taken from this as if this was a plural. What it really was, however, was a version of 'white arse', referring to the bird's white rump, which is in marked contrast to its black wings and tail and grey back. And the wheatear doesn't eat wheat anyway, but lives on a diet of insects intermingled with worms and snails when available. The bird's French name is *cul-blanc*, reflecting the true English origin. In fact 'wheat' itself is also related to 'white'. The wheatear shares the common cry usually written 'chack-chack' with the **fieldfare** (which see).

**whet** (stimulate, excite)
A short 'wet' (alcoholic drink) can serve as an aperitif and 'whet' your appetite, as can a 'whet' (appetizer) itself. So why not 'wet your whistle'? The two words are so similar in sound and association that they must surely be connected! But, since they feature here, they are obviously not, and 'whet', with its basic sense 'sharpen' (as 'whetting' a knife on a stone), comes from Old English *hwettan*, meaning just this. 'Wet', on the other hand, is one of those basic Germanic words that has links in many other languages (especially the various words for 'water'). However, the expression 'wet one's whistle' (i.e. take an alcoholic drink) was for some time spelt 'whet one's whistle', and is even entered under 'whet' in the *Oxford English Dictionary* (which is careful to point out, nevertheless, that the word should really be 'wet'). Today, the phrase is almost invariably spelt with 'wet', but from the seventeenth to the twentieth century

instances of the spelling with 'h' are found, as in Henry Fielding's *Joseph Andrews* of 1742 ('Give the gentleman a glass to whet his whistle before he begins') and Hardy's *The Dynasts* of 1908 ('See that they have plenty of Madeira to whet their whistles with'). No doubt the 'h' of 'whistle' helped to influence the alteration of 'wet' to 'whet', as well as the association mentioned with taking a drink to stimulate the appetite. The expression originated in Chaucer's *Canterbury Tales* ('So was hir ioly whistle wel y-wet', in *The Reeve's Tale*).

**Whigs** (major political party of the eighteenth and early nineteenth centuries)
The Whigs, who were the precursors of the Liberals, and in opposition to the Tories, were not so called because they wore wigs! The name is probably short for *Whiggamores*. These were members of a group of seventeenth-century Scottish rebels who went to Edinburgh in 1648 to oppose the court party. Their own name probably came from Scottish *whig*, 'to drive' and *more*, 'mare', 'horse'.

**while away** (make time pass in a leisurely way)
The expression is still sometimes spelt (and thought of) as 'wile away', as if ingenuity were needed to make time pass. This variant spelling seems to have been additionally influenced, in former times, by association with such phrases as Shakespeare's 'beguile the day', 'beguile the time' (as in *Twelfth Night*, where Antonio recommends that Sebastian should 'beguile the time' by 'viewing the town' while he arranges food and board), as well as with similar phrases in other languages, such as Latin *diem decipere* (literally 'to cheat the day') and French *tromper le temps* ('deceive time'). At any rate, for whatever reason, Dickens used this spelling in *Oliver Twist* ('I was reading a book to-night, to wile the time away') and other writers have followed this interpretation in more recent times. But the word here really is 'while', with the use of the old noun 'while' (meaning 'time') acquiring the verbal use only quite recently, probably not much before the seventeenth century.

**whippet** (breed of swift, slender dog used for racing)
The dog is not so called since you have to 'whip it' to make it run, but very likely because it was ordered to 'whip it!', or move quickly, with this expression already being in general use, and the verb 'whip' itself in the 'move briskly' sense a fairly old one (thus appearing rather incongruously, to modern eyes, in Shakespeare's *Much Ado About Nothing*, where Borachio says: 'I whipt me behind the arras'). A sixteenth-century sense of 'whippet' slightly earlier than that of the dog was 'lively young woman' (compare modern colloquial 'fast piece').

**whist** ('A game at cards, requiring close attention and silence' [Johnson, *Dictionary*])
'Whist' is or was also, of course, a word meaning 'silent', 'quiet', perhaps most common in its use as an interjection or exclamation to command silence, as in the famous quotation from Sterne's *Tristram Shandy*: 'Whist! cried one – st, st, – said a second – hush, quoth a third – poo, poo, replied a fourth – gramercy! cried the Lady Carnavallette'. But the card game is not so called for the reason suggested by Johnson above. The name is an alteration of earlier 'whisk', with the reference probably being to the way the tricks are 'whisked up'.

**whydah** (kind of African weaverbird)
The name of this bird, also spelt 'whidah', is sometimes said to derive from the town of Whydah, in Dahomey. In fact it is an alteration of the much more straightforward 'widow bird', this name referring to the bird's dark plumage, resembling a widow's black dress. This is an interesting example of a 'common' sense becoming altered to a more obscure or exotic one. Usually it is the other way round.

**wilderness** (barren place, desert)
The association with 'wild' is correct here, but perhaps not in the way the word actually originated. In Old English the word was *wildēornes*. This is really 'wild-deer-ness', from Old English *wilddēor*, literally 'wild deer', plus the '-ness' ending that means 'state', 'condition' (as in modern 'vastness'). 'Deer' here simply means

'animals', 'beasts', in a much more general sense than modern 'deer'. Compare **reindeer** for a similar sense.

**winsome** (pleasantly and unaffectedly agreeable)
This word is *related* to 'win', but does not directly derive from it (as if a 'winsome' person is able to 'win you over' or is attractive because of his or her 'winning' ways). It derives from Old English *wynsum*, 'pleasant', based on *wyn*, 'joy'. 'Win' itself, on the other hand, comes from Old English *winnan*, 'to struggle', 'to suffer'. Both words have a common sense of 'gaining', however, of getting over to one's own side – and what better way of winning than by being winsome?

**wiseacre** (person who claims to be knowledgeable, 'smart alec')
The word looks as if it somehow describes a person who 'spreads' his knowledge and smartness for the benefit of all around, or perhaps that his knowledge is itself extensive. Could it be that he has 'acres of wisdom', just as others have 'bags of common sense'? A story, repeated by *Brewer* (see Bibliography) and others, tells how Ben Jonson once said to a country gentleman: 'What care we for your dirt and clods? Where you have an acre of land, I have ten acres of wit.' The gentleman retorted by calling Jonson 'Good Mr Wiseacre'. However, the true origin of the word is nothing to do with acres, but is in Middle Dutch *wijssegger*, 'soothsayer', with this in turn seen in modern German *Weissager*. So a wiseacre is really a 'wise-sayer'. It is difficult to see why the latter part of the Dutch word should have been assimilated to 'acre', though.

**witch** (woman with supernatural powers, female wizard)
It could seem as if 'witch' and 'wizard' are related words, as many 'male/female' doublets are (for example 'fox/vixen', 'master/mistress' and 'man/woman' are etymologically linked). But here the two words have different origins. 'Witch' in Old English was *wicce*, and the masculine equivalent was *wicca*, with both words ultimately coming from some Germanic root that

meant 'strike' and that is also behind modern English 'victim'. 'Wizard', by contrast, comes from Middle English *wysard*, based on *wys* or *wis*, 'wise', with the '-ard' ending that so often indicates an undesirable or 'disapproving' sense (as in 'dastard', 'drunkard', 'laggard', 'sluggard' and **'coward'**). In modern colloquial English, of course, 'wizard' (as an adjective) has anything but a derogatory sense.

**witch hazel** (kind of tree whose bark yields a substance used in ointments)
The first word here is nothing to do with 'witch', as above, as if the tree, or its product, had some magic or supernatural power. It is alternatively spelt 'wych', and both these spellings were formerly used of a tree with pliant branches, i. e. one that was 'weak'. The same origin holds for the wych elm.

**wog** (nonwhite person)
This derogatory term is still explained in some contemporary 'word origin' books as deriving from the initials of '*w*ily *o*riental *g*entleman' (see Berlitz, in Bibliography, who inheriting his grandfather's linguistic background should have known much better). Other facetious or insulting sources have been similarly devised for the word, which is probably a shortening of **'golliwog'** (which see).

**wolverine** (kind of flesh-eating animal related to the weasel)
This animal is not a wolf, but does in fact have certain wolfish features and characteristics (if only its flesh-eating habits and solitary way of life, like a 'lone wolf'). Its name was probably given deliberately to suggest 'wolf', however, or at least a sort of diminutive of it (perhaps a 'wolvering'). Other names for the animal, which is found mainly in the northern forests of America, Asia and Europe, are 'glutton', 'carcajou' and 'skunk bear'.

**woman** (adult female human being)
Man (both generically and generally) has long pondered on this word, offering derivations ranging from the supposedly witty ('woe to man') to the extremely unlikely ('womb man'). In Old English, the word

was *wīfman,* in modern terms 'wife man', but in the original sense 'woman-human', having the much broader meaning that 'man' itself had (and still has in many contexts). Some modern 'campaigning' women elect to spell the plural of the word as 'wimmin' in order to avoid any suggestion of 'men' in 'women'. See also '**virago**' for more about the linguistic and etymological battle of the sexes.

**wombat** (kind of Australian animal resembling a small bear)
This animal only coincidentally has a name that suggests 'bat'. Its origin, as will be hardly surprising, is in an aboriginal word from New South Wales.

**woodchuck** (kind of North American burrowing rodent)
Most of us know the answer to the old tonguetwisting teaser, 'How much wood would a woodchuck chuck', etc. But here, yet again, as for the **wombat** (above) and many other creatures, the origin lies in a native name. For the woodchuck it is probably Ojibwa *otchig* or Cree *otcheck.*

**wormwood** (plant giving bitter green oil used to make absinthe)
The plant may have been used in the past as a cure for worms, but there are no worms and no wood behind its name. In Old English it was *wermōd,* and the modern version of this is seen better in German *Wermut* and in English 'vermouth' which is thus really the same word, and came into English from this German word via French (*vermout*). See also **absinthe.**

**worsted** (kind of smooth yarn made from wool, or fabric made from it)
The word looks like a kind of blend of 'wool' and 'twisted', with perhaps a 'weave' or 'woven' intertwined. But this is a genuine fabric name, and thus derives, as many fabric names do, from its place of origin. This is the village of Worstead (formerly Worsted) in Norfolk, north-east of Norwich. Both the fabric and the village are pronounced as 'woostid' – perhaps just as well, to differentiate from the identically spelt 'worsted' (pronounced 'werstid') that means 'defeated' (from the rarish verb 'to worst').

**wound** (past tense of 'wind')
This verb is sometimes found in poetry to mean 'blew', as of sounding a horn or other wind instrument, and as a past tense of an apparent present tense 'wind' (pronounced to rhyme with the same verb that means 'curve', 'coil'). Thus Walter Scott in *The Lady of the Lake* has the line:

But scarce again his horn he wound,

and Tennyson in one of the four *Idylls of the King* ('Elaine') has the line:

Thither he made and wound the
    gateway horn.

Scott also uses the alternative past tense 'winded', so that in *The Lord of the Isles* comes the line:

That blast was winded by the King!

In prose, too, the same usage can be found on occasions, as in Stevenson's *The Black Arrow:* 'He raised a little tucket to his mouth and wound a rousing call'. (Stevenson seems to have misunderstood 'tucket' here, since this is not a trumpet or other type of instrument but a fanfare on a trumpet.) So which 'winding' verb is this – the one that means 'coil' or the one that means 'blow'? Obviously the meaning is the latter, although the pronunciation (in the present tense) is the former. What has happened is that a sort of confused compromise has evolved, with a verb formed from the noun 'wind' (the air that blows), but associated with the 'coiling' verb 'wind', perhaps aided by the additional association with the coils and winding tubes of a horn or other brass instrument. And in fact the noun 'wind' (air) and the verb 'wind' (coil) are not even related anyway, since the former comes from a basic sense 'blow' and the latter from a general sense 'turn'. So the whole thing is rather convoluted.

**wrinkle** (valuable hint, device)
This word *may* be of the same origin as the 'wrinkle' that means 'crease', 'fold', although there was an Old English word *wrenc,* meaning 'trick' (related to 'wrench'), that may have had some role to play in giving the present sense. Some modern dictionaries give one and the same etymology for both meanings.

**yard** (measure of length)
This 'yard', meaning 'three feet', is not related to the other 'yard' meaning 'enclosure', despite the association with 'square yard' and the use of ordinary words ('foot', 'rod', 'chain' and the like) to give the name of measures of length. But the clue to the true origin here really lies in this second fact, since the length 'yard' comes from Old English *gierd,* meaning 'rod', 'twig'. The other 'yard' was *geard* in Old English, which is related to modern 'garden'.

**ye** ('the' in 'Olde Englishe')
This archaic word, still found today in twee or 'period' use (as for 'Ye Olde Tea Shoppe'), is sometimes wrongly associated with its archaic double, 'ye' meaning 'you'. Perhaps there is even some confusion of sense at times, too, especially when followed by an adjective or a noun, where the 'you' sense of 'ye' would be a vocative one, addressing whoever or whatever it was. (One example might be in the exclamation 'Ye gods!'.) The evolution of 'ye' to mean 'the' came about because in Middle English (and earlier in Old English) the sound 'th' (as in 'thin' and 'then') was represented by the single letter þ (called 'thorn', simply because it began this word). This gradually fell out of use from about the fourteenth century and was replaced by either the letter 'y', which was similar to it in shape (hence 'ye') or, more commonly and generally, by 'th', which eventually became the accepted rendering. Even so, the use of 'y' to represent 'th' continued until quite late in certain isolated instances, and even some eighteenth-century texts have it, as in a letter written by the Duke of Portland in 1741, where a typical sentence runs: 'j am to inform you yt ye Duchess continues as well as can be, and ye Babe too'. 'Ye' meaning 'you' was the spelling that evolved for the plural of 'thou'. In Old English its form was *gē,* and that and its modern spelling are related to German *ihr,* also meaning 'you'.

**yellowhammer** (finchlike bird the male of which is mainly yellow)
An earlier form of the name was *yelambre,* with this deriving from an assumed Middle English *yelwanbre,* consisting of *yelwe,* 'yellow' and *ambre,* the actual name of the bird, which itself comes from Old English *amore,* whose precise origin is uncertain. Still, the connection with modern 'hammer' continues to be popularly made, as if perhaps referring to the bird's distinctive call (traditionally represented as 'little-bit-of-bread-and-no-cheese'). This at least is the attribution made in a poem by the nineteenth-century hymn writer and Roman Catholic theologian Frederick William Faber, where the lines occur:
> Away he goes and hammers still
> Without a rule but his free will,
> A little gaudy elf [ ... ]
> And beats and beats his tune again.

**yokel** ('country bumpkin')
Perhaps the yokel is so called with reference to the yoke he carries, or to the yoke of oxen that he drives? Or possibly the word is an alteration of a personal name such as 'Jacob', in some language? The true origin has still not been conclusively established, but it seems probable that the word could come from a dialect term meaning either 'green woodpecker' or '**yellowhammer**' (see last entry). It is not an old word, and is first recorded only in the nineteenth century. If the origin, as seems likely, is in the bird name, then this in turn would be an imitative word, relating to the call. The green woodpecker's name in dialect forms has also been recorded as 'yockle' and 'yuckle' in Shropshire and Wiltshire. Not for nothing is it also called the 'laughing bird'. And here in this book it has the last laugh by being reincarnated as a rustic bumpkin. (See also **bumpkin** itself.)

# BIBLIOGRAPHY

The Bibliography is divided into three parts. Part I comprises the 'standard' dictionaries of English that were consulted during the course of work on the book. Such dictionaries contain, in varying degrees of detail, both definitions of words and phrases and etymologies. Dr. Johnson's unique *Dictionary* is included here since it fulfills these criteria, albeit basically and at times erratically, but it was a supreme pioneering work and in many ways was the true progenitor of all the dictionaries we know today. Part II consists of specialized dictionaries, ranging from etymological works (obviously of the most immediate importance for the present book) to dictionaries of phrases, bird names, plant names, and other clearly defined fields. The fact that some of these books call themselves 'encyclopaedia' or 'manual' does not prevent them from being a dictionary in the proper sense of the word. Part III includes books on the English language that are not dictionaries. Some of these have pages or even separate sections dealing exclusively with popular etymologies, and Eric Partridge's *Adventuring Among Words*, for example, has two whole chapters on the subject, while the two Palmer books are entirely devoted to it.

Unlike many bibliographies, the full titles of most books are given, including the subtitle. This enables the particular content or 'angle' of a work to be seen more clearly, and often gives an illuminating insight into the way the author himself sees his book.

As mentioned briefly at the end of the Introduction (page 7), not all the books included in the Bibliography can be equally recommended for providing the *true* origin of a word, and indeed some of them are featured here because they themselves contain a number of *false* etymologies, and so were useful sources for some of the entries in the present dictionary, if only because they provided a good 'story' for a word. So how is the reader to know which is which?

On the whole, the broad principle is that the more recent the work, the more reliable it will be. This particularly applies to the dictionaries in Part I, which with the exception of Johnson's opus can all qualify as 'recent'. The great *Oxford English Dictionary* is the oldest of these, but also the most substantial and detailed. Any unreliability it may have for determining the true origin of a word will be simply due to the advance of lexicographical scholarship and research techniques since it first appeared. Many of its entries, incidentally, have very readable commentaries on a word's etymology which themselves consider (and usually categorically dispose of) other suspect etymologies, include the 'popular' ones.

The same principle also generally holds for books in Parts II or III, where again, works dealing specifically with general etymology will be more dependable than some that select a more 'anecdotal' area, such as the origin of slang words. These are one or two exceptions to the rule, however, and occasionally one comes across a recent work whose scholarship is shaky and its authority suspect. Even so, it is still capable of providing 'origin stories', which is what is required for our present purpose. It would be invidious to brand such books by name, but the reader may have noted the odd oblique reference in the entries of this book and have seen the warning light come on. (A further gauge can be found in the publishers of the book: do they have a tried and trusted reputation for their reference works, and in particular for their dictionaries?)

Clearly, there are hundreds of other books dealing in one way or another with the English language, and some of them may also well provide good 'word origin' material. One must stop somewhere, however, and make a finite selection. The books that follow are the ones that were chosen for the present dictionary.

## 1  Standard English dictionaries

Burchfield, R.W. (ed.), *A Supplement to the Oxford English Dictionary*, OUP, Vol. I(A-G), 1972, Vol. II (H-N), 1976, Vol. III (O-Scz), 1982, Vol. IV (Se-Z), 1986.

Gove, Philip B. (ed.), *Webster's Third New International Dictionary of the English Language*, G. & C. Merriam, Springfield, Mass., 1971.

Hanks, Patrick (ed.), *Collins Dictionary of the English Language,* Collins, London and Glasgow, 2nd ed., 1986.

Hanks, Patrick (ed.), *Encyclopedic World Dictionary*, Hamlyn, London, 1971.

Johnson, Samuel, *A Dictionary of the English Language: in which the words are deduced from their originals, and illustrated by their different significations by examples from the best writers, to which are prefixed, A History of the Language and an English Grammar* (in two volumes), London, 1755.

Schwarz, Catherine, *et al.* (eds.), *Chambers Twentieth Century Dictionary*, W. & R. Chambers, Cambridge, 1988.

*Longman New Universal Dictionary*, Merriam-Webster, Springfield, MA, 1982.

Murray, James and others (eds.), *The Oxford English Dictionary*, OUP, 1888-1933.

Wyld, Henry Cecil, *The Universal Dictionary of the English Language*, Routledge & Kegan Paul, London, 1934.

## 2  Specialized dictionaries

Barnhart, Robert K. (ed.), *The Barnhart Dictionary of Etymology*, H.W. Wilson Company, New York, 1988.

Beavis, Bill and McCloskey, Richard G., *Salty Dog Talk: The Nautical Origins of Everyday Expressions*, Granada Publishing, St. Albans, 1983.

Beeching, Cyril Leslie, *A Dictionary of Eponyms*, Clive Bingley, London, 1979.
Boycott, Rosie, *Batty, Bloomers and Boycott: A Little Etymology of Eponymous Words*, Hutchinson, London, 1982.
Byrne, Mary, *Eureka! A Dictionary of Latin and Greek Elements in English Words*, David & Charles, England, 1987.
Bryson, Bill, *The Penguin Dictionary of Troublesome Words*, Penguin Books, Harmondsworth, 1984.
Chapman, Robert L., *The Dictionary of American Slang*, Harper & Row, New York, 1987.
Edwards, Eliezer, *Words, Facts and Phrases: A Dictionary of Curious, Quaint, and Out-of-the-way Matters*, Chatto & Windus, London, 1901.
Evans, Ivor H., *Brewer's Dictionary of Phrase and Fable*, Cassell, London, 1981.
Findlater, Andrew (ed.), *Chambers's Etymological Dictionary of the English Language*, W. & R. Chambers, Edinburgh, 1890.
Franklyn, Julian, *A Dictionary of Rhyming Slang*, Routledge and Kegan Paul, London, 1961.
Green, Jonathon, *Newspeak: A Dictionary of Jargon*, Routledge & Kegan Paul, London, 1984.
Grigson, Geoffrey, *A Dictionary of English Plant Names*, Allen Lane, London, 1974.
Grose, Francis, *Dictionary of the Vulgar Tongue: A Dictionary of Buckish Slang, University Wit, and Pickpocket Eloquence*, Bibliophile Books, London, 1984 [1811].
Hagan, S. F., *Which is Which?: A manual of homophones*, Macmillan, London, 1982.
Hargrave, Basil, *Origins and Meanings of Popular Phrases and Names*, Werner Laurie, London, 1925.
Hendrickson, Robert, *The Dictionary of Eponyms*, Dorset Press, New York, 1972.
_____. *The Encyclopedia of Word and Phrase Origins*, Facts on File, New York, 1987.
Hoad, T.F. (ed.), *The Concise Oxford Dictionary of English Etymology*, Clarendon Press, Oxford, 1986.
Hunt, Cecil, *Talk of the Town: The Place Names in our Language*, Herbert Jenkins, London, 1951.
Jeffs, Julian, *Little Dictionary of Drink*, Pelham Books, London, 1973.
Lockwood, W.B., *The Oxford Book of British Bird Names*, OUP, 1984.
McAdam, Jr., E.L., and Milne, George, *Johnson's Dictionary: A Modern Selection*, Book Club Associates, London, 1982.
Morris, William and Mary, *Morris Dictionary of Word and Phrase Origins*, Harper & Row, New York, 1977.
Onions, C. T. (ed.), with the assistance of G.W.S. Friedrichsen and R. W. Burchfield, *The Oxford Dictionary of English Etymology*, Clarendon Press, Oxford, 1966.
Palmer, A. Smythe, *Folk-Etymology: A Dictionary of Verbal Corruptions or Words Perverted in Form or Meaning, by False Derivation or Mistaken Analogy*, George Bell & Sons, London, 1882.

Partridge, Eric, *A Dictionary of Slang and Unconventional English*, Routledge & Kegan Paul, London, 1951.

Partridge, Eric, *Origins: A Short Etymological Dictionary of Modern English*, Routledge & Kegan Paul, London, 1966.

Picoche, Jacqueline, *Dictionnaire étymologique du français*, Robert, Paris, 1979.

Radford, Edwin (collator), *Crowther's Encyclopaedia of Phrases and Origins*, John Crowther, Bognor Regis, 1945.

Radford, Edwin and Smith, Alan, *To Coin a Phrase: A Dictionary of Origins*, Macmillan, London, 1981.

Room, Adrian, *Dictionary of Confusing Words and Meanings*, National Textbook Company, Lincolnwood (Chicago), 1990.

Shipley, Joseph T., *Dictionary of Word Origins*, Philosophical Library, New York, 1945.

Skeat, Rev. Walter W., *An Etymological Dictionary of the English Language*, Clarendon Press, Oxford, 1909.

Stenhouse, Rev. T., *Lives Enshrined in Language; or, Proper Names Which Have Become Common Parts of Speech*, The Walter Scott Publishing Co., London, 1922.

Vanstone, J.H., *Dictionary of the World's Commercial Products*, Sir Isaac Pitman, London, 1930.

Weekley, Ernest, *A Concise Etymological Dictionary of Modern English*, John Murray, London, 1924.

Weekley, Ernest, *An Etymological Dictionary of Modern English* (in two volumes), Dover Publications, New York, 1967 [1921].

## 3 Books on the English language

Asimov, Isaac, *Words from the Myths*, Faber & Faber, London, 1963.

Baugh, Albert C., and Cable, Thomas, *A History of the English Language*, Prentice Hall, Englewood Cliffs, NJ, 1978.

Berlitz, Charles, *Native Tongues*, Granada Publishing, St Albans, 1983.

Bolinger, Dwight, *Language – The Loaded Weapon: The use and abuse of language today*, Longman, London and New York, 1980.

Bombaugh, C.C., *Oddities and Curiosities of Words and Literature*, edited and annotated by Martin Gardner, Dover Publications, New York, 1961 [1890].

Burchfield, Robert, *The English Language*, OUP, 1985.

Editors of the American Heritage Dictionaries, *Word Mysteries and Histories*, Houghton Mifflin, Boston, MA, 1986.

Funk, Wilfred, *Word Origins and Their Romantic Stories*, Bell Publishing, New York, 1978.

Greenoak, Francesca, *All The Birds of the Air: The names, love and literature of British Birds*, André Deutsch, London, 1979.

Heller, Louis, Humez, Alexander, and Dror, Malcah, *The Private Lives of English Words*, Routledge & Kegan Paul, London, 1984.

Howard, Philip, *A Word in Your Ear*, Hamish Hamilton, London, 1983.

Howard, Philip, *New Words for Old: A survey of misused, vogue and cliché words*, Hamish Hamilton, London, 1977.

Howard, Philip, *The State of the Language: English Observed*, Hamish Hamilton, London, 1984.

McDonald, James, *Wordly Wise: A book about the origins of English words and phrases*, Constable, London, 1984.

Mencken, H. L., *The American Language: An Inquiry into the Development of English in the United States*, Alfred A. Knopf, New York, 1943.

Michaels, Leonard, and Ricks, Christopher (eds.), *The State of the Language*, University of California Press, Berkeley and Los Angeles, 1980.

Owen, Denis, *What's in a Name: A Look at the Origins of Plant and Animal Names*, BBC Publications, London, 1985.

Palmer, A. Smythe, *Leaves from a Word-Hunter's Note-Book: Being Some Contributions to English Etymology*, Trübner & Co., London, 1876.

Palmer, A. Smythe, *The Folk and Their Word-Lore: An Essay on Popular Etymologies*, Routledge, London, 1904.

Partridge, Eric, *Adventuring Among Words*, André Deutsch, London, 1961.

Pinkerton, Edward C., *Word for Word*, Verbatim Books, Essex, Ct., 1982.

Potter, Stephen and Sargent, Laurens, *Pedigree: Essays on the Etymology of Words from Nature*, Collins, London, 1973.

Ross, A. S. C., *Etymology: With Especial Reference to English*, André Deutsch, London, 1958.

Shipley, Joseph T., *In Praise of English: The Growth and Use of Language*, Times Books, New York, 1977.

Taylor, Isaac, *Words and Names: or Etymological Illustrations of History, Ethnology and Geography*, edited with corrections and additions by A. Smythe Palmer, Routledge, London, 1909.

Trench, Richard Chenevix, *On the Study of Words*, edited with emendations by A. Smythe Palmer, Routledge, London, n. d. [c. 1910].

Weekley, Ernest, *The Romance of Words*, John Murray, London, 1922.

Weekley, Ernest, *Words Ancient and Modern*, John Murray, London, 1926.

Weekley, Ernest, *More Words Ancient and Modern*, John Murray, London, 1927.

Weekley, Ernest, *Adjectives and Other Words*, John Murray, London, 1930.

Weekley, Ernest, *Words and Names*, John Murray, London, 1932.

Weekley, Ernest, *Something About Words*, John Murray, London, 1935.